Palgrave Macmillan Studies in Banking and Financial Institutions

Founding Editor
Philip Molyneux

Series Editor
Jonathan Williams, Surrey Business School, University of Surrey, Guildford, UK

The Palgrave Macmillan Studies in Banking and Financial Institutions series is international in orientation and includes studies of banking systems in particular countries or regions as well as contemporary themes such as Islamic Banking, Financial Exclusion, Mergers and Acquisitions, Risk Management, and IT in Banking. The books focus on research and practice and include up to date and innovative studies that cover issues which impact banking systems globally.

Abderazak Bakhouche

Banking in the GCC

Structure, Performance and Transformation

palgrave
macmillan

Abderazak Bakhouche
Higher Colleges of Technology
Dubai, United Arab Emirates

ISSN 2523-336X ISSN 2523-3378 (electronic)
Palgrave Macmillan Studies in Banking and Financial Institutions
ISBN 978-3-032-21736-3 ISBN 978-3-032-21737-0 (eBook)
https://doi.org/10.1007/978-3-032-21737-0

Zhou: Cover illustration: QQ7/shutterstock

This Palgrave Macmillan imprint is published by the registered company Springer Nature Switzerland AG
The registered company address is: Gewerbestrasse 11, 6330 Cham, Switzerland

To the memory of Professor Phil Molyneux

Preface

The economies of the Gulf Cooperation Council (GCC) have undergone a remarkable transformation over the past three decades. From modest, oil-dependent beginnings to increasingly diversified and globally connected financial systems, the GCC region now stands as one of the world's most dynamic economic blocs. This book, *Banking in the GCC: Structure, Performance, and Transformation*, was written to offer a comprehensive, research-driven, and accessible overview of the structural, financial, and institutional forces shaping this rapidly evolving landscape.

The work brings together eight thematic chapters that explore the foundational characteristics of GCC economies, the complex relationship between natural resource dependency and financial development, competition and profitability in the banking sector, the growing role of Environmental, Social and Governance (ESG) practices, and emerging challenges related to globalisation, institutional quality, stability, and cost efficiency. Each chapter employs empirical evidence, more recent available data, and relevant theoretical frameworks to examine how GCC financial systems are adapting to shifting global conditions—including technological innovation, oil price volatility, regulatory reforms, and sustainability imperatives.

This book is intended to serve multiple audiences. It provides scholars and students of economics, banking, finance, and public policy with rigorous empirical insights into a region often underrepresented in mainstream economic literature. At the same time, it offers practitioners, policy-makers, and industry professionals a structured analysis of the factors influencing financial performance, regulatory transformation, and competitiveness in GCC banking. For the general reader, the book presents a straightforward narrative on how financial systems evolve when shaped by both extraordinary resource endowments and ambitious national visions.

Writing this book has been both an academic exercise and a personal journey. Having lived, worked, and researched in the region, I have witnessed firsthand the rapid evolution of its financial architecture and the strategic efforts of governments, institutions, and market participants to pursue diversified, resilient growth. This work would not have been possible without the vast body of international and regional research and the continuous transformation that make the GCC an increasingly compelling subject of study.

I hope this book contributes meaningfully to ongoing discussions about the future of banking and finance in the GCC and the wider MENA region, and inspires further research into the region's unique economic pathways. As the GCC continues to diversify beyond hydrocarbons and integrate more deeply with global markets, its financial sector will undoubtedly remain central to shaping its long-term prosperity.

Dubai, United Arab Emirates
2026

Abderazak Bakhouche

Acknowledgements Writing this book has been an enriching journey, shaped by the generous support, intellectual engagement, and encouragement of many individuals and institutions.

I want to express my deepest gratitude to the late Professor Philip Molyneux, my former supervisor and mentor at Bangor University in North Wales. His backing was essential to the study of banking in GCC. His intellectual rigour, steadfast support, and views regarding the importance of this subject motivated my in-depth study of GCC banking.

I am equally grateful to my colleagues at the Higher Colleges of Technology, especially Randa El Chaar and Mohamed Boulkeroua, whose academic dialogue has continually motivated this work. Their feedback and encouragement have enriched this book in many ways.

Finally, special appreciation goes to my students at HCT. Their probing questions, intellectual curiosity, and engagement with GCC banking have deeply enhanced this book. You remind me daily of the transformative power of education.

Competing Interests The author has no competing interests to declare that are relevant to the content of this manuscript.

Praise for *Banking in the GCC*

"This book delivers a rigorous and insightful analysis of GCC banking, integrating competition, profitability, ESG, and financial development within a coherent empirical framework grounded in industrial organisation and institutional theory. It offers an original contribution, including the Israf-avoidance hypothesis, and provides timely insight into financial transformation in resource-based economies, making it valuable for scholars, policymakers, and practitioners."

—Zakaria Boulanouar, *United Arab Emirates University, Al Ain, UAE*

"This book offers a rigorous and well-structured contribution to the study of GCC banking, integrating economic context, institutional arrangements, and banking performance within a coherent analytical framework. A notable strength is its treatment of sustainability, where ESG considerations are positioned as a core component of the sector's ongoing transformation, underscoring their role in enhancing financial resilience and supporting long-term development in GCC banking systems."

—Faisal Alqahtani, *Riyadh, Saudi Arabia*

Contents

List of Figures

List of Tables

CHAPTER 1

Introduction to the Book

The Gulf Cooperation Council (GCC) represents one of the world's most distinctive and influential economic regions. Rich in hydrocarbon resources yet increasingly committed to economic diversification, the GCC offers a compelling environment for studying financial systems, institutional development, and macroeconomic transformation. This book brings together a series of research-driven chapters that explore the evolution, challenges, and prospects of banking and finance across the six GCC countries.

The book begins by examining the structural foundations of GCC economies, tracing how natural resource endowments, demographics, and government policies have shaped development trajectories over the past decades. It then investigates the complex relationship between financial development, diversification, and the long-debated resource curse or blessing hypotheses.

Subsequent chapters analyse competition, profitability, efficiency, and stability in GCC banking systems, drawing on empirical tools such as the Lerner Index, the Boone Indicator, the Panzar-Rosse H-statistic, and various regression models. These assessments provide insights into how GCC banks operate within concentrated yet dynamic financial landscapes.

A. Bakhouche, *Banking in the GCC*, Palgrave Macmillan Studies in Banking and Financial Institutions,
https://doi.org/10.1007/978-3-032-21737-0_1

Recognising the global shift towards sustainability, the book dedicates a chapter to the impact of ESG (Environmental, Social, and Governance) performance on bank profitability in the GCC. With the region increasingly integrating ESG principles into corporate governance and investment practices, this chapter provides timely empirical evidence on the link between responsible finance and financial performance.

The book also explores issues of globalisation, institutional quality, and financial stability, highlighting how external integration, geopolitical exposure, and regulatory reforms shape banking resilience. Finally, it examines cost efficiency and returns to scale, providing a rigorous quantitative understanding of operational performance across the region's banking sectors.

Throughout the book, the analysis is grounded in contemporary data, regional policies, and global trends, enabling readers to appreciate the complexities of economic and financial transformation in a region that lies at the intersection of energy markets, global trade routes, and strategic geopolitical interests.

This book aims to serve as both a reference for researchers and a practical guide for policy-makers, practitioners, and students seeking to understand the intricate dynamics of GCC banking and finance.

Chapter-by-Chapter Summaries

Chapter 2—Characteristics of the GCC Economies

This chapter provides an overview of GCC macroeconomic structures, focusing on economic growth, hydrocarbon dependency, sectoral composition, labour market dynamics, and demographic trends. It highlights the challenges of diversification, the dominance of oil revenues in government budgets, and the role of expatriate labour.

Chapter 3—Financial Development, Diversification, and the Resource Curse

This chapter examines theoretical and empirical debates surrounding the resource curse in the context of GCC economies. It analyses how financial development can mitigate or exacerbate resource dependence and investigates the channels through which financial systems enable diversification.

Chapter 4—Competition in GCC Banking Systems

Using industrial organisation theory, this chapter evaluates the level of competition in the GCC banking sector. Measures such as concentration ratios, the Herfindahl–Hirschman Index (HHI), the Lerner Index, the Boone Indicator, and the Panzar-Rosse H-Statistic are employed to assess market power and competitive behaviour.

Chapter 5—Profitability in GCC Banking Systems

This chapter identifies the key drivers of bank profitability across the GCC, including ROE, ROA, capital adequacy, net interest margins, and cost efficiency. It also considers regulatory reforms, Islamic vs. conventional banking, and major macroeconomic and bank-specific determinants.

Chapter 6—The Impact of ESG on Bank Profitability

In light of global financial trends, this chapter evaluates ESG developments within GCC banking systems. It examines how environmental, social, and governance performance influences profitability and how ESG interacts with factors such as bank size and Islamic banking practices.

Chapter 7—Globalisation, Institutional Quality, and Bank Stability

This chapter explores the interplay between globalisation, institutional quality, and financial stability in GCC banking—three dimensions increasingly relevant in an interconnected world. It uses empirical models to assess how openness, governance, and rule of law affect banking resilience.

Chapter 8—Cost Efficiency and Returns to Scale in GCC Banking

Employing Data Envelopment Analysis (DEA) and Generalised Method of Moments (GMM), this chapter investigates cost efficiency, returns to scale, and the implications of bank size and ownership. It also addresses calls for industry consolidation to improve efficiency.

CHAPTER 2

Characteristics of the GCC Economies

Introduction

The Gulf Cooperation Council (GCC) was established by an agreement concluded on 25 May 1981 in Riyadh, Saudi Arabia, among Bahrain, Kuwait, Oman, Qatar, Saudi Arabia, and the UAE in view of their special relations, geographic proximity, similar political systems based on Islamic beliefs, joint destiny, and common objectives. The GCC countries share standard features, including Arabic, Islam, and deep cultural and historical ties. Economically, they rely heavily on hydrocarbon exports, government-led infrastructure development, and business environments defined by low or no taxation. Growth has historically been driven by oil and gas exports, public spending, and a labour market dominated by expatriates, primarily from South Asia, due to domestic labour shortages.

The global significance of the GCC lies in its strategic geographic location and vast energy resources. Holding nearly 30% of global crude oil reserves (500.7 billion barrels) and 20% of natural gas output, the region is a significant energy supplier to Asia, Europe, and North America (EIA, 2014; OPEC, 2022). The Strait of Hormuz, a vital trade route through which one-fifth of global oil passes, further enhances the GCC's geopolitical importance (World Bank, 2023).

In recent years, the GCC has launched significant economic reforms to reduce its reliance on hydrocarbons amid volatility in global oil prices.

A. Bakhouche, *Banking in the GCC*, Palgrave Macmillan Studies in Banking and Financial Institutions,
https://doi.org/10.1007/978-3-032-21737-0_2

Strategies such as Saudi Arabia's Vision 2030, the UAE's Vision 2021, and Qatar's National Vision 2030 focus on diversifying their economies and fostering private-sector growth. These initiatives aim to mitigate the risks posed by oil price fluctuations and to encourage innovation, entrepreneurship, and sustainable development. Beyond hydrocarbons, the GCC's total GDP reached USD 2 trillion as of 2022. Member states are diversifying into sectors such as finance, technology, renewable energy, and tourism. They are leveraging support from sovereign wealth funds such as Saudi Arabia's Public Investment Fund (PIF) and the UAE's Abu Dhabi Investment Authority (ADIA) to drive regional and global investment and bolster economic resilience.

This chapter examines the GCC's macroeconomic and financial characteristics over the last two decades, analysing economic foundations, challenges, and diversification strategies. It explores key sectors such as energy, financial services, trade, and tourism, as well as emerging industries including technology and renewable energy, to provide a comprehensive understanding of the region's economic dynamics and prospects.

Economic Growth

The GCC economies are deeply linked in their abundant natural resource wealth, strategic geographic location, and distinct economic structures. These elements have shaped the economic trajectories of the six countries over the last few decades, influencing global energy markets while also presenting challenges that have driven efforts towards economic diversification.

The GCC made significant economic progress, expanding the size of GDP from USD 10 billion in 1970 to USD 2,114 billion in 2023, as shown in Fig. 2.1, reflecting the annualised growth rate of 10.4%. The region's GDP accounts for 50% of MENA's GDP but 2% of the World's, 8% of the US', 12% of the EU's and China's, and 60% of India's. As of 2023, Saudi Arabia has the largest economy in the region with about USD 1,067 billion, followed by the UAE and Qatar. Bahrain has the smallest economy, at about USD 43 billion, followed by Oman and Kuwait. The significant economic progress has led to an unprecedented surge in welfare, as measured by GDP per capita (Fig. 2.2).

Figure 2.2 shows that GCC countries have among the highest per capita incomes in the world.

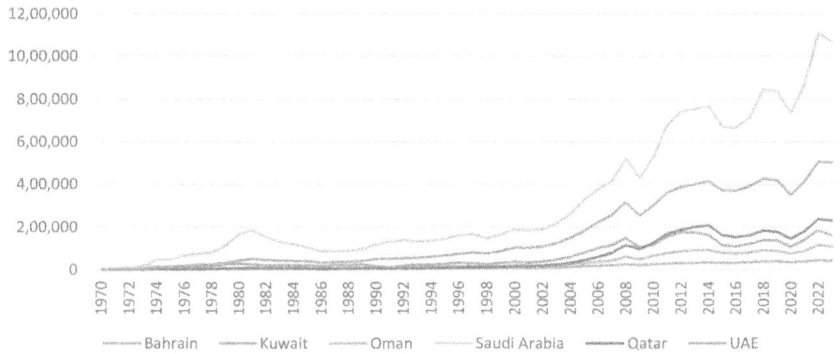

Fig. 2.1 Current GDP of GCC countries between 1970 and 2023 in million USD (*Source* World Bank database)

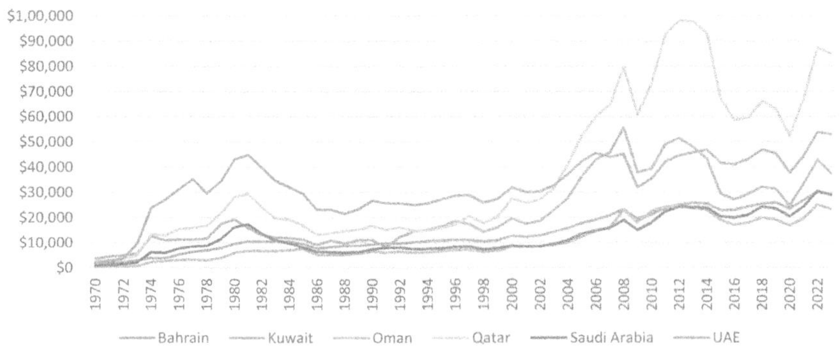

Fig. 2.2 Current GDP per capita of GCC countries between 1970 and 2023 in USD (*Source* World Bank Database)

The rapid economic growth of GCC countries since the 1970s has been primarily fuelled by oil and gas revenues. In 1970, the combined GDP of GCC economies stood at USD 10 billion, increasing to over USD 2 trillion by 2022. Saudi Arabia, the UAE, and Qatar led this growth, leveraging their vast hydrocarbon reserves. Saudi Arabia's GDP rose from USD 5.38 billion in 1970 to USD 1.1 trillion in 2022, making it the largest economy in the MENA region (IMF, 2022). Similarly, Qatar, buoyed by its substantial natural gas resources, grew from USD 0.30 billion in 1970 to USD 235.77 billion in 2022, achieving one of the world's highest GDP per capita levels (World Bank, 2023). The UAE's economy expanded from USD 0.69 billion in 1970 to USD 507.06 billion in 2022, supported by its oil wealth and significant growth in international trade and foreign investments (Antwi-Boateng & Al jaberi, 2022).

As shown in Table 2.1, during 1970–2023, the UAE and Qatar grew at an annualised rate of 13%, followed by Oman (12%) and Saudi Arabia (10%). Bahrain (7%) and Kuwait (7%) witnessed the lowest growth rates. GCC economies experienced rapid GDP growth during oil price booms, such as the 1970–1980 period, when annualised growth in current GDP averaged 38.4% across the region. However, over the subsequent decades, fluctuating oil prices highlighted the vulnerability of oil-dependent economies, with GDP contractions during periods of low prices, such as the 1980s and the mid-2010s.

Hydrocarbon Dependency in GCC Economies

The GCC countries possess some of the largest proven oil and natural gas reserves in the world, making them pivotal to the global energy supply. Saudi Arabia, the largest oil producer in the region, holds approximately 17% of the world's proven crude oil reserves, with production averaging 10 million barrels per day (BP, 2023). The UAE and Qatar also rank among the top energy producers, with Qatar being the leading exporter of liquefied natural gas (IEA, 2022). Together, the GCC accounted for nearly 30% of global crude oil production and 20% of natural gas output in 2022 (OPEC, 2022).

Hydrocarbons contribute significantly to the GDP, exports, and fiscal revenues of GCC countries. In 2021, oil revenues accounted for 68% of Saudi Arabia's government revenues (IMF, 2022). Qatar's LNG exports have been instrumental in its economic prosperity, funding massive infrastructure projects and contributing to one of the world's highest per capita incomes (World Bank, 2022). However, this dependence on hydrocarbons also exposes these economies to the volatility of global energy markets. The oil price crash of 2014–2016 highlighted the risks of revenue fluctuations, prompting GCC states to implement fiscal reforms and diversify their economies (Stocker et al., 2018).

The reliance on hydrocarbons has also underscored the urgency of transitioning to more sustainable growth models. Efforts such as Saudi

Table 2.1 Annualised growth rates of GCC's current GDP between 1970 and 2023

	1970–1980	*1980–1990*	*1990–2000*	*2000–2010*	*2010–2023*	*1970–2023*
Current GDP in USD						
Bahrain	24.5%	3.2%	6.5%	11.0%	4.1%	9.3%
Kuwait	25.8%	−4.3%	7.4%	11.8%	2.6%	7.9%
Oman	37.0%	6.9%	5.3%	12.8%	4.0%	12.1%
Qatar	38.5%	−0.6%	9.2%	21.6%	4.8%	13.3%
Saudi Arabia	40.8%	−3.3%	4.9%	10.8%	5.6%	10.5%
UAE	51.5%	1.5%	7.5%	11.1%	4.1%	13.3%
GCC	**38.4%**	**−1.9%**	**6.0%**	**11.9%**	**4.7%**	**10.7%**
Constant GDP in USD (base year = 2015)						
Bahrain	7.53%	1.55%	5.54%	5.36%	2.70%	4.41%
Kuwait	−2.19%	−2.67%	6.09%	4.58%	1.52%	1.41%
Oman	5.51%	8.97%	4.78%	2.99%	2.58%	4.81%
Qatar	5.63%	1.48%	6.67%	13.25%	2.96%	5.75%
Saudi Arabia	10.66%	−1.89%	2.58%	3.37%	3.21%	3.49%
UAE	23.88%	0.60%	4.66%	3.87%	3.29%	6.74%
GCC	9.76%	−0.81%	3.74%	4.31%	3.03%	3.90%
Current GDP per capita in USD						
Bahrain	18.54%	−0.36%	3.20%	5.22%	2.47%	5.44%
Kuwait	18.27%	−5.40%	5.89%	7.24%	−0.34%	4.53%
Oman	31.43%	0.97%	2.54%	10.48%	0.25%	8.06%
Qatar	27.14%	−5.13%	5.13%	10.26%	1.18%	6.83%
Saudi Arabia	33.79%	−7.59%	1.81%	7.40%	3.73%	6.81%
UAE	34.01%	−4.66%	1.79%	1.06%	3.15%	6.10%
GCC	26.69%	−4.45%	3.44%	6.77%	1.58%	6.04%
Constant GDP per capita in USD (base year = 2015)						
Bahrain	2.41%	−1.99%	2.24%	−0.12%	1.11%	0.74%
Kuwait	−8.08%	−3.77%	4.57%	0.28%	−1.41%	−1.75%
Oman	1.21%	2.90%	2.07%	0.88%	−1.12%	1.05%
Qatar	−3.03%	−3.13%	2.69%	2.73%	−0.56%	−0.31%
Saudi Arabia	5.15%	−6.24%	−0.42%	0.20%	1.42%	0.04%
UAE	9.61%	−5.53%	−0.89%	−5.56%	2.38%	−0.01%
GCC	1.23%	−4.06%	1.32%	−0.39%	0.23%	−0.32%
Population growth rate						
Bahrain	5.00%	3.62%	3.24%	5.49%	1.57%	3.65%

(continued)

Table 2.1 (continued)

	1970–1980	*1980–1990*	*1990–2000*	*2000–2010*	*2010–2023*	*1970–2023*
Kuwait	6.41%	1.15%	1.45%	4.28%	2.98%	3.22%
Oman	4.26%	5.90%	2.65%	2.09%	3.74%	3.72%
Qatar	8.93%	4.76%	3.87%	10.25%	3.61%	6.10%
Saudi Arabia	5.24%	4.64%	3.02%	3.16%	1.77%	3.45%
UAE	13.02%	6.48%	5.60%	9.98%	0.89%	6.75%
GCC	5.72%	4.54%	3.15%	4.35%	1.91%	3.81%

Source World Bank Database. Calculations by author

Arabia's Vision 2030 and the UAE's Vision 2021 aim to reduce oil dependency by expanding non-oil sectors such as renewable energy, technology, and tourism (Vision 2030, 2023). However, achieving diversification remains challenging, as oil revenues still dominate fiscal accounts and provide the capital required to fund diversification initiatives (Shadab, 2023).

One key feature underscoring the economic and geostrategic importance of GCC economies is their control of 40% of the world's proven crude oil reserves, 20% of global oil production, and 36% of global oil exports (Alsayegh, 2023). The strong integration with the oil market can also be emphasised in its role in affecting other economic features. Table 2.2 shows that across GCC economies, oil rents drive both total exports and government budgets, thereby indirectly affecting government spending, consumer spending, corporate earnings, and savings. Hydrocarbon revenues are the primary sources of funding for public spending, illustrating the role of fiscal policy in transmitting oil shocks into the real economy. GCC countries utilise hydrocarbon receipts to finance imports of consumer goods, inputs, and capital goods, and to support substantial labour remittances and financial outflows.

Oil rents drive several macroeconomic variables in GCC economies, including exports, fiscal budgets, and government spending. Table 2.2 illustrates the magnitude of oil's dominance across three key macroeconomic pillars: output, exports, and government revenues, over the last three decades. Oil accounted for about 30% of the GCC's GDP, 55% of exports, and 75% of government revenues, underscoring its outsized role in driving economic activity. The sensitivity of GCC economies to oil varies across countries. Kuwait and Saudi Arabia exhibit the highest

Table 2.2 Oil rents as a percentage of GDP, exports, and government revenues in GCC countries between 1991 and 2021

	Oil rents as % of GDP				*Oil rents as % of total goods exports*				*Oil rents as % of government revenues*			
Decade	1990s	2000s	2010s	Average	1990s	2000s	2010s	Average	1990s	2000s	2010s	Average
Bahrain	16.6	17.5	13.5	15.9	23.2	22.7	15	20.3	69	67.3	60.5	65.6
Kuwait	32.7	46.2	46	41.6	73.1	78.8	74	75.3	63.8	73	70.6	69.1
Oman	30.7	37.4	26.4	31.5	67.6	61.8	47.6	59	87.5	93.5	76	85.7
Qatar	30.8	33.5	18.8	27.7	64	53.8	30.3	49.4	66.4	87.4	46.5	66.8
Saudi Arabia	28.3	42.1	31.6	34	78.4	83	76.7	79.3	97.6	–	96.9	–
UAE	–	20.9	19	19.9	–	32.1	20.3	26.2	–	72.9	60.1	66.5
Average	**0.278**	**0.329**	**0.259**	**0.289**	**0.613**	**0.554**	**0.44**	**0.535**	**0.768**	**0.844**	**0.684**	**0.766**

Source Calculations based on World Bank database

degree of dependence, with oil rents accounting for a significant share of GDP and government revenues. At the same time, Bahrain and the UAE are comparatively less sensitive due to their more diversified economic structures (IMF, 2022). Between 1991 and 2021, Kuwait's oil rents averaged 41.6% of GDP and 75.3% of exports, reflecting its reliance on hydrocarbon revenues. Conversely, Bahrain and the UAE have steadily reduced their reliance on oil, focusing on expanding non-oil sectors such as finance, trade, and real estate (World Bank, 2023).

The reliance on oil rents exposes GCC economies to significant external shocks. Table 2.6 reveals fluctuations in oil rents as a percentage of GDP, exports, and government revenues, with peaks in the 2000s driven by oil price surges, followed by declines in the 2010s as global oil markets softened. This dependence implies that oil price shocks, such as price collapses, can affect economic growth, fiscal balances, and foreign exchange reserves (EIA, 2023). For instance, the Dutch Disease hypothesis suggests that prolonged reliance on oil rents can weaken non-oil sectors by causing exchange rate appreciation, making non-oil exports less competitive and hindering diversification efforts (Alssadek & Benhin, 2021).

Despite high oil prices supporting fiscal surpluses and aggregate demand, they may also lead to economic distortions. For instance, rising oil prices can increase the cost of imported inputs for oil-intensive industries, reducing competitiveness and slowing industrial growth (El Anshasy & Bradley, 2012). Moreover, the over-reliance on hydrocarbons restricts GCC governments' ability to implement countercyclical fiscal policies, as fluctuations in oil revenues directly affect government spending and, by extension, private consumption and investment (Hamdi & Sbia, 2013).

Table 2.2 confirms the dominance of oil rents in the macroeconomic frameworks of GCC countries, though with varying degrees of reliance. During 1991–21, Saudi Arabia and Kuwait were the most dependent on oil rents for exports and fiscal revenues, whereas the UAE and Bahrain exhibited greater diversification. In Saudi Arabia, oil rents accounted for an average of 34% of GDP and 79.3% of exports, underscoring the critical role of hydrocarbons in its economic structure. The UAE, in contrast, reduced oil rents to an average of 26.2% of exports during the same period, reflecting the success of its diversification efforts in sectors such as tourism, trade, and logistics (World Bank, 2023).

Numerous studies underscore the positive relationship between oil prices and economic growth in oil-exporting countries. Rising oil prices typically lead to higher export revenues and fiscal surpluses, which governments often use to stimulate aggregate demand (Charfeddine & Barkat, 2020). However, higher oil prices can also induce inflationary pressures, raise the cost of imported inputs, and limit industrial diversification. For instance, the appreciation of GCC currencies linked to oil price surges reduces the cost of imported consumer and capital goods, facilitating investment in infrastructure and industrial growth.

Nevertheless, the long-term economic implications of oil dependency remain challenging. The Dutch Disease effect, in which an over-reliance on oil rents crowds out investment in non-oil sectors, continues to pose a significant obstacle to economic diversification and sustainable growth in GCC economies.

Sectoral Composition of the GCC Economies

The economies of the GCC have undergone profound structural transformations over the past five decades. Initially driven by hydrocarbon exports, these economies have diversified, with significant growth in non-oil sectors such as finance, tourism, real estate, and manufacturing. Tables 2.4 and 2.5 explore key trends in sectoral composition, employment patterns, and economic growth in GCC countries.

The rapid economic growth of GCC countries since the 1970s has been fuelled mainly by oil and gas revenues. Despite this impressive growth, hydrocarbon dependency has posed challenges. Fluctuations in global oil prices have led to volatile GDP growth rates, as highlighted in Table 2.3. For example, the 1980s and mid-2010s witnessed economic slowdowns due to declining oil prices (EIA, 2023). Recognising the risks of over-reliance on hydrocarbons, GCC countries have prioritised diversification strategies to reduce economic vulnerability.

Data in Table 2.3 indicate that over the 1970–22 period, agriculture has had a minimal role in GCC economies, with contributions of less than 1% in Bahrain, Kuwait, Qatar, and the UAE, given the region's harsh desert environment and limited arable land. Oman and Saudi Arabia had relatively higher agricultural shares of GDP. Still, these have declined over time, driven by industrialisation, urbanisation, and diversification into other sectors such as tourism and logistics.

Table 2.3 Sectoral value-added contributions to GCC economies between 1970 and 2022

Years	*1970*	*1980*	*1990*	*2000*	*2010*	*2020*	*2022*	*1970*	*1980*	*1990*	*2000*	*2010*	*2020*	*2022*
Country	**GDP (current billions of USD)**							**Agriculture, forestry, and fishing, value added (% of GDP)**						
Bahrain	0.39	3.49	4.81	9.06	25.71	34.62	44.38	–	0.87	0.83	–	0.3	0.31	0.26
Kuwait	2.87	28.64	18.43	37.72	115.42	107.51	182.81	–	–	–	0.36	0.45	0.51	0.4
Oman	0.26	5.98	11.69	19.51	64.99	75.91	114.67	15.54	2.55	2.59	2.24	1.25	2.47	1.84
Qatar	0.3	7.83	7.36	17.76	125.12	144.41	235.77	–	–	–	0.37	0.12	0.34	0.26
Saudi Arabia	5.38	164.54	117.63	189.51	528.21	734.27	1,108.57	4.23	0.95	5.64	4.9	2.62	2.96	2.4
UAE	0.69	43.6	50.7	104.34	300.19	349.47	507.06	–	0.49	1.06	2.26	0.74	0.96	0.82
Country	**Industry (including construction), value added (% of GDP)**							**Manufacturing, value added (% of GDP)**						
Bahrain	–	51.97	40.22	–	44.98	39.87	47.9	–	14.27	14.71	–	14.48	18.29	21.44
Kuwait	–	–	–	–	66.07	48.91	66.96	–	–	–	6.92	5.98	8.12	6.87
Oman	77.25	69.36	54.1	59.16	63.27	47.15	56.98	0.19	–	–	5.73	10.05	8.36	10.5
Qatar	–	–	–	–	–	52.33	65.36	–	–	–	31.94	12.53	7.91	9.28
Saudi Arabia	58.27	71.22	48.55	53.45	58.03	39.47	53.14	8.22	3.98	8.3	9.23	10.83	12.64	14.44
UAE	–	72.66	58.9	48.52	51.68	42.17	51.46	–	3.73	7.49	9.07	8.48	10.29	9.73
Country	**Services, value added (% of GDP)**							**Trade in services (% of GDP)**						
Bahrain	–	32.05	–	–	53.68	56.94	47.93	–	23.09	17.32	19.18	23.87	61.09	57.46
Kuwait	–	–	–	–	47.04	66.03	43.62	–	14.99	25.17	17.88	21.48	24.51	20.87
Oman	21.54	29.41	–	39.99	39.94	55.02	44.48	–	8.8	6.73	11.33	12.57	14.1	13.27
Qatar	–	–	–	–	–	52.74	38.53	–	–	–	–	–	37.48	30.42
Saudi Arabia	36.32	27.36	44.22	40.29	38.61	53.31	39.86	–	21.53	21.6	15.83	16.56	8.89	10.55
UAE	–	26.85	40.04	49.22	47.59	56.86	47.71	–	–	–	–	–	–	–

Table 2.4 Labour force characteristics of GCC countries between 1991 and 2022

Year	*1995*	*2000*	*2005*	*2010*	*2015*	*2020*	*2022*	*1995*	*2000*	*2005*	*2010*	*2015*	*2020*	*2022*
Country	**Unemployment rate (%)**							**Employment in agriculture (% of total employment)**						
Bahrain	1.12	1.14	1.04	1.13	1.17	1.77	1.33	2.02	1.64	1.35	1.09	1.07	0.94	0.9
Kuwait	0.69	0.8	1.46	1.82	2.2	3.54	2.12	2.08	2.34	2.64	2.43	2.2	2	1.95
Oman	4.26	4.4	4.64	3.93	3.39	2.94	1.51	7.97	6.39	7.96	5.16	5.26	5.23	6.07
Qatar	0.87	0.87	0.87	0.45	0.17	0.14	0.13	3.99	2.6	2.87	1.46	1.23	1.35	1.3
Saudi Arabia	6.44	4.57	6.05	5.55	5.6	7.45	5.59	7.47	7.27	6.88	6.44	5.93	3.17	2.88
UAE	1.8	2.25	3.12	2.79	1.79	4.29	2.87	8.61	8.53	5.97	3.56	2.07	1.78	1.39
Country	**Employment in industry (% of total employment)**							**Employment in services (% of total employment)**						
Bahrain	28.57	28.46	31.01	35.72	35.16	34.89	34.82	69.41	69.9	67.64	63.19	63.77	64.17	64.28
Kuwait	23.11	19.37	22.46	24.17	24.92	24.94	25.16	74.81	78.29	74.9	73.41	72.89	73.06	72.89
Oman	7.63	11.19	18.92	36.88	37.33	46.75	46.89	84.4	82.42	73.12	57.96	57.41	48.02	47.05
Qatar	31.73	36.88	41.08	56.37	54.14	44.33	40.03	64.28	60.52	56.05	42.17	44.63	54.31	58.67
Saudi Arabia	25.21	24.14	23.73	23.29	23.77	22.9	16.88	67.32	68.58	69.4	70.27	70.3	73.93	80.23
UAE	28.59	28.03	27.55	26.26	31.45	27.58	29.58	62.8	63.43	66.48	70.18	66.48	70.64	69.03
Country	**Self-employed, total (% of total employment)**							**Wage and salaried workers, total (% of total employment)**						
Bahrain	4.62	3.84	4.05	2.66	2.7	2.73	2.68	95.38	96.16	95.95	97.34	97.3	97.27	97.32
Kuwait	3.41	3.29	2.67	1.21	1.06	2.08	2.09	96.59	96.71	97.33	98.79	98.94	97.92	97.91
Oman	14.07	12.54	7.31	4.44	4.26	4.48	4.4	85.93	87.46	92.69	95.56	95.74	95.52	95.6
Qatar	1.28	1.16	1.03	0.65	0.42	0.4	0.39	98.72	98.84	98.97	99.35	99.58	99.6	99.61
Saudi Arabia	7.08	5.8	4.62	3.71	2.97	5.54	6.45	92.92	94.2	95.38	96.29	97.03	94.46	93.55
UAE	2.71	2.75	3.09	4.09	2.88	4.61	4.47	97.29	97.25	96.91	95.91	97.12	95.39	95.53

Table 2.5 Demographic characteristics of GCC countries between 1970 and 2023. Population is divided by gender (male, female) and age (0–14 years, 15–64 years, and 65 years and over)

Year	*1970*	*1980*	*1990*	*2000*	*2010*	*2020*	*2023*	*1970*	*1980*	*1990*	*2000*	*2010*	*2020*	*2023*
Country	**Population, in million**							**Decennial growth of population (%)**						
Bahrain	0.22	0.36	0.52	0.71	1.21	1.48	1.49	–	62.9	42.7	37.5	70.6	21.7	0.5
Kuwait	0.80	1.49	1.67	1.93	2.94	4.36	4.31	–	86.1	12.1	15.5	52.1	48.1	−1.2
Oman	0.67	1.02	1.80	2.34	2.88	4.54	4.64	–	51.7	77.4	29.9	22.9	57.7	2.2
Qatar	0.12	0.28	0.44	0.65	1.71	2.76	2.72	–	135.1	59.2	46.2	165.3	61.1	−1.6
Saudi Arabia	6.11	10.17	16.00	21.55	29.41	36.00	36.95	–	66.6	57.3	34.6	36.5	22.4	2.6
UAE	0.30	1.01	1.90	3.28	8.48	9.29	9.52	–	240.2	87.4	72.4	159	9.5	2.5
GCC	**8.22**	**14.34**	**22.34**	**30.46**	**46.65**	**58.43**	**59.62**	–	**74.5**	**55.8**	**36.3**	**53.1**	**25.3**	**2.0**
Country	**Population, Female (% of total population)**							**Population, Male (% of total population)**						
Bahrain	44.94	41.19	41.47	41.03	37.87	37.7	38.16	55.06	58.81	58.53	58.97	62.13	62.3	61.84
Kuwait	43.96	43.24	44.22	41.45	43.07	38.74	39.3	56.04	56.76	55.78	58.55	56.93	61.26	60.7
Oman	50.02	49.14	43.11	42.68	40.7	37.91	39.3	49.98	50.86	56.89	57.32	59.3	62.09	60.7
Qatar	41.66	32.78	32.49	32.84	24.25	27.35	27.68	58.34	67.22	67.51	67.16	75.75	72.65	72.32
Saudi Arabia	48.6	45.24	43.05	42.84	42.66	41.98	42.5	51.4	54.76	56.95	57.16	57.34	58.02	57.5
UAE	32.72	29.56	33.09	31.68	27.2	30.28	30.82	67.28	70.44	66.91	68.32	72.8	69.72	69.18
GCC	**43.65**	**40.19**	**39.57**	**38.75**	**35.96**	**35.66**	**36.29**	**56.35**	**59.81**	**60.43**	**61.25**	**64.04**	**64.34**	**63.71**
Country	**Population ages 0–14 (% of total population)**							**Population ages 15–64 (% of total population)**						
Bahrain	44.99	35.79	33.82	29.27	20.45	20.3	19.88	52.42	62.08	64.04	68.26	77.41	76.5	76.09
Kuwait	44.66	41.72	38.84	28.68	23.02	20.97	20.13	53.57	57.02	59.64	69.76	75.17	75.04	74.43
Oman	45.32	46.87	43.85	37.18	26.91	25.64	27	51.14	49.98	53.66	60.37	70.56	71.6	70.19
Qatar	35.58	30.33	27.25	23.61	13.82	15.35	15.69	62.08	68.36	71.65	75.14	85.32	83.39	82.7
Saudi Arabia	45.5	45.26	41.36	35.9	29.48	26.04	25.6	51.31	52.01	56.06	61.46	68.37	71.56	71.35
UAE	32.17	27.32	29.68	22.17	13.74	14.94	15.22	66.27	71.46	69.29	76.93	86.08	83.41	82.92
GCC	**41.37**	**37.88**	**35.8**	**29.47**	**21.24**	**20.54**	**20.59**	**56.13**	**60.15**	**62.39**	**68.65**	**77.15**	**76.92**	**76.28**

Table 2.6 Labour force characteristics of GCC countries between 1991 and 2022

Year	*1991*	*2000*	*2010*	*2020*	*2022*	*1991*	*2000*	*2010*	*2020*	*2022*
Country	**Labour force participation rate, total (% of total population ages 15–64)**					**Employment to population ratio, 15 years and over (%)**				
Bahrain	66.93	67.51	73.07	73.27	74.13	64.65	65.16	70.94	70.08	70.88
Kuwait	65.54	67.15	69.89	71.29	73.8	63.56	65.4	67.45	67.1	69.97
Oman	58.43	57.32	62.16	68.47	69.98	54.17	53.1	58.01	64.36	66.67
Qatar	82.91	81.69	87.16	88.49	89.62	81.72	80.33	86.24	87.49	88.52
Saudi Arabia	54.7	52.37	54.38	61.41	63.07	49.2	48.92	50.26	55.6	58.19
UAE	74.54	75.05	77.83	83.2	83.66	72.43	72.68	75.57	78.65	79.88
Country	**Employment to labour force population (%)**					**International migration stock-to-total population (%)**				
Bahrain	96.59	96.52	97.09	95.65	95.62	35.89	35.89	52.16	55	–
Kuwait	96.98	97.4	96.51	94.12	94.82	58.44	58.44	61.17	72.8	–
Oman	92.7	92.62	93.32	93.99	95.28	27.85	27.85	27.73	46.5	–
Qatar	98.57	98.34	98.95	98.87	98.77	60.61	60.61	82.49	77.3	–
Saudi Arabia	89.95	93.4	92.42	90.55	92.26	24.6	24.6	30.01	38.6	–
UAE	97.17	96.84	97.09	94.53	95.49	80.22	80.22	87.84	88.1	–

The industrial sector, which includes oil and gas extraction, construction, and manufacturing, has historically dominated GCC economies. In 2022, the industrial sector accounted for 56.98% of GDP in Oman and 53.14% in Saudi Arabia (Table 2.3). Manufacturing has become a key driver of diversification. Saudi Arabia expanded its manufacturing base from 8.30% of GDP in 1990 to 14.44% in 2022, with a focus on petrochemicals, construction materials, and consumer goods (Vision 2030, 2023). Bahrain and Oman have similarly developed their manufacturing sectors, investing in aluminium, cement, and steel production (Kuna, 2021). Qatar has leveraged its natural gas reserves to develop energy-intensive industries, including petrochemicals and liquefied natural gas (LNG) facilities. However, the industrial sector's share of GDP has fluctuated over time, driven by oil price volatility and efforts to diversify into services (IMF, 2022).

The services sector has grown significantly across the GCC, overtaking industry in some years and reflecting the broader efforts to diversify economies into high-value-added activities such as finance, tourism, trade, and logistics. Bahrain and the UAE have become regional hubs for finance, international trade, and tourism, highlighting the role of Dubai and Abu Dhabi as major global cities. In Saudi Arabia, growth in the services sector may reflect the country's efforts to develop tourism, retail, healthcare, and financial services (as part of Vision 2030).

The services sector has emerged as a growing contributor to the GDP of the GCC, as shown Table 2.3, reflecting their efforts to diversify into high-value-added activities. Table 2.4 shows that the services sector accounted for over 80% of employment in Saudi Arabia by 2022, driven by growth in tourism, finance, retail, and logistics (Table 2.4). In the UAE, the services sector contributed 47.71% of GDP in 2022, supported by Dubai and Abu Dhabi's positions as global hubs for trade, tourism, and finance (World Economic Forum, 2023).

Tourism has been a particularly dynamic sector, with Saudi Arabia leveraging religious tourism to become one of the world's top 20 tourist destinations. As part of Vision 2030, the country aims to increase tourism's contribution to GDP from 3 to 10% by 2030, supported by mega-projects such as NEOM and Red Sea resorts (Vision 2030, 2023). Similarly, Dubai has capitalised on its strategic location, attracting millions of international visitors each year through luxury resorts, shopping malls, and cultural attractions.

Agriculture plays a minimal role in GCC economies, contributing less than 1% to GDP in most countries due to harsh desert climates and limited arable land (Table 2.3). Oman and Saudi Arabia have relatively higher agricultural shares, but these have declined over time due to urbanisation and industrialisation.

Employment trends reflect the structural shift from agriculture to services. By 2022, over 80% of employment in Saudi Arabia and 69.03% in the UAE was in services (Table 2.4). Oman and Qatar have experienced increased industrial employment, reflecting their focus on manufacturing and energy-intensive sectors. However, agriculture remains relatively significant in Oman, accounting for 6.07% of employment in 2022, supported by favourable weather conditions and rural development programmes (ILO, 2021).

Population and Labour Market Characteristics

As shown in Table 2.5, the population of the GCC countries grew from 8 million in 1970 to 60 million in 2023, with 60% in Saudi Arabia and 15% in the UAE, reflecting an annualised growth rate of 3.8%. Population growth rates were higher in the 1970s, 1980s, and 2000s. Still, they slowed in the post-financial-crisis and post-COVID eras, suggesting a stabilisation of the expatriate population and potential policy shifts in 2020 and beyond. The highest historical growth rates are observed in Qatar (165.3% between the 2000s and 2010s) and the UAE (159.0% between the 1990s and 2000s), mainly due to an influx of expatriate workers during periods of economic expansion, particularly in construction, oil, and services.

Based on data in Tables 2.5 and 2.6, the population growth and demographic structure of the GCC exhibit distinct features and trends that emphasise what has been referred to as a "*demographic imbalance*" at multiple levels. These imbalances are evident in rapid population growth, disproportionately low female representation, and a high proportion of working-age males attributable to expatriate labour.

Gender Structure

A key structural feature of GCC demographics is the overwhelming reliance on expatriate labour, which has led to a significant gender imbalance across the region. In 2023, male populations outnumbered female populations in all GCC countries except Oman. In Qatar, the sex ratio is three males per 1 female, whereas in the UAE it is two males per 1 female. Bahrain and Kuwait have the highest proportion of women, at approximately 40%. This imbalance can be attributed to the recruitment of male expatriates, who are often single, into labour-intensive industries such as construction and energy, which employ fewer women. The gender imbalance underscores the temporary nature of expatriate employment.

Age Structure

The age structure of the GCC population reveals another layer of demographic imbalance characterised by a decline in the proportion of younger people (aged 0–14) and an increase in the working-age group (15–64). In 2023, only 15.7% of Qatar's population and 15.2% of the UAE's population were below 15 years of age. This decline in the youth population indicates lower fertility rates and a higher share of the working-age population, particularly foreign workers. Over 80% of the populations in Qatar and the UAE were working-age adults, compared to just over 70% in Saudi Arabia and Oman.

This demographic shift reflects the importation of expatriate labour to meet labour market demands and sustain economic growth. On the other hand, although the proportion of older adults (aged 65 and above) remains low, the ageing population is gradually increasing across the GCC. Bahrain and Kuwait are experiencing increases in their elderly populations, with Kuwait's elderly population reaching 5.44% in 2023. The growing elderly population poses a future challenge for social services, healthcare systems, and pensions, mainly because the region's nationals are ageing and constitute a small share of the overall population. This trend may necessitate long-term reforms in social policy and healthcare infrastructure.

Prevalence of Expatriate Labour

Unemployment rates in GCC countries, particularly in Qatar and the UAE, have been low by global standards, owing to high demand for expatriate labour and job availability linked to economic growth. However, the unemployment rate in Saudi Arabia rose from 4.57% in 2000 to 7.45% in 2020, possibly due to increased female labour participation and challenges in integrating Saudi nationals into the workforce despite strong economic growth. Oman experienced a significant decrease in unemployment, from 4.64% in 2005 to 1.51% in 2022, reflecting favourable labour market conditions, possibly attributable to Omanisation policies aimed at increasing national employment.

The GCC countries have some of the highest percentages of expatriates in their populations globally. The international migration stock-to-total population data underscore the structural dependence on foreign labour to meet labour market demands despite labour nationalisation efforts. The UAE and Qatar have the highest expatriate-to-population ratios, with 88.1% and 77.3% of their populations, respectively, comprising expatriates as of 2020. By 2020, the expatriate population accounted for 72.8% of Kuwait's total population; in Oman and Bahrain, the ratio increased sharply between 1995 and 2020. Saudi Arabia's expatriate population rose from 24.60% in 1991 to 38.60% in 2020 (ILO, 2021).

The over-reliance on expatriate labour has created a dual labour market, in which nationals are primarily employed in the public sector while expatriates dominate the private sector. This dynamic has led to high wage differentials between the two groups and has created long-term challenges for the sustainability of economic growth and national employment.

Dominance of Wage and Salaried Workers

A further analysis of GCC labour market dynamics shows that the proportion of self-employed individuals is low, as most employed individuals, particularly expatriates, are salaried. This means that most workers in the GCC are wage or salaried employees, with Qatar and Kuwait showing nearly 100% wage employment. These levels reflect the dominance of formal employment contracts in sectors such as oil and gas, construction, and services, a stronger dependence on government for consumer spending, and possibly a relatively small entrepreneurial culture.

In response to demographic imbalances in labour markets, GCC countries have launched workforce nationalisation programmes. For instance, "Saudization" and "Emiratization" aim to increase nationals' participation in the private sector by imposing quotas and offering incentives to companies. However, significant progress is still needed to reduce the overwhelming reliance on foreign labour, particularly in sectors such as construction, retail, and hospitality.

Government Budgets and Recent Fiscal Reforms

Trends in Government Budgets

The government budgets of GCC countries are primarily shaped by their dependence on hydrocarbon revenues, expenditure patterns, and efforts to diversify their economies. As shown in Fig. 2.3, oil and gas account for more than 60% of total revenues, making their budgets vulnerable to fluctuations in global energy prices. The significant and rapid decline in oil prices has led to sharp cuts in government revenues (Fig. 2.4) and therefore government spending (Fig. 2.5).

In addition, government spending in the GCC focuses on social services, subsidies, and public-sector wages, with significant outlays on infrastructure projects as part of long-term national development plans. The large public-sector workforce in these countries, combined with extensive subsidies for fuel, electricity, and food, contributes to high levels of government spending (Table 2.7).

Additionally, the fiscal balances of GCC countries fluctuate with global oil prices; many countries experience deficits when oil prices decline. However, during periods of high oil prices, some countries, particularly Qatar and Kuwait, have recorded budget surpluses, leading to borrowing and the use of sovereign wealth funds to cover shortfalls (Figs. 2.6 and 2.7).

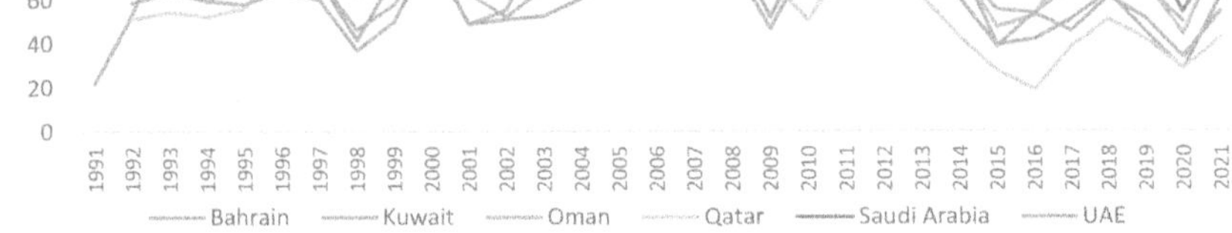

Fig. 2.3 Oil revenues to government revenues between 1991 and 2021 in the GCC countries (%)

Fig. 2.4 Government revenues to GDP between 1991 and 2021 in the GCC countries (%)

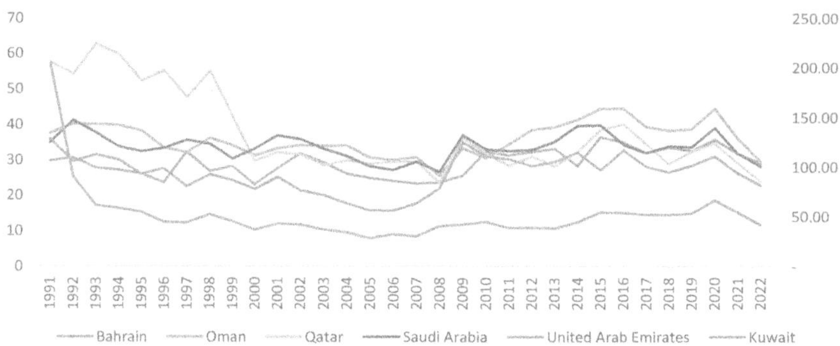

Fig. 2.5 Government spending to GDP between 1991 and 2021 in the GCC countries (%)

To finance budget deficits, GCC countries resorted to borrowing in recent years. Bahrain and Oman have particularly high debt-to-GDP ratios due to persistent fiscal deficits and lower fiscal reserves than wealthier neighbours such as the UAE and Qatar.

Table 2.7 Government expenditure categories as a percentage of total expenditure (2022)

Country	*Wages and -Salaries (%)*	*Social Spending (%)*	*Infrastructure and Capital Projects (%)*
Bahrain	42	25	33
Kuwait	50	20	30
Oman	40	22	38
Qatar	35	25	40
Saudi Arabia	45	28	27
UAE	38	20	42

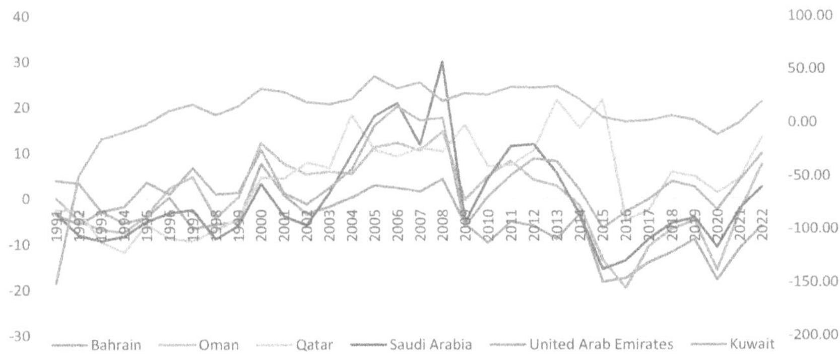

Fig. 2.6 Budget balance to GDP between 1991 and 2021 in the GCC countries (%)

Efforts Towards Fiscal Consolidation and Tax Reforms

The GCC countries have traditionally relied on hydrocarbon revenues to finance government budgets, leading to limited taxation. The absence of a personal income tax in the national economic models may have attracted a skilled expatriate workforce and enhanced perceptions of a favourable business environment. However, in recent years, GCC nations have introduced tax reforms, notably by implementing value-added tax (Table 2.8) and corporate tax (Table 2.9) measures, to achieve three primary goals. First, VAT may help diversify government revenues away from oil and gas, especially during periods of low oil prices. It is a mechanism for generating revenue from consumption, particularly in sectors like

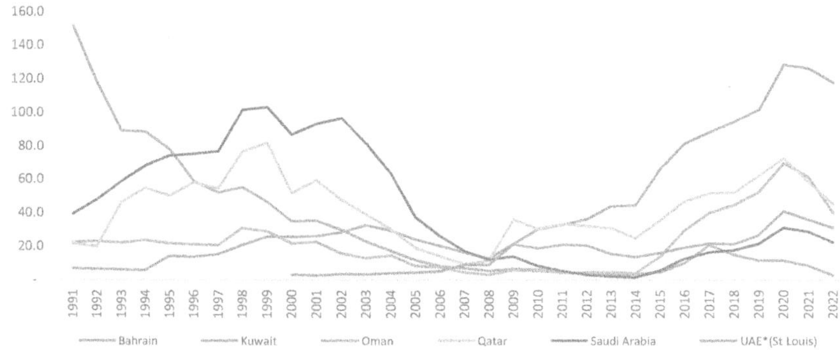

Fig. 2.7 Central Government debt to GDP between 1991 and 2021 in the GCC countries (%)

retail, hospitality, and luxury goods. Second, the introduction of VAT may improve the fiscal sustainability of GCC countries. For instance, in Saudi Arabia and the UAE, VAT has significantly reduced fiscal deficits and financed social services and infrastructure projects. Third, the corporate tax regimes in other GCC countries, particularly for foreign companies, reflect the growing importance of aligning with international tax standards. This has been influenced by the global push for tax transparency and by the OECD Base Erosion and Profit Shifting (BEPS) framework.

Sovereign Funds

Sovereign Wealth Funds (SWFs) are state-owned investment vehicles funded primarily through revenues from resource exports, particularly oil and natural gas. SWFs contribute to the region's long-term financial sustainability by managing excess liquidity from these revenues and investing it in assets such as equities, bonds, real estate, infrastructure, and other alternative investments. The establishment of SWFs in the GCC dates to the 1950s, driven by the need to manage the region's growing oil revenues. Over the decades, these funds have evolved into multi-billion-dollar portfolios that represent a significant portion of the world's sovereign wealth. Table 2.10 summarises the significant sovereign wealth funds (SWFs) in the GCC countries, including their year of establishment, current president (or managing director), estimated size of assets, and significant activities:

Table 2.8 Introduction of Value-Added Tax (VAT) in GCC countries

Country	*Year*	*VAT*	*Rationale for introduction and change*
Bahrain	January 2019	5% in 2019, then 10% in 2022	– Address fiscal deficits exacerbated by low oil prices – Public Reduce debt and achieve fiscal balance by 2024, under the Fiscal Balance Program
Oman	April 2021	5%	– Fiscal consolidation and reducing the budget deficit, particularly as part of its Vision 2040 initiative – Improving public services and reducing the reliance on oil revenues
Saudi Arabia	January 2018	5% in 2019; then 15% in July 2020	– Raise non-oil revenues in response to lower oil prices and the economic impacts of the COVID-19 pandemic. – Implement the Vision 2030 plan to diversify the economy and reduce reliance on hydrocarbons
UAE	January 2018	5%	– Strengthen public finances by contributing to non-oil revenue generation – VAT has been an effective tool for increasing fiscal revenues without imposing direct income taxes on individuals in a country with significant consumer activity
Kuwait and Qatar	Not yet implemented VAT Relatively minor fiscal deficits may have delayed the implementation of such taxes Both signal potential plans for tax reforms as part of regional agreements		

In the GCC, SWFs perform four roles. First, the stabilising role entails serving as a financial buffer, enabling governments to better manage the cyclical nature of oil revenues. During periods of low oil prices, governments can draw on SWF assets to fund budget deficits and maintain spending levels without incurring excessive borrowing or depleting central bank reserves. Countries like Kuwait and Saudi Arabia have relied on their SWFs to balance their budgets during economic downturns. In Kuwait, the Future Generations Fund (FGF) is often drawn on to meet fiscal needs during economic stress. The stabilising role can also be intertwined with the function of "*lenders of last resort*" performed by SWFs during crises. GCC SWFs can invest counter-cyclically. This was especially evident during the 2008 Global Financial Crisis, when GCC funds injected liquidity into struggling Western financial institutions.

Table 2.9 Corporate income tax rates in the GCC countries (as of 2024)

Country	*Details*
Bahrain	No corporate tax
Oman	A flat corporate income tax rate of 15% on most businesses, although small businesses with annual revenues below a particular threshold benefit from reduced rates
Saudi Arabia	20% on non-GCC businesses GCC businesses are required to pay zakat, a religious wealth tax, at a rate of 2.5% on their net worth Oil and gas companies face tax rates of 50%-85% on their profits, depending on production volumes
UAE	Firms in the oil and gas sector pay between 55 to 85%, Foreign banks pay a 20% corporate tax In 2022, the UAE announced plans to introduce a 9% corporate income tax on profits exceeding AED 375,000 (approximately $102,000) starting from June 2023. This is to align the UAE with international tax practices
Kuwait	Nationals and GCC citizens are exempt 15% for foreign businesses
Qatar	Nationals and GCC citizens are exempt 10% corporate tax on profits earned by foreign companies 35% for forms in oil and gas activities

Second, the diversification role entails supporting national economic diversification strategies by investing in sectors beyond oil and gas to reduce volatility and prepare for a post-oil era. The role is carried out through three channels. First, the funds are used to develop key infrastructure projects, such as airports, roads, and logistics hubs. Investments in infrastructure support long-term economic growth and help diversify the economy by encouraging tourism, trade, and foreign direct investment. Second, SWFs invest in domestic and global non-oil sectors, including finance, technology, real estate, and healthcare. For example, Saudi Arabia's PIF has invested heavily in NEOM, a futuristic megacity. At the same time, Qatar's QIA has made significant global investments in sectors such as sports (e.g., Paris Saint-Germain) and technology. Third, SWFs invest in domestic enterprises in key sectors, such as banking, telecommunications, and energy, thereby enhancing their competitiveness and supporting economic growth. The Investment Corporation of Dubai (ICD) manages Dubai's crown jewels in sectors such as aviation (Emirates), real estate (Emaar), and banking (Dubai Islamic Bank),

Table 2.10 Sovereign funds in the GCC countries

Country	*SWF Name*	*Year of Establishment*	*President/ Managing Director*	*Asset Size (USD Billion) in 2023*	*Major Activities*
Kuwait	Kuwait Investment Authority (KIA)	1953	Sheikh Faisal Al-Sabah	803	Short- and long-term Global investments in equities, bonds, infrastructure, and real estate
UAE (Abu Dhabi)	Abu Dhabi Investment Authority (ADIA)	1976	Hamed bin Zayed Al Nahyan	853	Global equities, fixed income, private equity, real estate, and infrastructure
Qatar	Qatar Investment Authority (QIA)	2005	Sheikh Mohammed bin Hamad	450	Diversified global investments, including real estate, sports, and technology
Saudi Arabia	Public Investment Fund (PIF)	1971, and revitalised in 2016	Yasir Al-Rumayyan	776	Investments in domestic infrastructure, technology, the NEOM project, and Vision 2030
UAE (Dubai)	Investment Corporation of Dubai (ICD)	2006	Mohammed Ibrahim Al Shaibani	320	Investments in banking, real estate, hospitality, transportation, and infrastructure
UAE (Abu Dhabi)	Mubadala Investment Company	2002	Khaldoon Khalifa Al Mubarak	284	Diversified global investments, including technology, aerospace, energy, real estate, and healthcare

(continued)

Table 2.10 (continued)

Country	*SWF Name*	*Year of Establishment*	*President/ Managing Director*	*Asset Size (USD Billion) in 2023*	*Major Activities*
Oman	Oman Investment Authority (OIA)	OIA was formed in 2020 after the merger of the State General Reserve Fund and the Oman Investment Fund	Abdulsalam Al Murshidi	17	Investments in domestic and global infrastructure, real estate, tourism, aviation, and industrial sectors
Bahrain	Mumtalakat Holding Company	2006	Khalid Al Rumaihi	18	Focus on manufacturing, financial services, tourism, and real estate

making it central to Dubai's growth strategy. GCC SWFs have increasingly diversified their portfolios into international assets. For example, ADIA has a global portfolio spanning sectors such as finance, real estate, and technology. ADIA is one of the largest SWFs globally and is known for its highly diversified portfolio across asset classes and geographies. Similarly, KIA and QIA have substantial holdings in global financial markets, including stakes in companies such as Volkswagen, Barclays, and Glencore.

Amar et al. (2018) examine the investment strategies of GCC SWFs over 2006–15, highlighting their tendency to acquire majority stakes in foreign companies. GCC SWFs do not consider the financial characteristics of the target firm nor the economic, institutional, and financial factors of the target country. The existence of trade agreements between the two countries is irrelevant to their acquisition/control decision. GCC SWFs target firms operating in strategic sectors for diversification and geopolitical influence purposes beyond pure profit maximisation or acquisition or control. Amar et al. (2018) support the hypothesis that GCC SWFs differ from other institutional investors in their acquisition decision strategies and that financial and commercial motives are not the exclusive targets of these strategies, which aligns with the broader strategic goal of economic diversification.

Conners (2024) explores how GCC SWFs align their investment strategies with national development plans and geopolitical goals. The study employs a qualitative case study approach to analyse major SWFs, including ADIA, Mubadala, QIA, and PIF. The findings reveal that these funds prioritise investments in strategic sectors and geographical regions that support their respective countries' long-term economic and geopolitical objectives. Conners (2024) explores how GCC SWFs align their investment strategies with national development plans and geopolitical goals. The study employs a qualitative case study approach to analyse major SWFs, including ADIA, Mubadala, QIA, and PIF. The findings reveal that these funds prioritise investments in strategic sectors and geographical regions that support their respective countries' long-term economic and geopolitical objectives. Al-Hassan et al. (2013) assess the role of SWFs in economic diversification efforts in the GCC. The research concludes that SWFs have been instrumental in reducing the region's dependence on oil revenues by investing in a diverse range of asset classes and sectors.

Third, SWFs serve as intergenerational wealth managers, saving current surplus wealth and oil revenues for future generations. This is especially important for countries like Qatar and the UAE, where the population expects high living standards to be maintained even as oil revenues decline.

Fourth, the large asset size of SWPs enables them to serve as a vehicle for global influence and strategic partnerships, particularly in global financial markets, real estate, and infrastructure projects. GCC SWFs have established strategic partnerships with global financial institutions, leveraging their capital to gain access to expertise, investment opportunities, and geopolitical influence. For instance, PIF has partnered with SoftBank's Vision Fund and global private equity firms to invest in cutting-edge technologies and innovation.

However, GCC sovereign wealth funds face several issues. First, most of them remain heavily reliant on oil revenues to expand their capital base. A sustained downturn in oil prices could affect their ability to make new investments or meet future obligations. Second, given their substantial international investments, GCC SWFs are exposed to geopolitical risks. For instance, diplomatic tensions between Qatar and other GCC states in 2017 caused some economic disruptions. Third, some SWFs are seen as lacking transparency regarding their investment strategies and governance structures. Increased global scrutiny of ESG (Environmental, Social, and

Governance) factors may push these funds to adopt more sustainable and transparent investment practices.

Global Importance of the GCC

The GCC economies are extensively linked to globalised economic growth due to their high degree of economic openness. Figure 2.8 shows that more than 50% of GCC economies depend on foreign trade, with the UAE and Bahrain exhibiting the highest exposure. In Fig. 2.9, The KOF index of globalisation, a measure of the economic dimensions of globalisation, shows that the GCC countries are more "globalised" than the MENA region and the rest of the world.

Economic exposures to foreign factors can be examined at four levels: goods trade, remittances, foreign direct investment, and foreign exchange reserves.

First, most GCC countries historically recorded significant current account surpluses owing to large oil export revenues. Qatar, Kuwait, and Saudi Arabia consistently maintain surpluses, while Bahrain and Oman face greater challenges in maintaining positive balances due to their smaller economies and higher import dependency. Large current account surpluses typically characterise periods of high oil prices, while lower prices can lead to deficits. The capital and financial accounts have also been affected by foreign investment and capital flows, including those associated with sovereign wealth funds.

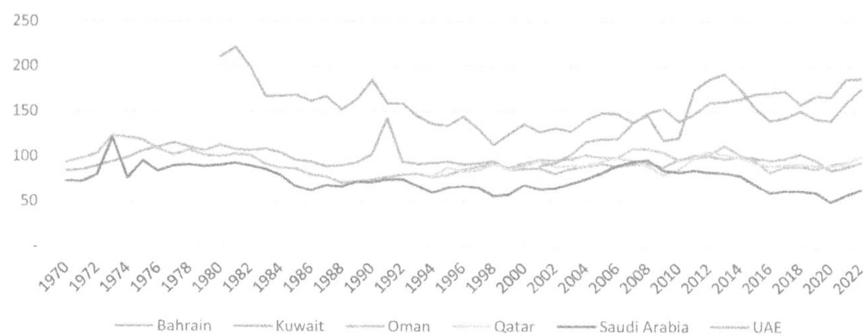

Fig. 2.8 Total foreign trade to GDP in GCC countries from 1970 to 2020 (%)

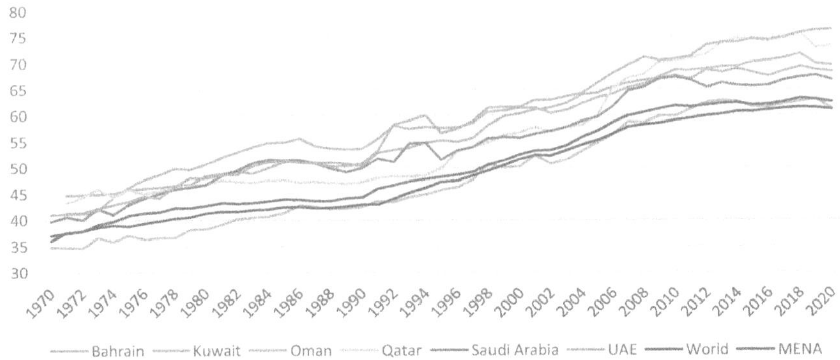

Fig. 2.9 The KOF Globalisation Index for GCC countries from 1970 to 2020 (%)

As shown in Table 2.11, the trade balance in GCC countries is dominated by oil and gas exports, which account for more than 60% of total exports. As a result, global oil price fluctuations directly affect export values and the trade balance. Kuwait, Qatar, Saudi Arabia, and Oman are more oil-dependent, while the UAE has the lowest concentration of oil revenue. On the other hand, GCC trade imbalances outside the hydrocarbon sector reflect non-oil trade deficits, as they are major importers of technology, services, and consumer and non-consumer goods, including food, vehicles, machinery, and electronics.

Second, since the 1970s, the substantial size of foreign workers' remittances repatriated from GCC economies has placed the region as an

Table 2.11 Trade balance and export composition (2022)

Country	*Trade Balance (US$ Billion)*	*Oil Exports (%)*	*Non-Oil Exports (%)*	*Imports (US$ Billion)*
Bahrain	3.2	60	40	12.3
Kuwait	45.6	85	15	23.2
Oman	18.4	65	35	26.7
Qatar	90.2	92	8	32.1
Saudi Arabia	221.9	85	15	183.7
UAE	64.5	74	26	222.7

important source of private and public foreign exchange flows, particularly in the Middle East (i.e., Egypt and Jordan) and the Indian subcontinent.

Third, supported by persistent current account surpluses driven by oil revenues, the GCC countries directed some of these surpluses from oil exports into direct foreign investment, thereby increasing their global economic importance. The capital and financial accounts are influenced by fluctuations in global capital markets, foreign direct investment (FDI), and the activities of GCC sovereign wealth funds. When oil prices drop, governments may draw down reserves or issue bonds to finance deficits.

Fourth, foreign reserves play a stabilising role by supporting long-term fiscal sustainability, particularly during periods of oil price declines, and serve as a buffer against external shocks, thereby supporting the fixed-exchange-rate regime. As shown in Fig. 2.10, GCC countries hold significant foreign reserves, owing to their high oil export revenues and strong current account surpluses, particularly during 2004–14. The value of the reserves increased significantly from 2004 to 2014. Saudi Arabia and the UAE hold more reserves than other GCC countries, but the share of reserves in GDP has declined since 2014 as GCC countries have invested some of these reserves in sovereign funds. Bahrain and Oman have relatively low foreign reserves compared with their GCC counterparts. They have had to rely more on external borrowing and drawdowns from reserves to finance fiscal deficits.

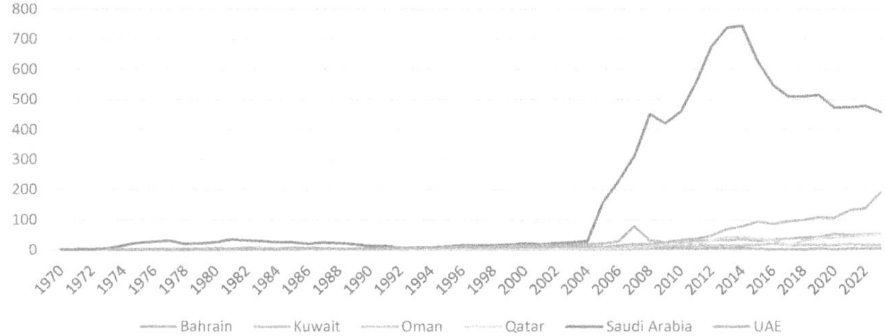

Fig. 2.10 The reserves (including gold) for GCC countries from 1970 to 2020 (USD billion)

In addition, the GCC's geographic location at the crossroads of Asia, Africa, and Europe enhances its strategic importance in global trade and energy supply. The region controls key maritime trade routes, including the Strait of Hormuz, through which nearly 20% of the world's oil passes daily (EIA, 2023). This chokepoint underscores the GCC's role in ensuring energy security for importing countries and highlights the potential economic and geopolitical disruptions arising from regional instability.

The GCC countries maintain strong economic and trade relationships with key global partners, including China, the EU, and the US. China has emerged as the largest importer of GCC hydrocarbons, driven by its growing energy demands and strategic Belt and Road Initiative partnerships (IMF, 2022). The EU and the US also remain important trading partners, with significant investments in GCC infrastructure, defence, and technology sectors. These relationships have allowed the GCC to leverage its energy resources for economic development while strengthening its geopolitical influence.

However, the region's strategic importance has also made it a focal point for political tensions and security challenges. Conflicts such as the Iran-Iraq War, the Gulf War, and the recent blockade of Qatar by its neighbours underscore the vulnerabilities associated with its geopolitical positioning. Despite these challenges, the GCC continues to play a central role in stabilising energy markets and fostering international trade.

Other Features of GCC Economies

Business Environment and Competitiveness in the GCC Region

The quality of the business environment and regulatory efficiency are directly linked to growth, and they serve as benchmarks for institutional change. These dimensions can be measured using the World Bank's "Doing Business"indicator, which covers 10 areas of business.

- Starting a business: Procedures, time, cost, and minimum capital to open a new business
- Dealing with construction permits: Procedures, time, and cost to build a warehouse

- Getting electricity: Procedures, time, and cost required for a business to obtain a permanent electricity connection for a newly constructed warehouse
- Registering property: Procedures, time, and cost to register commercial real estate
- Getting credit: Strength of legal rights index, depth of credit information index
- Protecting investors: Indices on the extent of disclosure, the extent of director liability, and ease of shareholder suits
- Paying taxes: Number of taxes paid, hours per year spent preparing tax returns, and total tax payable as a share of gross profit
- Trading across borders: Number of documents, cost, and time necessary to export and import
- Enforcing contracts: Procedures, time, and cost to enforce a debt contract
- Resolving insolvency: The time, cost, and recovery rate (%) under a bankruptcy proceeding

Table 2.12 presents the performance of GCC countries in the "Doing Business" environment from 2010 to 2020. It.

shows that the index increased from 66.8 in 2010 to 71.4 in 2020, suggesting that the introduced structural and regulatory reforms have improved the business environment regarding the establishment of new businesses, the growth of small and medium-sized enterprises (SMEs), and the attraction of foreign direct investment (Djankov et al., 2006; World Bank, 2020). Overall, the indicator presents a mixed picture of the business environment. While the UAE scores highly on the "Doing Business" indicators, Kuwait has the lowest score, and other GCC countries rank relatively below the GCC average. Across the GCC, identified problem areas include contract enforcement, access to credit, insolvency resolution, and the protection of minority investors.

Table 2.12 Doing business indicators for GCC between 2010 and 2020

Country	*Year*	*Ease of doing business*	*Starting a business*	*Dealing with construction permits*	*Getting electricity*	*Registering property*	*Getting credit*	*Protecting minority investors*	*Paying taxes*	*Trading across borders*	*Enforcing contracts*	*Resolving insolvency*
Bahrain	2010	66.3	75.9	72.6	79.0	90.4	37.5	50.0	87.8	74.5	52.4	42.8
Bahrain	2020	76.6	89.6	81.2	82.8	87.9	55.0	66.0	100.0	81.1	63.9	58.2
Average Bahrain	**2010–20**	**68.5**	**80.0**	**72.8**	**79.4**	**85.2**	**41.4**	**53.6**	**94.2**	**77.5**	**54.7**	**45.3**
Kuwait	2010	60.3	69.0	53.8	70.7	67.6	43.8	50.0	92.5	66.3	52.3	37.0
Kuwait	2020	67.4	88.4	71.9	81.9	75.1	45.0	66.0	92.5	52.6	61.4	39.2
Average Kuwait	**2010–20**	**61.4**	**73.4**	**58.7**	**71.9**	**67.5**	**39.1**	**57.3**	**92.5**	**57.6**	**56.8**	**39.1**
Oman	2010	65.6	69.8	74.9	82.3	81.3	37.5	50.0	92.7	74.8	50.1	42.8
Oman	2020	70.4	93.5	76.3	87.1	73.9	35.0	58.0	90.1	84.1	61.9	44.0
Average Oman	**2010–20**	**67.8**	**79.6**	**75.7**	**81.6**	**77.0**	**38.8**	**52.9**	**91.6**	**77.9**	**56.0**	**43.7**
Qatar	2010	66.2	82.3	80.9	84.0	83.8	18.8	43.3	100.0	75.2	56.7	37.0
Qatar	2020	68.6	86.0	84.2	83.6	95.4	45.0	28.0	99.4	71.5	54.6	38.0
Average Qatar	**2010–20**	**66.8**	**82.0**	**82.3**	**82.4**	**84.4**	**32.0**	**37.9**	**99.6**	**72.7**	**55.6**	**37.8**
Saudi Arabia	2010	66.0	73.1	71.6	81.6	87.8	56.3	66.7	92.9	77.8	52.7	0.0
Saudi Arabia	2020	70.8	93.1	76.8	91.8	84.5	55.0	86.0	79.1	76.0	65.3	0.0
Average Saudi Arabia	**2010–20**	**65.1**	**84.3**	**84.2**	**81.1**	**82.9**	**35.0**	**28.0**	**99.4**	**71.5**	**54.6**	**38.4**
UAE	2010	71.8	83.8	82.4	89.0	91.3	56.3	40.0	93.9	90.4	51.8	39.5
UAE	2020	80.3	94.8	89.8	100.0	90.1	65.0	80.0	83.8	74.1	75.9	49.3
Average UAE	**2010–20**	**75.9**	**88.9**	**85.1**	**95.0**	**90.5**	**52.7**	**60.7**	**96.5**	**81.2**	**64.6**	**42.9**
GCC	2010	66.8	79.0	73.6	82.8	83.2	41.5	53.2	91.0	76.2	54.8	33.2
GCC	2020	71.4	89.4	81.2	86.1	84.2	46.7	54.3	94.2	72.5	62.1	44.5
Average	**2010–20**	**68.7**	**81.3**	**76.2**	**83.2**	**82.6**	**43.4**	**50.4**	**94.7**	**76.2**	**56.6**	**41.4**

For instance, easier access to credit can facilitate investment in emerging sectors, while reduced regulatory burdens can encourage new business ventures and expansion beyond traditional industries (Djankov, 2009). Moreover, a positive business environment can foster innovation, enabling countries to develop new areas of comparative advantage and reducing reliance on a narrow set of exports (Amin & Djankov, 2019).

The UAE has the highest "Doing Business" score (75.9) among GCC countries and ranks highest in 9 of 10 categories. The UAE's comparative advantage is stimulated by reducing red tape, enhancing property rights, and improving access to finance. By contrast, Kuwait has the lowest "Doing Business" score (61.4), driven by issues related to red tape, access to credit, and property registration.

Human Development and Welfare: Education, Health, and Infrastructure

It is recognised that long-term, sustainable economic growth depends not only on the quality of infrastructure and the business environment, but also on progress in human development, including population access to health, education, and standards of living. This dimension is measured by the World Bank's Human Development Index (HDI), which combines life expectancy, educational attainment, and per capita income. A country with favourable human development conditions enables longer life expectancy, greater access to education, and higher incomes.

Table 2.13 presents trends in the HDI for all GCC countries from 1990 to 2002. In 2002, all GCC countries were classified as "very high human development" countries, reflecting higher per capita incomes attributable to oil resources and substantial investments in education and healthcare infrastructure. The region has a welfare system that offers extensive social benefits and a high life expectancy. The UAE recorded the highest human development index (HDI), followed by Bahrain (34), whereas Oman recorded the lowest (59).

Table 2.13 Human Development Index trends for GCC countries, 1990–2022

HDI rank (2002)	*Country*	*Human Development Index (HDI)*								*Change in HDI rank*	*Average annual HDI growth (%)*			
		1990	*2000*	*2010*	*2015*	*2019*	*2020*	*2021*	*2022*	*2015–2022*	*1990–2000*	*2000–2010*	*2010–2022*	*1990–2022*
17	UAE	0.717	0.790	0.828	0.860	0.933	0.930	0.931	0.937	19	0.97	0.47	1.04	0.84
34	Bahrain	0.733	0.775	0.807	0.859	0.888	0.884	0.884	0.888	3	0.56	0.41	0.80	0.60
40	Qatar	0.764	0.793	0.829	0.852	0.869	0.863	0.864	0.875	0	0.37	0.44	0.45	0.42
40	Saudi Arabia	0.699	0.746	0.805	0.842	0.862	0.861	0.867	0.875	6	0.65	0.76	0.70	0.70
49	Kuwait	0.698	0.780	0.811	0.829	0.838	0.826	0.836	0.847	0	1.12	0.39	0.36	0.61
59	Oman	.	0.702	0.798	0.824	0.841	0.823	0.810	0.819	–7	.	1.29	0.22	.
OTHER REGIONS														
Arab States		0.550	0.615	0.672	0.691	0.709	0.704	0.704	0.704	–	1.12	0.89	0.39	0.77
East Asia and the Pacific		0.507	0.594	0.689	0.728	0.757	0.760	0.761	0.766	–	1.60	1.49	0.89	1.30
Europe and Central Asia		0.663	0.680	0.746	0.782	0.802	0.792	0.797	0.802	–	0.25	0.93	0.61	0.60
Latin America and the Caribbean		0.637	0.686	0.735	0.758	0.768	0.755	0.754	0.763	–	0.74	0.69	0.31	0.57
South Asia		0.444	0.500	0.574	0.616	0.635	0.635	0.631	0.641	–	1.19	1.39	0.92	1.15
Sub-Saharan Africa		0.404	0.429	0.502	0.533	0.549	0.547	0.546	0.549	–	0.60	1.58	0.75	0.96
World		0.601	0.645	0.698	0.724	0.739	0.736	0.735	0.739	–	0.71	0.79	0.48	0.65

Conclusion

The sectoral structure of GCC economies has shifted markedly over the past five decades, with significant progress in economic diversification, particularly in services and manufacturing. However, the region remains heavily dependent on oil and gas exports and achieving a more balanced and sustainable economic structure will require continued reforms, investment in non-oil sectors, and enhanced global integration through trade in services. Balancing these structural shifts with demographic challenges, including the need to create employment for nationals, will shape the future trajectory of GCC economies.

While the GCC countries have made strides in diversifying their economies, reducing reliance on oil and gas remains a key challenge. The service sector's expansion and the growing role of manufacturing are positive signs, but heavy reliance on hydrocarbons persists in some countries, particularly in Qatar and Kuwait.

Each GCC country developed a strategic economic vision to diversify its economy and reduce its dependency on oil. Some of the key strategies include:

- Saudi Arabia's Vision 2020: This plan aimed to diversify the economy by investing in petrochemicals, mining, and manufacturing. The focus was also on privatisation, subsidy reduction, and encouraging private-sector participation. Vision 2020 refers to the first phase of the broader Vision 2030.
- Oman's Vision 2020: This plan focused on reducing the country's reliance on hydrocarbons and promoting sectors such as tourism, logistics, and fisheries.
- UAE's Vision 2021: The UAE invested heavily in infrastructure, real estate, and tourism, particularly in Dubai, positioning itself as a global financial and tourism hub.
- Qatar National Vision 2030: Qatar's strategy focused on sustainable development, with an emphasis on human capital, infrastructure, and education. It also sought to develop the liquefied natural gas sector.

CHAPTER 3

Financial Development, Diversification, and Resource Curse in GCC

Introduction

Economic diversification has become a fundamental strategy for reducing vulnerabilities and achieving sustainable growth in resource-dependent economies. In GCC countries, diversification is of indisputable importance given their heavy reliance on hydrocarbon revenues. Since the 1970s, GCC nations have used their oil and gas wealth as the foundation for economic development, facilitating substantial advancements in infrastructure, education, healthcare, and living standards (Fasanya et al., 2021; IMF, 2022; Abdelkawy, 2024). However, this resource-driven model has left them exposed to external shocks, such as sharp declines in oil prices during 1986, 2014–2016, and the COVID-19 pandemic, highlighting the need for structural reforms to reduce hydrocarbon dependency and foster broader economic resilience (Gately, 1987; IMF, 2023).

Diversification reduces the exposure of resource-dependent economies to global price volatility while addressing structural challenges such as rent-seeking behaviour, inefficient resource allocation, and weak governance (Leite & Weidmann, 1999; Dell'Anno & Maddah, 2022). It also enhances inclusive growth by generating employment across various sectors and strengthening human capital through investments in education and innovation (Morakabati, Beavis, & Fletcher, 2014). Moreover, diversification improves industrial competitiveness, positions economies

A. Bakhouche, *Banking in the GCC*, Palgrave Macmillan Studies in Banking and Financial Institutions,
https://doi.org/10.1007/978-3-032-21737-0_3

to participate in global value chains, and supports long-term stability by reducing reliance on volatile resource markets (Woertz, 2018; Poghosyan, 2022). The Sovereignty Retention Hypothesis underscores the importance of diversification in reducing external dependencies, enabling nations to mobilise domestic resources and pursue policies aligned with their national interests (Barry, 2014). Similarly, the Portfolio Effect Hypothesis highlights that diversification, akin to a balanced investment portfolio, minimises exposure to sector-specific shocks, stabilising growth and promoting economic resilience (Markowitz, 1952).

Despite these recognised benefits, the degree of economic diversification across the GCC remains uneven. As shown in Table 3.1, Bahrain and the UAE have made notable progress, with natural resource rents accounting for less than 20% of GDP in recent years. These nations have leveraged advanced financial systems to channel resource revenues into productive non-oil sectors, thereby reducing dependency (Davidson, 2011; IMF, 1996). In contrast, Kuwait and Saudi Arabia remain heavily reliant on their abundant hydrocarbons, with oil rents exceeding 30% of GDP. Qatar and Oman fall in between, reflecting mixed success in their diversification efforts (World Bank, 2024). Such disparities underscore the role of financial development (FD) as a key enabler of diversification, facilitating investment, improving access to credit, and promoting entrepreneurship in non-resource sectors.

Table 3.2 presents significant differences in FD across GCC countries. Bahrain and the UAE exhibit higher levels of financial development supported by efficient financial institutions and advanced financial markets. Conversely, Oman and Saudi Arabia lag in the depth and efficiency of their financial institutions, constraining their ability to support diversification-based structural transformation.

FD plays a transformative role in promoting economic diversification by efficiently allocating resource revenues, mitigating price volatility, and supporting structural changes in resource-dependent economies. Erdoğan et al. (2020) argue that integrating FD with natural resource sectors enhances economic resilience by attracting foreign investment, improving project financing, and enabling risk diversification. However, the relationship between FD and resource dependency in the GCC is complex. Qatar, for instance, achieved significant financial market development despite an average oil rent of 33.66% of GDP between 1995 and 2021. Conversely, Oman, despite moderate resource dependency, has made limited progress

Table 3.1 Oil rents as a percentage of current GDP over 1970–2021

Country	*1970–74*	*1975–79*	*1980–84*	*1985–89*	*1990–94*	*1995–99*	*2000–04*	*2005–09*	*2010–14*	*2015–19*	*2020–21*	*Ave*	*St. dev*
Total natural resources rents (% of GDP)													
Bahrain			46.74	31.49	25.68	19.29	19.67	22.53	22.03	12.31	13.67	23.71	10.40
Kuwait	47.02	61.73	46.96	29.64	31.98	36.42	44.22	49.55	52.97	38.29	29.28	42.55	10.38
Oman	49.25	59.20	44.25	38.83	35.56	31.76	39.69	41.34	35.60	22.50	24.05	38.37	10.55
Qatar	53.65	61.73	48.96	32.42	35.10	35.79	41.10	36.89	30.13	20.06	23.76	38.15	12.53
Saudi Arabia	40.52	58.31	46.45	28.40	33.44	28.77	38.27	47.99	42.09	24.96	21.44	37.33	11.15
UAE		38.88	29.89	23.84	25.34	16.93	19.53	24.98	24.68	15.05	14.80	23.39	7.38
MENA	22.72	40.25	31.46	17.43	21.83	16.33	22.43	30.03	26.00	17.14	15.65	23.75	7.66
World	1.72	4.18	4.42	2.09	1.73	1.45	2.10	3.64	3.49	1.99	2.25	2.64	1.07
Oil rents (% of GDP)													
Bahrain			44.18	27.60	22.19	15.11	15.97	19.11	18.61	9.53	8.82	20.12	10.75
Kuwait	46.42	60.96	46.35	28.84	31.24	35.31	43.24	48.85	52.21	37.37	27.58	41.67	10.55
Oman	49.25	59.06	43.81	37.93	34.67	30.56	36.88	37.96	32.90	19.95	19.27	36.57	11.63
Qatar	52.20	60.52	47.11	29.67	32.09	31.40	35.25	31.75	23.64	13.71	12.94	33.66	14.84
Saudi Arabia	40.42	58.19	46.23	27.68	32.67	27.85	37.21	46.94	41.06	24.00	19.83	36.55	11.46
UAE		38.53	29.45	22.52	23.98	15.33	18.00	23.73	23.59	14.09	13.08	22.23	7.75
MENA	22.13	39.54	30.91	16.58	20.77	15.15	20.96	28.16	24.05	15.35	12.60	22.38	7.99
World	0.96	2.83	3.11	1.38	1.13	0.88	1.34	2.29	2.20	1.15	1.01	1.66	0.80
Gas rents (% of GDP)													
Bahrain	-	-	2.57	3.88	3.49	4.18	3.70	3.42	3.42	2.79	4.86	3.59	1.58
Kuwait	0.61	0.77	0.62	0.81	0.74	1.11	0.98	0.70	0.76	0.92	1.70	0.88	0.31
Oman	0.00	0.14	0.43	0.90	0.89	1.20	2.81	3.38	2.71	2.55	4.78	1.80	1.54
Qatar	1.46	1.21	1.85	2.75	3.01	4.39	5.85	5.14	6.49	6.36	10.82	4.48	2.86

(continued)

Table 3.1 (continued)

Country	*1970–74*	*1975–79*	*1980–84*	*1985–89*	*1990–94*	*1995–99*	*2000–04*	*2005–09*	*2010–14*	*2015–19*	*2020–21*	*Ave*	*St. dev*
Saudi Arabia	0.10	0.12	0.22	0.72	0.77	0.92	1.06	1.05	1.02	0.96	1.61	0.78	0.47
UAE	-	0.35	0.44	1.32	1.36	1.61	1.53	1.25	1.09	0.96	1.72	1.16	0.56
MENA	0.60	0.71	0.55	0.84	1.06	1.18	1.47	1.87	1.95	1.79	3.05	1.37	0.76
World	0.77	1.35	1.30	0.71	0.60	0.57	0.76	1.35	1.29	0.83	1.24	0.98	0.32

Source World Bank (https://data.worldbank.org/, accessed 12/01/2025). Oil rents are the difference between the value of crude oil production at regional prices and the total production costs. Total natural resources rents are the sum of oil rents, natural gas rents, coal rents (hard and soft), mineral rents, and forest rent in financial development. These mixed outcomes highlight the importance of governance quality, effective policies, and institutional strength in mediating the relationship between FD and resource dependency (Stiglitz & Weiss, 1983; Guru & Yadav, 2019).

Although existing studies extensively examine the resource curse and the finance-growth nexus, they have paid limited attention to the relationship between FD and economic diversification in resource-dependent economies such as those in the GCC. Sachs and Warner (2001) and Sala-i-Martin and Subramanian (2013) focus on the negative effects of resource dependency, while Beck and Levine (2004) explore the broader finance-growth relationship without addressing its implications for diversification. Furthermore, many studies overlook the combined and moderating effects of FD and resource dependency on structural transformation, creating a gap in the literature (Hunjra et al., 2022).

This study addresses these gaps by investigating the multidimensional role of FD—measured through the access, depth, and efficiency of financial institutions and markets—in reducing resource dependency in GCC economies between 1995 and 2021. Using the IV-2SLS regression method, the research examines how FD supports economic diversification, mitigates the resource curse, and identifies the financial channels that influence structural transformation. The findings can help enhance FD's role in fostering sustainable economic development across the GCC.

Theoretical Framework

The relationship between financial development (FD) and economic diversification in resource-dependent economies is nuanced, shaped by the interplay of resource management, institutional quality, and the financial system's capacity to allocate capital efficiently. The theoretical perspectives underpinning this relationship draw on the resource curse and blessing hypotheses, as well as frameworks on financial systems and structural transformation.

Resource Curse Hypothesis (RCH)

The Resource Curse Hypothesis (RCH) posits that resource dependency can hinder economic diversification and long-term growth. This occurs through mechanisms such as weakened institutional quality, rent-seeking behaviour, and misallocation of financial resources. Resource rents often lead to corruption and bureaucratic inefficiencies, diverting revenues away from productive investments (Dell'Anno & Maddah, 2022). Sachs and Warner (2001) and Badeeb et al. (2017) demonstrate how resource dependency distorts capital allocation, limiting credit availability for non-resource sectors and stifling entrepreneurial activity. These mechanisms erect structural barriers that prevent economies from shifting to high-value sectors, thus perpetuating dependency on extractive industries.

Resource Blessing Hypothesis (RBH)

In contrast, the Resource Blessing Hypothesis (RBH) posits that resource wealth can catalyse economic diversification and sustainable growth under appropriate conditions. Robust financial systems and strong institutional frameworks are essential to this transformation. Financial development enables resource-rich economies to mobilise savings, allocate resources efficiently, and support innovation (Beck & Levine, 2004). Institutions play a complementary role, ensuring that resource revenues are managed transparently and directed towards infrastructure, human capital development, and technological advancement (North, 1990). Countries with strong governance structures and well-developed financial systems can use resource revenues to diversify into manufacturing, services, and high-tech industries, thereby mitigating the risk of dependency (Morakabati et al., 2014).

Saborowski Hypothesis

Saborowski (2011) proposes a theoretical framework suggesting that financial development (FD) serves as an effective mechanism for mitigating resource dependence and promoting economic diversification. It begins with the mobilisation of savings and the efficient allocation of resources, in which FD channels capital from low-productivity sectors, such as extractive industries, into high-productivity sectors, including manufacturing, services, and technology. This should be achieved by improving access to credit and supporting entrepreneurship, thereby reinforcing innovation and enabling the development of competitive industries. This reallocation of resources reduces reliance on resource-based activities and drives structural transformation, ultimately leading to economic diversification. The framework emphasises that diversification not only balances industrial structures but also enhances resilience to external shocks and ensures long-term sustainable growth. Within this framework, which emphasises the important role of FD in reshaping economic structures and promoting diversification, we may argue that FD enables resource-dependent economies to channel financial resources from the resource sector to upgrade their non-resource sectors, including the industrial and tertiary sectors.

Review of Past Studies

Empirical studies examining the relationship between FD and economic diversification in resource-dependent economies produce mixed findings. While FD is often cited as a key enabler of diversification, resource dependency can distort financial systems, which limits their effectiveness.

Several studies highlight how resource dependency undermines financial development. Sala-i-Martin and Subramanian (2013) argue that resource-based economies often prioritise short-term gains over long-term investments, perpetuating dependency on extractive sectors (Hattendorff, 2014). Similarly, they argue that resource-rich countries tend to have underdeveloped financial systems, which can affect welfare and lead to export concentration. Mlachila and Ouedraogo (2020) find evidence of a "*financial development curse*", in which commodity price shocks negatively affect FD in 68 resource-dependent economies between 1980 and 2014. However, they note that strong institutions, better governance and the effective use of resource windfalls can mitigate these effects.

In contrast, other studies identify a positive relationship between FD and economic diversification. Erdoğan et al. (2020) argue that FD transforms resource revenues into long-term economic growth by supporting entrepreneurship, innovation, and export diversification. Ogbonna et al. (2020) find that in Nigeria, FD positively impacts the non-oil sector by reallocating oil revenues to broader economic activities. Nwani et al. (2023) emphasise that institutional quality enhances FD's capacity to increase the share of manufacturing and services in GDP while reducing reliance on extractive industries.

Export diversification is one dimension of economic diversification. Han et al. (2022) find a relationship between FD and export diversification in ten resource-rich countries, showing that financial intermediation reduces resource dependency. Mazengia et al. (2023) highlight that FD in Ethiopia supports export diversification by improving access to credit and aligning trade and interest-rate policies. Kainat et al. (2024) show that expanding access to financial markets improves export performance in South Asia. However, Agosin et al. (2011) claim that FD does not always lead to export diversification, depending on structural and institutional conditions.

The role of institutional quality is widely recognised as an important factor for economic diversification. Boschini et al. (2007) argue that institutional quality moderates the adverse effects of resource dependency, such that resource rents contribute positively to FD. Bhattacharyya and Hodler (2014) show that resource abundance is negatively associated with FD in countries with weak institutions, while stronger governance frameworks help channel resource revenues into productive uses.

For GCC countries, the empirical evidence emphasises unique dynamics due to their reliance on hydrocarbon revenues. Ibrahim (2019) finds a positive relationship between oil price changes and banking-sector performance in GCC economies, reflecting the dependence of financial systems on resource revenues. Samargandi et al. (2014) show that FD positively affects non-oil GDP growth in Saudi Arabia, thereby demonstrating its role in reducing resource dependence. However, Haque et al. (2022) argue that the stronger institutional and governance frameworks in GCC countries could enhance the effectiveness of FD in promoting diversification.

In line with the liquidity constraint hypothesis (Nieminen, 2020) and the finance-growth literature (Guru & Yadav, 2019), access to domestic financial services may contribute to economic diversification by easing the credit constraints that diversification firms may face (Hermes & Lensink, 2000; Hausmann & Rodrik, 2003; Beck & Demirgüç-Kunt, 2006; Chaney, 2016). A developed financial sector can support the growth of the non-resource sector through loans, purchases of non-equity securities, trade credits, and other accounts receivable (King & Levine, 1993). Therefore, the following hypothesis is developed:

H0: There is a positive relationship between financial development and economic diversification.

Methodology

Regression Model

This study examines the factors influencing economic diversification in GCC countries, focusing on the role of financial development, institutional characteristics, and macroeconomic controls. The relationship between economic diversification and its potential determinants is captured using the following regression model:

$$\begin{aligned} ED =& \alpha + \lambda ED_{t-1} + \beta_1 FINDEV + \beta_2 GROWTH + \beta_3 INFLATION \\ &+ \beta_4 SAVING + \beta_5 TRAOPE + \beta 6\ GOV \\ &+ \beta_7 REG\_QUA + \beta_8 STABILITY + \varepsilon \end{aligned} \tag{3.1}$$

where ED denotes economic diversification, proxied by resource dependency, FINDEV represents financial development, the primary independent variable, and is proxied by the Financial Development Index and its constituent sub-indices. GROWTH and INFLATION are measured by the percentage change in country-level real GDP and CPI; TRAOPE is trade openness, SAVING is gross saving ratio; REG_QUA and STABILITY are estimates of regulation quality and political stability, capturing institutional quality; GOV measures the size of government, measured by government spending; ϵ is the error term.

To address potential endogeneity arising from reverse causality or omitted variable bias, the model produces robust, unbiased estimates using the two-stage least squares (2SLS) method with instruments. In this approach, we employ lagged values and external instruments to address simultaneity and endogeneity.

Data and Variables

This study employs annual data for six GCC countries (Bahrain, Kuwait, Oman, Qatar, Saudi Arabia, and the UAE) from 1995 to 2021. The data are obtained from the International Monetary Fund (IMF) Financial Development Index Database and the World Bank's World Development Indicators (WDI). In addition to the data in Tables 3.1 and 3.2, Table 3.3 summarises the descriptive statistics for the variables used in the analysis. Economic Diversification (ED) is the primary dependent variable, measured by the ratio of natural resource rents to GDP. This proxy reflects the extent of resource dependence in GCC economies, which rely heavily on hydrocarbons as their primary source of revenue. Bahrain and the UAE exhibit lower resource dependence, with average natural resource rents of approximately 20%, whereas Kuwait remains the most resource-dependent, with rents averaging 44.15%.

Financial Development (FINDEV) is the primary independent variable, measured using the IMF's Financial Development Index (FDI) and its sub-indices. The FDI is a composite index assessing the depth, access, and efficiency of financial systems, ranging from 0 (least developed) to 1 (most developed). It comprises two sub-indices: the Financial Institutions Development Index (FIDI), which evaluates the performance of banks and non-bank institutions, and the Financial Markets Development Index (FMDI), which captures the size and activity of stock and bond markets. Within the GCC, Qatar has the highest FDI score (mean = 0.525), supported by strong institutional and market performance, whereas Oman has the lowest (mean = 0.293), indicating gaps in financial infrastructure.

Institutional Variables, i.e., REG_QUA and STABILITY, capture governance quality and political stability in the countries under study. These factors are essential for creating a business-friendly environment that supports financial development and diversification. Qatar and the UAE show higher regulatory quality and political stability. At the same time, Saudi Arabia and Kuwait have relatively low institutional scores, underscoring the need for governance reforms to improve diversification outcomes.

Macroeconomic variables include GROWTH, which measures the annual percentage change in real GDP and serves as an indicator of economic stability. The GCC countries recorded an average growth rate of 4.23% during the study period, with Qatar achieving the highest growth (8.54%), driven by liquefied natural gas exports. INFLATION is generally stable, averaging 2.41%, but exhibits significant variability across countries. TRAOPE reflects the degree of trade integration, with an average trade-to-GDP ratio of 105%, primarily driven by hydrocarbon exports. SAVING highlights the role of domestic savings in financing diversification projects, with GCC countries maintaining a high average savings rate of 44.91%. GOV, representing government spending as a share of GDP, underscores the fiscal policies that influence resource allocation and public investment.

Table 3.2 Core indicators of financial development in GCC countries 1995–2021

	Financial Development Index (FDI)							*Financial Institutions Development Index (FIDI)*						
Country	*Bahrain*	*Kuwait*	*Oman*	*Qatar*	*Saudi Arabia*	*UAE*	*Average*	*Bahrain*	*Kuwait*	*Oman*	*Qatar*	*Saudi Arabia*	*UAE*	*Average*
1995–1999	0.416	0.412	0.354	0.519	0.307	0.249	**0.376**	0.351	0.367	0.418	0.403	0.323	0.337	**0.367**
2000–2004	0.412	0.338	0.322	0.548	0.351	0.288	**0.376**	0.346	0.381	0.416	0.388	0.283	0.313	**0.355**
2005–2009	0.450	0.456	0.402	0.541	0.436	0.472	**0.460**	0.354	0.411	0.417	0.386	0.267	0.372	**0.368**
2010–2014	0.423	0.443	0.335	0.522	0.460	0.457	**0.440**	0.347	0.424	0.405	0.401	0.295	0.391	**0.377**
2015–2019	0.413	0.470	0.377	0.491	0.457	0.489	**0.450**	0.336	0.485	0.408	0.444	0.347	0.400	**0.403**
2020–2021	0.444	0.403	0.380	0.540	0.449	0.486	**0.451**	0.341	0.520	0.414	0.477	0.353	0.370	**0.413**
Average	**0.424**	**0.422**	**0.360**	**0.525**	**0.406**	**0.398**	**0.423**	**0.347**	**0.422**	**0.413**	**0.410**	**0.307**	**0.363**	**0.377**

	Financial Markets Development Index (FMDI)						
Country	*Bahrain*	*Kuwait*	*Oman*	*Qatar*	*Saudi Arabia*	*UAE*	*Average*
1995–1999	0.465	0.441	0.275	0.615	0.279	0.151	**0.371**
2000–2004	0.461	0.281	0.214	0.687	0.405	0.251	**0.383**
2005–2009	0.528	0.483	0.372	0.674	0.589	0.553	**0.533**
2010–2014	0.482	0.444	0.252	0.622	0.607	0.505	**0.485**
2015–2019	0.475	0.438	0.332	0.518	0.550	0.560	**0.479**
2020–2021	0.530	0.270	0.332	0.583	0.527	0.584	**0.471**
Average	**0.486**	**0.406**	**0.292**	**0.620**	**0.489**	**0.417**	**0.452**

(continued)

Table 3.2 (continued)

Country	*Financial Institutions Development Index—Access (FIDI_Access)*							*Financial Institutions Development Index—Depth (FIDI_Depth)*						
	Bahrain	*Kuwait*	*Oman*	*Qatar*	*Saudi Arabia*	*UAE*	*Average*	*Bahrain*	*Kuwait*	*Oman*	*Qatar*	*Saudi Arabia*	*UAE*	*Average*
1995–1999	-	0.286	0.422	0.492	0.253	0.300	**0.351**	0.359	0.117	0.105	0.087	0.097	0.097	**0.144**
2000–2004	-	0.283	0.466	0.466	0.238	0.274	**0.345**	0.364	0.135	0.106	0.077	0.105	0.101	**0.148**
2005–2009	-	0.374	0.416	0.431	0.282	0.333	**0.367**	0.385	0.136	0.101	0.105	0.127	0.161	**0.169**
2010–2014	-	0.415	0.389	0.391	0.367	0.389	**0.390**	0.344	0.140	0.116	0.107	0.114	0.177	**0.166**
2015–2019	-	0.470	0.338	0.361	0.423	0.415	**0.401**	0.318	0.215	0.168	0.211	0.157	0.214	**0.214**
2020–2021	-	0.507	0.349	0.342	0.379	0.320	**0.379**	0.343	0.256	0.181	0.302	0.173	0.237	**0.249**
Average	-	**0.376**	**0.402**	**0.422**	**0.318**	**0.341**	**0.372**	**0.353**	**0.156**	**0.124**	**0.131**	**0.124**	**0.156**	**0.174**

Country	*Financial Institutions Development Index—Efficiency (FIDI_Efficiency)*						
	Bahrain	*Kuwait*	*Oman*	*Qatar*	*Saudi Arabia*	*UAE*	*Average*
1995–1999	0.722	0.715	0.706	0.569	0.638	0.612	**0.660**
2000–2004	0.695	0.745	0.629	0.571	0.498	0.559	**0.616**
2005–2009	0.691	0.709	0.718	0.576	0.333	0.589	**0.603**
2010–2014	0.731	0.684	0.695	0.689	0.323	0.544	**0.611**
2015–2019	0.732	0.701	0.701	0.729	0.357	0.474	**0.616**
2020–2021	0.711	0.705	0.687	0.734	0.427	0.477	**0.623**
Average	**0.714**	**0.710**	**0.690**	**0.635**	**0.430**	**0.550**	**0.621**

	Financial Markets Development Index—Access (FMDI_Access)							*Financial Markets Development Index—Depth (FMDI_Depth)*						
Country	*Bahrain*	*Kuwait*	*Oman*	*Qatar*	*Saudi Arabia*	*UAE*	*Average*	*Bahrain*	*Kuwait*	*Oman*	*Qatar*	*Saudi Arabia*	*UAE*	*Average*
1995–1999	0.707	0.173	0.332	0.652	0.175	0.234	**0.379**	0.575	0.418	0.163	0.689	0.217	0.093	**0.359**
2000–2004	0.644	0.106	0.301	0.661	0.248	0.358	**0.386**	0.646	0.386	0.190	0.762	0.318	0.184	**0.414**
2005–2009	0.720	0.077	0.397	0.766	0.390	0.680	**0.505**	0.730	0.601	0.366	0.669	0.464	0.467	**0.549**
2010–2014	0.763	0.066	0.302	0.685	0.403	0.674	**0.482**	0.615	0.565	0.287	0.588	0.485	0.472	**0.502**
2015–2019	0.769	0.158	0.503	0.762	0.448	0.852	**0.582**	0.580	0.573	0.348	0.596	0.533	0.567	**0.533**
2020–2021	0.873	0.141	0.581	0.852	0.557	0.864	**0.645**	0.640	0.465	0.323	0.677	0.716	0.685	**0.584**
Average	**0.732**	**0.118**	**0.383**	**0.716**	**0.349**	**0.582**	**0.480**	**0.630**	**0.505**	**0.275**	**0.662**	**0.427**	**0.381**	**0.480**

	Financial Markets Development Index—Efficiency (FMDI_Efficiency)						
Country	*Bahrain*	*Kuwait*	*Oman*	*Qatar*	*Saudi Arabia*	*UAE*	*Average*
1995–1999	0.069	0.719	0.342	0.462	0.446	0.131	**0.361**
2000–2004	0.036	0.318	0.147	0.591	0.650	0.214	**0.326**
2005–2009	0.069	0.728	0.337	0.558	0.914	0.506	**0.519**
2010–2014	0.019	0.659	0.150	0.572	0.932	0.354	**0.448**
2015–2019	0.033	0.535	0.126	0.157	0.648	0.233	**0.289**
2020–2021	0.030	0.153	0.078	0.173	0.247	0.157	**0.140**
Average	**0.044**	**0.559**	**0.210**	**0.446**	**0.683**	**0.278**	**0.370**

Table 3.3 Descriptive statistics of the variables used in regression for all GCC countries between 1995 and 2021

Variable	*Description*	*No. obs*	*Mean*	*St. dev*	*Min*	*Max*
Dependent variable						
ED	Economic diversification, measured by natural resources dependency: it is oil and gas rents as a share of GDP	161	30.88	11.81	9.65	59.07
Financial development indices (FINDEV)						
FDI	Financial Development Index: aggregate of FIDI and FMDI	162	0.423	0.082	0.232	0.586
FIDI	Financial Institutions Development Index: aggregate of access, depth, and efficiency sub-indices	135	0.377	0.053	0.224	0.526
FID_ACCESS	Financial institutions access index: accounts per 1,000 adults (commercial banks); % of firms with a line of credit	162	0.372	0.076	0.215	0.516
FID_DEPTH	Financial institutions depth index: banks' assets to GDP, credit to GDP, M2 to GDP	162	0.174	0.094	0.069	0.432
FID_ EFFICIENCY	Financial institutions' efficiency index: net interest margin; overhead costs (% of total assets)	162	0.621	0.125	0.273	0.781
FMDI	Financial Market Development Index: aggregate of access, depth, and efficiency sub-indices	162	0.452	0.155	0.115	0.739

(continued)

Table 3.3 (continued)

Variable	*Description*	*No. obs*	*Mean*	*St. dev*	*Min*	*Max*
FMD_ACCESS	Financial market access index: capitalisation outside of the top largest companies; total number of debt issues per 100,000 adults	162	0.480	0.263	0.025	1.000
FMD_DEPTH	Financial market depth index: market capitalisation to GDP; stock traded to GDP; debt securities to GDP	162	0.480	0.188	0.058	0.782
FMD_EFFICIENCY	Financial markets efficiency index: stock market turnover ratio	162	0.370	0.301	0.012	1.000
Other variables						
GROWTH	Real GDP growth: Annual percentage change in constant GDP	162	0.042	0.052	(0.071)	0.300
INFLATION	Inflation rate: annual percentage change in CPI	152	0. 241	0.314	−0.049	0.1515
SAVING	Gross domestic savings: GDP minus final consumption expenditure, expressed as a percentage of GDP	152	0.449	0.128	0.112	0.755
TRADE	Trade openness: sum of exports and imports of goods and services as a share of GDP	154	1.050	0.305	0.497	1.919

(continued)

Table 3.3 (continued)

Variable	*Description*	*No. obs*	*Mean*	*St. dev*	*Min*	*Max*
GOV	Government size: total government spending as a percentage of GDP, including current expenditures for goods and services	152	0.189	0.0589	0.0633	0.330
REG_QUA	Regulatory quality: the government's ability to formulate and implement sound policies that promote private-sector development	138	0.42	0.34	(0.31)	1.10
STABILITY	Political stability: perceptions of the likelihood of instability, politically motivated violence, or terrorism	138	0.324	0.636	(1.335)	1.224

Results and Discussion

Financial Development Results

The IV-2SLS regression estimations are presented in Table 3.4. The results highlight the relationship between financial development and economic diversification, where economic diversification is proxied by the natural resource rents-to-GDP ratio. A lower ratio indicates reduced resource dependency and higher diversification. The analysis includes nine regression models, with Model 1 assessing the overall impact of the Financial Development Index (FDI) and Models 2–9 examining the sub-components of the FDI, including the Financial Institutions Development Index (FIDI) and the Financial Markets Development Index (FMDI), along with their dimensions of depth, access, and efficiency. The models underscore the transformative potential of financial development in reducing resource dependency and enhancing diversified economic structures.

Table 3.4 IV-2SLS regression results for the specification where the ratio of natural resources rents to GDP is the proxy of economic diversification

	Model 1: Financial Development Index (FDI)	*Panel 1: Financial Institutions development*				*Panel 2: Financial markets development*			
		Model 2: Financial Institutions Index	*Model 3: FI Access Index*	*Model 4: FI depth Index*	*Model 5: FI Efficiency Index*	*Model 6: Financial Markets Index*	*Model 7: FM Access Index*	*Model 8: FM depth Index*	*Model 9: FM Efficiency Index*
CONSTANT	−0.4924 (0.598)	−1.9898 (0.272)	−5.3018 (0.009)***	0.1713 (0.873)	2.0029 (0.066)*	0.3369 (0.707)	0.467 (0.555)	−0.2912 (0.742)	0.8017 (0.569)
FINDEV	−0.6878 (0.001)***	−1.0569 (0.049)**	−1.8725 (0.003)***	−0.5061 (0.000)***	−0.5861 (0.0.000)**	−0.3988 (0.000)***	−0.2346 (0.000)***	−0.32 (0.000)***	+ 0.0925 (0.012)**
GROWTH	0.9367 (0.089)*	0.5151 (0.523)	0.4189 (0.610)	0.0069 (0.99)	1.1083 (0.077)*	1.1211 (0.038)**	1.2794 (0.004)***	1.1179 (0.048)**	3.0518 (0.000)***
INFLATION	0.2704 (0.001)***	0.2447 (0.000)***	0.2963 (0.011)**	0.1000 (0.089)*	0.2209 (0.001)***	0.2625 (0.002)***	0.1831 (0.001)***	0.2602 (0.000)***	0.1401 (0.136)
SAVING	0.6405 (0.000)***	0.5341 (0.000)***	0.7814 (0.000)***	0.3886 (0.000)***	0.5031 (0.000)***	0.6339 (0.000)***	0.5187 (0.000)***	0.615 (0.000)***	0.3130 (0.006)***
TRAOPE	−0.0372 (0.759)	−0.1351 (0.421)	0.4079 (0.052)*	0.183 (0.247)	−0.1914 (0.180)	−0.0845 (0.484)	−0.041 (0.685)	0.0139 (0.905)	0.0236 (0.898)
GOV	0.215 (0.043)**	0.3759 (0.011)**	0.5112 (0.011)**	0.1327 (0.155)	0.1166 (0.328)	0.1443 (0.3579)	0.1789 (0.055)*	0.2481 (0.012)**	0.3044 (0.024)***
REGQUAL	−1.1511 (0.000)***	−1.2963 (0.000)***	−1.6668 (0.000)***	−0.71 (0.000)***	−1.3176 (0.000)***	−1.1648 (0.000)***	−0.6952 (0.000)***	−1.1058 (0.000)***	−0.8694 (0.000)***
STABILITY	0.3714 (0.000)***	0.7641 (0.002)***	0.7586 (0.024)**	−0.2536 (0.048)**	0.293 (0.021)**	0.2501 (0.4764)	0.2601 (0.007)***	0.2542 (0.021)**	0.3685 (0.010)**
Model Diagnostics									
No. of obs	96	123	101	124	123	135	135	135	87

(continued)

Table 3.4 (continued)

	Model 1: Financial Development Index (FDI)	*Panel 1: Financial Institutions development*				*Panel 2: Financial markets development*			
		Model 2: Financial Institutions Index	*Model 3: FI Access Index*	*Model 4: FI depth Index*	*Model 5: FI Efficiency Index*	*Model 6: Financial Markets Index*	*Model 7: FM Access Index*	*Model 8: FM depth Index*	*Model 9: FM Efficiency Index*
Wald Chi^2 (p-value)	293.21 (0.000) ***	217.31 (0.000) ***	115.79 (0.000) ***	216.01 (0.000) ***	265.16 (0.000) ***	241.14 (0.000***	389.07 (0.000) ***	243.42 (0.000) ***	144.73 (0.000) ***
R-Squared	0.6647	0.5608	0.1245	0.657	0.599	0.5973	0.695	0.608	0.5674
Root MSE	0.22195	0.2838	0.3599	0.28	0.271	0.2665	0.232	0.263	0.2751
Diagnostic Tests									
Overidentification Test (p-value)	1.588 (0.0.2076)	1.788 (0.1811)	2.217 (0.1365)	4.569 (0.1018)	2.308 (0315)	1.55 (0.213)	0.911 (0.340)	0.706 (0.401)	2.062 (0.1501)
First Stage F-Test (p-value)	77.99 (0.000) ***	11.83 (0.000)***	8.64 (0.000)***	24.344 (0.000)***	12.18 (0.000)***	73.77 (0.000)***	67.31 (0.000)***	186.14 (0.000)***	1,807 (0.000)***

The regression results in Table 3.4 exhibit strong explanatory power, with R-squared values ranging from 0.568 to 0.695. The Wald Chi-square statistics are significant across all models, confirming the relevance of the explanatory variables. Overidentification tests and first-stage F-tests assess the robustness of the instruments used in the IV-2SLS approach, ensuring that the results are reliable and free of endogeneity.

Financial Development as an Enabler of Diversification

The significant negative coefficient for the Financial Development Index (FDI) in Model 1 (−0.6878, $p < 0.001$) supports the hypothesis that financial development enables economic diversification by reducing resource dependency. This aligns with Schumpeter's finance-growth nexus (Schumpeter, 1911) and Patrick's supply-leading hypothesis (Patrick, 1966), which emphasises the role of financial systems in mobilising savings, allocating resources efficiently, and funding non-resource sectors. The findings also resonate with the Resource Blessing Hypothesis (Sachs & Warner, 1995), which argues that financial development can transform resource revenues into productive investments under sound institutions.

Several studies emphasise the importance of financial development in resource-rich economies. Levine (2002) proposes the financial service view, emphasising the role of financial institutions and markets in directing resources to productive sectors. Beck and Levine (2004) demonstrate that financial development reduces financing constraints on entrepreneurship and innovation, thereby promoting economic growth. Dogan et al. (2020) find that natural resource rents have a positive effect on financial development, supporting the financial resource blessing rather than the financial resource curse for developed countries. Erdoğan et al. (2020) further argue that financial development in resource-dependent economies facilitates the allocation of revenues from resource sectors to non-resource industries, a mechanism that may be applicable to the GCC context, as supported by our results.

The Dominance of Financial Institutions

The results reveal that financial institutions exert a stronger influence on economic diversification than financial markets. The Financial Institutions Development Index (FIDI) in Model 2 has a larger, more significant negative coefficient (−1.0569, p = 0.049) than the Financial Markets Development Index (FMDI) in Model 6 (−0.3988, p < 0.001). This indicates that the institutional side of financial systems, including banks, insurance companies, and pension funds, is more effective at channelling resources to non-resource sectors.

This finding aligns with Greenwood and Jovanovic's (1990) view that financial institutions play a pivotal role in facilitating private-sector investment by reducing information asymmetries and lowering the cost of capital. In this context, financial development enables a transition from a resource-based to a more developed, diversified economy. Similarly, Samargandi et al. (2014) show that financial institutions in Saudi Arabia support growth in the non-oil sector, highlighting their relevance in the GCC context.

Conversely, the relatively weaker performance of financial markets may reflect their sensitivity to resource revenues, as evidenced by the positive coefficient for financial market efficiency (Model 9: 0.0925, p = 0.012). This result suggests that, while financial markets in the GCC continue to mature, their activities remain closely tied to the hydrocarbon sector, potentially limiting their ability to drive diversification through the financial market channel.

Channels for Diversification: Access, Depth, and Efficiency

Among the sub-dimensions of financial development, "Access" emerges as the most effective channel for promoting diversification. The coefficients for ACCESS in financial institutions in Model 3 (−1.8725, p = 0.003) and in financial markets in Model 7 (−0.2346, p < 0.001) are more significant and more impactful than those for depth and efficiency. This indicates that expanding financial inclusion—by increasing access to credit, expanding the number of financial service providers, and improving financial literacy—is necessary to enable diversification.

Depth also plays a significant role, as evidenced by the negative coefficients for financial institutions' depth in Model 4 (−0.5061, p < 0.001) and for financial market depth in Model 8 (−0.32, p < 0.001). This supports the idea that mobilising and allocating sufficient capital is essential for large-scale investments in non-resource sectors, such as technology, logistics, and renewable energy.

The mixed results for efficiency highlight the complex nature of the finance-diversification nexus. While financial institution efficiency (β =

−0.5861, $p < 0.001$) is positively associated with diversification, financial market efficiency remains associated with resource dependence. This suggests that financial markets in the GCC need to diversify their asset bases and reduce their reliance on resource-linked revenues to support economic diversification fully.

Comparison with Existing Literature

The findings contribute to the ongoing debate on the relationship between financial development and resource dependency. In contrast to Beck (2011), who highlights the "natural resource curse" in financial development, our results for the GCC indicate that highly developed financial systems can mitigate the effects of resource dependency. This aligns with the endogenous growth theory (Solow, 1956), which supports that financial development facilitates structural transformation by reallocating resources to innovative and entrepreneurial activities.

The emphasis on the "Access" dimension is consistent with Beck et al. (2013) and Brixiová et al. (2020), who demonstrate that financial inclusion enables SMEs to thrive, fostering job creation and economic diversification. Similarly, the role of financial institution depth resonates with findings by Greenwood and Jovanovic (1990), who argue that deep financial systems enable economies to mobilise capital for high-return sectors.

The positive coefficient for financial market efficiency in the GCC contrasts with global findings by Rajan and Zingales (2003), who highlight the efficiency of capital markets in promoting diversification. This divergence may be attributed to the unique structure of GCC markets, which remain closely tied to hydrocarbon revenues despite significant financial reforms.

The results of this work underline the complementary role of institutional quality, governance, and macroeconomic policies. Financial institutions, through enhanced access, depth, and efficiency, mobilise resources for entrepreneurial and industrial activities, leading to a diversified economic structure. Similarly, financial markets provide capital for emerging sectors, encouraging private investment in technology, logistics, and renewable energy. The positive coefficient on financial market efficiency highlights a persistent challenge: GCC financial markets' continued reliance on oil revenues. This indicates the need for further reforms to dissociate financial systems from resource sectors to make a sustainable transition towards economic diversification.

Other Control Variables

The regression results in Table 3.4 reveal essential relationships between the control variables and economic diversification in the GCC region.

Constant and Resource Dependency

The negative constant term in most models suggests that, in the absence of significant control variables, the inherent baseline conditions of the economies studied are associated with lower resource dependency. This aligns with the view that some economies, even without active interventions, possess inherent structural conditions—such as demographic composition or geographic location—that favour diversification over resource dependency. According to Sachs and Warner (1997), countries with smaller natural resource endowments tend to have inherently lower dependency ratios due to necessity-driven diversification.

The Role of Real GDP Growth

Real GDP growth exhibits a positive and significant relationship with resource dependency, particularly in Panel 2, which presents regression results for financial market development (e.g., Model 6: coefficient = 1.1211, $p < 0.005$). This suggests that resource sectors, rather than non-resource industries, predominantly drive higher economic growth in the GCC region. This finding aligns with the literature. Sachs and Warner (1997) argue that resource-rich countries often experience growth driven by extractive industries, which may limit broader diversification. Hamdi and Sbia (2013) find that higher oil revenues promote economic growth in Bahrain through the government-spending channel. (Fuinhas, Marques, & Couto, 2015) find that, in a panel of oil-producing countries over 1970–12, oil rents depress growth in both the short and long run, suggesting that resources are a curse rather than a blessing for the economies. Ari et al. (2019) and Jolo et al. (2022) demonstrate that resource-based economies, including those of the GCC, remain rentier despite diversification efforts. Nusair (2016) finds that increases in oil prices are associated with higher real GDP in GCC countries.

The significant impact of GDP growth on financial market models supports growth theory, which posits that financial markets are more responsive to macroeconomic performance. During periods of economic expansion, financial markets in resource-dependent economies tend to channel capital towards hydrocarbon-related activities due to their high profitability and established infrastructure. However, the lack of significance in financial institution models indicates that banks and financial institutions may play a less direct role in redirecting growth towards non-resource sectors. These findings align with those of Samargandi et al. (2014), who find that financial institutions in Saudi Arabia primarily support the oil sector rather than foster diversification.

Inflation and Resource Dependency

Inflation is consistently positively and significantly associated with resource dependency across most models (e.g., Model 1: coefficient = 0.2704, $p = 0.001$). While this result may indicate that oil prices drive inflation, it may also imply that higher inflation in the GCC exacerbates resource dependency, likely by discouraging investments in non-resource sectors and increasing reliance on resource revenues to stabilise fiscal deficits. This finding aligns with the Resource Curse Hypothesis, which posits that resource-driven inflation has adverse economic effects. Auty (2001) argues that resource windfalls often lead to inflationary pressures through increased government spending, strengthening the resource curse. In this context, inflation undermines competitiveness in non-resource sectors by raising production costs and distorting investment incentives. This will reinforce dependence on resource exports and limit the potential for economic diversification.

The Paradox of Savings

Savings have a significant positive effect on resource dependence across all models (e.g., Model 1: 0.6405, $p < 0.001$), indicating a negative relationship between savings and economic diversification. In resource-based economies such as the GCC, high savings rates often reflect the accumulation of resource revenues in sovereign wealth funds or their reinvestment in the resource sector rather than in non-resource industries. This finding is consistent with Collier and Goderis (2012), who argue that excessive savings in resource-rich economies can perpetuate resource dependency by funding subsidies or resource-linked investments rather than supporting diversification.

The theoretical framework highlights the role of financial development in mobilising savings towards productive sectors (Solow, 1956). However, the results suggest that in the GCC, high savings rates have not been effectively channelled into non-resource sectors, possibly due to weak institutional frameworks and limited or ineffective private-sector participation (Banwo et al., 2019). This underscores the need for policies directing savings towards innovative and entrepreneurial activities in non-resource industries.

Government Spending and Resource Dependency

The positive and significant coefficient for government spending (e.g., Model 1: 0.215, $p = 0.043$) suggests that higher fiscal expenditures in the GCC reinforce reliance on resource sectors. It may also indicate that government spending in the GCC depends on oil revenues. This aligns with van der Ploeg's (2011) view that public spending in resource-dependent economies often disproportionately benefits resource sectors or inefficient state-led projects. The findings also align with the broader literature on rentier economies, in which fiscal revenues are heavily tied to resource rents, creating "spending inertia" and discouraging diversification (Ross, 2012).

The Resource Curse Hypothesis supports the results on the saving-dependency nexus, emphasising how resource revenues can weaken incentives for fiscal discipline and public investment in productive sectors. In the GCC, high government spending often supports welfare systems and public-sector employment rather than promoting private-sector growth. Policymakers should consider reallocating fiscal resources towards infrastructure, education, and technology to support diversification.

Trade Openness and Diversification

Trade openness has an insignificant effect on resource dependency across most models (e.g., Model 1: coefficient = −0.0372, $p = 0.759$). This finding can be attributed to the GCC's resource-based trade structure, in which hydrocarbons dominate exports. The lack of a diversified export base limits the potential for trade openness to promote economic transformation. These results align with Auty's (2001) claim that resource exports often lead to exchange rate appreciation, thereby reducing the competitiveness of non-resource sectors. To leverage trade openness for diversification, the GCC should strengthen its manufacturing base and develop export-oriented non-resource industries. Rodrik et al. (2004) propose addressing institutional weaknesses, improving regulatory frameworks, and implementing targeted industrial strategies.

Regulatory Quality and Political Stability

Regulatory quality consistently shows a negative and significant impact on resource dependency (e.g., Model 1: −1.1511, $p < 0.001$), indicating that strong institutions promote diversification by promoting a stable and transparent investment environment. This finding aligns with the Institutional Theory (North, 1990), which argues that robust institutions create the conditions for economic agents to invest across diverse industries. Mehlum et al. (2006) support this view, demonstrating that high regulatory quality channels resource revenues into productive sectors while curbing rent-seeking behaviours. Hao et al. (2021) argue that effective regulatory frameworks can help counter Dutch disease by fostering trade policies and investments that strengthen non-resource industries, thereby reducing resource dependence.

Political stability, however, has a positive and significant impact on resource dependency (e.g., Model 1: 0.3714, $p = 0.000$), suggesting that while stability attracts investment, it may strengthen reliance on resources rather than promote diversification. This result reflects the unique context of the GCC, where political stability has facilitated large-scale investments in resource sectors, given their high profitability and appeal to foreign investors. This result is consistent with Nganga (2021), who finds that political stability can hinder economic diversification in resource-reliant regions, and with Mehlum et al. (2006), who argue that in resource-based economies, political stability often strengthens extractive institutions unless accompanied by strong diversification policies. However, while political stability is essential, the absence of policies to support non-resource sectors risks perpetuating the dependency that economic diversification seeks to overcome (Table 3.5).

Table 3.5 IV-2SLS regression results for the export diversification specifications. The dependent variable is the Export diversification ratio

	Model 10: Financial Development Index	*Panel 1: Financial Institutions development*				*Panel 2: Financial markets development*			
		Model 11: Financial Institutions Index	*Model 12: FI Access Index*	*Model 13: FI depth Index*	*Model 14: FI Efficiency Index*	*Model 15: Financial Markets Index*	*Model 16: FM Access Index*	*Model 17: FM depth Index*	*Model 18: FM Efficiency Index*
COSTANT	0.7606 (0.002) ***	−0.5638 (0.083) *	0.6327 (0.304)	−0.4133 (0.132)	0.7172 (0.024) **	−0.8651 (0.000) ***	−0.5525 (0.496)	−0.5744 (0.051)*	−0.8435 (0.017)**
FINANCIAL DEVELOPMENT	0.0706 (0.073) *	0.1345 (0.005) ***	0.2416 (0.128)	0.0652 (0.024) **	0.4335 (0.000)***	0.0282 (0.311)	0.2152 (0.094)*	0.0863 (0)***	−0.0134 (0.762)
GROWTH	0.5509 (0.001) ***	0.5087 (0.001)***	0.2053 (0.375)	0.5926 (0)***	0.2376 (0.145)	0.5352 (0.001)**	2.5093 (0.001)***	0.5158 (0.001)***	0.5382 (0.001)***
INFLATION	0.0138 (0.381)	0.0165 (0.291)	0.035 (0.025)**	0.04 (0.038)**	0.022 (0.181)	0.0148 (0.355)	0.0174 (0.753)	0.0143 (0.355)	0.0223 (0.418)
REGULATION	−0.0615 (0.159)	−0.0358 (0.456)	−0.1472 (0.048)**	−0.07 (0.077)**	−0.0926 (0.053)*	−0.0629 (0.151)	−0.1339 (0.444)	−0.0612 (0.171)	−0.105 (0.305)
TRADE	−0.1031 (0.007)***	−0.1625 (0.000)***	−0.3774 (0)***	−0.1931 (0.000)***	−0.3518 (0.000)***	−0.098 (0.009)***	−0.1407 (0.167)	−0.126 (0.004)***	−0.1172 (0.203)
SAVING	0.0727 (0.008)***	0.1531 (0.000)***	0.1045 (0.079)*	0.086 (0.001)***	0.1836 (0.000)***	0.0785 (0.008)***	−0.0874 (0.297)	0.0513 (0.035)**	0.0944 (0.007)***
GOVERNMENT	0.2337 (0.000)***	0.1945 (0.1286)	0.142 (0.000)***	0.2323 (0.000)***	0.0962 (0.004)***	0.2385 (0.1838)	0:3867 (0.004)***	0.226 (0.000)***	0.2249 (0.000)***
STABILITY	−0.0192 (0.482)	−0.0891 (−0.1633)	0.1753 (0.004)***	0.0159 (0.692)	−0.1952 (0.000)***	−0.0105 (0.0687)*	0.0555 (0.531)	0.0115 (0.680)	0.001 (0.987)
Model Diagnostics									

	Model 10: Financial Development Index	*Panel 1: Financial Institutions development*				*Panel 2: Financial markets development*			
		Model 11: Financial Institutions Index	*Model 12: FI Access Index*	*Model 13: FI depth Index*	*Model 14: FI Efficiency Index*	*Model 15: Financial Markets Index*	*Model 16: FM Access Index*	*Model 17: FM depth Index*	*Model 18: FM Efficiency Index*
No. obs	135	123	87	124	123	135	87	135	137
Wald Chi^2 *p*-value)	290.44	268.03	420.11	338.28	346.60	276.08	78.21	313.35	285.37
	(0.000) ***	(0.000) ***	().000) ***	(0.000) ***	(0.000) ***	(0.000) ***	(0.000) ***	(0.000) ***	(0.000) ***
R-Squared	0.5993	0.6351	0.771	0.658	0.556	0.595	0.0287	0.631	0.6197
Root MSE	0.082	0.07823	0.071	0.0784	0.0863	0.0821	0.131	0.0784	0.0794
Diagnostic Tests									
Overidentification	7.811	28.62	2.523	1.839	1.527	1.59	4.31	3.06	2.499
Test (*p*-value)	(0.0501) *	(0.000) ***	(0.1122)	(0.0399)	(0.466)	(0.02058)	(0.1158)	(0.08)*	(0.1139)
First Stage *F*-Test	1,584.69	231.56	3.21	24.34	12.18	73.77	1.343	186.14	1.856
(p-value)	(0.000) ***	(0.000) ***	(0.046) **	(0.000) ***	(0.000) ***	(0.000) ***	(0.267)	(0.000) ***	(0.161)

Conclusion

This study examines the impact of financial development on economic diversification in GCC countries over 1995–2021, measured by resource dependency, proxied by the ratio of natural resource rents to GDP. Using an IV-2SLS estimation framework, the analysis highlights the pivotal role of financial development in reducing resource dependency and promoting diversification in resource-based economies. The findings provide evidence that, while financial development enables GCC economies to diversify, these countries are simultaneously striving to overcome the persistent challenges posed by the resource curse.

The results demonstrate a significant negative relationship between financial development, as measured by the Financial Development Index (FDI), and resource dependency. This indicates that higher financial development fosters greater economic diversification, supporting the theoretical frameworks of the Resource Blessing Hypothesis and endogenous growth theory. The results reveal that, under appropriate financial and institutional conditions, resource wealth in the GCC can act as a catalyst for diversification rather than perpetuating dependency. By mobilising savings, efficiently allocating capital, and fostering entrepreneurship, financial systems in the GCC provide a pathway to shift from resource-driven growth models to diversified, sustainable economic structures.

A closer analysis of the components of financial development underscores the transformative role of financial institutions, which emerge as the most effective channel for diversification. The Financial Institutions Development Index (FIDI) and its sub-dimensions—access, depth, and efficiency—consistently show significant negative relationships with resource dependency, highlighting the importance of inclusive and efficient banking systems. Financial institutions have proven instrumental in expanding credit access, mobilising resources, and facilitating private-sector growth, particularly in non-resource sectors. While financial markets also play a significant role in reducing resource dependency, their efficiency remains partially tied to oil revenues, reflecting residual sensitivity to resource cycles. This duality highlights that, although financial blessings exist, GCC countries continue to grapple with structural barriers inherent in the resource curse.

The study offers further insight into the complex dynamics of diversification. Positive relationships between GDP growth, inflation, savings, government spending, and resource dependency suggest that these variables, when coupled with resource-based economic structures, reinforce reliance on natural resources. However, regulatory quality is identified as a key enabler of diversification, underscoring the importance of strong governance and institutional frameworks in mitigating the resource curse. Interestingly, political stability, while a hallmark of GCC economies, appears to reinforce resource dependency when not accompanied by diversification policies, reflecting the dual-edged nature of stability in resource-based economies.

This study contributes to the existing literature by bridging the gap between financial development and economic diversification in resource-dependent economies, particularly in the GCC context. While existing studies focus on aggregate growth or export diversification, this analysis emphasises the relationship between financial development and resource dependency, offering a more direct measure of diversification. The results highlight the need to strengthen financial systems—both institutions and markets—to mobilise savings, expand access to credit, and allocate resources efficiently to non-resource sectors.

Policy implications emerge from the findings. First, GCC countries must further develop their financial systems, with particular emphasis on improving access to credit for SMEs and non-resource industries. Second, governance reforms should aim to strengthen regulatory frameworks, propagating transparency and investor confidence in non-resource sectors. Third, fiscal policies need to prioritise investment in education, technology, and infrastructure, redirecting resource revenues towards high-value-added industries.

Despite progress, the persistence of the resource curse in the GCC underscores the need for continued reforms. While financial development has provided a means to channel resource revenues into productive sectors, the over-reliance on oil and gas revenues continues to limit the potential for transformative diversification. Future efforts should focus on addressing institutional and structural barriers that perpetuate resource dependency and on ensuring that financial systems align with broader economic policies to achieve sustainable growth.

Future research can employ alternative measures of diversification, such as sectoral contributions to GDP or export composition, to provide a more comprehensive understanding of diversification dynamics. Additionally, longitudinal analyses of individual GCC countries could offer deeper insights into country-specific factors and policy effectiveness.

CHAPTER 4

Competition in GCC Banking Systems

Introduction

There is a view that the degree of competition in the banking sector can have substantial implications for financial development, economic growth, and social welfare (Alfaihani et al., 2024; Bakhouche & El Ghak, 2003; Claessens & Laeven, 2004; Maudos & De Guevara, 2007). Competition in the banking sector influences bank stability through many channels such as innovation (Claessens & Laeven, 2004), profitability and asset quality (Boyd & De Nicoló, 2005; Goetz, 2018), efficiency (Schaeck & Cihák, 2008), lowering monopoly rents and weakening quiet life (Koetter et al., 2012), and reducing borrowing costs and improving access of firms and households to financial services and external financing (Bamaceda et al., 2014), which leads to more efficient allocation of capital (Berger, 1995).

However, the relationship between competition and financial stability is complex. While greater competition can increase efficiency and lower costs, excessive pressure to maintain market share can lead to riskier lending practices, as observed in past financial crises (Beck et al., 2013). As a result, policymakers face the challenge of balancing competition with stability. This goal is particularly relevant in economies where the banking

A. Bakhouche, *Banking in the GCC*, Palgrave Macmillan Studies in Banking and Financial Institutions,
https://doi.org/10.1007/978-3-032-21737-0_4

sector plays a dominant role in financial intermediation and is often influenced by government policies, regulatory frameworks, and the presence of dominant financial institutions.

The banking sector in the GCC region differs from that in advanced economies, owing to its reliance on banks as the primary financial intermediaries. At the end of 2020, GCC banks' total assets amounted to $2.6 trillion, representing approximately 180% of the region's GDP (Al-Hassan et al., 2022), and contributing by 20% to the region's GDP, just after oil (Ali et al., 2022). Unlike many emerging and developed economies, where liberalisation measures largely shape competition, GCC banking operates within a framework of significant government involvement, regulatory constraints, structural linkages across social and economic sectors, and geopolitical factors. Many banks in the region are state-owned or have substantial government shareholding, which can influence their competitive behaviour and strategic objectives (Shome et al., 2024). These banks often serve both commercial and policy-driven functions, acting as *quasi-stakeholder banks* (Prieg & Greenham, 2013), supporting national economic initiatives while maintaining financial stability. Additionally, the region features a dual-banking system in which Islamic and conventional banks operate under different regulatory frameworks. Islamic banking has expanded significantly, attracting customers seeking Sharia-compliant financial services. However, assessing competition in Islamic banking is complex due to its unique risk-sharing mechanisms and regulatory structures (Čihák & Hesse, 2010). Moreover, foreign bank participation in GCC markets is subject to restrictive policies, further shaping competition dynamics. Saudi Arabia and Kuwait impose strict limits on foreign bank branches, while the UAE and Bahrain have adopted a more liberal approach (IMF, 2019). Given these structural characteristics, traditional measures of competition—such as market concentration ratios—may not fully capture the competitive environment. High concentration does not necessarily imply weak competition, as regulatory barriers and product differentiation can influence market outcomes (Bikker & Haaf, 2002).

This study examines competition in GCC banking using structural and non-structural indicators. Concentration measures such as the Herfindahl–Hirschman Index (HHI) and Concentration Ratios (CR3 and CR5) allow for an overview of market structure. At the same time, the behavioural indicators of the Panzar-Rosse H-statistic and the Boone Indicator provide a more direct assessment of competition based on market conduct. The H-statistic distinguishes between monopolistic and competitive market structures by measuring the responsiveness of bank revenues to input costs. The Boone Indicator examines the relationship between efficiency and profitability, offering further insights into competitive dynamics.

The analysis follows the approach of Carbo-Valverde et al. (2009), which compares both structural and non-structural indicators to assess the consistency of different competition measures. The study aims to contribute to the discussion regarding the nature of competition in GCC banking by addressing three main issues:

- Does high market concentration necessarily indicate low competition?
- Are non-structural indicators more reflective of actual competitive behaviour?
- How has competition evolved across different countries and over pre-defined sub-periods?

This study provides a broader understanding of banking competition in the GCC and contributes to the literature on market structure and financial development. Because no single measure fully captures competitive conditions, the study integrates multiple approaches to assess how regulatory frameworks, market entry barriers, and economic conditions may have influenced competition. The findings are expected to inform both policymakers and financial institutions on the implications of market structure for efficiency, financial inclusion, and stability.

Theoretical Framework: The Industrial Organisation Theory (IO) and New Empirical Industrial Organisation Theory (NEIO)

Competition is a complex process of rivalry between decision-making units and is not directly measurable (Bikker & Haaf, 2002). The literature on industrial organisation theory that examines competition in banking markets can be classified into two principal streams: the traditional or structural approach and the new empirical or non-structural approach.

The Traditional or Structural Approach

The structural approach argues that individual banks' performance is sensitive to market competition, as reflected in concentration levels and market power. Fewer, larger banks in a market indicate lower competition, whereas a more fragmented market suggests higher competition (Bikker & Haaf, 2002). Two major hypotheses within the traditional approach are the Structure-Conduct-Performance (SCP) and Efficient Structure (ES) hypotheses.

The *SCP* hypothesis (Bain, 1951; Mason, 1939) asserts that concentration is negatively related to competition (Khan et al., 2016). In highly concentrated markets, a few large banks may exploit their market power, forming collusive agreements that allow them to set less favourable prices for customers and earn monopoly rents (Berger, 1995).

The ES hypothesis (Demsetz, 1973) argues that concentration results from a change in cost efficiency rather than reduced competition. Efficient banks tend to lower costs and improve profitability, leading to market expansion and higher concentration (Berger, 1995). That is, competition drives efficiency, and the most efficient banks expand at the expense of less efficient ones.

Smirlock (1985) proposes the relative-market-power or product-differentiation hypothesis, which suggests that higher profits arise not only from cost efficiency but also from market power. Banks with well-differentiated, high-quality products can charge premium prices, increasing market share and profits (Mueller, 1983; Ravenscraft, 1983, 1984; Shepherd, 1982). Another related framework is the Quiet Life (QL) hypothesis (Hicks, 1935), which suggests that firms in concentrated markets earn higher profits due to monopoly power rather than efficiency (Berger & Hannan, 1998; Hicks, 1935).

K-Bank Concentration Ratio

The k-bank concentration ratio (CRk) is a widely used structural measure. It is calculated by summing the market shares of the k largest banks in the market:

$$\mathrm{CRk} = \mathrm{MS1} + \mathrm{MS2} + \ldots . + \mathrm{MSn} \tag{4.1}$$

where *MS* is the market share of the *i*th bank, ranked in descending order. The ratio ranges from zero to unity, with higher values indicating greater concentration and potentially lower competition. Commonly used values are CR3 and CR5. These measure the market share of the three or five largest banks by total assets, deposits, or loans. "Concentration" reflects the number and relative size of firms competing to offer a product or service to a group of customers (The US Department of Justice, 2024).

Herfindahl–Hirschman Index (HHI)

The Herfindahl–Hirschman Index (HHI) (Herfindahl, 1950; Hirschman, 1964) measures market concentration by summing the squares of market shares:

$$HHI = MS_1^2 + MS_2^2 + \ldots + MS_n^2 \quad (4.2)$$

where MSn denotes the market share of firm n. A higher HHI indicates a more concentrated market with greater market power, increasing the risk of collusion and reducing competition (Bolt & Humphrey, 2015). The US Department of Justice uses the HHI to assess mergers and acquisitions (The US Department of Justice, 2024), classifying markets as follows:

- HHI < 1,000: more competitive market
- 1,000 ≤ HHI ≤ 1,800: moderately concentrated market
- HHI > 1,800: highly concentrated market

A transaction that changes the HHI by more than 100 points in a highly concentrated market is likely to enhance market power.

The HHI is used in various forms, including the HHI of total assets, total loans, total deposits, total revenue, and total profit (Saif-Alyousfi et al., 2020). Following Chen and Liao (2011), Fiordelisi and Mare (2014) and Kasman and Kasman (2015), we use alternative measures of HHI: HHI of total assets, HHI of total loans, and HHI of total deposits. We also compute the HHI for total revenue and for total profit.

The Lerner Index of Market Power

The Lerner index of market power (Lerner, 1934) is a firm-level measure of competition directly from firms' conduct (Khan et al., 2016) (Ariss, 2010; Fiordelisi & Mare, 2014; Soedarmono et al., 2013). It measures market power by assessing the pricing markup over marginal cost. It is computed as:

$$Lerner_{it} = \frac{P_{it} - MC_{it}}{P_{it}} \quad (4.3)$$

where P_{it} is the price of the total assets proxied by the ratio of total interest and non-interest income to total assets; MC_{it} is the marginal cost of producing an additional unit of output derived from the cost function. The Lerner index ranges from "less than zero" to "one", with higher values indicating greater market power and less competitive conditions. The values "zero", "one", and "less than one" imply perfect completion, monopoly, and a non-optimal state (in which banks price their product below marginal cost), respectively. The Lerner Index is typically estimated over time, enabling dynamic analysis of competition. Estimates the degree of market power by comparing a bank's pricing behaviour with its marginal cost. A higher Lerner Index suggests weaker competition and stronger pricing power.

Following Chen and Liao (2011), Soedarmono et al. (2013), Fu et al. (2014), Fiordelisi and Mare (2014), and Tan (2016), the marginal cost (MC) is estimated from a translog cost function with assets as an output and three inputs as follows:

$$\begin{aligned}\ln\left(\frac{TC}{p_3}\right) &= \alpha + \beta_1 \ln Q + \frac{1}{2}\beta_2 \ln Q^2 + \gamma_1 \ln\left(\frac{p_1}{p_3}\right)Q \\ &+ \gamma_2 \ln\left(\frac{p_2}{p_3}\right)Q + \delta_1 \ln\left(\frac{p_1}{p_3}\right)^2 + \delta_2 \ln\left(\frac{p_2}{p_3}\right)^2 \\ &+ \delta_3 \ln\left(\frac{p_1}{p_3}\right)\ln\left(\frac{p_2}{p_3}\right) + \rho \end{aligned} \tag{4.4}$$

where:

- TC = total cost (sum of interest and non-interest expenses) for bank i at time t.
- Q = bank output (proxied by total assets
- P_1, P_2 and P_3 = input prices: purchased funds, labour, and physical capital, respectively. P1 is measured by the ratio of interest expenses/ total deposits; P2 is proxied by the ratio of personnel expenses to total assets; P3 is approximated by the ratio of operating and administrative expenses to total assets.

The marginal cost (MC) is then computed as:

$$\mathrm{MC} = \frac{TC}{Q}\left[\beta_1 + \beta_2 \ln Q + \gamma_1 \ln\left(\frac{p_1}{p_3}\right) + \gamma_2 \ln\left(\frac{p_2}{p_3}\right)\right] \tag{4.5}$$

The New Empirical or Non-structural Approach

The non-structural approach, also known as the New Empirical Industrial Organisation (NEIO) approach, assesses competition by analysing banks' pricing behaviour and market conduct. Panzer-Rosse *H-statistic* and *Boone* indicator as the main measures of competition for this approach.

The Panzar-Rosse H-Statistic

The Panzar-Rosse model measures the responsiveness of firm revenue to changes in input prices (Molyneux et al., 1996). The Panzar-Rosse H-statistic is based on the intermediation model (Sealey & Lindley, 1977), under which a bank employs purchased funds, labour, and physical capital to generate revenue. Therefore, the PR H-statistic is computed as the sum of elasticities of total revenue with respect to the bank's input prices:

$$\text{H} - \text{statistic} \; = \beta 1 + \beta 2 + \beta 3 \tag{4.6}$$

where β1, β2, and β3 represent the estimated coefficients of factor input prices (PF for purchased funds' PL for Labour, and PK for capital), and capital (PK)). The H-statistic helps determine market structure:

- $H \leq 0$: Monopoly or collusive oligopoly
- $0 < H < 1$: Monopolistic competition
- $H = 1$: Perfect competition or a perfectly contestable market

The model assumes that banks operate in a long-run equilibrium, where returns should not be correlated with input prices (Casu & Girardone et al., 2006). Equilibrium is tested by replacing revenue with return on assets or equity in the regression. If $H < 0$, it indicates disequilibrium, whereas $H = 0H = 0$ confirms equilibrium (Molyneux et al., 1994).

The reduced-form revenue equation follows the intermediation approach, which views banks as financial intermediaries producing loans and other earning assets using purchased funds, labour, and capital as inputs. Following Bikker and Haaf (2002), the revenue function is specified as follows:

$$\text{LnTR}_{\text{it}} = \alpha + \beta_1 \text{lnPF} + \beta_2 \text{lnPLK} + \lambda \text{ lnGDPG} + \varepsilon_{\text{it}} \tag{4.7}$$

where:

- TR = Total revenue (interest and non-interest income over total assets)
- PF = Cost of purchased funds (interest expenses to total deposits and borrowing)
- PL = Cost of labour and fixed capital (personnel expenses and other expenses to total assets)
- GDP = GDP growth (macroeconomic control)

Following Rakshit & Bardhan (2020), we apply ordinary least squares (OLS) regression.

After estimating the H-statistic, we test two hypotheses regarding market structure. First, we test the Null hypothesis (H = 0); if it is not rejected, then the market is a monopoly. If rejected, it suggests some level of competition. Second, the Null hypothesis (H = 1) is not rejected, then the market is perfectly competitive. If rejected, this suggests that the market is likely monopolistically competitive.

The model assumes that banks operate in a long-run equilibrium, in which returns are not correlated with input prices (Casu & Girardone, 2006). Equilibrium is tested by replacing revenue with ROA in the regression and estimating a new H-statistic, denoted E-Equilibrium. If E = 0 fails to reject, it indicates long-term equilibrium, implying that banks are not earning significant abnormal profit and input prices do not affect profitability. If H = 0 is rejected, the market is not in equilibrium, suggesting that input prices affect profitability and that banks adjust to shocks or competitive pressures through entry/exit (Molyneux et al., 1994).

The Boone Indicator

The Boone approach (Boone, 2008), which is based on the ES hypothesis, measures the reallocation effect (Schaeck & Čihák, 2014). It assesses how efficient banks with lower marginal costs gain market share. It is estimated using the following regression model:

$$\mathrm{lnMS}_{\mathrm{it}} = \alpha + \beta \mathrm{lnMC}_{\mathrm{it}} + \varepsilon_{\mathrm{it}} \quad (4.8)$$

where:

- MS_{it} = Market share of Q of bank iii in year t (proxied by four indicators: assets, loans and deposits. We also use ROA or robustness checks)
- MC_{it} = Marginal cost (derived from a Translog Cost Function, as explained earlier)
- β = Boone Indicator (expected to be negative; a lower value indicates stronger competition)

Results and Discussion

There is empirical evidence for the significant role of bank competition in shaping financial stability, market efficiency and economic growth. In the GCC, examining competition in banking is essential for assessing the sector's ability to support economic diversification and financial development.

Analysis of CR3, CR5, and HHI

Over the period 2002–22, the traditional structural indicators for the GCC banking sector do show strikingly different conclusions across countries. Tables 4.1, 4.2, and 4.3 present the annual 3-bank concentration ratio (CR3), 5-bank concentration ratio (CR5), and HHI, based on total assets, total equity, total loans, and total purchased funds, for individual GCC markets. Table 4.4 presents the yearly values for the Lerner index of market power for individual countries over the same period.

The CR3 and CR5 values indicate a moderate-to-high degree of concentration in GCC banking markets, with significant variation across countries. Bahrain, followed by Qatar and Oman, consistently exhibits the highest concentration, with CR3 values exceeding 0.8, reflecting a banking sector dominated by a few large banks. This is a common characteristic of smaller banking systems (Beck et al., 2013). In contrast, Saudi Arabia, the UAE, and Kuwait have less concentrated markets, with CR3 values below 0.65. The Herfindahl–Hirschman Index (HHI) follows a similar pattern, with the UAE, Saudi Arabia, and, to a lesser extent, Kuwait maintaining HHI values below 1800, suggesting a moderately

Table 4.1 3-bank concentration ratio (CR3) of GCC banks for different aggregates: assets, equity, loans, and deposits between 2002 and 2022

	Assets							*Equity*						
Year	*Bahrain*	*Kuwait*	*Oman*	*Qatar*	*Saudi Arabia*	*UAE*	*Average GCC*	*Bahrain*	*Kuwait*	*Oman*	*Qatar*	*Saudi Arabia*	*UAE*	*Average GCC*
2002	0.984	0.641	0.884	0.858	0.859	0.585	0.755	0.954	0.622	0.818	0.893	0.855	0.568	0.737
2003	0.906	0.645	0.843	0.857	0.850	0.542	0.713	0.834	0.628	0.794	0.908	0.836	0.507	0.686
2004	0.847	0.593	0.833	0.864	0.685	0.536	0.669	0.833	0.545	0.805	0.927	0.717	0.473	0.643
2005	0.852	0.610	0.826	0.846	0.667	0.541	0.673	0.825	0.586	0.836	0.850	0.686	0.471	0.646
2006	0.844	0.629	0.851	0.818	0.657	0.537	0.681	0.756	0.613	0.834	0.691	0.662	0.453	0.624
2007	0.849	0.644	0.843	0.821	0.620	0.598	0.696	0.658	0.665	0.842	0.708	0.646	0.529	0.643
2008	0.812	0.640	0.864	0.800	0.534	0.608	0.676	0.658	0.732	0.816	0.720	0.599	0.536	0.648
2009	0.798	0.658	0.847	0.780	0.570	0.612	0.682	0.684	0.695	0.811	0.718	0.598	0.540	0.644
2010	0.808	0.658	0.826	0.758	0.563	0.610	0.677	0.752	0.669	0.822	0.699	0.533	0.545	0.638
2011	0.801	0.655	0.857	0.742	0.560	0.631	0.681	0.758	0.656	0.856	0.733	0.532	0.559	0.648
2012	0.799	0.680	0.440	0.753	0.554	0.629	0.648	0.762	0.651	0.416	0.738	0.525	0.569	0.611
2013	0.798	0.678	0.729	0.759	0.543	0.614	0.670	0.756	0.665	0.697	0.715	0.524	0.560	0.634
2014	0.790	0.684	0.727	0.750	0.536	0.611	0.666	0.733	0.663	0.708	0.719	0.516	0.563	0.632
2015	0.787	0.667	0.751	0.758	0.326	0.604	0.629	0.716	0.659	0.718	0.716	0.364	0.564	0.604
2016	0.786	0.666	0.731	0.785	0.533	0.554	0.651	0.709	0.656	0.721	0.706	0.518	0.543	0.622
2017	0.783	0.664	0.724	0.790	0.530	0.633	0.671	0.710	0.647	0.721	0.720	0.517	0.641	0.649
2018	0.771	0.655	0.719	0.800	0.535	0.638	0.671	0.727	0.636	0.721	0.724	0.499	0.634	0.645
2019	0.772	0.639	0.702	0.783	0.528	0.676	0.673	0.746	0.634	0.717	0.715	0.515	0.670	0.659
2020	0.762	0.643	0.680	0.784	0.557	0.673	0.673	0.741	0.641	0.723	0.717	0.512	0.672	0.659
2021	0.761	0.642	0.678	0.769	0.614	0.674	0.681	0.747	0.634	0.708	0.714	0.601	0.672	0.672
2022	0.729	0.686	0.671	0.783	0.611	0.694	0.690	0.753	0.723	0.684	0.721	0.610	0.681	0.691
Average	**0.804**	**0.653**	**0.755**	**0.787**	**0.573**	**0.611**	**0.675**	**0.744**	**0.650**	**0.745**	**0.739**	**0.568**	**0.570**	**0.647**

Year	*Assets*							*Equity*						
	Bahrain	*Kuwait*	*Oman*	*Qatar*	*Saudi Arabia*	*UAE*	*Average GCC*	*Bahrain*	*Kuwait*	*Oman*	*Qatar*	*Saudi Arabia*	*UAE*	*Average GCC*
St.dev	**0.06**	**0.02**	**0.10**	**0.04**	**0.11**	**0.05**	**0.02**	**0.07**	**0.04**	**0.10**	**0.07**	**0.12**	**0.07**	**0.03**
	Loans							**Deposits**						
2002	0.979	0.635	0.914	0.862	0.844	0.626	0.767	0.986	0.643	0.894	0.853	0.857	0.590	0.758
2003	0.920	0.635	0.844	0.896	0.889	0.608	0.745	0.909	0.646	0.851	0.851	0.849	0.550	0.717
2004	0.829	0.668	0.864	0.856	0.751	0.597	0.714	0.849	0.592	0.830	0.851	0.679	0.544	0.669
2005	0.845	0.699	0.872	0.884	0.755	0.584	0.725	0.797	0.605	0.804	0.848	0.790	0.555	0.686
2006	0.850	0.723	0.904	0.879	0.737	0.620	0.749	0.857	0.626	0.849	0.855	0.652	0.556	0.692
2007	0.871	0.692	0.888	0.834	0.655	0.577	0.713	0.868	0.633	0.837	0.854	0.614	0.611	0.703
2008	0.842	0.732	0.876	0.809	0.572	0.654	0.719	0.823	0.634	0.865	0.820	0.521	0.622	0.681
2009	0.807	0.634	0.846	0.769	0.544	0.617	0.675	0.810	0.647	0.851	0.782	0.562	0.625	0.685
2010	0.865	0.631	0.838	0.759	0.591	0.557	0.671	0.812	0.651	0.828	0.770	0.569	0.620	0.682
2011	0.820	0.635	0.869	0.751	0.531	0.635	0.678	0.801	0.650	0.858	0.759	0.566	0.646	0.688
2012	0.837	0.642	0.424	0.760	0.528	0.624	0.640	0.797	0.675	0.442	0.773	0.560	0.645	0.655
2013	0.831	0.642	0.761	0.770	0.522	0.626	0.673	0.798	0.678	0.730	0.788	0.547	0.630	0.678
2014	0.839	0.635	0.744	0.749	0.515	0.606	0.661	0.795	0.680	0.730	0.774	0.539	0.621	0.673
2015	0.825	0.621	0.735	0.760	0.339	0.593	0.623	0.790	0.661	0.754	0.785	0.320	0.611	0.632
2016	0.814	0.618	0.737	0.788	0.512	0.566	0.647	0.788	0.661	0.729	0.810	0.532	0.558	0.654
2017	0.809	0.619	0.734	0.796	0.519	0.620	0.664	0.783	0.660	0.721	0.811	0.529	0.633	0.673
2018	0.794	0.611	0.724	0.801	0.525	0.616	0.659	0.768	0.654	0.715	0.817	0.539	0.641	0.673
2019	0.793	0.591	0.703	0.784	0.517	0.669	0.665	0.769	0.633	0.696	0.812	0.537	0.680	0.678

(continued)

Table 4.1 (continued)

	Assets							*Equity*						
Year	*Bahrain*	*Kuwait*	*Oman*	*Qatar*	*Saudi Arabia*	*UAE*	*Average GCC*	*Bahrain*	*Kuwait*	*Oman*	*Qatar*	*Saudi Arabia*	*UAE*	*Average GCC*
2020	0.779	0.602	0.685	0.781	0.554	0.652	0.661	0.761	0.637	0.669	0.812	0.568	0.676	0.676
2021	0.771	0.617	0.681	0.782	0.603	0.647	0.670	0.764	0.646	0.673	0.814	0.619	0.679	0.689
2022	0.744	0.648	0.674	0.792	0.611	0.672	0.681	0.726	0.679	0.665	0.824	0.610	0.692	0.693
Average	**0.827**	**0.643**	**0.767**	**0.796**	**0.577**	**0.617**	**0.682**	**0.805**	**0.649**	**0.753**	**0.809**	**0.578**	**0.619**	**0.680**
St. dev	**0.05**	**0.04**	**0.11**	**0.05**	**0.13**	**0.03**	**0.04**	**0.06**	**0.02**	**0.10**	**0.03**	**0.12**	**0.05**	**0.02**

Table 4.2 5-bank concentration ratio (CR5) of GCC banks for different aggregates: assets, equity, loans, and deposits between 2002 and 2022

	Assets							*Equity*						
Year	*Bahrain*	*Kuwait*	*Oman*	*Qatar*	*Saudi Arabia*	*UAE*	*Average GCC*	*Bahrain*	*Kuwait*	*Oman*	*Qatar*	*Saudi Arabia*	*UAE*	*Average GCC*
2002	1.000	0.865	1.000	1.000	1.000	0.855	0.932	1.000	0.840	1.000	1.000	1.000	0.789	0.908
2003	1.000	0.863	1.000	1.000	1.000	0.797	0.905	1.000	0.843	1.000	1.000	1.000	0.715	0.873
2004	1.000	0.781	1.000	1.000	0.966	0.787	0.880	1.000	0.757	1.000	1.000	0.958	0.706	0.846
2005	1.000	0.807	1.000	0.939	0.961	0.780	0.878	1.000	0.794	1.000	0.955	0.941	0.689	0.843
2006	0.982	0.813	1.000	0.971	0.936	0.772	0.880	0.935	0.794	1.000	0.946	0.885	0.705	0.839
2007	0.969	0.828	1.000	0.957	0.885	0.803	0.882	0.860	0.828	1.000	0.933	0.858	0.751	0.844
2008	0.951	0.832	1.000	0.959	0.786	0.790	0.859	0.848	0.871	1.000	0.941	0.802	0.717	0.831
2009	0.940	0.833	1.000	0.954	0.804	0.784	0.859	0.876	0.842	1.000	0.930	0.806	0.713	0.827
2010	0.945	0.828	1.000	0.942	0.782	0.768	0.849	0.915	0.817	1.000	0.898	0.729	0.711	0.811
2011	0.944	0.825	1.000	0.927	0.783	0.781	0.850	0.916	0.804	1.000	0.894	0.732	0.714	0.810
2012	0.946	0.836	0.951	0.922	0.772	0.776	0.844	0.931	0.804	0.947	0.898	0.737	0.721	0.811
2013	0.943	0.827	0.920	0.919	0.762	0.770	0.838	0.939	0.808	0.886	0.902	0.737	0.718	0.810
2014	0.948	0.824	0.913	0.918	0.747	0.764	0.833	0.941	0.808	0.893	0.900	0.737	0.724	0.813
2015	0.943	0.806	0.913	0.918	0.470	0.760	0.781	0.928	0.803	0.896	0.902	0.523	0.728	0.774
2016	0.939	0.802	0.904	0.930	0.740	0.732	0.818	0.928	0.800	0.902	0.898	0.741	0.724	0.810
2017	0.933	0.795	0.896	0.932	0.730	0.783	0.828	0.925	0.792	0.896	0.904	0.741	0.785	0.826
2018	0.930	0.787	0.887	0.934	0.724	0.791	0.827	0.947	0.785	0.903	0.909	0.720	0.792	0.827
2019	0.933	0.771	0.878	0.916	0.734	0.814	0.829	0.953	0.776	0.899	0.885	0.739	0.811	0.832
2020	0.936	0.781	0.881	0.914	0.747	0.821	0.834	0.942	0.784	0.896	0.887	0.736	0.815	0.830
2021	0.933	0.782	0.882	0.914	0.775	0.819	0.838	0.941	0.776	0.873	0.892	0.784	0.816	0.835
2022	0.928	0.804	0.883	0.922	0.773	0.837	0.848	0.938	0.832	0.862	0.894	0.786	0.835	0.849
Average	**0.951**	**0.812**	**0.940**	**0.938**	**0.783**	**0.788**	**0.848**	**0.932**	**0.807**	**0.937**	**0.916**	**0.775**	**0.746**	**0.828**

(continued)

Table 4.2 (continued)

Year	*Assets*							*Equity*						
	Bahrain	*Kuwait*	*Oman*	*Qatar*	*Saudi Arabia*	*UAE*	*Average GCC*	*Bahrain*	*Kuwait*	*Oman*	*Qatar*	*Saudi Arabia*	*UAE*	*Average GCC*
St.dev	**0.026**	**0.026**	**0.053**	**0.029**	**0.122**	**0.028**	**0.033**	**0.042**	**0.027**	**0.055**	**0.038**	**0.113**	**0.046**	**0.027**
	Loans							**Deposits**						
2002	1.000	0.851	1.000	1.000	1.000	0.838	0.924	1.000	0.869	1.000	1.000	1.000	0.865	0.935
2003	1.000	0.830	1.000	1.000	1.000	0.846	0.916	1.000	0.866	1.000	1.000	1.000	0.808	0.909
2004	1.000	0.849	1.000	1.000	0.972	0.850	0.916	1.000	0.781	1.000	1.000	0.966	0.799	0.885
2005	1.000	0.833	1.000	0.947	0.959	0.821	0.897	1.000	0.804	1.000	0.935	0.967	0.795	0.883
2006	0.981	0.853	1.000	0.999	0.951	0.833	0.912	0.994	0.811	1.000	0.998	0.945	0.782	0.890
2007	0.974	0.927	1.000	0.970	0.906	0.782	0.899	0.981	0.824	1.000	0.974	0.888	0.809	0.887
2008	0.972	0.917	1.000	0.953	0.819	0.780	0.879	0.962	0.829	1.000	0.965	0.781	0.800	0.863
2009	0.954	0.816	1.000	0.965	0.798	0.756	0.850	0.955	0.827	1.000	0.962	0.802	0.795	0.864
2010	0.965	0.799	1.000	0.966	0.799	0.781	0.857	0.953	0.825	1.000	0.956	0.790	0.776	0.856
2011	0.948	0.800	1.000	0.945	0.772	0.781	0.847	0.947	0.825	1.000	0.951	0.790	0.793	0.858
2012	0.947	0.812	0.967	0.935	0.760	0.767	0.838	0.947	0.837	0.955	0.949	0.777	0.791	0.854
2013	0.936	0.801	0.924	0.924	0.747	0.764	0.830	0.942	0.829	0.925	0.947	0.766	0.781	0.846
2014	0.936	0.791	0.917	0.919	0.729	0.755	0.821	0.947	0.823	0.917	0.944	0.749	0.775	0.840
2015	0.930	0.781	0.915	0.922	0.489	0.750	0.776	0.943	0.803	0.916	0.944	0.467	0.767	0.785
2016	0.924	0.771	0.905	0.933	0.719	0.736	0.809	0.938	0.799	0.904	0.957	0.738	0.738	0.823
2017	0.927	0.770	0.904	0.932	0.719	0.769	0.818	0.930	0.794	0.896	0.953	0.726	0.787	0.831
2018	0.924	0.762	0.905	0.933	0.721	0.767	0.816	0.925	0.787	0.885	0.953	0.727	0.790	0.828
2019	0.931	0.748	0.897	0.913	0.721	0.795	0.820	0.927	0.770	0.875	0.948	0.733	0.813	0.831

Year	*Assets*							*Equity*						
	Bahrain	*Kuwait*	*Oman*	*Qatar*	*Saudi Arabia*	*UAE*	*Average GCC*	*Bahrain*	*Kuwait*	*Oman*	*Qatar*	*Saudi Arabia*	*UAE*	*Average GCC*
2020	0.937	0.758	0.906	0.910	0.739	0.799	0.825	0.933	0.780	0.877	0.945	0.746	0.821	0.836
2021	0.933	0.768	0.906	0.914	0.765	0.783	0.827	0.932	0.784	0.881	0.952	0.773	0.819	0.842
2022	0.933	0.778	0.910	0.923	0.766	0.814	0.840	0.925	0.798	0.883	0.957	0.767	0.834	0.848
Average	**0.951**	**0.807**	**0.948**	**0.944**	**0.781**	**0.787**	**0.849**	**0.952**	**0.811**	**0.940**	**0.959**	**0.784**	**0.795**	**0.853**
St. dev	**0.028**	**0.049**	**0.046**	**0.031**	**0.124**	**0.033**	**0.043**	**0.028**	**0.027**	**0.054**	**0.021**	**0.123**	**0.026**	**0.033**

Table 4.3 Herfindahl–Hirschman Index (HHI) of GCC banks for different aggregates: assets, equity, loans, and deposits between 2002 and 2022

	Assets						
Year	*Bahrain*	*Kuwait*	*Oman*	*Qatar*	*Saudi Arabia*	*UAE*	*Average GCC*
2002	6,740.24	2,098.79	3,063.99	2,731.51	2,693.55	1,599.11	2,781.64
2003	5,465.82	1,998.71	2,910.36	2,751.96	2,607.60	1,401.84	2,488.58
2004	3,511.05	1,679.50	3,063.63	2,774.96	2,031.32	1,371.70	2,097.04
2005	3,567.93	1,707.08	2,924.48	3,146.44	1,988.30	1,365.87	2,142.47
2006	3,599.99	1,688.76	3,314.90	2,986.36	1,905.87	1,327.46	2,207.03
2007	3,800.47	1,787.12	3,428.29	3,121.35	1,776.06	1,630.21	2,344.37
2008	3,244.18	1,787.84	3,702.52	3,008.88	1,469.69	1,571.87	2,199.43
2009	2,891.77	1,874.77	3,523.55	3,039.29	1,540.69	1,537.22	2,157.03
2010	2,905.69	1,883.91	3,319.46	3,036.39	1,493.58	1,497.60	2,126.37
2011	2,689.11	1,878.61	3,544.46	3,138.92	1,469.09	1,552.96	2,134.50
2012	2,600.68	1,948.05	3,110.18	3,241.17	1,454.16	1,563.78	2,108.70
2013	2,605.61	1,911.08	2,606.16	3,249.83	1,418.75	1,533.03	2,063.17
2014	2,565.25	1,955.74	2,612.69	3,168.18	1,411.80	1,520.32	2,051.53
2015	2,518.29	1,958.15	2,899.46	3,124.95	1,415.40	1,494.44	2,068.34
2016	2,530.92	1,943.31	2,526.18	3,619.41	1,391.81	1,391.09	2,049.57
2017	2,496.69	1,945.47	2,489.49	3,736.05	1,375.93	1,684.76	2,133.15
2018	2,463.35	1,932.84	2,545.47	3,906.56	1,370.57	1,727.79	2,164.65
2019	2,442.42	1,884.25	2,439.69	3,780.99	1,363.82	1,781.11	2,139.01
2020	2,367.61	1,889.55	2,365.57	3,834.24	1,428.34	1,815.04	2,143.71
2021	2,388.13	1,926.58	2,327.34	3,645.63	1,686.91	1,831.26	2,174.79
2022	2,269.05	2,110.43	2,269.54	3,938.48	1,648.22	1,924.70	2,252.21
Average	**2,973.48**	**1,896.50**	**2,840.80**	**3,330.66**	**1,592.16**	**1,577.74**	**2,175.81**
St.dev	**1,109.28**	**115.13**	**447.17**	**390.79**	**387.34**	**166.79**	**169.05**

	Assets						
Year	*Bahrain*	*Kuwait*	*Oman*	*Qatar*	*Saudi Arabia*	*UAE*	*Average GCC*
	Loans						
2002	7,056.88	1,824.84	4,076.31	2,710.59	2,597.34	1,684.16	2,915.82
2003	5,026.11	1,825.58	2,928.16	3,319.08	3,024.70	1,584.30	2,578.26
2004	3,074.51	2,107.74	3,489.49	2,937.65	2,272.50	1,564.35	2,291.46
2005	3,126.23	2,237.85	3,932.79	3,715.19	2,196.08	1,482.87	2,436.21
2006	2,782.83	2,260.53	4,530.47	3,985.56	2,183.58	1,724.14	2,602.81
2007	3,249.91	1,990.49	4,505.65	3,951.59	1,813.72	1,490.05	2,475.24
2008	3,319.34	2,427.27	4,530.23	3,840.78	1,570.23	1,923.89	2,622.88
2009	2,699.17	1,786.06	3,256.51	2,375.89	1,463.54	1,549.30	2,003.14
2010	3,632.92	1,738.67	3,231.80	2,493.83	1,558.17	1,413.25	2,118.56
2011	2,728.88	1,751.49	3,427.05	3,308.17	1,381.87	1,552.60	2,112.48
2012	2,831.55	1,824.08	3,130.00	3,352.28	1,375.89	1,525.35	2,110.24
2013	2,780.10	1,782.73	2,767.34	3,470.41	1,337.39	1,565.56	2,106.13
2014	2,808.39	1,755.91	2,631.21	3,215.60	1,323.90	1,483.33	2,033.21
2015	2,738.47	1,783.89	2,486.64	3,212.10	1,347.52	1,452.98	2,006.22
2016	2,682.00	1,751.86	2,527.90	3,728.72	1,320.69	1,435.22	2,050.71
2017	2,700.83	1,749.90	2,508.65	3,872.31	1,332.71	1,550.48	2,101.85
2018	2,583.55	1,752.77	2,524.13	4,017.05	1,331.74	1,547.50	2,104.51
2019	2,645.42	1,706.44	2,424.47	3,914.98	1,308.71	1,707.62	2,120.91
2020	2,474.92	1,717.74	2,320.93	3,865.73	1,401.85	1,672.92	2,080.59
2021	2,412.31	1,784.11	2,282.54	3,729.75	1,586.40	1,628.70	2,083.09
2022	2,305.22	1,856.24	2,236.23	4,005.19	1,620.84	1,751.78	2,165.86
Average	**2,998.82**	**1,868.29**	**3,025.30**	**3,505.08**	**1,590.80**	**1,581.57**	**2,216.76**
St.dev	**1,067.70**	**205.00**	**781.61**	**506.70**	**487.17**	**123.48**	**255.72**

(continued)

Table 4.3 (continued)

	Equity						
Year	*Bahrain*	*Kuwait*	*Oman*	*Qatar*	*Saudi Arabia*	*UAE*	*Average GCC*
2002	4,396.81	1,896.14	2,441.48	2,963.64	2,839.70	1,460.26	2,392.09
2003	3,612.60	1,823.47	2,421.71	3,172.69	2,714.46	1,220.08	2,157.00
2004	3,630.07	1,546.47	2,603.61	3,125.99	2,137.13	1,139.45	1,999.04
2005	3,331.17	1,600.28	2,824.78	3,073.29	2,036.39	1,116.12	1,997.92
2006	2,601.74	1,665.53	2,841.67	2,098.86	1,943.51	1,111.98	1,842.61
2007	1,982.09	1,948.94	3,345.79	2,361.08	1,819.76	1,413.20	1,961.33
2008	2,003.66	2,229.28	3,247.25	2,263.48	1,524.52	1,291.90	1,902.07
2009	2,168.25	2,174.00	3,089.57	2,276.58	1,531.59	1,267.49	1,888.37
2010	2,881.02	2,113.23	3,191.04	2,212.70	1,333.06	1,262.33	1,946.17
2011	2,962.32	2,039.02	3,463.33	2,714.57	1,335.82	1,285.99	2,041.81
2012	2,931.03	2,028.14	3,238.24	2,849.83	1,326.11	1,303.36	2,035.44
2013	2,884.00	2,040.94	2,631.39	2,921.24	1,319.62	1,280.31	2,000.53
2014	2,746.94	2,000.76	2,692.58	2,984.18	1,310.85	1,294.67	1,992.13
2015	2,594.00	2,009.64	2,699.81	3,028.15	1,318.01	1,306.09	1,983.13
2016	2,484.58	2,009.91	2,719.67	2,910.33	1,325.05	1,259.62	1,944.66
2017	2,464.39	1,972.16	2,738.00	3,011.01	1,324.38	1,775.01	2,091.79
2018	2,594.65	1,908.67	2,738.29	3,054.25	1,285.82	1,737.61	2,087.10
2019	2,621.60	1,922.50	2,757.46	2,974.08	1,302.30	1,714.26	2,082.24
2020	2,551.26	1,973.30	2,827.51	2,986.42	1,307.32	1,725.24	2,087.13
2021	2,563.61	1,926.12	2,755.98	2,778.35	1,756.12	1,735.86	2,127.75
2022	2,464.51	2,442.60	2,414.49	2,850.96	1,723.11	1,776.78	2,193.49
Average	**2,713.33**	**1,975.01**	**2,818.95**	**2,782.94**	**1,557.60**	**1,404.40**	**2,030.80**
St.dev	**571.68**	**201.70**	**304.91**	**334.35**	**464.57**	**235.13**	**121.05**
	Deposits						

Year	*Equity*						
	Bahrain	*Kuwait*	*Oman*	*Qatar*	*Saudi Arabia*	*UAE*	*Average GCC*
2002	6,786.90	2,126.41	3,190.00	2,717.97	2,672.50	1,642.77	2,818.42
2003	5,560.86	2,018.40	3,012.50	2,727.13	2,587.16	1,445.56	2,526.94
2004	3,487.21	1,703.84	3,047.88	2,746.01	2,017.35	1,407.58	2,104.84
2005	2,571.13	1,711.41	2,804.86	3,178.95	2,304.94	1,430.98	2,085.46
2006	3,774.83	1,679.72	3,309.25	3,181.47	1,917.01	1,382.01	2,271.95
2007	3,970.92	1,746.75	3,347.66	3,333.32	1,788.55	1,673.35	2,393.28
2008	3,393.69	1,735.16	3,685.68	3,183.80	1,468.40	1,629.02	2,246.16
2009	2,992.96	1,817.23	3,561.22	3,131.33	1,550.95	1,593.58	2,195.26
2010	2,863.41	1,827.16	3,295.47	3,245.89	1,544.47	1,542.61	2,157.76
2011	2,641.89	1,834.75	3,522.68	3,355.10	1,506.50	1,624.35	2,172.08
2012	2,546.89	1,921.00	3,083.95	3,489.91	1,491.10	1,638.37	2,152.84
2013	2,568.38	1,895.84	2,623.67	3,548.50	1,446.47	1,597.86	2,116.23
2014	2,555.38	1,946.51	2,595.92	3,402.06	1,437.89	1,563.25	2,091.12
2015	2,509.14	1,941.78	2,972.17	3,355.22	1,429.72	1,522.15	2,110.93
2016	2,525.05	1,922.00	2,520.09	3,920.11	1,398.86	1,421.72	2,090.31
2017	2,485.93	1,933.95	2,447.84	4,000.95	1,381.03	1,680.36	2,156.29
2018	2,437.10	1,934.81	2,525.09	4,137.52	1,383.96	1,734.73	2,191.01
2019	2,422.20	1,868.75	2,386.09	4,111.89	1,379.12	1,807.14	2,176.84
2020	2,344.59	1,869.47	2,301.09	4,178.08	1,452.16	1,832.73	2,180.81
2021	2,381.02	1,927.15	2,302.70	4,101.33	1,680.42	1,867.49	2,235.98
2022	2,232.92	2,068.49	2,229.65	4,416.72	1,632.00	1,922.83	2,292.35
Average	**2,955.14**	**1,878.13**	**2,829.09**	**3,564.25**	**1,614.98**	**1,617.60**	**2,212.01**
St.dev	**1,147.52**	**118.89**	**459.32**	**511.57**	**393.75**	**155.06**	**172.81**

Table 4.4 Lerner index of market power for GCC banks between 2002 and 2022

Year	*Bahrain*	*Kuwait*	*Oman*	*Qatar*	*Saudi Arabia*	*UAE*	*Average GCC*
2002	0.35	0.53	0.63	0.65	0.67	0.60	0.58
2003	0.45	0.61	0.65	0.65	0.66	0.66	0.62
2004	0.44	0.57	0.67	0.61	0.73	0.62	0.61
2005	0.38	0.56	0.65	0.42	0.54	0.61	0.55
2006	0.30	0.46	0.56	0.51	0.36	0.46	0.44
2007	0.29	0.41	0.57	0.52	0.53	0.14	0.36
2008	0.35	0.41	0.58	0.53	0.64	0.11	0.38
2009	0.40	0.52	0.66	0.54	0.73	0.53	0.56
2010	0.53	0.64	0.55	0.64	0.80	0.56	0.62
2011	0.49	0.62	0.61	0.78	0.80	0.62	0.65
2012	0.50	0.66	0.65	0.78	0.79	0.62	0.66
2013	0.55	0.66	0.68	0.74	0.79	0.69	0.69
2014	0.55	0.64	0.67	0.71	0.79	0.72	0.69
2015	0.53	0.67	0.69	0.69	0.78	0.73	0.69
2016	0.56	0.60	0.65	0.57	0.74	0.69	0.65
2017	0.53	0.58	0.62	0.53	0.74	0.69	0.63
2018	0.48	0.55	0.60	0.48	0.74	0.63	0.59
2019	0.45	0.53	0.60	0.52	0.73	0.61	0.58
2020	0.53	0.59	0.61	0.61	0.78	0.68	0.64
2021	0.54	0.64	0.61	0.65	0.82	0.73	0.68
2022	0.48	0.55	0.61	0.59	0.75	0.67	0.62
Average	**0.47**	**0.57**	**0.63**	**0.61**	**0.72**	**0.59**	0.60
St.dev	**0.09**	**0.08**	**0.04**	**0.10**	**0.11**	**0.17**	**0.09**

concentrated banking system. Meanwhile, Qatar, Oman, and Bahrain exceed 2500, indicating higher concentration and lower competition.

Concentration levels vary across banking aggregates (assets, loans, equity, and deposits), providing insight into market segmentation. While asset and loan concentration trends are similar, deposit concentration remains consistently high across all countries, underscoring the dominance of large banks in deposit-taking. The alignment between loan and deposit concentration with asset concentration further reinforces the dominance of leading banks in both lending and funding markets.

Between 2002 and 2022, most GCC countries experienced a slight decline in concentration, particularly following the 2008–09 financial crisis, suggesting increased competition. Between 2010 and 2016, concentration remained relatively stable, fluctuating within a narrow range. Since 2016, most markets have experienced a moderate decline, driven by regulatory reforms, new entrants, and the growth of digital banking.

Saudi Arabia, Oman, and Qatar saw a reduction in concentration over time, reflecting improved competitive conditions. Bahrain also experienced a decline in the concentration of loans and deposits, suggesting greater competition in the lending and funding markets. Kuwait followed a similar trend, aligning with broader financial liberalisation and regulatory reforms that encouraged competition (Al-Muharrami et al., 2006). Conversely, the UAE saw increases in CR3 and CR5 between 2013 and 2022, alongside rising HHI values. This was primarily due to domestic bank mergers and policies that support national champions. Additionally, state-owned and family-owned banks may have constrained competition through ownership structures rather than market forces alone.

Overall, concentration indicators (CR3, CR5, and HHI) suggest that the smaller banking sectors of Qatar, Oman, and Bahrain are highly concentrated, with the largest banks dominating total assets, equity, loans, and deposits. In contrast, Saudi Arabia, the UAE, and Kuwait—home to the region's largest banking systems—exhibit lower concentration levels, implying greater competition. Differences in financial-sector policies, market openness, and bank-specific factors contribute to cross-country disparities. Countries with fewer banks, such as Bahrain and Oman, naturally exhibit higher concentration, whereas the UAE and Kuwait, with more diversified banking systems, exhibit lower concentration (Sufian, 2007).

A comparison of CR3, CR5, and HHI shows consistent trends across these measures. High CR3 and CR5 values indicate market dominance by a few banks, while HHI offers a more nuanced assessment by incorporating the entire market distribution. Over time, the concentration trends suggest that the largest banks primarily drive market structure (Bikker & Haaf, 2002).

Lerner Index of Market Power

The Lerner Index is a measure of market power that captures banks' ability to set prices above marginal cost. A higher index value indicates stronger market power and reduced competition, whereas a lower value reflects a more competitive banking environment. The analysis of GCC banks between 2002 and 2022 reveals significant trends in market power, highlighting fluctuations over time and across countries.

Over the entire period, in Table 4.4, the average Lerner Index for GCC banks was 0.60, indicating moderate market power, with notable cross-country variation. Saudi Arabia exhibited the highest market power (0.72), followed by Oman (0.63) and Qatar (0.61), while Bahrain recorded the lowest (0.47). The UAE experienced considerable volatility, with an average of 0.59 and the highest standard deviation (0.17), indicating substantial fluctuations in market power.

The annual data highlights three key trends. First, market power peaked between 2010 and 2015, with the GCC-wide average reaching 0.69. Saudi Arabia and Qatar recorded particularly high values, exceeding 0.78 in some years. Second, the 2007–2009 period saw a temporary decline, particularly in the UAE, where the Lerner Index fell to 0.11 in 2008, reflecting heightened competition during the Global Financial Crisis (GFC). Third, from 2016 onward, market power declined, particularly in Oman and Qatar, while Saudi Arabia maintained relatively stable levels, peaking at 0.82 in 2021. By 2022, the index had declined to 0.62, suggesting a modest improvement in competition.

A sub-period analysis reinforces these observations. Between 2002 and 2006, market power was relatively moderate (0.56) but varied significantly across countries, with Oman exhibiting the highest index (0.63) and Bahrain the lowest (0.38). During 2007–2012, some regions declined, particularly the UAE (0.43), while Saudi Arabia's market power increased to 0.72. The highest levels were recorded between 2013 and 2018, with the GCC average reaching 0.66 and Saudi banks leading at 0.76. However, during 2019–2022, the average decline was slight (0.63), although Saudi Arabia remained dominant (0.77).

The observed trends align with empirical literature on banking competition and market power. Studies on GCC banking (e.g., Al-Muharrami & Matthews, 2009; Bikker & Spierdijk, 2010) suggest that financial liberalisation and regulatory changes have influenced competition. The GFC disrupted market structures, temporarily reducing pricing power. In the post-crisis period, consolidation and capital adequacy reforms contributed to the resurgence of market power, particularly in Saudi Arabia and Qatar.

Saudi banks' consistently high Lerner Index aligns with research by Beck et al. (2013), which highlights how concentrated banking sectors with strong government ties tend to exhibit greater pricing power. In contrast, Bahrain's more open financial market resulted in lower market power and greater competition. The UAE's volatility reflects shifts in competition intensity, driven by market liberalisation and regulatory interventions (Mirzaei et al., 2013).

From 2013 to 2019, the Lerner Index declined across the GCC, reflecting increased competition, particularly in Saudi Arabia, Oman, and Kuwait. Financial-sector reforms, market liberalisation, and regulatory incentives to attract new banking institutions likely contributed to this trend (GCC Financial Stability Report, 2018). The expansion of digital banking and Islamic finance may have further pressured traditional banks to reduce mark-ups and adopt more customer-centric strategies.

The COVID-19 pandemic and subsequent economic slowdown had a significant impact on GCC banking. Between 2019 and 2021, the Lerner Index increased, particularly in Kuwait, Saudi Arabia, and the UAE, reflecting reduced competition as banks prioritised financial stability. The decline in lending activity and the implementation of government-backed financial support programmes may have favoured established banks, reinforcing market concentration (BIS, 2021). However, the slight decline in 2022 suggests a modest improvement in competition, particularly in Qatar, Bahrain, and the UAE, possibly driven by post-pandemic recovery efforts, regulatory initiatives, and banking-sector diversification.

The evolution of market power in GCC banking over the past two decades has followed a cyclical pattern, shaped by regulatory changes, economic conditions, and financial crises. Periods of increased competition were observed due to liberalisation and market entry, whereas crises reinforced the dominance of large banks. The recent decline in the Lerner Index suggests a potential shift towards greater competition, supported by economic recovery, financial-sector reforms, and digital transformation. However, continued monitoring of regulatory policies, competitive dynamics, and technological advancements is necessary to determine whether increased competition will be sustained in the long run.

Boone Indicator: Market Share and Cost Efficiency

The Boone indicator is widely used in empirical banking literature to assess competition by measuring the impact of marginal costs on firm performance. A more negative Boone coefficient suggests higher competition, whereas a positive or near-zero value implies weaker competitive pressures. In Table 4.12, Bahrain's banking sector has exhibited fluctuating levels of competition over the years. On average, the overall Boone coefficient for assets is −0.4346 ($p = 0.098$), indicating strong competition, particularly in the loan market, whereas competition in assets and deposits is weaker. The sub-period analysis reveals an unusual trend. Negative Boone indicators (assets or loans) were observed during the period 2007–12 and 2019–22, whereas they were insignificant for other periods. This suggests that Bahrain's banking competition, as measured by Boone, may be cyclical, with phases of strong competition followed by relative stabilisation.

Kuwait shows limited competition, with an insignificant period Boone coefficient for assets (0.0387, $p = 0.81$) but significant and negative values for loans (−0.4259, $p = 0.029$), suggesting greater competition in the loan market. The sub-period analysis highlights a competitive banking environment in the loan markets in the early years (2002–2012), as indicated by all Boone indicators being significantly negative. However, competition diminishes in subsequent years, particularly from 2013 onward, where Boone coefficients become insignificant. The weak competition in Kuwait aligns with its historically concentrated banking sector, where government-backed banks dominate and limit market contestability.

Oman remains the least competitive market in the GCC, with no statistically significant Boone coefficients across the whole period. The 2013–18 sub-period is an exception, where highly negative Boone values indicate a brief period of heightened competition (−1.6164 to −1.9159, $p < 0.001$). However, this intensity does not persist during the 2019–2022 period, during which all coefficients become insignificant. This suggests that structural barriers continue to limit competitive pressures in Oman's banking sector.

Qatar's banking sector exhibits an unusual pattern, with positive Boone indicators across all variables over the entire period (e.g., 0.843 for deposits, $p = 0.000$), suggesting an inverse relationship between costs and market share. This could indicate regulatory distortions or state intervention in pricing. The sub-period breakdown shows that Qatar's banking market became increasingly uncompetitive after 2013, with significantly positive Boone values, particularly in deposits (1.5114, $p = 0.008$) during 2019–22. This supports the argument that Qatar's banking sector operates under strong government influence, limiting the role of cost efficiency in determining market power.

Saudi Arabia exhibits strong competition, with negative and significant Boone indicators across all market segments. The most competitive periods are 2013–2022, during which the Boone coefficients exceed −1.0 for all variables. This suggests that cost efficiency plays a dominant role in shaping market dynamics, particularly in recent years. The results are consistent with Saudi Arabia's efforts to modernise its banking sector and introduce market-driven reforms that intensify competition.

The UAE remains the most competitive market in the GCC, with consistently negative Boone coefficients for all banking activities. Competition is extreme in the 2013–18 period (−1.5209 for assets, −1.3967 for loans, $p = 0.000$), coinciding with major regulatory reforms and increased market liberalisation. While competition slightly weakens in 2019–22, Boone values remain significantly negative, confirming that the UAE's banking sector continues to operate under intense competitive pressure.

Across the GCC, the 2013–2018 period emerges as the most competitive, with highly negative Boone coefficients in Saudi Arabia, the UAE, and Bahrain. This period coincides with post-global financial crisis regulatory adjustments and increased financial liberalisation efforts. In contrast, the 2019–22 period shows a mixed trend. While Saudi Arabia and the UAE maintain strong competition, Bahrain and Kuwait see a decline in competitive intensity, suggesting that certain regulatory changes may have dampened competitive forces. Qatar's Boone coefficients become even more positive in this period, reinforcing the view that its banking sector is becoming less competitive over time (Table 4.5).

In Table 4.6, Islamic banks in Bahrain, Kuwait, and Qatar face less competition than their conventional counterparts. The positive Boone coefficients for Qatar's Islamic banks in multiple periods suggest market power, likely due to regulatory advantages or government support. Conversely, Saudi Arabia and the UAE exhibit strong competition across both conventional and Islamic banking, with no significant divergence between the two. This indicates that Islamic banking in these two markets is sufficiently developed to face competitive pressures comparable to those faced by conventional banks.

The analysis of Boone indicator estimates confirms that GCC banking competition varies significantly across countries, banking types, and time periods. First, the UAE, Saudi Arabia, and Bahrain exhibit strong competition, as indicated by significantly negative Boone coefficients. By contrast, Qatar's banking sector demonstrates weak competition, with

Table 4.5 Boone indicator for GCC banks between 2002 and 2022 per country and per sub-period

Dependent variable		*Market share of assets*		*Market Share of Loans*		*Market Share of Deposits*		*ROA*	
Country	*Sub-periods*	*Boone_Assets*	P-*value*	*Boone_Loans*	P-*value*	*Boone_Deposits*	P-*value*	*Boone_ROA*	P-*value*
Bahrain	All period: 2002:2022	−0.4346	0.098*	−0.9712	0.004***	−0.3536	0.185	−0.0554	0.019*
Bahrain	1: 2002–2005	1.1667	0.077*	1.0621	0.136	1.4328	0.055*	1.1667	0.077*
Bahrain	2: 2007–2012	−1.4472	0.002***	−1.6246	0.003***	−1.6525	0.001***	−1.4472	0.002***
Bahrain	3: 2013–2018	0.2762	0.61	−0.1151	0.863	0.4805	0.356	0.2762	0.61
Bahrain	4: 2019:2022	−0.758	0.15	−2.4243	0.009***	−0.3324	0.435	−0.758	0.15
Kuwait	All period: 2002:2022	0.0387	0.81	−0.4259	0.029**	0.0208	0.902	0.001	0.014**
Kuwait	1: 2002–2005	−0.7474	0.017**	−0.9687	0.021**	−0.7656	0.017**	−0.7474	0.017**
Kuwait	2: 2007–2012	−0.0523	0.875	−0.9521	0.05**	−0.0709	0.848	−0.0523	0.875
Kuwait	3: 2013–2018	0.1696	0.665	0.1066	0.3575	0.1618	0.68	0.1696	0.665
Kuwait	4: 2019:2022	−0.2347	0.602	−0.1616	0.689	−0.2132	0.633	−0.2347	0.602
Oman	All period: 2002–2022	−0.2945	0.253	−0.5604	0.115	−0.3512	0.204	−0.001	0.232
Oman	1: 2002–2005	1.9326	0.106	−1.5966	0.509	2.1338	0.089*	1.9326	0.106
Oman	2: 2007–2012	0.5051	0.292	0.788	0.124	0.5739	0.231	0.5051	0.292
Oman	3: 2013–2018	−1.6164	0.000***	−1.7218	0.001***	−1.9159	0.000***	−1.6164	0.000***
Oman	4: 2019:2022	−0.6949	0.163	−0.3996	0.472	0.6887	0.159	−0.6949	0.163

Dependent variable		*Market share of assets*		*Market Share of Loans*		*Market Share of Deposits*		*ROA*	
Country	*Sub-periods*	*Boone_Assets*	*P-value*	*Boone_Loans*	*P-value*	*Boone_Deposits*	*P-value*	*Boone_ROA*	*P-value*
Qatar	All period: 2002–2022	0.6253	0.000***	0.6503	0.000***	0.843	0.000***	0.0003	0.604
Qatar	1: 2002–2005	0.6317	0.019**	1.6933	0.000***	1.6055	0.000***	0.6317	0.019**
Qatar	2: 2007–2012	0.0717	0.769	−0.1975	0.478	0.0832	0.788	0.0717	0.769
Qatar	3: 2013–2018	0.9864	0.01**	0.8748	0.026**	0.9028	0.071*	0.9864	0.01**
Qatar	4: 2019:2022	1.4029	0.002***	1.2509	0.006***	1.5114	0.008***	1.4029	0.002***
Saudi Arabia	All period: 2002–2022	−0.4526	0.001***	−0.5416	0.000***	−0.4516	0.001***	0.0007	0.095*
Saudi Arabia	1: 2002–2005	−0.81	0.036**	−0.8297	0.062*	−0.9077	0.029**	−0.81	0.036**
Saudi Arabia	2: 2007–2012	−0.5192	0.036**	−0.6276	0.014**	−0.4861	0.065*	−0.5192	0.036**
Saudi Arabia	3: 2013–2018	−1.0942	0.000**	−1.1659	0.000***	−1.0321	0.000***	−1.0942	0.000**
Saudi Arabia	4: 2019:2022	−1.0654	0.000***	−1.0723	0.000***	−1.0272	0.001***	−1.0654	0.000***
UAE	All period	−0.7892	0.000***	−0.898	0.000***	−0.7959	0.000***	0.00	0.923
UAE	1: 2002–2005	−0.6667	0.086 *	−1.5072	0.004***	−0.6758	0.10*	−0.6667	0.086 *
UAE	2: 2007–2012	−1.3772	0.000***	−1.1147	0.001***	−1.3941	0.000***	−1.3772	0.000***
UAE	3: 2013–2018	−1.5209	0.000***	−1.3967	0.000***	−1.4706	0.000***	−1.5209	0.000***
UAE	4: 2019:2022	−1.1943	0.008***	−1.065	0.014**	−1.1077	0.016**	−1.1943	0.008***

Four specifications of the MS-based dependent variable. P-value is the significance level for the Boone coefficient; *, ** and *** indicate 10%, 5% and 1% significance level

Table 4.6 Boone indicator for GCC banks between 2002 and 2022, per country and per type of bank

Dependent variable		*Market share of assets*		*Market Share of Loans*		*Market Share of Deposits*		*ROA*	
Country	*Type of banking*	*Boone_assets*	*P-value*	*Boone_Loans*	*P-value*	*Boone_Deposits*	*P-value*	*Boone_ROA*	*P-value*
Bahrain	**All**	−0.4346	0.098*	−0.9712	0.004***	−0.3536	0.185	−0.0554	0.019*
Bahrain	**Islamic**	1.6804	0.464	1.6371	0.000***	1.7927	0.000***	0.0008	0.464
Bahrain	**Conventional**	−1.3859	0.000***	−2.1236	0.000***	−1.3213	0.000***	−0.0798	0.029**
Kuwait	**All**	0.0387	0.81	−0.4259	0.029**	0.0208	0.902	0.001	0.014**
Kuwait	**Islamic**	0.5004	0.036**	−0.503	0.856	0.4667	0.066*	0.002	0.000***
Kuwait	**Conventional**	0.0638	0.757	−0.3166	0.256	0.0964	0.64	0.0008	0.259
Oman	**All**	−0.2945	0.253	−0.5604	0.115	−0.3512	0.204	−0.001	0.232
Oman	**No Islamic banks in Oman**								
Oman	**Conventional**	−0.2945	0.253	−0.5604	0.115	−0.3512	0.204	−0.001	0.232
Qatar	**All**	0.6253	0.000***	0.6503	0.000***	0.843	0.000***	0.0003	0.604
Qatar	**Islamic**	0.3085	0.016**	0.5282	0.005***	0.6054	0.000***	0.001	0.235
Qatar	**Conventional**	0.5956	0.042**	0.395	0.225	0.9466	0.017**	0.0011	0.027**
Saudi Arabia	**All**	−0.4526	0.001***	−0.5416	0.000***	−0.4516	0.001***	0.0007	0.095*
Saudi Arabia	**Islamic**	−0.9221	0.000***	−1.0118	0.000***	−0.8958	0.000***	0.0003	0.631
Saudi Arabia	**Conventional**	0.1349	0.271	0.0465	0.738	0.1045	0.411	0.0011	0.002***
UAE	**All**	−0.7892	0.000***	−0.898	0.000***	−0.7959	0.000***	0.000001	0.923
UAE	**Islamic**	−0.6256	0.002***	−0.7291	0.000***	−0.6902	0.001***	0.0006	0.3334
UAE	**Conventional**	−0.8455	0.000***	−1.3562	0.000***	−0.8331	0.000***	−0.0002	0.748

positive Boone coefficients indicating market power and regulatory distortions. Oman and Kuwait also exhibit limited competition, with Boone values that are largely insignificant. Second, Islamic banks in Bahrain and Qatar exhibit weaker competition, whereas those in Saudi Arabia and the UAE face competitive pressures comparable to those of conventional banks. Finally, the 2013–2018 period was the most competitive across the GCC. Still, recent trends suggest a divergence, with Qatar becoming increasingly uncompetitive while Saudi Arabia and the UAE sustain competitive market conditions. These findings align with broader literature on GCC banking, highlighting the role of regulatory structures, market concentration, and financial liberalisation in shaping competitive dynamics.

Revenue Elasticity and the Panzar-Rosse H-Statistic

The Panzar-Rosse H-statistic is estimated for each sub-period and country to assess the prevailing market structure in GCC banking. Table 4.7 presents the estimation results alongside the required market-structure tests. The results consistently reject the null hypotheses of H = 0 (monopoly) and H = 1 (perfect competition), confirming that the banking sector in the GCC operates under monopolistic competition. This implies that while banks compete for customers, they retain significant pricing power, allowing them to sustain profit margins above those expected in a perfectly competitive market. Across all time periods, the banking markets in GCC countries have remained within this competitive structure, with no substantial shift towards either monopoly or perfect competition.

One significant finding is that the H-statistic exceeds one across all sub-periods and countries. While this may seem counterintuitive, it does not alter the core conclusion of monopolistic competition. The Panzar-Rosse framework emphasises that the interpretation of H-values should be strictly confined to the accepted market-structure tests (H = 0 and H = 1). The empirical literature suggests that H-statistics greater than one can arise from specific banking characteristics, such as high income elasticity of demand for banking services, economies of scale, or variations in cost structures across banks. These factors can lead to an overestimation of revenue sensitivity to input prices without implying a departure from monopolistic competition.

Table 4.7 H-statistic of Panzar-Rosse for GCC banks between 2002 and 2022 per country and per sub-period

Country	*Period*	*Price of funds (P1)*	p-*value on P1*	*Price of labour and physical capital (P2)*	p-*value on P2*	*GDP GROWTH*
Bahrain	1: 2002–2006	0.2993	0.000***	1.0042	0.000***	6.0383 (0.000)***
Bahrain	2: 2007–2012	0.4628	0.000***	0.9998	0.000***	4.6542 (0.000)***
Bahrain	3: 2013–2018	0.4897	0.000***	0.9994	0.000***	−1.0540 (0.10)*
Bahrain	4: 2019:2022	0.2636	0.000***	0.9965	0.000***	−0.1549 (0.289)
Kuwait	1: 2002–2006	0.1856	0.000***	0.9993	0.000***	.2446 (0.003)***
Kuwait	2: 2007–2012	0.5125	0.000***	0.9976	0.000***	0.6188 (0.000)***
Kuwait	3: 2013–2018	0.4702	0.000***	0.9999	0.000***	−0.0241 (0.748)
Kuwait	4: 2019:2022	0.3416	0.000***	0.9996	0.000***	0.0803 (0.004)***
Oman	1: 2002–2006	0.5157	0.000***	0.9991	0.000***	1.859 (0.000)***
Oman	2: 2007–2012	0.6651	0.000***	0.9957	0.000***	4.5416 (0.000)***
Oman	3: 2013–2018	0.2406	0.000***	1.0001	0.000***	0.9720 (0.000)***
Oman	4: 2019:2022	0.9379	0.000***	0.9984	0.000***	0.0433 (0.758)
Qatar	1: 2002–2006	0.4333	0.000***	1.0058	0.000***	1.6324 (0.000)***
Qatar	2: 2007–2012	−0.1704	0.021	0.9719	0.000***	−0.9502 (0.20)
Qatar	3: 2013–2018	0.3478	0.000***	0.9964	0.000***	−0.1620 (0.828)
Qatar	4: 2019:2022	0.1951	0.000***	0.9991	0.000***	1.7537 (0.000)***
Saudi Arabia	1: 2002–2005	0.2989	0.000***	1.0037	0.000***	0.1801 (0.768)
Saudi Arabia	2: 2007–2012	0.1697	0.000***	1.0006	0.000***	−0.3058 (0.000)***
Saudi Arabia	3: 2013–2018	0.1296	0.000***	0.9993	0.000***	−0.5248 (0.035)**
Saudi Arabia	4: 2019:2022	0.0765	0.000***	0.9989	0.000***	1.0701 (0.000)***
UAE	1: 2002–2005	0.5679	0.000***	1.0067	0.000***	−1.2714 (0.007)***
UAE	2: 2007–2012	0.1759	0.000***	0.9985	0.000***	0.0636 (0.834)
UAE	3: 2013–2018	0.2738	0.000***	0.9991	0.000***	−1.1701 (0.000)***
UAE	4: 2019:2022	0.1915	0.000***	0.9993	0.000***	0.7948 (0.000)***

Country	*Constant*	*Um of obs*	*F (p = value)*	*R2*	*Adj_R2*	*H-statistic of Panzer Rosse*	*Test H = 0*	*Test H = 1*	*Type*
Bahrain	2.0992 (0.000)***	26	10,102.16 (0.000)***	0.9993	0.9992	1.3035	3293.21 (0.000)***	178.49 (0.000)***	Monopolistic competition
Bahrain	2.8790 (0.000)***	46	75,035.06 (0.000)***	0.9998	0.9998	1.4626	4659.82 (0.000)***	466.10 (0.000)***	Monopolistic competition
Bahrain	3.7352 (0.000)***	48	68,241.17 (0.000)***	0.9998	0.9998	1.4891	521.94 (0.000)***	56.30 (0.000)***	Monopolistic competition
Bahrain	2.7625 (0.000)***	29	39,808.40 (0.000)***	0.9998	0.9998	1.2601	2404.74 (0.000)***	102.40 (0.000)***	Monopolistic competition
Kuwait	2.8631 (0.000)***	39	33,919.52 (0.000)***	0.9997	0.9996	1.1849	14,323.72 (0.000)***	348.77 (0.000)***	Monopolistic competition
Kuwait	3.9812 (0.000)***	56	5732 (0.000)***	0.997	0.9968	1.5101	5861.01 (0.000)***	668.72 (0.000)***	Monopolistic competition
Kuwait	3.8777 (0.000)***	60	92,219.71 (0.000)***	0.9998	0.9998	1.4701	27,055.57 (0.000)***	2766.79 (0.000)***	Monopolistic competition
Kuwait	3.3118 (0.000)***	40	85,279.08 (0.000)***	0.9999	0.9999	1.3412	39,336.86 (0.000)***	2546.28 (0.000)***	Monopolistic competition
Oman	3.553 (0.000)***	25	25,492.19 (0.000)***	0.9997	0.9997	1.5148	3724.54 (0.000)***	430.17 (0.000)***	Monopolistic competition
Oman	3.8049 (0.000)***	30	1011.80 (0.000)***	0.9915	0.9905	1.6608	716.62 (0.000)***	112.82 (0.000)***	Monopolistic competition
Oman	2.6517 (0.000)***	42	21,748.79 (0.000)***	0.9994	0.9994	1.2407	4096.97 (0.000)***	154.20 (0.000)***	Monopolistic competition
Oman	5.5161 (0.000)***	28	13,083.26 (0.000)***	0.9994	0.9993	1.9363	117.44 (0.000)**	27.46 (0.000)***	Monopolistic competition
Qatar	3.1498 (0.000)***	23	4028.27 (0.000)***	0.9984	0.9982	1.4391	2501.13 (0.000)***	232.86 (0.000)***	Monopolistic competition
Qatar	1.4652 (0.001)***	39	544.27 (0.000)***	0.979	0.9772	0.8015	121.97 (0.000)***	7.84 (0.0097)***	Monopolistic competition
Qatar	3.7326 (0.000)***	42	3200.19 (0.000)***	0.9959	0.9956	1.3442	994.04 (0.000)***	65.16 (0.000)***	Monopolistic competition
Qatar	3.1153 (0.0000)***	28	3282.96 (0.000)***	0.9976	0.9973	1.1942	824.23 (0.000)***	21.81 (0.000)***	Monopolistic competition

(continued)

Table 4.7 (continued)

Country	*Constant*	*Um of obs*	*F (p = value)*	*R2*	*Adj_R2*	*H-statistic of Panzer Rosse*	*Test H = 0*	*Test H = 1*	*Type*
Saudi Arabia	3.1286 (0.000)***	29	552.53 (0.000)***	0.9851	0.9834	1.3026	447.58 (0.000)***	24.16 (0.000)***	Monopolistic competition
Saudi Arabia	2.6803 (0.000)***	56	55,094.87 (0.000)***	0.9997	0.9997	1.1703	72,270.83 (0.000)***	1530.48 (0.000)***	Monopolistic competition
Saudi Arabia	2.499 (0.000)***	60	26,542.94 (0.000)***	0.9993	0.9993	1.1289	10,353.63 (0.000)***	134.91 (0.000)***	Monopolistic competition
Saudi Arabia	2.1328 (0.000)***	40	21,285.06 (0.000)***	0.9994	0.9994	1.0754	19,942.73 (0.000)***	98.05 (0.000)***	Monopolistic competition
UAE	4.3368 (0.000)***	69	3866.54 (0.000)***	0.9944	0.9942	1.5746	2189.86 (0.000)***	291.60 (0.000)***	Monopolistic competition
UAE	2.5059 (0.000)***	94	5247.22 (0.000)***	0.9943	0.9941	1.1744	894.05 (0.000)***	19.72 (0.000)***	Monopolistic competition
UAE	3.2405 (0.000)***	96	70,401.51 (0.000)***	0.9996	0.9996	1.2729	7179.56 (0.000)***	330.04 (0.000)***	Monopolistic competition
UAE	2.7181 (0.000)***	62	99,999 (0.000)***	0.9998	0.9998	1.1908	14,534.78 (0.000)***	373.27 (0.000)***	Monopolistic competition

The Panzar-Rosse H-statistic is a widely used measure for assessing competitive conditions in banking markets. An H-statistic greater than one is unusual and may be attributable to characteristics inherent in the banking sector. For instance, high income elasticity of demand for banking services can lead to disproportionate increases in revenues relative to input costs, resulting in an H-statistic exceeding unity. Additionally, significant economies of scale or variations in cost structures across banks can make revenue overly sensitive to input price changes, thereby inflating the H-statistic beyond the typical range. However, it is crucial to note that such values do not necessarily indicate a departure from monopolistic competition. The critical aspect is testing the null hypotheses $H = 0$ and $H = 1$; rejection of both suggests that the market operates under monopolistic competition, regardless of the H-statistic's magnitude.

Empirical studies have highlighted that the Panzar-Rosse model's interpretation requires careful consideration. Bikker et al. (2012) emphasise that the value of the H-statistic must be contextualised within the market's structural and operational nuances, as factors such as scale economies and cost heterogeneity can influence the results. Furthermore, Shaffer (2020) argues that the H-statistic is more closely related to the pass-through rate than to a direct measure of market power, implying that values greater than 1 may reflect specific market dynamics rather than contradict the presence of monopolistic competition.

Additionally, the evolution of the banking sector in the GCC indicates that market forces have been active, with banks adjusting their pricing strategies in response to competitive pressures. Sustained monopolistic competition suggests a dynamic environment in which banks differentiate their products and services while retaining some pricing discretion. This aligns with findings in the empirical banking literature, which show that banking sectors in emerging markets often exhibit monopolistic competition due to regulatory frameworks, market concentration, and the presence of both domestic and international players.

To assess whether GCC banking systems were in long-run equilibrium, we examine the sum of elasticities (E-Equilibrium) in the ROA regression. If the equilibrium test p-value is greater than or equal to 10% ($p \geq 0.10$), the long-run equilibrium is not rejected; if $p < 0.10$, the equilibrium is rejected. The findings indicate disequilibrium during the early period (2002–2006) across all GCC countries, suggesting abnormal profits or losses in the early 2000s. Disequilibrium persisted in Qatar and the UAE following the financial crisis, reflecting ongoing structural adjustments.

However, from 2013 onward, GCC banking systems reached a long-run equilibrium, as evidenced by the failure to reject the null hypothesis.

Despite the persistence of monopolistic competition, the attainment of long-run equilibrium suggests that banks do not generate excess profits. This reinforces the view that the sector operates under competitive constraints, in which entry and exit dynamics prevent abnormal returns from persisting. The results align with broader empirical literature, which finds that monopolistic competition in banking does not necessarily imply inefficiency; rather, it reflects product differentiation, regulatory conditions, and evolving market dynamics. Thus, while GCC banking markets retain pricing power, they function within a competitive structure that promotes long-term equilibrium and stability.

While H-statistics exceeding one are atypical, they can result from specific market characteristics and do not inherently contradict a monopolistic competition framework. The essential result is the rejection of the null hypotheses H = 0 and H = 1, confirming the monopolistic competition market structure. The shift from disequilibrium in the pre-crisis era to equilibrium in the post-crisis period further underscores the dynamic nature of the GCC banking sector's competitive environment (Table 4.8).

Log of Total revenue over total assets is the dependent variable. H-statistic is the sum of the coefficients on P1 and P2, *, ** and *** indicate 10%, 5%, and 1% significance level.

Sub-periods of GCC Banking Sectors (2002–2022)

Based on the consistent trends observed in CR3, CR5, HHI, and the Lerner Index of market power across GCC countries from 2002 to 2022, the period can be divided into four distinct sub-periods. These sub-periods reflect changes in market concentration, competition, and banking-sector dynamics, shaped by economic cycles, financial crises, regulatory reforms, and technological advancements.

The four identified sub-periods (2002–2006, 2007–2012, 2013–2018, 2019–2022) apply to all six GCC countries (Bahrain, Kuwait, Oman, Qatar, Saudi Arabia, and the UAE). Still, the extent and specific nature of the trends vary across countries. While the overall patterns of banking concentration and market power follow these timeframes, individual countries exhibit some differences in the magnitude and timing of changes, reflecting variations in market structure, regulatory policies, and

Table 4.8 Testing equilibrium using E-statistic for GCC banks between 2002 and 2022 per country and per sub-period (Log ROA is the dependent variable. E-Equilibrium is the sum of the coefficients on P1 and P2, *, **, and *** indicate 10%, 5%, and 1% significance level)

Country	*Period*	*E-Equilibrium of Panzar-Rosse*	*Test E = 0 (p-value)*	*Comment on the significance of the p-value*	*Equilibrium or No Equilibrium*
Bahrain	**1: 2002–2006**	0.0055	0.001 ***	$p < 10\%$ (Significant)	No Equilibrium
Bahrain	**2: 2007–2012**	0.0067	0.452	$p > 10\%$ (Not significant)	Equilibrium
Bahrain	**3: 2013–2018**	−0.4318	0.4662	$p > 10\%$ (Not significant)	Equilibrium
Bahrain	**4: 2019–2022**	−0.0141	0.3365	$p > 10\%$ (Not significant)	Equilibrium
Kuwait	**1: 2002–2006**	0.003	0.0020 ***	$p < 10\%$ (Significant)	No Equilibrium
Kuwait	**2: 2007–2012**	0.0001	0.9617	$p > 10\%$ (Not significant)	Equilibrium
Kuwait	**3: 2013–2018**	0.0015	0.4064	$p > 10\%$ (Not significant)	Equilibrium
Kuwait	**4: 2019–2022**	−0.0002	0.776	$p > 10\%$ (Not significant)	Equilibrium
Oman	**1: 2002–2006**	0.0033	0.5482	$p > 10\%$ (Not significant)	Equilibrium
Oman	**2: 2007–2012**	0.0015	0.1408	$p > 10\%$ (Not significant)	Equilibrium
Oman	**3: 2013–2018**	−0.0016	0.4001	$p > 10\%$ (Not significant)	Equilibrium
Oman	**4: 2019–2022**	0.0112	0.2297	$p > 10\%$ (Not significant)	Equilibrium
Qatar	**1: 2002–2006**	0.0662	0.0798 *	$p < 10\%$ (Significant)	No Equilibrium

(continued)

Table 4.8 (continued)

Country	*Period*	*E-Equilibrium of Panzar-Rosse*	*Test E = 0* (p-*value*)	*Comment on the significance of the* p-*value*	*Equilibrium or No Equilibrium*
Qatar	**2: 2007–2012**	0.0047	0.0075 ***	$p < 10\%$ (Significant)	No Equilibrium
Qatar	**3: 2013–2018**	−0.0005	0.4028	$p > 10\%$ (Not significant)	Equilibrium
Qatar	**4: 2019–2022**	0.0005	0.5001	$p > 10\%$ (Not significant)	Equilibrium
Saudi Arabia	**1: 2002–2005**	0.0065	0.0077 ***	$p < 10\%$ (Significant)	No Equilibrium
Saudi Arabia	**2: 2007–2012**	−0.0008	0.1058	$p > 10\%$ (Not significant)	Equilibrium
Saudi Arabia	**3: 2013–2018**	0.0011	0.1104	$p > 10\%$ (Not significant)	Equilibrium
Saudi Arabia	**4: 2019–2022**	0.002	0.9852	$p > 10\%$ (Not significant)	Equilibrium
UAE	**1: 2002–2005**	0.0022	0.0275 **	$p < 10\%$ (Significant)	No Equilibrium
UAE	**2: 2007–2012**	0.0021	0.0255 **	$p < 10\%$ (Significant)	No Equilibrium
UAE	**3: 2013–2018**	−0.0027	0.1173	$p > 10\%$ (Not significant)	Equilibrium
UAE	**4: 2019–2022**	−0.0002	0.8511	$p > 10\%$ (Not significant)	Equilibrium

economic conditions. Below is a country-by-country assessment within the sub-period framework:

Between 2002 and 2006, the GCC banking sector experienced a period of market expansion and intensifying competition. The declining values of concentration ratios (CR3, CR5), the Herfindahl–Hirschman Index (HHI), and the Lerner Index suggest that market structures were becoming less concentrated, fostering a more competitive environment. This trend aligns with the predictions of Contestability Theory, which posits that even in markets with a few dominant players, the threat of new entrants can enhance competition (Baumol, 1982). During this period, financial liberalisation and regulatory reforms, particularly in the UAE, Kuwait, and Saudi Arabia, enabled new entrants to challenge incumbents, thereby reducing pricing power and increasing efficiency. Bahrain exhibited the lowest market power, supporting the Efficient Structure Hypothesis (ESH), which posits that competition drives efficiency gains rather than merely market-structure changes (Demsetz, 1973). The negative and significant Boone Indicator further indicates that cost-efficient banks gained market share, reinforcing the idea that competitive pressures were driving improvements in banking performance.

The 2007–2012 period marked a phase of market consolidation and rising market power following the global financial crisis. The previous trend reversed as CR3, CR5, and HHI values rose across all GCC countries, indicating a shift towards greater concentration. The financial crisis led to the exit or weakening of smaller institutions, favouring the survival of large banks—a pattern consistent with the Survivor Bias Theory (Beck, Demirgüç-Kunt, & Levine, 2006). The increase in the Lerner Index, particularly in Saudi Arabia and Qatar, suggests that surviving banks capitalised on reduced competition to enhance their pricing power. The rise in market power without proportional increases in efficiency suggests that banks leveraged their dominant positions rather than achieving efficiency gains, lending support to the Relative Market Power Hypothesis (RMPH) (Shepherd, 1982). While Bahrain, the UAE, and Kuwait exhibited lower Lerner values, indicating sustained competitive pressures, banks in Saudi Arabia, Qatar, and Oman experienced stronger market power, potentially due to regulatory barriers and economies of scale favouring incumbent institutions.

Between 2013 and 2018, regulatory reforms and market diversification efforts were instrumental in shaping competition in the GCC banking sector. Saudi Arabia, Bahrain, and Oman experienced declining concentration ratios (CR3, CR5, and HHI), indicating increased competition driven by regulatory intervention and financial innovation. The introduction of digital banking initiatives and open banking frameworks has intensified competition, aligning with Contestability Theory, which argues that removing entry barriers can enhance competition even in concentrated markets. Despite declining concentration levels, the Lerner Index remained relatively high in certain jurisdictions, particularly Kuwait, suggesting that pricing power was retained through brand differentiation and customer loyalty, supporting the Relative Market Power Hypothesis. The Boone Indicator results indicate that Saudi Arabia, the UAE, and Oman had the most competitive banking environments, as efficiency improvements played a more significant role in shaping market dynamics. Meanwhile, Qatar exhibited weaker competition, as evidenced by persistently high HHI values.

The period from 2019 to 2022 was characterised by economic uncertainty, a surge in market power, and early signs of increased competition. The COVID-19 pandemic and global economic slowdown led to increased concentration in the banking sector, particularly in the UAE and Saudi Arabia, as larger banks consolidated their positions to ensure financial stability. The peak of the Lerner Index in 2021, especially in Saudi Arabia and the UAE (0.73), suggests that dominant banks capitalised on crisis conditions to strengthen their market power. This trend reflects the Quiet Life Hypothesis (QLH) (Hicks, 1935), which suggests that firms in concentrated markets may avoid competitive pressures and focus on maintaining stable profits. However, by 2022, signs of a recovery in competition emerged, particularly in the UAE, where concentration ratios (CR3 and CR5) declined, and the Lerner Index fell across most GCC economies, except in Oman. This shift suggests that regulatory reforms and fintech innovations were beginning to counteract the effects of market concentration. The Boone Indicator results reinforce this trend, indicating stronger competition in the post-crisis period, with Saudi and UAE banks—particularly conventional banks—exhibiting greater competitiveness than Islamic banks.

Overall, the analysis highlights distinct phases in GCC banking competition dynamics, shaped by economic cycles, regulatory interventions, and market structures. On average, banks in Bahrain exhibited the lowest market power (Lerner Index: 0.47), followed by Kuwait (0.57) and the UAE (0.59), whereas Saudi Arabia (0.72), Oman (0.63), and

Qatar (0.61) had the highest market power. The Structure-Conduct-Performance (SCP) paradigm is particularly relevant for explaining the persistence of market power in concentrated markets, where dominant banks employ pricing strategies that limit competition. However, the findings also support elements of the *Efficient Structure Hypothesis* (ESH), particularly in jurisdictions in which cost efficiency contributed to market success. The Boone Indicator suggests increasing competition over time, particularly in the UAE and Saudi Arabia, while Qatar remains the least competitive market. The contrast between declining concentration and persistent market power in some countries underscores the importance of regulatory frameworks, financial innovation, and institutional factors in shaping competition dynamics beyond structural market conditions alone. Importantly, the Panzar-Rosse values indicate that all GCC banking markets exhibit monopolistic competition, emphasising that while banks exert some pricing power, competitive forces remain present across periods and countries.

The following tables propose the factors and events shaping competition indicators for each sub-period and GCC country (Tables 4.9, 4.10, 4.11, and 4.12).

Discussion

The competitive dynamics of the GCC banking sector can be better understood by examining the relationship between market concentration and market power. The Three-Bank Concentration Ratio (CR3), Five-Bank Concentration Ratio (CR5), Herfindahl–Hirschman Index (HHI), and Lerner Index collectively provide insight into how concentration influences competition. A key question is whether high concentration, as measured by CR3, CR5, and HHI, directly translates into greater market power, reflected in the Lerner Index. If a strong relationship exists, the underlying factors must be considered, whereas inconsistencies require further investigation.

Over the past two decades, market concentration and market power in GCC banking have fluctuated in response to economic cycles, financial crises, regulatory changes, and technological advancements. Between 2002 and 2006, increased competition was evident, as evidenced by declines in the Lerner Index in Bahrain, Kuwait, and the UAE. CR3, CR5, and HHI either stabilised or slightly decreased, suggesting a more even distribution of market share. This period coincided with economic

Table 4.9 Market expansion and competition during 2002–2006

Country	*Factors shaping competition*	*Key events influencing trends*
UAE	– Entry of foreign banks – Regulatory and ownership reforms promoting competition – Technological advancements improved efficiency: Banks like Emirates NBD introduced early online banking services, enhancing competition	– Expansion of free zones (e.g., Dubai International Financial Centre in 2004) – Central Bank of the UAE easing restrictions on foreign banks – Growth in oil revenues is increasing banking-sector activity
Saudi Arabia	– Increased financial-sector openness by allowing foreign banks – Regulatory relaxation for new banking services – Growth in private-sector lending led to more competition for corporate clients	– The Saudi Arabian Monetary Authority (SAMA) is allowing more competition in retail banking, like HSBC and BNP Paribas – Boom in oil-driven economic expansion, increasing banking-sector activity
Kuwait	– Reduced state control over the banking sector – Increased competition among private banks – Foreign investment in the financial sector	– Privatisation of key financial institutions (Gulf Bank) – Expansion of foreign bank operations in Kuwait
Bahrain	– Established financial hub status – Progressive regulatory framework to allow more offshore banks to establish operations – Strong fintech adoption: Bahrain was the first GCC country to introduce mobile banking services	– Bahrain is promoting itself as a regional financial centre – Financial-Sector Development strategy introduced
Qatar	– State-driven banking-sector growth – Financing of large-scale infrastructure projects – Limited foreign bank presence due to restrictive licensing	– Pre-2006 economic boom – Rapid development due to oil and gas revenues – State-backed infrastructure projects increased demand for banking services
Oman	– Gradual financial liberalisation kept competition moderate to low- Entry of new banking institutions – Foreign bank presence remained limited due to regulatory restrictions	– The Central Bank of Oman is allowing more flexibility in banking-sector reforms – The Central Bank of Oman maintained conservative policies on foreign bank entry

Table 4.10 Crisis, consolidation, and market power during 2007–2012

Country	*Factors shaping competition*	*Key events influencing trends*
UAE	– Banking-sector consolidation – Liquidity constraints post-2008 crisis reduced new bank entry – Government intervention to stabilise banks: Government bailouts favoured larger banks, reducing competition	– **Global Financial Crisis (GFC) impact**—UAE government launching support programmes (e.g., 2009 liquidity support scheme) Post-crisis lending reforms
Saudi Arabia	– Reduced market competition due to bank failures – State support for major financial institutions – Rising dominance of large banks – State-owned banks absorbed weaker institutions, reducing competition – Increased banking regulations tightened lending policies, discouraging new banks	– GFC is reducing lending activities – The government is injecting capital into banks to maintain stability – Saudi banks faced liquidity shortages due to the GFC, leading to government capital injections
Kuwait	– Weaker competition due to financial instability – Merger of struggling banks (e.g., Kuwait Finance House acquired smaller Islamic banks) – Credit restrictions reduced competitive lending activities	– GFC-related credit crunch: Kuwait's banking system suffered significant losses during the GFC – Central Bank of Kuwait tightening regulations
Bahrain	– Decline in offshore banking activities – Increased reliance on the domestic market – More cautious lending practices – Islamic banking growth increased market segmentation	– **Impact of the global recession** – Declining international banking operations:—International investors pulled out post-GFC, reducing offshore banking strength

(continued)

Table 4.10 (continued)

Country	*Factors shaping competition*	*Key events influencing trends*
Qatar	– Government backing national banks through capital injection – M&As are reducing competition	– Qatar Investment Authority is supporting key banks during the crisis, preventing collapse- Expansion of government-backed financial institutions
Oman	– Higher capital requirements may reduce competition and force smaller banks to merge – Weaker competition among private banks – Government supporting key banks	– **Financial reforms post-GFC** – Stricter regulatory supervision of banking practices: Basel II regulations implemented, leading to stricter capital adequacy rules

growth and financial liberalisation, which encouraged sector expansion and greater competition.

The fluctuations in HHI values, particularly during 2008–2010, suggest that the global financial crisis significantly shaped market concentration. Economic instability led to asset consolidation, with larger banks strengthening their positions while smaller institutions struggled. CR3, CR5, and HHI values increased, indicating that banking assets, loans, and deposits became more concentrated among the largest banks. The Lerner Index also rose, particularly in Saudi Arabia and Qatar, suggesting growing pricing power among dominant banks. This trend aligns with the Survivor Bias Theory, which posits that economic downturns strengthen only the most prominent institutions, thereby increasing concentration and reducing competition. However, as the financial sector recovered, competition intensified, leading to a gradual decline in HHI.

Between 2013 and 2018, regulatory reforms and bank diversification contributed to a decline in concentration and market power in some GCC countries. Many GCC countries undertook banking-sector reforms to increase competition and financial stability. Regulatory measures, such as capital adequacy requirements, risk-management frameworks, and market liberalisation, contributed to the decline in concentration ratios observed in Saudi Arabia, Kuwait, and the UAE (Al-Muharrami et al., 2006; Hasan & Dridi, 2010). CR3 and CR5 fell in Saudi Arabia and the UAE, while HHI values declined, reinforcing market diversification. Similarly, the Lerner Index fell in Bahrain and Qatar, reflecting reduced pricing

Table 4.11 Regulatory reforms and market diversification during 2013–2018

Country	*Factors shaping competition*	*Key events influencing trends*
UAE	– Fintech and digital banking expanded, forcing traditional banks to innovate – Declining concentration levels – Open banking frameworks are increasing competition	– Introduction of fintech regulations (2017) – Rise of digital banking platforms (e.g., Emirates NBD digital strategy)
Saudi Arabia	– Regulatory intervention to promote competition – Increasing role of fintech firms – Competitive pressures from foreign banks	– SAMA launching Vision 2030 reforms – Growth in SME lending programmes
Kuwait	– Market competition stabilising – The sector is dominated by the National Bank of Kuwait – Strong customer loyalty to established banks	– Kuwait National Development Plan 2015 – Gradual opening of the financial sector
Bahrain	– Adoption of digital banking and fintech innovations – Regulatory efforts to diversify banking activities – Strengthening of financial regulations	– Bahrain launching Fintech Bay initiative (2018) – Development of a regulatory sandbox for fintech startups
Qatar	– Continued state-driven banking sector – Less foreign bank competition – High dependency on government financing	– 2017 GCC crisis affecting banking flows – Increased government intervention in the financial sector
Oman	– Strengthened banking-sector regulations – Moderate decline in market concentration – Adoption of digital banking	– The Central Bank of Oman is implementing Basel III regulations – The Central Bank of Oman maintained strict control over banking licences

power. These changes were primarily driven by financial-sector reforms aimed at increasing competition.

The broader economic diversification strategies pursued by GCC governments have also influenced market concentration trends. By encouraging private-sector growth and reducing reliance on state-backed financial institutions, these initiatives have fostered greater competition in the banking sector. The UAE and Saudi Arabia, in particular, have experienced increased participation by international and mid-sized banks,

Table 4.12 COVID-19, market power & competition during 2019–2022

Country	*Factors shaping competition*	*Key events influencing trends*
UAE	– Increased banking-sector concentration during the pandemic (e.g., ADCB merged with Union National Bank) – Larger banks strengthening market dominance – Post-crisis fintech expansion reviving competition:	– COVID-19 pandemic (2020) affecting financial stability and causing stress – Post-pandemic fintech adoption increased banking competition (2022)
Saudi Arabia	– Dominant banks benefiting from crisis conditions – Signs of competition recovery post-pandemic – Regulatory measures to support financial resilience	– Saudi Vision 2030 reforms continuing post-pandemic – Increase in digital banking services post-crisis
Kuwait	– Market power remained high – Concentration ratios are declining slightly – Government stimulus measures supporting the banking sector	– Kuwaiti banking-sector stabilising post-COVID
Bahrain	– Fintech adoption accelerating post-pandemic – Increased digital banking competition – Lower banking-sector concentration	– Post-pandemic financial recovery policies (2021–2022)
Qatar	– High government influence on the banking sector – Strong state backing for major banks – Limited foreign banking presence	– Qatar continues national banking consolidation efforts
Oman	– Banking competition is fluctuating – Stronger digital banking presence – Regulatory changes impacting market dynamics	– Fintech regulations introduced post-pandemic

resulting in lower concentration ratios. Economic uncertainty from 2019 to 2021, particularly due to the COVID-19 pandemic, reversed these trends, leading to higher market concentration and reduced competition. CR3, CR5, and HHI rose across the region, whereas the Lerner Index peaked in 2021, suggesting that banks exerted greater pricing power as competition weakened. This trend aligns with the Market Power Hypothesis, which posits that dominant banks can sustain profitability during economic distress due to limited competitive pressure.

By 2022, signs of recovery in competition emerged: CR3 and CR5 declined slightly in the UAE and Qatar, and HHI values showed a broader distribution of market share. The Lerner Index also fell marginally, indicating a resurgence of competitive pressures. These changes suggest that market liberalisation and regulatory reforms contributed to the reversal of concentration trends. Technological advancements and the rise of digital banking and financial technology (fintech) solutions have also contributed to reducing market concentration. As new banking channels emerge, consumers and businesses have greater access to a broader range of financial services, reducing reliance on a small number of dominant banks. This trend is particularly evident in the decline in the HHI for deposits, suggesting a broader distribution of banking services.

The relationship between market concentration and market power is influenced by economic and sector conditions, regulatory policies, and technological changes. The Structure-Conduct-Performance (SCP) Hypothesis posits that higher concentration leads to greater market power and reduced competition, as observed in Kuwait, Saudi Arabia, and Bahrain, where large banks maintain strong pricing control. However, the Efficient Structure Hypothesis argues that concentration may result from efficiency rather than anti-competitive behaviour. This may explain why the UAE and Qatar experienced declining concentration alongside a reduction in the Lerner Index, suggesting that competition, rather than dominance, is the driving force.

Additionally, the Contestable Market Theory suggests that even in concentrated markets, the potential for new entrants can limit market power. This explains why some GCC countries, despite high concentration, did not consistently exhibit rising Lerner Index values. The slight decline in market power in 2022, despite persistent concentration, suggests that regulatory reforms and digital banking innovations may have increased market contestability.

These findings highlight the evolving nature of competition in GCC banking, shaped by structural factors, regulatory policies, technological advancements, and economic fluctuations. While market concentration remains high, its impact on market power is not uniform across countries or time periods. Theoretical frameworks such as the SCP Hypothesis, Efficient Structure Hypothesis, and Contestable Market Theory help interpret these dynamics, providing insights into the relationship

Table 4.13 Evaluation of competitive conditions across the GCC banking sectors using different measures

Country	*Sub-Period*	*CR3*	*CR5*	*HHI*	*Lerner Index*	*H-Statistic*	*Boone Indicator (Assets)*	*Boone Indicator (Loans)*	*Boone Indicator (Deposits)*	*Boone ROA*
Bahrain	2002–2005	High	Very High	High	Moderate	1.30 (MC)	1.1667 (*Weak comp*)	1.0621 (*Weak comp*)	1.4328 (*Weak comp*)	−0.0011 (*Stable profitability*)
	2007–2012	Very High	Very High	Very High	High	1.46 (MC)	−1.4472 (Strong comp)	−1.6246 (Strong comp)	−1.6525 (Strong comp)	−0.0074 (*Profitability decline*)
	2013–2018	High	High	Moderate	Moderate	1.49 (MC)	0.2762 (*Weak comp*)	−0.1151 (*Weak comp*)	0.4805 (*Weak comp*)	−0.2146 (Sharp profitability drop)
	2019–2022	High	High	Moderate	High	1.26 (MC)	−0.758 (Moderate comp)	−2.4243 (Strong comp)	−0.3324 (*Weak comp*)	−0.008 (Profitability stabilised)
Kuwait	2002–2005	High	High	High	High	1.18 (MC)	−0.7474 (Moderate comp)	−0.9687 (Moderate comp)	−0.7656 (Moderate comp)	– 0.000001 (*Stable profitability*)
	2007–2012	Very High	Very High	High	High	1.51 (MC)	−0.0523 (*Weak comp*)	−0.9521 (Moderate comp)	−0.0709 (*Weak comp*)	0.0008 (*Slight profitability increase*)
	2013–2018	High	High	Moderate	High	1.47 (MC)	0.1696 (*Weak comp*)	0.1066 (*Weak comp*)	0.1618 (*Weak comp*)	−0.0002 (*Stable profitability*)
	2019–2022	High	High	High	High	1.34 (MC)	−0.2347 (*Weak comp*)	−0.1616 (*Weak comp*)	−0.2132 (*Weak comp*)	−0.0003 (*Stable profitability*)
Oman	2002–2005	High	Very High	High	Moderate	1.51 (MC)	1.9326 (*Weak comp*)	−1.5966 (Strong comp)	2.1338 (*Weak comp*)	−0.0106 (Profitability decline)

Country	*Sub-Period*	*CR3*	*CR5*	*HHI*	*Lerner Index*	*H-Statistic*	*Boone Indicator (Assets)*	*Boone Indicator (Loans)*	*Boone Indicator (Deposits)*	*Boone ROA*
	2007–2012	High	High	Moderate	Moderate	1.66 (MC)	0.5051 (*Weak comp*)	0.788 (*Weak comp*)	0.5739 (*Weak comp*)	0.00016 (*Stable profitability*)
	2013–2018	Moderate	High	Declining	Moderate	1.24 (MC)	−1.6164 (Strong comp)	−1.7218 (Strong comp)	−1.9159 (Strong comp)	−0.004 (Profitability drop)
	2019–2022	Moderate	Moderate	Low	Low	1.93 (**PC**)	−0.6949 (Moderate comp)	−0.3996 (*Weak comp*)	0.6887 (*Weak comp*)	−0.0003 (*Stable profitability*)
Qatar	2002–2005	High	High	High	High	1.43 (MC)	0.6317 (*Weak comp*)	1.6933 (*Weak comp*)	1.6055 (*Weak comp*)	0.001 (*Stable profitability*)
	2007–2012	Very High	Very High	Very High	High	0.80 (MC)	0.0717 (*Weak comp*)	−0.1975 (*Weak comp*)	0.0832 (*Weak comp*)	−0.0019 (Profitability decline)
	2013–2018	High	High	Moderate	Moderate	1.34 (MC)	0.9864 (Moderate comp)	0.8748 (Moderate comp)	0.9028 (*Weak comp*)	−0.0016 (Profitability decline)
	2019–2022	High	High	Moderate	Moderate	1.19 (MC)	1.4029 (*Weak comp*)	1.2509 (*Weak comp*)	1.5114 (*Weak comp*)	0.00001 (*Stable profitability*)
Saudi Arabia	2002–2005	High	High	High	High	1.30 (MC)	−0.81 (Moderate comp)	−0.8297 (Moderate comp)	−0.9077 (Moderate comp)	0.0024 (*Stable profitability*)
	2007–2012	High	High	Moderate	High	1.17 (MC)	−0.5192 (Moderate comp)	−0.6276 (Moderate comp)	−0.4861 (Moderate comp)	−0.0007 (*Stable profitability*)
	2013–2018	Moderate	Moderate	Moderate	Moderate	1.12 (MC)	−1.0942 (Strong comp)	−1.1659 (Strong comp)	−1.0321 (Strong comp)	−0.0011 (Profitability decline)
	2019–2022	Moderate	Moderate	Low	Moderate	1.07 (MC)	− 1.0654 (Strong comp)	− 1.0723 (Strong comp)	− 1.0272 (Strong comp)	− 0.0008 (*Stable profitability*)

(continued)

between market structure and competition in the region's banking sector (Table 4.13).

Conclusion

Empirical evidence from concentration ratios (CR3, CR5, and HHI) indicates that the GCC banking sector remains highly concentrated, though patterns vary across countries and over time. The CR3 ratio, averaging 0.675, indicates that the three largest banks in each country dominate a substantial share of the market. In contrast, the CR5 ratio, at 0.848, further underscores the dominance of the five largest banks. The Herfindahl–Hirschman Index (HHI) value exceeding 2,000 indicates a moderately concentrated market under US Department of Justice guidelines. These findings align with global trends in banking-sector consolidation, particularly in markets where regulatory frameworks favour large incumbents (Claessens & Laeven, 2004; Bikker & Haaf, 2002).

The Boone indicator, which measures competition via profit elasticity, exhibits negative correlations with CR3, CR5, and HHI, consistent with the expectation that greater concentration diminishes competitive intensity. However, lower competition does not necessarily translate into greater market power, as monopolistic or oligopolistic structures can lead to inefficiencies. The Panzar-Rosse H-statistic indicates that GCC banks operate under monopolistic competition, in which firms maintain some pricing power but remain subject to competitive pressures—an observation consistent with global banking markets (Shaffer, 1982; Molyneux et al., 1996).

The Structure-Conduct-Performance (SCP) paradigm, initially proposed by Mason (1939) and Bain (1951), provides a relevant framework for interpreting these results. The SCP model posits that higher market concentration enables dominant banks to exert pricing power, reducing competition and driving profitability. Evidence from Saudi Arabia, Oman, and Qatar supports this perspective, in which a few large banks dominate market conditions, often benefiting from regulatory barriers and economies of scale. These dynamics are well documented in the literature, with studies confirming that concentrated banking systems face lower competitive pressures and higher profitability (Berger, 1995; Delis, 2012).

Conversely, the Efficient Structure Hypothesis (ESH), introduced by Demsetz (1973), suggests that high concentration may stem from superior efficiency rather than anti-competitive behaviour. Large banks in the UAE and Kuwait, for example, may achieve dominance through

Country	*Sub-Period*	*CR3*	*CR5*	*HHI*	*Lerner Index*	*H-Statistic*	*Boone Indicator (Assets)*	*Boone Indicator (Loans)*	*Boone Indicator (Deposits)*	*Boone ROA*
UAE	2002–2005	High	High	High	High	1.57 (MC)	– 0.6667 (Moderate comp)	– 1.5072 (Strong comp)	– 0.6758 (Moderate comp)	0.0003 (*Stable profitability*)
	2007–2012	Moderate	Moderate	Moderate	Moderate	1.17 (MC)	– 1.3772 (Strong comp)	– 1.1147 (Strong comp)	– 1.3941 (Strong comp)	0.001 (*Stable profitability*)
	2013–2018	Moderate	Moderate	Low	Low	1.27 (MC)	– 1.5209 (Strong comp)	– 1.3967 (Strong comp)	– 1.4706 (Strong comp)	– 0.0029 (Profitability decline)
	2019–2022	Moderate	Low	Low	Low	1.19 (MC)	– 1.1943 (Strong comp)	– 1.065 (Strong comp)	– 1.1077 (Strong comp)	– 0.0038 (Profitability decline)

cost advantages, technological superiority, or superior management practices, rather than by exploiting market power. This view aligns with studies indicating that efficient banks can thrive in concentrated markets without necessarily reducing competition (Berger & Humphrey, 1997; Beck, 2008). The observed divergence between SCP and ESH perspectives underscores the complexity of competition dynamics in the GCC banking sector.

An additional explanation emerges from the Relative Market Power (RMP) Hypothesis, proposed by Shepherd (1982). Unlike the SCP paradigm, which assumes that all firms in a concentrated market benefit from reduced competition, the RMP Hypothesis suggests that only the largest firms with strong brand recognition, customer loyalty, and specialised services can sustain pricing power. This is particularly relevant for GCC banks, where government backing, extensive retail networks, and expertise in Islamic finance create differentiation advantages. Studies such as Berger (1995) and Delis (2012) support this hypothesis, demonstrating how market power persists even in concentrated banking environments with partial contestability.

The Contestability Theory (Baumol et al., 1982) further refines this analysis by suggesting that concentrated markets can still exhibit competitive behaviour if entry barriers remain low. Although the GCC banking sector is concentrated, the presence of foreign banks, advances in digital banking, and regulatory reforms have introduced elements of contestability. The rise of Islamic banking and fintech players has also intensified competition, challenging traditional incumbents. This aligns with research highlighting how technological innovation and regulatory openness can mitigate the adverse effects of concentration (Boot & Thakor, 2000; Claessens et al., 2018).

Macroeconomic shocks have also influenced competition levels in the GCC banking sector. The 2008 financial crisis and the 2014 oil price decline had varying impacts across countries: Bahrain, Kuwait, and the UAE experienced increased competitive pressures post-2008, whereas Saudi Arabia saw a rise in market power. The prolonged effects of the 2014 oil price collapse contributed to a sector-wide decline in competition between 2014 and 2018, as banks consolidated their positions amid economic uncertainty. Policy interventions, including the implementation of Basel III and economic diversification efforts, also shaped market concentration and competitive dynamics. The UAE, for instance, has fostered competition in its banking sector through a more diversified economy and open regulatory approach.

Over the past two decades, shifts in concentration and market power have followed key economic events and regulatory changes. The post-2007 period saw an increase in market concentration due to financial crisis-induced consolidation, leading to a temporary rise in market power, particularly in Saudi Arabia, Qatar, and Oman. Between 2015 and 2019, liberalisation efforts and new entrants contributed to increased competition, particularly in Bahrain and the UAE. However, the COVID-19 pandemic (2019–2021) reversed this trend, reinforcing market power among established banks as competition weakened amid economic instability.

These findings highlight the evolving nature of competition in the GCC banking sector. While market concentration remains high, competitive pressures are influenced by regulatory policies, economic conditions, and technological advancements. Future research could further explore how digital banking, cost structures, and evolving regulatory frameworks shape competition. A nuanced approach that integrates elements of the SCP paradigm, the Relative Market Power Hypothesis, and the Contestability Theory is essential for understanding the complex interplay between concentration and competition in GCC banking markets.

CHAPTER 5

Profitability in GCC Banking Systems

Introduction

The GCC region holds more than 45% of the world's oil reserves, 25% of crude oil exports, and 17% of proven gas reserves (OPEC, 2023). This hydrocarbon wealth was utilised to stimulate economic growth and enhance citizens' welfare through substantial fiscal surpluses and sustained government spending. Recently, several post-oil transformation plans, such as Saudi Vision 2030, UAE Vision 2050, and Qatar National Vision 2030, have focused on developing non-oil industries and on private-sector-led growth (Khan et al., 2021). In this context, a well-functioning banking system is essential for financing investment in infrastructure, technology, entrepreneurship and other economic diversification projects. The success of this role depends on the extent to which banks are profitable, strong, and efficient. Therefore, understanding the factors that drive bank profitability is crucial for sound managerial decision-making and informed policymaking.

While existing empirical studies have examined bank profitability in developed and emerging markets, research on the GCC remains limited. This chapter examines the key bank-specific, industry-wide, and macroeconomic determinants of bank profitability in the GCC between 2003 and 2021. It employs ROE, ROA, and NIM as primary indicators of financial profitability. It examines the impact of bank-level size, capital, liquidity,

A. Bakhouche, *Banking in the GCC*, Palgrave Macmillan Studies in Banking and Financial Institutions,
https://doi.org/10.1007/978-3-032-21737-0_5

overhead costs (cost efficiency), income diversification, and credit risk. Second, it examines the impact of market concentration, GDP growth, inflation, rule of law and external shocks on banking performance. This research provides policymakers, regulators, and banking practitioners with insights to strengthen bank profitability and enhance the banking sector's role in supporting the GCC's long-term economic objectives.

The remainder of this chapter is structured as follows: Sects. "Other Features of GCC Banks" and "Regulatory Reforms and Their Impact on GCC Banking Performance (2000–2024)" review trends in profitability and other performance measures across GCC banking systems; Sect. "Islamic vs Conventional Banking in the GCC" examines prior studies of the factors influencing bank profitability; Sects. "Determinants of Bank Profitability: Literature Review" and "Data and Methodology" present the methodology and variables; and Sect. "Regression Results and Discussion" presents and discusses the results. Section "Conclusion" concludes.

Profitability and Capitalisation in GCC Countries

Return on Equity (ROE)

The Return on Equity (ROE) measures the efficiency with which banks generate profits from shareholders' equity. Table 5.1 presents annual ROE values for GCC banking systems between 2000 and 2021. Figure 5.1 and Fig. 5.2 compare trends with those of Egypt, the UK, and the US. All bank-level data are obtained from the World Bank's Global Financial Development database.[1]

Between 2000 and 2021, the ROE of the GCC banking sector fluctuated sharply. Saudi Arabia (17.5%) and Qatar (16.3%) had the highest average ROE, maybe driven by strong credit demand and economic growth. In contrast, Bahrain (10.5%) and Oman (12.4%) had the lowest average ROE, which may be attributable to smaller market sizes and lower income diversification. The UAE and Kuwait (14%) posted stable but moderate ROE.

The trends in ROE of GCC banks can be divided into four phases. First, the ROE increased from an average of 15% in 2000–03 to 25%

[1] https://www.worldbank.org/en/publication/gfdr/data/global-financial-development-database.

Table 5.1 Bank before-tax Return on Equity (%)

Year	*Bahrain*	*Kuwait*	*Oman*	*Qatar*	*Saudi Arabia*	*UAE*	*GCC*	*Egypt*	*UK*	*USA*
2000	10.36	19.49	13.23	9.76	19.79	14.73	14.56	14.33	20.73	20.97
2001	12.74	20.74	1.11	13.48	21.24	14.67	13.99	11.07	9.05	19.00
2002	7.92	19.27	12.79	15.77	21.19	14.70	15.27	8.26	10.37	20.58
2003	12.34	20.01	−7.55	16.85	21.51	14.69	12.97	7.93	11.36	22.07
2004	16.31	22.90	14.06	16.67	25.42	18.33	18.95	9.38	38.04	19.46
2005	24.09	26.82	21.46	21.52	30.89	27.77	25.43	9.62	17.02	18.77
2006	9.97	27.20	23.11	20.84	31.62	21.37	22.35	11.05	17.31	18.23
2007	5.64	24.89	22.52	21.48	23.77	20.84	19.86	16.16	22.81	12.45
2008	9.45	2.18	18.81	19.91	16.77	16.63	13.96	15.93	1.47	1.61
2009	3.92	9.81	13.52	17.06	14.66	10.89	11.64	18.13	−1.66	2.21
2010	7.76	13.27	14.22	19.17	13.77	10.86	13.18	21.71	−0.37	8.48
2011	10.38	11.06	12.59	19.09	14.81	11.64	13.26	20.31	1.23	10.78
2012	13.10	10.36	14.45	17.30	14.61	12.24	13.68	26.52	−5.08	12.42
2013	16.73	8.91	14.81	16.72	14.80	12.59	14.09	27.20	3.79	13.57
2014	13.58	9.88	13.43	16.77	15.52	14.49	13.94	30.25	4.56	13.10
2015	9.79	9.14	13.59	15.78	14.84	13.64	12.80	33.74	6.27	13.85
2016	9.98	9.23	11.64	14.58	12.49	12.39	11.72	34.41	5.28	13.91
2017	9.98	9.68	10.83	13.98	12.56	11.06	11.35	30.92	7.22	14.22
2018	8.37	10.43	10.64	14.46	13.45	11.48	11.47	27.44	6.18	15.74
2019	10.03	9.31	9.72	14.32	12.57	12.42	11.39	32.12	6.43	15.08
2020	1.98	4.02	6.32	11.45	8.29	5.56	6.27	25.12	3.77	8.32
2021	7.51	8.30	7.40	12.60	10.09	9.72	9.27	27.97	8.42	15.81
Average	10.54	13.95	12.39	16.34	17.48	14.21	14.15	20.89	8.83	14.12
St.dev	4.64	7.34	6.77	3.16	6.23	4.67	4.24	9.06	9.62	5.48
Average/ St.dev	2.27	1.90	1.83	5.17	2.81	3.05	3.34	2.31	0.92	2.58

in 2006. High oil prices, economic expansion, and rising credit demand characterised this sub-period (Al-Hassan et al., 2013). Second, the global financial crisis of 2007–09 reduced credit growth, and the average ROE fell to its lowest level in 2009 at 11.64%. Kuwaiti and Bahraini banks are the most affected. However, GCC banks remained more profitable than those in the UK and the US, due to their lower exposure to bad assets and government ownership. Third, between 2010 and 2014, the ROE of GCC banks recovered and stabilised at an average of 14%. Banks in Qatar and Saudi Arabia maintained high ROE values of 17–19%, supported by strong government spending and high credit demand. **Fourth**, the oil price downturn from mid-2014 onwards led to a decline

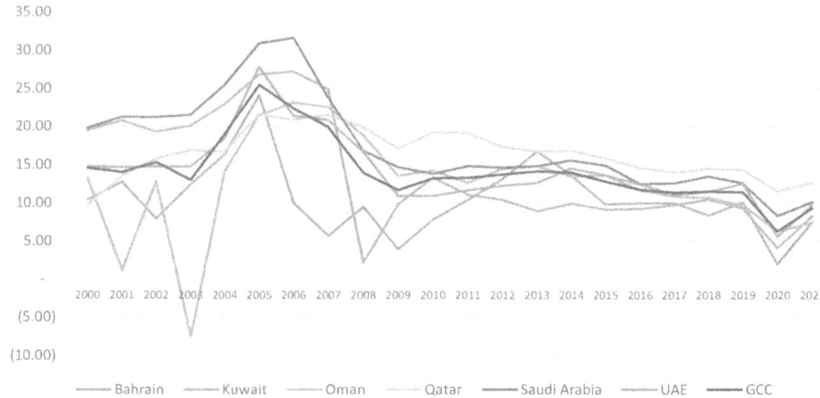

Fig. 5.1 Pre-tax ROE for GCC banks

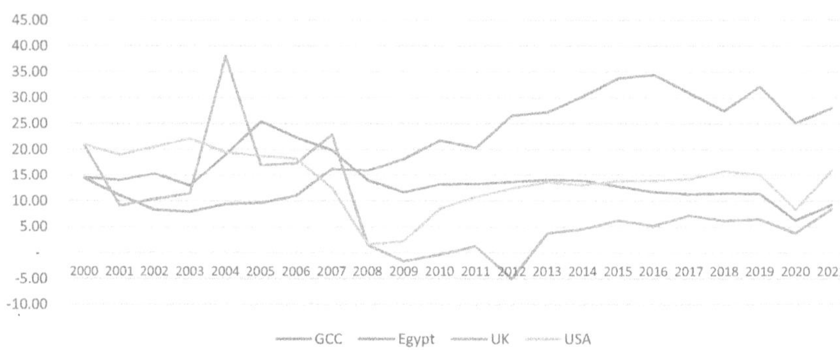

Fig. 5.2 Pre-tax ROE for GCC, Egypt, UK, and US banks

in ROE to an average of 11.72% between 2015 and 2019. In Bahrain and Oman, average ROE dropped to 9.98% and 10.83%, respectively, in 2017. The COVID-19 pandemic further exacerbated profitability declines, with the average ROE for GCC banks plummeting to 6.27% in 2020. However, ROE increased to 9.27% in 2021, driven by rising oil prices and government stimulus measures.

Capital Adequacy Ratio (CAR)

Capital adequacy (CAR) measures the extent to which a bank has built a capital buffer against bad assets to maintain solvency and withstand financial shocks. Table 5.2 and Figure 5.3 present trends in CAR for GCC banking systems from 2000 to 2021, while Fig. 5.4 provides a comparative analysis with Egypt, the UK, and the US. Between 2000 and 2021, GCC banks maintained capital ratios between 9 and 18%, with an average of 13%. This level may indicate overcapitalisation, as it is significantly higher than that of the US (10.3%), Egypt (7.42%), and the UK (6.91%). Two factors may explain the high CARs in GCC banking systems. First, the reliance on hydrocarbon revenues has provided a stable funding base for the government-dominated banks in the GCC. Second, GCC regulators have adopted the Basel capital adequacy requirements. Overcapitalisation may provide a substantial buffer against financial instability, but it may also reduce ROE due to the opportunity cost of holding excess capital (Berger, 1995).

Return on Assets (ROA)

Return on Assets (ROA) measures how efficiently a bank utilises its assets, mainly loans, to generate earnings. ROA is influenced by multiple factors, including net interest margin (NIM), cost efficiency, market structure, income diversification, and economic conditions. Table 5.3 presents the after-tax annual ROA values for individual GCC countries from 2000 to 2021.

Figure 5.5 depicts trends in ROA across GCC banking systems. Figure 5.6 compares with banks in Egypt, the UK, and the US.

Table 5.3 and Figs. 5.5 and 5.6 show that between 2000 and 2021, the average ROA for GCC banks was 1.77%, higher than Egypt (1.04%), the US (1.02%), and the UK (0.55%). Banks in Qatar (2.18%) and Saudi Arabia (2.15%) had the highest ROA values, followed by the UAE (1.88%), Kuwait (1.65%), Oman (1.48%), and Bahrain (1.25%). These variations may be attributed to the differences in economic performance, market competition, and banking regulations.

The trends in GCC banks' average ROA show that it increased from 1.6% in 2000–01 to 3.45% in 2005, driven by high oil prices and increased credit demand. Qatar and Saudi Arabia had the highest ROA. The indicator fell to 1.42% in 2009 due to the 2007–09 global financial crisis,

Table 5.2 Capital ratios (%) for GCC, Egypt, UK, and US banking systems

Year	*Bahrain*	*Kuwait*	*Oman*	*Qatar*	*Saudi Arabia*	*UAE*	*GCC*	*Egypt*	*UK*	*USA*
2000	10.7	11.1	12.4	14.4	9.4	14.0	11.7	6.2	7.2	8.5
2001	11.0	10.9	12.0	13.6	10.0	14.1	11.7	5.9	8.1	8.9
2002	10.9	10.7	12.1	13.4	10.4	14.6	11.9	5.6	9.6	9.3
2003	10.8	10.9	12.8	13.8	10.7	15.0	12.1	5.7	10.7	9.3
2004	12.1	11.8	13.6	15.9	10.7	14.3	12.8	6.0	6.4	9.7
2005	13.8	12.8	14.8	18.3	11.5	14.5	14.1	5.9	4.7	10.2
2006	12.8	12.8	15.2	16.0	12.5	13.4	13.7	5.8	3.8	10.2
2007	12.0	12.6	14.3	14.1	12.3	11.2	12.8	5.8	3.8	10.2
2008	12.9	11.3	13.8	13.7	11.8	10.4	12.6	6.1	3.3	7.4
2009	12.7	11.2	13.7	13.6	12.2	11.7	12.7	6.7	3.1	10.0
2010	12.2	13.7	13.7	13.8	13.1	13.4	13.4	6.9	4.1	11.1
2011	11.8	14.9	12.7	14.3	13.7	13.7	13.6	7.0	4.7	11.3
2012	11.5	14.7	11.7	14.4	13.8	13.9	13.3	7.6	4.9	11.2
2013	11.9	14.0	11.7	13.6	13.7	13.9	13.0	8.1	4.9	11.2
2014	12.3	13.1	11.6	13.1	13.6	13.7	12.9	8.3	5.5	11.2
2015	12.9	13.1	12.4	12.6	14.0	13.9	13.2	8.1	9.4	11.3
2016	13.4	13.3	13.1	11.7	14.8	13.7	13.3	7.5	9.5	11.2
2017	14.0	13.4	14.6	11.1	15.8	14.0	13.8	7.4	8.5	11.1
2018	13.7	13.5	15.3	11.2	16.2	14.1	14.0	8.1	8.8	11.2
2019	13.8	13.9	15.5	11.1	16.3	13.5	13.9	8.5	9.6	11.3
2020	13.3	13.9	15.7	10.8	16.2	13.0	13.6	8.9	9.4	10.7
2021	12.7	13.5	15.8	10.5	16.7	12.6	13.4	8.4	9.2	10.1
Mean	12.4	12.8	13.6	13.4	13.2	13.5	13.1	7.0	6.8	10.3
St. dev	1.0	1.3	1.4	1.9	2.2	1.1	0.7	1.1	2.5	1.1
Mean/ St. dev	12.01	9.96	9.58	7.06	5.91	12.07	18.13	6.36	2.68	9.51

which reduced credit growth and tightened liquidity. However, GCC banks maintained higher ROA levels than UK banks (–0.05%). Between 2010 and 2015, the ROA stabilised at an average of 1.7%, but fell to 1.45% by 2019 due to the decline in oil prices. Because of the COVID-19 pandemic, ROA fell to 0.76%, driven by economic contraction, declining credit demand, and higher provisions for NPLs. However, the subsequent economic reopening, rising oil prices, and government stimulus measures supported an improvement in ROA to 1.10%.

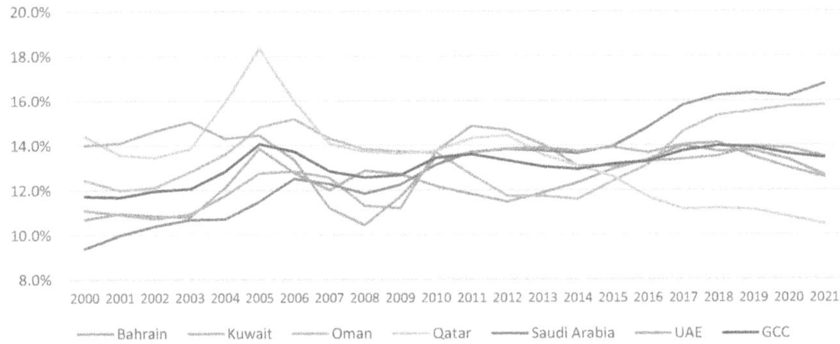

Fig. 5.3 Capital ratios for GCC banking systems

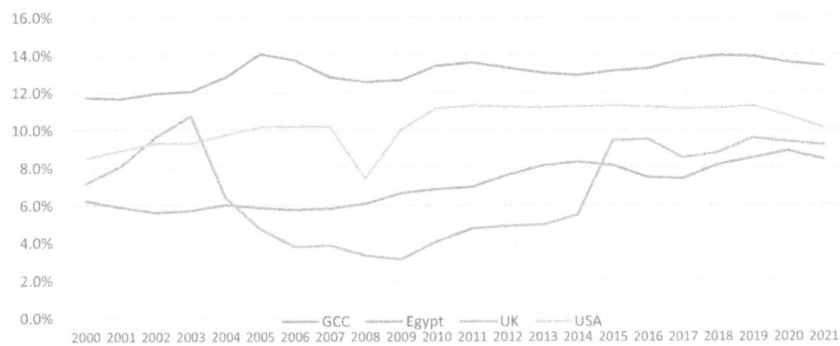

Fig. 5.4 CARs for GCC, Egypt, UK and US banking systems

Net Interest Margin (NIM)

Net Interest Margin (NIM) reflects the difference between interest income earned on loans and investments and the interest expenses paid on deposits and borrowings. A higher NIM indicates higher revenues from financial intermediation, signalling favourable economic conditions, monetary policies, and competition. Table 5.4, Figs. 5.7, and 5.8 show that between 2000 and 2021, GCC banks had an average NIM of 2.84%, which is higher than that of the UK (1.73%) and Egypt (2.76%), but lower than that of the US (3.45%). However, NIM declined gradually from 3.23% in 2005 to 2.31% in 2021. Banks in Oman (3.23%)

Table 5.3 Bank after-tax Return on Assets (%)

Year	*Bahrain*	*Kuwait*	*Oman*	*Qatar*	*Saudi Arabia*	*UAE*	*GCC*	*Egypt*	*UK*	*USA*
2000	1.08	2.09	1.42	1.41	1.86	2.04	1.65	0.81	1.29	1.16
2001	1.37	2.14	0.00	1.81	2.12	2.03	1.58	0.57	0.69	1.13
2002	0.83	1.98	1.51	2.11	2.20	2.12	1.79	0.41	0.95	1.28
2003	1.31	2.11	–0.92	2.31	2.30	2.18	1.55	0.41	1.16	1.38
2004	1.99	2.58	1.66	2.64	2.72	2.60	2.36	0.50	2.40	1.29
2005	3.30	3.29	2.75	3.94	3.55	3.98	3.47	0.52	0.79	1.29
2006	1.25	3.35	3.07	3.32	3.95	2.84	2.96	0.56	0.64	1.27
2007	0.65	3.00	2.89	3.01	2.92	2.32	2.46	0.85	0.87	0.87
2008	1.22	0.18	2.32	2.72	1.99	1.73	1.69	0.86	0.05	0.10
2009	0.49	1.03	1.63	2.33	1.79	1.26	1.42	0.83	–0.05	0.16
2010	0.90	1.73	1.70	2.63	1.81	1.44	1.70	1.04	–0.02	0.66
2011	1.17	1.56	1.40	2.73	2.03	1.57	1.74	0.82	0.05	0.86
2012	1.42	1.44	1.48	2.48	2.02	1.68	1.75	1.14	–0.25	0.99
2013	1.89	1.17	1.52	2.19	2.03	1.72	1.75	1.25	0.18	1.05
2014	1.58	1.20	1.38	2.09	2.12	1.95	1.72	1.49	0.25	1.02
2015	1.22	1.14	1.49	1.90	2.07	1.83	1.61	1.74	0.50	1.08
2016	1.19	1.12	1.36	1.60	1.85	1.63	1.46	1.72	0.33	1.07
2017	1.29	1.20	1.34	1.47	1.98	1.51	1.46	1.55	0.48	0.97
2018	1.09	1.30	1.38	1.52	1.59	1.57	1.41	1.42	0.43	1.39
2019	1.32	1.19	1.29	1.49	1.80	1.61	1.45	1.82	0.45	1.34
2020	0.31	0.49	0.83	1.15	1.13	0.67	0.76	1.25	0.26	0.72
2021	0.89	1.02	0.99	1.22	1.48	1.04	1.11	1.32	0.65	1.26
Mean	1.26	1.65	1.48	2.18	2.15	1.88	1.77	1.04	0.55	1.02
St.dev	0.60	0.84	0.86	0.72	0.64	0.67	0.59	0.45	0.57	0.35
Mean/ st.dev	2.09	1.96	1.71	3.05	3.36	2.78	3.00	2.29	0.96	2.89

recorded the highest average NIM, followed by Saudi Arabia (3.15%). In contrast, banks in Bahrain (2.11%) had the lowest average NIM, likely due to higher competition. The UAE (2.80%), Kuwait (2.77%), and Qatar (2.81%) reported similar NIM levels.

The trends in GCC banks' NIM can be divided into several sub-periods. First, NIM increased from 2.90% in 2000 to 3.23% in 2005, supported by favourable economic conditions and increased lending. Second, NIM fell to 2.84% in 2008, due to the effect of the financial crisis on credit growth and interest rates. Third, the 2014–15 oil price shock was associated with a decline in NIM to 2.58% in 2015, particularly in Qatar (2.55%). Finally, monetary easing policies, economic uncertainty,

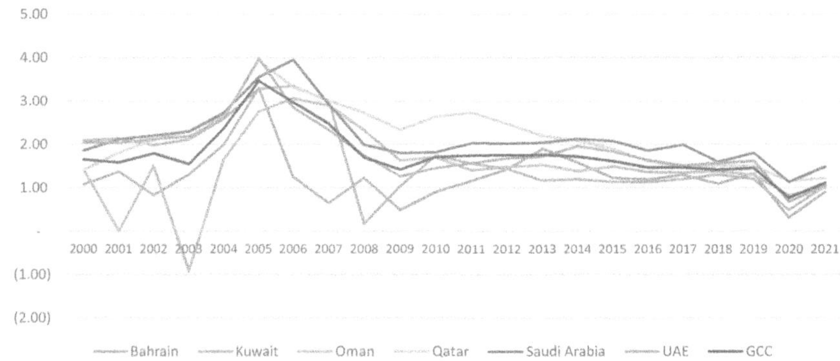

Fig. 5.5 After-tax ROA for GCC banking systems

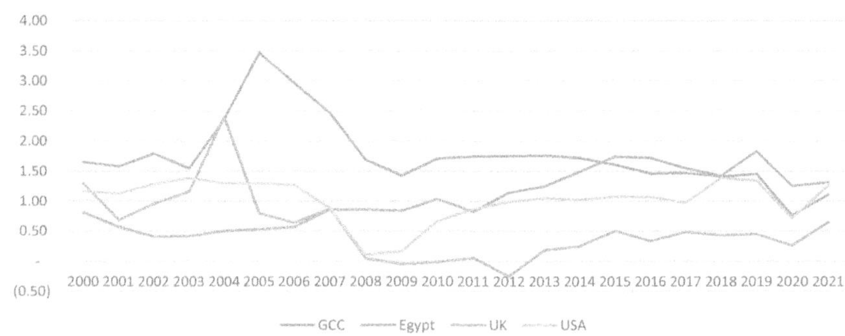

Fig. 5.6 After-tax ROA for GCC, Egypt, UK and US banking systems

and lower credit demand in 2020, due to the COVID-19 pandemic, weakened the NIM for GCC banks to an average of 2.40%. Although NIMs recovered in 2021, persistent pressures on profitability did not lift them above pre-2014 levels.

Table 5.5 compares the NIMs of GCC banks with those of global banks. The NIMs of GCC banks are highly correlated with those of the US, with a coefficient of 0.616. This close relationship is explained by GCC banks' exposure to monetary arrangements aligned with US interest-rate policies under the fixed-exchange-rate regime. The UAE, Oman, and Qatar exhibit the highest correlation with US NIMs. In

Table 5.4 Net Interest Margin (%) of GCC banks, Egypt, the UK, and the US

Year	*GCC*	*Bahrain*	*Kuwait*	*Oman*	*Qatar*	*Saudi Arabia*	*UAE*	*Egypt*	*UK*	*USA*
2000	2.90	1.75	2.66	4.03	2.70	3.35	2.91	1.65	1.26	3.83
2001	2.86	1.83	2.66	3.30	3.02	3.59	2.78	1.28	0.95	3.83
2002	3.09	1.75	2.41	4.56	3.38	3.69	2.77	1.33	1.40	3.95
2003	2.95	1.63	2.32	4.28	3.16	3.52	2.76	1.25	1.88	3.71
2004	2.97	1.58	2.80	4.29	2.82	3.54	2.79	1.63	2.27	3.51
2005	3.23	1.68	3.66	4.40	3.10	3.56	2.97	1.74	2.66	3.47
2006	3.21	1.88	3.69	4.28	3.02	3.69	2.68	1.35	1.53	3.21
2007	2.89	1.95	3.08	3.63	2.77	3.53	2.39	1.90	1.87	3.14
2008	2.84	1.89	3.05	3.39	2.72	3.26	2.73	2.05	1.70	3.10
2009	2.87	2.37	2.83	3.61	2.66	3.07	2.67	2.39	1.60	3.41
2010	2.99	2.09	3.01	3.69	3.18	2.92	3.04	2.44	2.13	3.81
2011	3.00	2.14	3.06	3.39	3.30	2.87	3.23	2.63	1.65	3.65
2012	2.94	2.56	2.94	3.23	2.89	2.76	3.23	3.70	1.04	3.53
2013	2.90	2.58	3.00	3.00	2.97	2.72	3.12	3.86	1.50	3.43
2014	2.84	2.62	2.74	3.05	2.77	2.68	3.15	3.77	1.48	3.46
2015	2.58	2.12	2.40	2.81	2.55	2.59	2.99	4.18	1.97	3.25
2016	2.62	2.25	2.47	2.70	2.78	2.74	2.77	3.69	1.86	3.29
2017	2.64	2.41	2.63	2.63	2.46	2.99	2.69	3.70	1.77	3.39
2018	2.75	2.54	2.72	2.68	2.40	3.26	2.91	3.34	1.55	3.53
2019	2.69	2.48	2.59	2.65	2.38	3.30	2.71	4.77	2.25	3.49
2020	2.40	2.11	2.14	2.53	2.34	2.98	2.32	4.13	1.85	3.05
2021	2.31	2.14	2.10	2.45	2.41	2.72	2.02	3.85	1.84	2.77
Average	2.84	2.11	2.77	3.39	2.81	3.15	2.80	2.76	1.73	3.45

contrast, Kuwait has the lowest correlation with US NIMs, likely due to its adoption of a basket-based exchange rate regime.

Other Features of GCC Banks

Credit Risk and Non-performing Loans (NPLs)

The NPLs ratio, calculated as non-performing loans to total gross loans, measures the quality of a bank's loan portfolio. Lower NPL ratios indicate less exposure to credit risk, suggesting effective risk management and asset quality control. Table 5.6 presents trends in the NPL ratio for GCC banking systems from 2000 to 2021. The average NPL ratio for GCC banks peaked at 4.57% in 2009, possibly due to the adverse effects of the 2007–09 global financial crisis on credit quality. However, the average

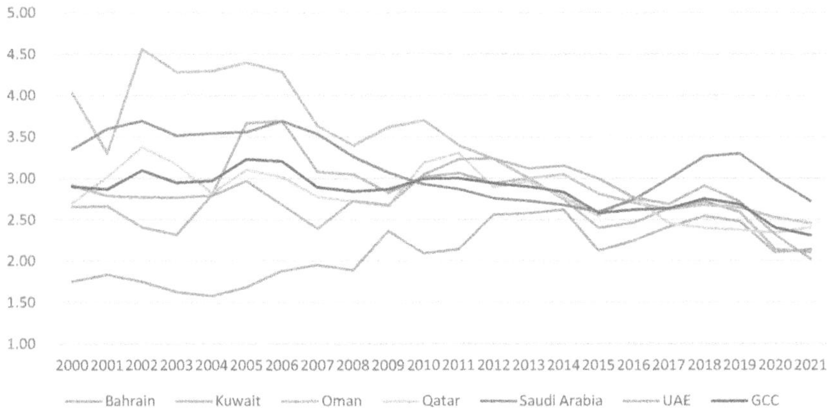

Fig. 5.7 Trends in GCC NIM between 2000 and 2021

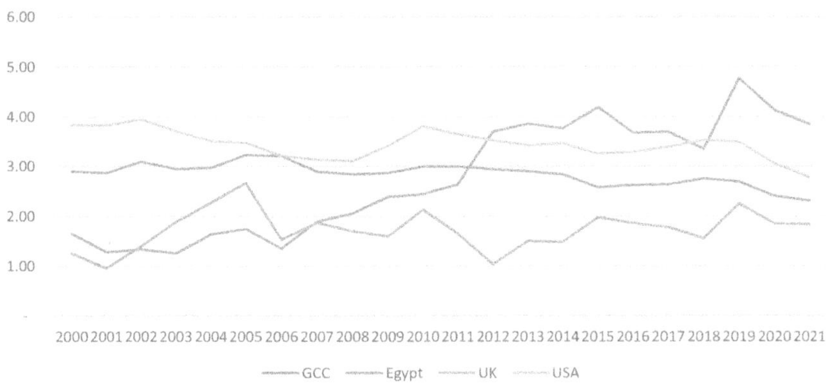

Fig. 5.8 Trends in GCC, Egypt, UK, and US' NIMs between 2000 and 2021

NPL ratio fell to 3.44% in 2021, attributable to improved lending conditions and enhanced oversight. Kuwait recorded the highest NPL ratio of 19.2% in 2000, which declined to 1.4% by 2021, possibly due to write-offs of bad debt. The UAE also experienced high NPL ratios in the early 2000s, peaking at 15.7% in 2001, before gradually declining to 7.3% in 2021. In contrast, Saudi Arabia maintained consistently lower NPL ratios, with a rate of 2.18% in 2020.

Table 5.5 Correlation values between Net Interest Margin of GCC, Egypt, UK, and US banking systems (%)

	Bahrain	*Kuwait*	*Oman*	*Qatar*	*Saudi Arabia*	*UAE*	*GCC*	*Egypt*	*UK*
NIM_Levels									
Kuwait	−0.107	1.000							
Oman	−0.738	0.474	1.000						
Qatar	−0.438	0.427	0.729	1.000					
Saudi Arabia	−0.702	0.316	0.712	0.327	1.000				
UAE	0.239	0.397	0.195	0.478	−0.209	1.000			
GCC	−0.389	0.770	0.851	0.794	0.572	0.536	1.000		
Egypt	0.806	−0.393	−0.879	−0.652	−0.789	−0.006	−0.714	1.000	
UK	−0.239	0.123	0.079	−0.114	0.063	−0.191	−0.032	0.107	1.000
USA	−0.197	0.079	0.498	0.604	0.336	0.618	0.579	−0.434	−0.264
NIM_Percentage change									
	Bahrain	Kuwait	Oman	Qatar	Saudi Arabia	UAE	GCC	Egypt	UK
Kuwait	0.227	1.000							
Oman	0.002	0.069	1.000						
Qatar	−0.148	0.230	0.252	1.000					
Saudi Arabia	0.286	0.390	0.098	0.085	1.000				
UAE	0.001	0.485	0.212	0.214	0.084	1.000			
GCC	0.351	0.695	0.609	0.512	0.508	0.595	1.000		
Egypt	0.094	−0.048	0.042	−0.402	−0.267	0.131	−0.111	1.000	
UK	−0.521	0.019	0.298	0.175	−0.118	0.101	0.057	0.368	1.000
USA	0.308	0.198	0.358	0.354	0.330	0.566	0.616	0.108	0.199

Generally, the fluctuations in the NPL ratios were driven by global events, oil price volatility, and regulatory reforms. First, between 2000 and 2007, high levels of non-performing loans may have been driven by rapid loan growth, which coincided with inefficient loan monitoring mechanisms and weak regulatory oversight. However, regulatory reforms in the mid-2000s, along with improved credit screening processes, led to a gradual decline in NPL ratios. The UAE experienced a significant improvement, decreasing from 15.7% in 2001 to 2.6% in 2008. Second, the 2007–09 global financial crisis weakened asset quality across GCC banks, with an average NPL ratio of 4.57% in 2009, but fell to 2.98% in 2014. Improved economic conditions and stricter credit-risk assessment procedures drove this improvement. Third, the mid-2014 decline

Table 5.6 Non-performing loans to total gross loans (NPL, %) for all banking systems during 2000–21

Year	*Bahrain*	*Kuwait*	*Oman*	*Qatar*	*Saudi Arabia*	*UAE*	*GCC*	*Egypt*	*UK*	*US*
2000	–	19.2		–	10.4	12.7	14.10	13.6	2.5	1.1
2001	–	10.3	10.6	–	10.1	15.7	11.68	16.9	2.6	1.3
2002	–	7.8	8.8	–	8.8	15.3	10.18	20.2	2.6	1.4
2003	–	6.1	12.5	–	5.4	14.3	9.58	24.2	2.5	1.1
2004	–	5.3	11	–	2.8	12.5	7.90	23.6	1.9	0.8
2005	–	4.1	7	–	1.9	8.3	5.33	26.5	1	0.7
2006	–	4.6	–	–	2.0	6.4	4.33	18.2	0.9	0.8
2007	–	3.8	3.2	–	2.1	2.6	2.92	19.3	0.9	1.4
2008	2.3	6.8	2.00	1.2	1.4	2.3	2.67	14.8	1.6	3
2009	3.9	11.5	2.7	1.7	3.3	4.3	4.57	13.4	3.5	5
2010	5.1	8.9	2.7	2	2.97	5.27	4.49	13.60	3.95	4.39
2011	4.9	7.3	2.2	1.7	2.22	6.09	4.07	10.90	3.96	3.78
2012	5.84	5.2	2.1	1.7	1.67	7.13	3.94	9.80	3.59	3.32
2013	5.60	3.6	2.00	1.9	1.31	6.66	3.51	9.30	3.11	2.45
2014	4.62	2.9	1.94	1.7	1.08	5.64	2.98	8.50	1.65	1.85
2015	4.41	2.8	1.8	1.6	1.24	5.03	2.81	7.20	1.01	1.47
2016	5.9	2.4	1.7	1.3	1.38	5.07	2.96	6.80	0.94	1.32
2017	5.5	2.2	1.9	1.6	1.61	5.30	3.02	5.80	0.73	1.13
2018	5.5	1.9	2.4	1.9	1.95	5.61	3.21	3.87	1.07	0.91
2019	4.4	1.5	2.8	1.8	1.86	6.46	3.14	4.15	1.08	0.86
2020	4.00	2	3.5	2	2.18	8.15	3.64	3.60	1.22	1.07
2021	3.5	1.4	4.2	2.4	1.85	7.3	3.44	3.5	1.00	1.3

in global oil prices triggered an economic slowdown, weakened corporate lending, and led to a gradual increase in NPL ratios through 2019. The COVID-19 pandemic in 2020 caused distress to businesses and households, pushing the average NPL ratio for GCC banks to 3.64%. In 2021, it improved to 3.44% due to government stimulus measures and economic recovery.

Trends in NPLs indicate several characteristics of GCC banks. First, the GCC economy remains highly dependent on oil revenues, making credit risk cyclical and sensitive to fluctuations in global oil prices. Second, GCC banks rely heavily on corporate lending, particularly in construction and real estate, thereby increasing their vulnerability to sector-specific downturns. Third, the global financial crisis and the COVID-19 pandemic heightened GCC banks' sensitivity to external shocks.

Cost Efficiency Ratios

Cost efficiency measures the ability to manage operating expenses in relation to income and assets. We capture cost efficiency in GCC banking from 2000 to 2021 through two ratios: the cost-to-income ratio (Table 5.7) and the overhead-to-total-assets ratio (Table 5.8). Lower values indicate greater efficiency.

Between 2000 and 2021, the average cost-to-income ratio for GCC banks was 35.92%, significantly lower than the averages for Egypt (42.54%), the UK (62.73%), and the US (59.42%). This suggests that

Table 5.7 Bank cost-to-income ratio (%) for all banking systems during 2000–21

Year	*Bahrain*	*Kuwait*	*Oman*	*Qatar*	*Saudi Arabia*	*UAE*	*GCC*	*Egypt*	*UK*	*US*
2000	43.71	31.42	47.95	36.15	43.95	36.68	39.98	49.59	47.57	60.50
2001	43.16	30.30	46.28	34.46	40.15	36.86	38.54	51.43	75.00	58.74
2002	40.71	28.61	43.51	30.47	40.51	36.06	36.64	50.95	77.54	55.96
2003	39.69	27.35	49.59	30.88	37.94	35.98	36.90	47.63	63.97	56.24
2004	31.54	23.87	50.00	31.95	34.10	32.19	33.94	50.36	55.87	58.32
2005	21.41	22.02	45.00	28.68	29.71	23.34	28.36	41.75	55.23	57.90
2006	37.46	22.62	41.72	29.36	27.36	31.77	31.72	51.32	54.24	58.21
2007	27.19	23.83	43.56	28.28	31.14	32.50	31.09	56.82	53.03	61.55
2008	31.89	28.43	41.34	27.10	36.53	35.86	33.52	39.37	56.43	64.02
2009	37.41	31.28	43.28	26.24	34.04	30.58	33.81	47.36	59.74	58.35
2010	40.50	29.14	47.65	24.89	35.44	30.63	34.71	37.67	57.92	58.14
2011	37.64	29.28	47.54	23.21	36.40	32.80	34.48	51.88	61.40	60.47
2012	36.42	31.26	52.39	23.98	35.18	32.91	35.36	44.24	74.28	60.98
2013	35.65	32.00	55.58	27.32	35.46	32.33	36.39	42.83	64.93	59.97
2014	33.77	31.58	52.71	26.79	35.06	31.40	35.22	38.54	71.35	61.12
2015	44.59	35.05	45.24	27.82	35.40	35.52	37.27	35.14	69.09	61.04
2016	43.67	37.12	45.75	33.76	36.53	34.95	38.63	28.69	65.97	58.14
2017	44.25	35.13	47.04	31.41	35.10	36.11	38.17	30.02	63.59	58.86
2018	44.91	34.15	45.73	28.04	34.31	36.20	37.23	33.60	61.02	57.14
2019	46.95	35.92	46.11	27.15	34.27	34.73	37.52	35.47	63.36	57.16
2020	54.02	39.09	48.51	25.61	35.48	39.25	40.33	35.96	64.61	61.68
2021	51.67	40.83	48.57	24.17	38.03	39.04	40.38	35.34	63.92	62.73
Mean	39.46	30.92	47.05	28.53	35.55	33.99	35.92	42.54	62.73	59.42
St.dev	7.60	5.14	3.56	3.48	3.52	3.47	3.08	8.05	7.61	2.13
mean/St.dev	5.19	6.02	13.20	8.19	10.11	9.80	11.65	5.29	8.24	27.96

Table 5.8 Overhead to total assets ratio (%) for all banking systems during 2000–21

	Bahrain	*Kuwait*	*Oman*	*Qatar*	*Saudi Arabia*	*UAE*	*GCC*	*Egypt*	*UK*	*US*
2000	1.09	1.44	1.10	2.31	1.25	1.65	1.48	1.60	1.80	3.52
2001	1.15	1.41	1.08	1.86	1.30	1.61	1.40	1.31	2.17	3.40
2002	1.06	1.41	0.95	2.45	1.26	1.70	1.47	1.24	3.14	3.33
2003	1.01	1.47	0.98	2.68	1.27	1.68	1.51	1.16	2.87	3.26
2004	0.92	1.38	0.95	2.68	1.24	1.56	1.45	1.47	2.71	3.13
2005	0.93	1.34	1.12	2.47	1.57	1.58	1.50	1.48	2.50	3.07
2006	0.93	1.40	1.16	2.29	1.37	1.60	1.46	1.37	1.49	2.90
2007	0.90	1.25	1.04	2.25	1.23	1.50	1.36	2.18	1.71	2.87
2008	0.97	1.34	1.04	1.99	1.18	1.55	1.35	1.47	0.94	2.79
2009	1.26	1.11	1.09	1.90	1.02	1.34	1.29	1.46	0.73	2.86
2010	1.14	1.21	1.13	2.02	0.99	1.36	1.31	1.50	0.39	2.93
2011	1.11	1.28	1.13	1.99	0.95	1.35	1.30	1.62	0.71	2.87
2012	1.21	1.28	1.15	2.07	0.88	1.30	1.31	1.80	1.14	2.87
2013	1.18	1.24	1.13	2.01	1.01	1.28	1.31	1.87	0.96	2.74
2014	1.16	1.25	1.02	1.92	0.92	1.27	1.26	1.68	1.42	2.72
2015	1.29	1.44	1.12	1.67	0.86	1.32	1.28	1.63	1.80	2.84
2016	1.33	1.31	1.19	1.59	1.14	1.36	1.32	1.27	1.53	2.59
2017	1.37	1.27	1.18	1.65	0.92	1.35	1.29	1.18	1.49	2.71
2018	1.40	1.29	1.16	1.63	0.80	1.37	1.28	1.30	1.21	2.74
2019	1.41	1.25	1.19	1.63	0.77	1.37	1.27	1.73	1.66	2.74
2020	1.32	1.16	1.11	1.59	0.67	1.31	1.19	1.48	1.43	2.68
2021	1.32	1.17	1.19	1.62	0.66	1.27	1.20	1.47	1.39	2.41
Mean	1.16	1.31	1.10	2.01	1.06	1.44	1.35	1.51	1.60	2.91
St.dev	0.17	0.10	0.07	0.35	0.24	0.15	0.10	0.24	0.72	0.27
mean/St.dev	6.96	13.09	14.72	5.71	4.38	9.71	14.02	6.19	2.23	10.63

GCC banks manage operational costs effectively. Qatar exhibited the lowest cost-to-income ratio (28.53%), followed by Kuwait (30.92%) and the UAE (33.99%). Oman recorded the highest average cost-to-income ratio (47.05%), while Bahrain (39.46%) and Saudi Arabia (35.55%) maintained moderate levels.

Similarly, GCC banks maintained an average overhead-to-assets ratio of 1.35% over the study period, which is lower than the averages for Egypt (1.51%), the UK (1.60%), and the US (2.91%). While Saudi Arabia (1.06%) and Bahrain (1.16%) recorded the lowest overhead-to-assets ratios, Qatar had the highest (2.01%). The UAE (1.44%) and Kuwait (1.31%) exhibited moderate growth rates.

The analysis reveals that the cost-to-income ratio improved from 39.98% in 2000 to 28.36% in 2005. However, the 2007–09 global financial crisis disrupted this progress, leading to an increase to 33.81% in 2009. The 2010–14 period saw relative stability, but the 2014–15 global oil crisis and the COVID-19 pandemic in 2020 led to a gradual deterioration in the cost ratio, which reached 40.38% in 2021.

Income Diversification

Income diversification may enhance bank performance by reducing reliance on traditional income sources and generating interest-based revenue from fees, commissions, and financial advisory services. Table 5.9 presents trends in income diversification across GCC banking systems from 2000 to 2021, using the ratio of non-interest income to total income as the key measure. On average, GCC banks derived 31.63% of their total income from non-interest sources, which is lower than that of banks in the UK (48.83%), the US (39.59%), and Egypt (36.90%). The UAE had the highest income diversification ratio at 36.40%, followed by Bahrain (35.08%) and Kuwait (32.51%). In contrast, Qatar (28.35%), Oman (28.64%), and Saudi Arabia (28.77%) exhibit greater dependence on traditional lending.

In 2000, the average diversification ratio of GCC banks was 25.90%, increasing to 42.62% by 2005. This growth was primarily driven by policies that encouraged banks to expand their service offerings beyond traditional lending. The 2007–09 global financial crisis led to a decline in the ratio to 30.90% in 2009, primarily due to market volatility and reduced investment activity. Overall, during the 2010s, income diversification stabilised, averaging approximately 30%.

Market Concentration in GCC Countries

Tables 5.10 and 5.11 present trends in concentration across GCC banking systems from 2000 to 2021. The average 3-bank and 5-bank asset concentration ratios were 74.74% and 90.14%, respectively, far exceeding the corresponding figures in the US (32.07% and 44.55%), the UK (50.47% and 67.36%), and Egypt (63.76% and 71.54%).

Table 5.9 Non-interest income to total income (%) for all banking systems during 2000–21

	Bahrain	*Kuwait*	*Oman*	*Qatar*	*Saudi Arabia*	*UAE*	*GCC*	*Egypt*	*UK*	*US*
2000	33.28	27.19	21.64	25.54	18.63	29.15	25.90	53.73	74.08	41.71
2001	34.29	28.10	22.31	24.09	18.08	30.75	26.27	54.75	74.93	41.71
2002	35.25	30.48	23.66	21.97	19.47	32.75	27.27	51.59	71.00	41.70
2003	38.15	38.51	25.20	26.50	26.80	36.22	31.90	54.21	62.91	43.29
2004	51.41	33.08	24.60	31.62	27.89	39.95	34.76	50.14	56.53	42.14
2005	62.88	31.98	24.29	46.81	37.29	52.47	42.62	56.44	48.44	42.23
2006	32.77	33.60	25.77	38.93	41.48	44.28	36.14	53.66	54.06	43.15
2007	42.90	37.73	33.66	40.76	33.06	44.84	38.83	55.59	50.28	40.90
2008	40.58	28.68	36.22	42.03	29.67	35.03	35.37	49.98	47.29	38.14
2009	31.07	29.06	27.61	36.14	28.42	33.12	30.90	31.30	49.08	41.00
2010	29.53	31.36	24.55	28.61	31.04	30.47	29.26	45.61	49.73	37.02
2011	34.27	29.28	28.85	26.60	31.45	26.27	29.45	27.75	59.85	36.76
2012	27.81	30.23	27.32	26.20	33.80	28.08	28.91	20.95	57.17	38.28
2013	28.14	28.23	27.01	25.26	32.95	30.76	28.73	22.78	50.86	38.01
2014	29.02	29.93	27.06	25.98	33.23	31.86	29.51	23.29	44.54	36.59
2015	34.68	36.52	35.01	24.41	34.25	37.97	33.81	24.28	37.45	41.58
2016	35.57	34.44	33.13	24.04	30.70	38.75	32.77	25.13	32.10	37.54
2017	32.45	33.92	33.35	23.25	27.26	37.88	31.35	21.30	36.15	37.19
2018	30.30	32.73	33.08	23.42	23.40	35.61	29.76	28.89	36.05	36.28
2019	30.75	33.41	32.76	23.02	23.04	40.58	30.59	20.23	27.32	36.09
2020	27.87	36.77	29.89	18.54	25.89	37.53	29.42	18.30	27.88	39.86
2021	28.88	40.06	32.99	19.99	25.18	46.49	32.27	21.82	26.53	39.80
Mean	35.08	32.51	28.64	28.35	28.77	36.40	31.63	36.90	48.83	39.59
St.dev	8.38	3.67	4.45	7.68	6.00	6.57	4.05	15.06	14.55	2.43
Mean/ St.dev	4.19	8.85	6.43	3.69	4.80	5.54	7.81	2.45	3.36	16.28

Qatar has the highest concentration, with average 3-bank ratios of 89.60% and 5-bank ratios of 98.90%. In Saudi Arabia, both ratios averaged 56.31% and 79.74%, respectively. The UAE has the lowest concentration, with 3-bank and 5-bank asset concentration ratios averaging 56.92% and 77.14%, respectively. The 3-bank ratio declined from 52.66% in 2000 to 44.09% in 2006, but rose to 72.78% by 2020. The 5-bank ratio followed a similar pattern, falling from 77.08% in 2000 to 66.73% in 2006, then rising to 85.22% in 2021. Mergers and acquisitions drive these fluctuations.

Table 5.10 3-bank asset concentration ratio (%) for all banking systems during 2000–21

Year	*Bahrain*	*Kuwait*	*Oman*	*Qatar*	*Saudi Arabia*	*UAE*	*GCC*	*Egypt*	*UK*	*US*
2000	78.73	76.14	79.88	93.06	61.06	52.66	73.59	58.44	33.89	21.45
2001	78.59	75.05	81.32	92.70	59.99	50.71	73.06	60.80	35.85	23.12
2002	79.45	74.85	84.66	93.12	57.88	49.96	73.32	59.55	36.48	23.45
2003	82.58	74.88	84.06	93.13	57.45	49.34	73.57	59.83	33.84	23.33
2004	83.33	73.76	82.80	90.97	55.21	47.33	72.23	57.97	68.17	28.07
2005	80.22	74.10	84.42	88.97	54.37	47.98	71.68	58.34	50.46	29.97
2006	81.89	76.24	83.32	88.39	53.69	44.09	71.27	59.34	52.32	32.81
2007	80.51	78.26	76.64	85.77	55.44	49.98	71.10	53.93	59.36	34.06
2008	79.01	87.48	72.73	83.38	53.15	49.49	70.87	58.32	63.02	35.52
2009	80.32	100.00	69.76	83.32	57.01	59.60	75.00	58.07	57.05	35.07
2010	80.69	100.00	69.14	84.75	57.78	59.64	75.33	59.62	56.82	34.71
2011	89.06	100.00	72.95	87.06	57.16	60.93	77.86	59.44	57.39	35.63
2012	89.79	100.00	69.21	87.76	55.94	61.18	77.31	58.16	54.90	35.10
2013	90.25	100.00	69.79	89.63	54.93	63.43	78.00	57.32	51.62	35.03
2014	90.48	100.00	68.38	91.58	54.24	63.09	77.96	60.15	55.14	36.17
2015	84.89	80.9	80.56	89.24	54.86	54.03	74.06	72.03	42.57	35.31
2016	84.97	81.20	78.38	90.42	53.99	55.11	74.01	79.31	46.55	35.44
2017	85.87	81.46	77.68	91.37	54.28	65.64	76.05	74.30	51.57	35.27
2018	86.35	81.64	78.06	92.14	55.74	66.15	76.68	74.96	48.66	34.42
2019	87.47	81.12	76.28	92.41	57.87	72.28	77.91	75.73	50.73	34.43
2020	87.04	82.29	76.79	92.49	60.49	72.78	78.65	83.37	53.42	35.22
Mean	83.88	84.73	76.99	89.60	56.31	56.92	74.74	63.76	50.47	32.07
St.dev	4.08	10.45	5.55	3.22	2.28	8.34	2.58	8.68	9.43	4.98
mean/ St.dev	20.57	8.11	13.87	27.85	24.69	6.82	28.98	7.34	5.35	6.44

Bahrain had high levels of concentration, with a 3-bank ratio averaging 83.88% and a 5-bank ratio averaging 95.98%. The 3-bank ratio exhibited distinct phases, characterised by stable levels of approximately 80% between 2000 and 2010, an increase to 90% between 2011 and 2014, and a subsequent decline to 86% between 2015 and 2020. In Kuwait, the 3-bank ratio increased during the global financial crisis, peaking at 100% between 2009 and 2014, before declining to 81.20% in 2016. Meanwhile, the 5-bank ratio remained close to 100% throughout the period, reflecting a highly concentrated banking sector.

Oman followed a different trajectory. The 3-bank asset concentration ratio increased from 79.88% in 2000 to 84.66% in 2002 but declined

Table 5.11 5-bank asset concentration ratio (%) for all banking systems during 2000–21

Year	*Bahrain*	*Kuwait*	*Oman*	*Qatar*	*Saudi Arabia*	*UAE*	*GCC*	*Egypt*	*UK*	*US*
2000	94.86	100.00	95.03	100.00	81.62	77.08	91.43	71.77	46.55	28.12
2001	95.13	100.00	100.00	100.00	80.25	76.33	91.95	73.88	50.22	29.43
2002	95.63	100.00	100.00	100.00	78.92	74.91	89.89	72.52	50.42	30.91
2003	97.89	100.00	100.00	100.00	79.47	73.75	90.22	73.36	48.18	31.11
2004	96.66	100.00	100.00	100.00	77.89	71.98	89.30	72.15	81.31	36.79
2005	94.40	100.00	100.00	100.00	76.33	71.39	88.42	71.25	65.82	39.33
2006	95.41	100.00	100.00	100.00	76.33	66.73	87.70	71.38	67.48	41.67
2007	94.11	100.00	100.00	97.67	78.10	69.72	89.93	66.68	74.23	43.89
2008	92.56	100.00	100.00	96.66	77.58	69.40	87.24	69.08	77.86	44.89
2009	93.90	100.00	100.00	95.52	79.79	80.14	89.87	68.50	75.67	44.29
2010	93.87	100.00	100.00	95.46	80.11	79.55	89.80	69.80	76.14	46.14
2011	95.57	100.00	100.00	96.34	80.80	81.13	90.77	69.54	76.40	47.30
2012	96.65	100.00	100.00	96.99	79.88	81.49	91.00	68.39	75.11	47.17
2013	96.73	100.00	100.00	97.51	79.15	83.42	91.36	68.02	73.98	47.61
2014	96.50	100.00	100.00	100.00	77.79	83.64	91.59	70.60	74.06	48.42
2015	96.20	99.70	85.14	99.89	77.32	73.73	88.67	68.39	74.38	56.35
2016	96.76	99.69	84.47	99.91	77.58	74.04	88.74	74.68	75.02	55.77
2017	97.20	99.68	84.54	99.94	77.53	77.61	89.42	70.08	74.85	54.97
2018	97.37	99.70	83.99	99.94	78.27	78.01	89.55	70.84	61.81	53.32
2019	97.48	99.70	83.34	99.93	82.55	83.40	91.07	71.40	61.59	51.45
2020	98.12	99.70	83.96	100.00	84.09	84.35	91.70	77.39	60.95	51.49
2021	98.43	99.72	84.91	100.00	92.87	85.22	93.52	84.17	59.85	49.68
Mean	95.98	99.86	93.26	98.90	79.74	77.14	90.14	71.54	67.36	44.55
St.dev	1.56	0.16	7.79	1.68	3.52	5.39	1.51	3.75	10.78	8.66
mean/ St.dev	61.37	639.95	11.97	58.88	22.63	14.31	59.78	19.07	6.25	5.14

to 68.38% in 2014. The ratio increased to 80.56% in 2015 but fell to 76.79% in 2020. The 5-bank ratio remained at 100% between 2001 and 2014, but decreased to 84.91% by 2021. Regulatory changes and new market entrants may have impacted these trends.

GCC banking systems are more concentrated than those in other countries. In the US, the market is the least concentrated, with average 3-bank and 5-bank ratios of 32.07% and 44.55%, respectively. The UK banking system has ratios of 50.47% and 67.36%, respectively. Egypt has average 3-bank and 5-bank ratios of 63.76% and 71.54%, respectively, mainly attributable to the dominance of state-owned banks.

Regulatory Reforms and Their Impact on GCC Banking Performance (2000–2024)

The GCC banking sector has undergone significant regulatory transformations that have enhanced stability over the past two decades.

Table 5.12 lists selected regulatory measures taken between 2000 and 2024. First, the implementation of Basel I (2000), Basel II (2007), and Basel III (2015) may have profound implications for ROE, ROA, NIM, capital adequacy, cost efficiency, and credit risk. The introduction of the Basel III liquidity coverage ratio (LCR) and net stable funding ratio (NSFR) required banks to hold higher-quality liquid assets, affecting their NIM and ROE. Second, GCC countries introduced several reforms in corporate governance and risk management. For instance, the Kuwaiti Corporate Governance Code (2016) and Bahrain's Capital Market Reforms (2012) may have helped reduce non-performing loans (NPLs) and enhance cost efficiency by improving transparency, risk management, and financial disclosure. Qatar's banking supervision guidelines (2005) enhanced liquidity risk monitoring, reducing credit risk and improving ROA over time.

Third, the global financial crisis prompted emergency regulatory responses across the GCC. Measures included liquidity injections, loan restructuring programmes, and relaxations of capital requirements. GCC regulators have taken steps to modernise the banking sector and encourage financial innovation. The UAE's fintech regulatory framework (2017) and Saudi Arabia's Open Banking Initiative (2019) have facilitated the entry of digital banks and fintech firms. This should increase competition and influence banks' operating efficiency, income diversification, and ROA. Similarly, the introduction of Islamic banking regulations in Oman (2010) and the growth of sustainable finance guidelines in 2023 have encouraged banks to diversify revenue streams.

Another critical regulatory change impacting bank performance is anti-money laundering (AML) compliance. Based on FATF recommendations (2018), GCC countries introduced AML reforms, focusing on implementing more stringent customer due diligence (CDD) procedures. While this may enhance financial integrity and reduce reputational risks, it may also increase compliance costs and pose operational challenges, particularly for smaller banks with limited resources.

The introduction of Saudi Arabia's Deposit Protection Fund (2014) contributes to public confidence and bank stability. However, this may

Table 5.12 Key regulatory changes in GCC Banking (2000–2024) and their potential impact on bank performance

Year	*Country*	*Regulatory change*	*Description*	*Impact on banks*	*Source*
2000	GCC	Basel I Implementation	Adoption of Basel I capital adequacy requirements	Strengthened capital buffers but increased compliance costs	Below
2003	UAE	UAE Banking Law Amendment	Strengthened loan classification and provisioning rules	Improved asset quality and credit-risk management	Al-Hassan et al. (2013)
2004	Saudi Arabia	SAMA Banking Reform	Allowed foreign banks to enter the market	Increased competition and banking-sector diversification	IMF (2004)
2005	Qatar	Banking Supervision Guidelines	Introduced liquidity risk and stress testing requirements	Improved resilience against liquidity shocks	QCB (2005)
2006	Kuwait	Foreign Investment Liberalisation	Allowed 100% foreign ownership in some financial services	Increased foreign bank presence and financial innovation	CBK (2006)
2007	GCC-wide	Basel II Implementation	Transition to risk-based capital requirements	Strengthened risk management but increased regulatory costs	BIS (2007)
2008–2009	GCC-wide	Financial Crisis Response	Central banks injected liquidity, eased capital requirements, and introduced loan restructuring programmes	Stabilised banks during the global financial crisis, but this led to short-term profitability pressures	IMF (2010)

(continued)

Table 5.12 (continued)

Year	*Country*	*Regulatory change*	*Description*	*Impact on banks*	*Source*
2010	Oman	Islamic Banking Law	Allowed the establishment of Islamic banks and required separate Islamic banking windows for conventional banks	Expanded Islamic banking and financial inclusion	CBO (2010)
2011	UAE	Mortgage Lending Regulations	Imposed loan-to-value (LTV) limits for real estate lending	Reduced credit risk but slowed mortgage lending growth	CBUAE (2011)
2012	Bahrain	Capital Market Reforms	Strengthened corporate governance and risk disclosures	Enhanced transparency and investor confidence	CBB (2012)
2013	Qatar	Capital Market Authority (CMA) Reforms	Introduced new financial reporting standards for banks	Improved financial transparency and risk assessment	QCB (2013)
2014	Saudi Arabia	New Deposit Insurance Scheme	Launched the Saudi Deposit Protection Fund to insure retail deposits	Increased depositor confidence and financial stability	SAMA (2014)
2015	GCC-wide	Basel III Implementation	Phased introduction of higher capital requirements and liquidity coverage ratios (LCRs)	Strengthened financial resilience but reduced lending capacity	BIS (2015)
2016	Kuwait	Corporate Governance Code	Imposed stricter board independence and risk governance requirements	Enhanced corporate oversight and reduced conflicts of interest	CBK (2016)
2017	UAE	Fintech Regulation	Created licensing frameworks for digital banks and fintech startups	Encouraged financial innovation and digital transformation	CBUAE (2017)

(continued)

Table 5.12 (continued)

Year	*Country*	*Regulatory change*	*Description*	*Impact on banks*	*Source*
2018	GCC-wide	Anti-Money Laundering (AML) Reforms	Implemented stricter AML compliance measures following FATF recommendations	Increased compliance costs but reduced financial crime risks	FATF (2018)
2019	Saudi Arabia	Open Banking Initiative	Allowed third-party financial service providers to access banking data with customer consent	Boosted competition and digital banking innovation	SAMA (2019)
2020	GCC-wide	COVID-19 Economic Stimulus	Central banks lowered interest rates, implemented loan deferrals, and provided liquidity support to mitigate the impact of the pandemic	Helped banks maintain solvency but compressed interest margins (NIMs)	IMF (2021)
2021	UAE	Digital Currency Exploration	The Central Bank of the UAE (CBUAE) announced plans for a central bank digital currency (CBDC)	Increased focus on digital banking and payments modernisation	CBUAE (2021)
2022	Bahrain	Crypto Asset Regulations	Introduced licensing frameworks for crypto exchanges and digital assets	It has led to increased financial innovation, but has also posed new regulatory challenges	CBB (2022)
2023	Oman	Sustainable Finance Guidelines	Launched green finance and ESG banking incentives	Encouraged banks to develop climate-friendly investment products	CBO (2023)
2024	GCC-wide	Basel IV Transition	GCC central banks prepared banks for compliance with Basel IV capital rules	Increased capital adequacy requirements affect profitability and lending capacity	BIS (2024)

introduce moral hazard concerns. Banks may engage in riskier lending practices due to the implicit safety net provided by deposit protection mechanisms.

The evolving nature of these regulatory reforms underscores the need for a balanced approach—one that ensures financial stability without excessively constraining profitability. Policymakers must focus on maintaining strong capitalisation, encouraging banking innovation, and ensuring efficient risk management, all of which are crucial for navigating future economic transformations in the GCC region.

Islamic vs Conventional Banking in the GCC

The GCC banking sector operates as a dual-banking system, with Islamic and conventional banks coexisting. Both types of banking follow distinct financial principles, risk structures, and income-generating mechanisms. Islamic banks adhere to Shariah law, which prohibits transactions involving interest (riba) and speculative activities (gharar). The Islamic model relies on profit-and-loss sharing contracts, asset-backed financing, and ethical investment principles. In contrast, conventional banks operate on interest-based lending and employ traditional financial instruments commonly used in global banking markets.

As shown in Table 5.13, Islamic banking has expanded rapidly across the GCC, growing from approximately 20% of total banking assets in 2000 to 40% in 2023 (Islamic Financial Services Board, 2023). In Saudi Arabia and Kuwait, Islamic banks hold over 50% of total banking assets, while in the UAE and Bahrain, their market share ranges between 30 and 40%.

This expansion has been actively supported by governments and regulators, who have established Shariah-compliant financial frameworks and regulatory bodies to ensure the stability of Islamic banking. The growing role of Islamic banks in financial intermediation, trade financing, and corporate lending underscores the need to explicitly account for banking type when assessing the determinants of performance and profitability.

Table 5.14 shows the extent to which Islamic and conventional banks differ in their profitability, cost structures, and risk characteristics. This difference affects profitability indicators, including ROE, ROA, and NIM.

In Table 5.14, Islamic banks tend to have lower ROE (13.4%) and ROA (1.5%) than conventional banks (15.2% and 1.9%, respectively). This may be due to three factors: (i) higher compliance costs associated with

Table 5.13 Importance of Islamic banking in each GCC country

Country	*Islamic Banking Share of Total Banking Assets (2023)*	*Growth Rate of Islamic Banking Assets (2010–2023, %)*	*Largest Islamic Bank*
Saudi Arabia	53%	12.1%	Al Rajhi Bank
Kuwait	52%	10.8%	Kuwait Finance House
UAE	38%	9.5%	Dubai Islamic Bank
Bahrain	34%	8.2%	Al Baraka Islamic Bank
Qatar	28%	11.7%	Qatar Islamic Bank
Oman	21%	14.4%	Bank Nizwa
GCC Average	40%	11.1%	–

Table 5.14 Performance of Islamic and conventional banking for the GCC region

Indicator	*Islamic Banks (2000–2023 Average, %)*	*Conventional Banks (2000–2023 Average, %)*
Return on Equity (ROE)	13.4%	15.2%
Return on Assets (ROA)	1.5%	1.9%
Net Interest Margin (NIM)	2.8%	2.9%
Cost-to-Income Ratio	45.3%	38.1%
Capital Ratio (CAR)	16.2%	13.1%
Non-Performing Loan (NPL) Ratio	2.9%	3.4%

Shariah governance and structuring Islamic financial products; (ii) limited income diversification, as Islamic banks cannot engage in interest-based investments or speculative trading, and (iii) lower financial leverage, since Islamic banks rely more on equity-based financing rather than debt.

Islamic banks have higher cost-to-income ratios (45.3%) than conventional banks (38.1%). This may be attributable to costs associated with Shariah supervisory boards and compliance audits, as well as the complex financial structuring of Islamic contracts, which increases administrative expenses. Additionally, higher costs are incurred for managing short-term funding needs due to limited access to interbank liquidity markets.

Islamic banks also maintain higher capital ratios (16.2%) compared to their conventional counterparts (13.1%). This may be driven by the alignment of the capital structure of Islamic banks with Shariah principles, which discourages excessive leverage. Regulatory conditions for Islamic banks require them to maintain higher capital buffers because of the limited risk-mitigation tools available to them.

Similarly, Islamic banks have slightly lower NPL ratios (2.9%) compared to conventional banks (3.4%). They rely on profit-sharing and asset-backed transactions and engage in stronger borrower-bank relationships.

Determinants of Bank Profitability: Literature Review

Empirical studies on bank profitability can be classified into country-specific and cross-country analyses. Country-specific studies typically focus on developed economies such as the US (Chronopoulos et al., 2015; Rezvanian & Mehdian, 2024; Schreiber, 2024) and European banking markets (Dietrich & Wanzenried, 2011; O'Connell, 2023; Athanasoglou et al., 2008). More recent research focuses on emerging and developing economies, such as China (Tan, 2016; Li, Gao, & Gu, 2023), Latin America (Saona, 2016; Guillén et al., 2014), MENA (Mateev & Bachvarov, 2021; Caporale et al., 2017), and cross-country studies (Molyneux & Thornton, 1992; Demirguc-Kunt & Huizinga, 1999; Asteriou et al., 2021; Klein & Weill, 2022; Karkowska et al., 2025).

A significant strand of the literature focuses on internal bank-specific determinants, including capital adequacy, cost efficiency, risk exposure, and asset quality. Molyneux and Thornton (1992) find a positive correlation between managerial efficiency and bank performance in a study of 18 European banking systems. Conversely, Bourke (1989) reported mixed findings across 12 economies in North America, Europe, and Australia. Zimmerman (1996) reinforced the idea that management quality, particularly in loan portfolio selection, is a significant determinant of profitability. Another critical variable in the literature is capital adequacy. Bourke (1989) suggested that well-capitalised banks have access to lower-cost funding, thereby enhancing profitability. Berger (1995) introduced the expected bankruptcy cost hypothesis, arguing that banks with higher capital ratios are better positioned to withstand economic shocks. However, other studies, such as Hoffman (2011), found a negative relationship between capital ratios and profitability, suggesting that excessive capital accumulation may lead to overly conservative lending strategies, thereby reducing income-generating opportunities.

Bank size is another prominent determinant, introduced to account for economies or diseconomies of scale in banking operations. Larger banks benefit from cost efficiencies in information processing and risk diversification (Boyd & Runkle, 1993), and are less vulnerable to profit volatility (McMillan & McMillan, 2016). Short (1979) argued that size is closely linked to capital adequacy, as larger institutions can raise funds at lower costs, thereby increasing profitability. Smirlock (1985) found a strong positive relationship between size and profitability across a sample of multinational banks. In contrast, Berger et al. (1987) suggested that cost efficiencies from increased size were minimal for US banks. Some researchers, such as Berger and Humphrey (1997) and Altunbas et al. (2001), have provided evidence of economies of scale. In contrast, others, including Pallage (1991) and Vander Vennet (1998), have identified diseconomies of scale, particularly in huge banking institutions.

More recent studies have shifted focus towards the regulatory and supervisory environment. Barth et al. (2003, 2004) examined the impact of banking regulations on profitability, though no conclusive relationship was established. Demirgüç-Kunt and Huizinga (2000) emphasised the role of legal and institutional frameworks in shaping profitability, linking bank size and market structure to regulatory constraints. Further research by Bikker and Hu (2002) and Goddard et al. (2004) reinforced the idea that regulatory capital requirements influence profitability by affecting banks' risk-taking behaviour and funding costs.

External macroeconomic determinants also play a significant role in profitability. These factors are typically divided into core economic indicators, such as GDP growth and inflation, and market-specific characteristics, including market concentration and ownership structure. The SCP hypothesis remains central to much of the literature on market structure and profitability, asserting that greater concentration yields monopoly profits. However, competing theories, such as the efficient structure hypothesis, challenge this view. Studies testing these hypotheses (Demsetz, 1973; Pelzman, 1977; Carter, 1978; Marshall, 1984) found mixed evidence, with some supporting the efficient structure perspective. McMillan and McMillan (2016) examined the effect of market concentration (measured by the Herfindahl–Hirschman Index) on bank profitability, finding that while concentration had little impact on profits, market power—measured via the Lerner Index—led to higher profitability and profit persistence, indicating lower competitive pressure.

Demirgüç-Kunt and Huizinga (1998) analyse bank profitability across 80 countries between 1988 and 1995, identifying strong links between bank characteristics, market structure, and macroeconomic conditions. They found that well-capitalised banks were more profitable but less diversified. Banks that rely on deposits for funding are less profitable due to high operating costs. Inflation had a positive impact on bank margins, while increased financial market development reduced reliance on bank financing. Institutional factors such as credit rights enforcement and financial market structure also played a more pronounced role in emerging economies than in advanced markets.

Studies focusing on the GCC and broader MENA region are relatively scarce. Zeitun (2012) examines the determinants of profitability for Islamic and conventional banks in the GCC between 2002 and 2009 and finds that cost, inflation, and reserve holdings negatively affect ROE. In contrast, larger, well-capitalised banks achieve higher profit margins. Foreign ownership has an insignificant effect on profitability. Al-Matari (2023) highlights the significant roles of bank size and liquidity in moderating the relationships among capital adequacy, asset quality, and overall performance. The study uses GCC data between 2000 and 2018.

Macroeconomic factors, particularly inflation and interest rates, have also been widely studied in relation to profitability. Hanson and Rocha (1986) identified a strong positive correlation between inflation and bank interest margins across 29 countries between 1975 and 1983. Barth, Nolle, and Rice (1997) examined market power, bank concentration, and deposit insurance across 19 industrialised nations and found no significant relationship with profitability. More recent studies, such as those by Chronopoulos et al. (2013), have found evidence that bank profits in the US are pro-cyclical, aligning with earlier findings by Demirgüç-Kunt and Huizinga (2000) and Bikker and Hu (2002), who demonstrated that bank profitability tends to move in line with the business cycle. Revell (1979) was among the first to examine the impact of inflation on banking, while Perry (1992) argued that inflation affects profitability only when it is unanticipated, allowing banks to adjust their pricing strategies accordingly. Kohlscheen et al. (2018) further supported this view, showing that long-term interest rate increases boost bank profitability, while short-term rate hikes reduce it by raising funding costs.

While extensive literature exists on banking profitability in advanced economies, empirical research on the determinants of bank profitability in the GCC remains relatively underdeveloped. Most studies on the region examine bank efficiency or financial stability rather than specific profitability drivers. Given the unique economic and regulatory environment of the GCC, along with its exposure to oil price fluctuations and global financial cycles, further research is needed to understand how internal bank characteristics, regulatory policies, and macroeconomic conditions interact to shape bank profitability.

Data and Methodology

Data and Sample

The analysis employs a panel of 55 banks from GCC countries, comprising 657 observations from 2003 to 2022. The sample is representative of the GCC banking system because it includes the largest banks by market capitalisation, which collectively account for a significant proportion of the system's assets. The period encompasses the 2007–09 global financial crisis, the 2014–15 global oil crisis, and the COVID-19 crisis, thereby enabling an examination of their impact on bank profitability. All bank-level variables are derived from balance sheets and income statements obtained from the Thomson Reuters database. The economy-level information is obtained from the World Bank's economic and financial databases.

Regression Model

In this study, we examine the determinants of bank profitability, capturing the effect of bank-level factors—such as size, liquidity, capitalisation, credit risk, and diversification—and external influences, including market concentration, economic cycles, governance structures, and financial crises. Accordingly, the following regression specification is proposed:

$$\begin{aligned} PROFITABILITY_{it} = {} & \beta_0 + \beta_1\ PROFITABILITY_{it-1} + \gamma_1 SIZE_t \\ & + \gamma_2 CAPITAL_t + \gamma_3\ DIVERSIFICATION_t + \gamma_4\ LIQUIDITY_t \\ & + \gamma_5\ CREDIT_t\ +\ \gamma_6\ OVERHEADS_t \\ & + \gamma_7\ ISLAMIC + \delta_1\ CONCENTRATION_t + \delta_2\ GROWTH_t \\ & + \delta_3\ INFLATION_t + \delta_4 RULE\_OF\_LAW_t \\ & + \zeta_1 GFC + \zeta_2 OGC + \zeta_3 COVID + \varepsilon \end{aligned} \tag{5.1}$$

The dependent variable, PROFITABILITY, is measured using three financial indicators: Return on Equity (ROE), Return on Assets (ROA), and Net Interest Margin (NIM). $PROFITABILITY_{t-1}$ is a lagged dependent variable capturing the persistence of profitability over time. The coefficient β_1 measures the speed of mean reversion. Values between 0 and 1 indicate that profits are persistent but gradually return to their equilibrium level. A coefficient close to zero suggests a high speed of adjustment, implying a more competitive market structure. On the other hand, a coefficient closer to one indicates slow mean reversion, suggesting a less competitive banking environment.

Several bank-specific variables are included as explanatory factors. SIZE is measured as the natural logarithm of total assets (Demirgüç-Kunt et al., 2004). CREDIT RISK is proxied by the loan loss provision-to-total-loans ratio (Lin et al., 2012). CAPITAL is measured by the ratio of book value of equity to total assets (Angbazo, 1997; Ben Naceur & Goaied, 2008; Saona, 2011). DIVERSIFICATION is measured by the ratio of non-interest income to total operating income. Higher values indicate greater reliance on non-traditional banking activities. EFFICIENCY is measured as the ratio of total operating and financial expenses to total assets. LIQUIDITY is defined as the proportion of liquid assets to total assets. Annual GDP growth and inflation rates are also included to consider economic conditions. Demirgüç-Kunt and Huizinga (1999) expect that banks benefit from higher inflation if they can adjust lending rates more quickly than they can adjust funding costs. The model also incorporates the RULE OF LAW as a governance variable to assess the impact of institutional quality on banking performance. Major exogenous shocks are also accounted for by including three dummy variables: GFC for the 2008–09 Global Financial Crisis (1 for the year 2009), OGC for the 2014–15 oil price collapse (1 for the year 2015), and COVID for the COVID-19 pandemic in 2020 (1 for the year 2020). The ISLAMIC dummy variable is included to assess the differences in profitability across banking models.

The model is estimated following the approach outlined by Saona (2016), utilising the generalised method of moments (GMM) to address unobservable heterogeneity and endogeneity (Arellano, 2002).

Variables and Research Hypotheses

Measures of Profitability

This study employs three key measures of bank profitability: NIM, ROA and ROE.

Net Interest Margin (NIM) measures the efficiency of financial intermediation. It is calculated as the difference between interest income and interest expense, divided by total earning assets. A higher NIM suggests that a bank is effectively managing its interest-bearing assets and liabilities. NIM serves as an indicator of a bank's ability to convert deposits into profitable loans (Islam & Nishiyama, 2016).

Return on Assets (ROA) is calculated as pre-tax profits divided by total assets. It measures the bank's ability to generate earnings from its asset management functions. It is frequently used as a key metric for evaluating bank profitability (Molyneux & Thornton, 1992; Golin, 2001; Claessens & Laeven, 2004; Athanasoglou et al., 2008; Flamini et al., 2009; Sufian & Habibullah, 2010; Dietrich & Wanzenried, 2011; Mamatzakis & Bermpei, 2016). ROA provides a view of operating profitability, free from distortions caused by capital structure decisions (Djalilov & Piesse, 2016).

Return on Equity (ROE) indicates the return generated on invested equity. It is calculated as pre-tax profits divided by total equity. It incorporates the impact of financial leverage by reflecting the risks and returns associated with debt. Since banks operate under strict regulatory constraints and face informational asymmetries, ROE provides insight into how effectively banks balance profitability with capital requirements (Flamini et al., 2009).

Bank-Specific Variables

Bank Size (SIZE)

Bank size captures economies of scale for larger banks. It assesses the extent to which larger banks extract profitability from cost efficiencies or market power (Smirlock, 1985; Boyd & Runkle, 1993; Hailegebreal, 2016; Berger & Humphrey, 1997). Larger banks enjoy bargaining power in funding, lower cost of capital, and diversified income streams. However, a few studies argue that size may negatively impact profitability due to operational inefficiencies, increased bureaucracy, and higher agency costs (Goddard et al., 2004; Akhtar et al., 2011; Mazviona et al., 2017; Kazeem, 2015). Empirical results remain mixed, with some studies finding an insignificant relationship.

Given that GCC banks have expanded significantly over the last three decades through business growth and consolidation, the following hypothesis is made:

H1: Bank size affects bank profitability in the GCC countries

Capital adequacy (CAPITAL)

Capitalisation is measured by the equity-to-assets ratio to assess a bank's resilience to financial shocks. The impact of capital on profitability is a topic of debate. The bankruptcy cost hypothesis suggests that higher capital buffers protect against financial distress (Berger, 1995). The signalling hypothesis posits that better capitalisation conveys positive expectations to investors, enabling them to absorb unexpected losses (Berger & Bouwman, 2009). Conversely, the opportunity cost hypothesis suggests that excessive capital may lead to the maximisation of returns, thereby affecting performance (Jensen, 1986).

Generally, empirical studies support a positive relationship between capital and profitability (Athanasoglou et al., 2008; Dietrich & Wanzenried, 2014). We posit the following hypothesis:

> H2: Capital adequacy significantly affects bank profitability in the GCC countries.

Cost Efficiency (OVERHEADS)

Overheads, measured as total operating and financial costs relative to total assets, reflect a bank's operational efficiency. A higher overhead ratio indicates cost inefficiencies and lower earnings (Hassan & Bashir, 2003; Kunt & Huizinga, 1998; Rashid & Jabeen, 2016). We hypothesise the following:

> H3: Overhead costs affect bank profitability in the GCC countries.

Credit Risk (CREDIT)

Credit risk, proxied by loan loss provisions relative to total loans (LLPs), measures the quality of a bank's loan portfolio. A higher LLP ratio indicates deteriorating asset quality, potential loan defaults, and reduced profitability (Miller & Noulas, 1997; Athanasoglou et al., 2008). Three hypotheses explain the impact of bad loans on profitability. The bad luck hypothesis (Berger & DeYoung, 1997) posits that external shocks increase banks' NPLs, thereby reducing their earnings. The bad management hypothesis posits that inadequate loan screening results in higher default rates. However, the risk-return hypothesis (Saona, 2016) suggests that riskier loans may yield higher returns when adequately priced.

Empirical studies confirm that high credit risk hurts profitability (Flamini et al., 2009; Messai & Jouini, 2013; Apergis, 2014; Kjosevski et al., 2019). Therefore, we hypothesise that:

H4: Credit risk affects bank profitability in the GCC countries.

Income DIVERSIFICATION

Income DIVERSIFICATION, measured as the ratio of non-interest income to total operating income, captures a bank's reliance on non-traditional banking activities. The conglomeration hypothesis posits that diversification reduces costs and increases risk (Smith et al., 2003; De Jonghe & Vennet, 2007; Nisar et al., 2018; Bakhouche, 2024). In contrast, the strategic focus hypothesis argues that banks should specialise in specific areas to improve efficiency and management. Berger et al. (2000) find that both strategies have their advantages. We hypothesise the following:

H5: Diversification affects bank profitability in the GCC countries.

Liquidity

LIQUIDITY, measured as liquid assets to total assets, reflects a bank's ability to meet short-term obligations. While adequate liquidity contributes to stability (Al-Tamimi, 2012), excessive liquidity reduces interest income due to underutilised resources (Bourke, 1989; Kosmidou et al., 2005). Therefore, we hypothesise the following:

H6: Liquidity affects bank profitability in the GCC countries.

ISLAMIC Dummy Variable

Islamic banking operates under Sharia law, which prohibits the charging of interest (*riba*), speculation, and unethical investments. Islamic banks (IBs) operate on an asset-based, risk-sharing model that uses profit-loss-sharing mechanisms. Some studies suggest that IBs outperform conventional banks (CBs) in terms of risk management and stability. Others find no significant difference in profitability between IBs and CBs. We propose the following hypothesis:

H7: Islamic banks are not different from conventional banks in terms of profitability in the GCC countries.

Country-Level Variables

Market Concentration

Market concentration measures the extent to which a few large firms dominate the banking sector. The Structure-Conduct-Performance (SCP) hypothesis suggests that in highly concentrated banking markets, banks with higher market power charge higher interest rate spreads and earn higher profits due to economies of scale. In contrast, the Efficient Structure (ES) hypothesis argues that high profitability stems from superior cost efficiency and innovation. Empirical findings on this relationship remain inconclusive. Demirgüç-Kunt & Huizinga (2000) and Claeys & Vander Vennet (2008) report a positive correlation between bank concentration and profitability, while Naceur & Omran (2011) find a negative relationship. Al-Muharrami & Matthews (2009) support the SCP hypothesis in the GCC banking. We propose the following hypothesis:

H8: Market concentration affects bank profitability in the GCC countries.

GDP Growth

Higher GDP growth typically stimulates demand for loans and reduces default rates, thereby increasing banks' earnings (Rajan & Zingales, 1998; Dietrich & Wanzenried, 2014). Al-Hussaini & Al-Shammari (2013) find that, in the GCC, rising GDP levels expanded lending and improved banks' ROA and ROE. Conversely, economic slowdowns lead to lower loan demand, deteriorating credit quality, and declining profitability (Djalilov & Piesse, 2016). Thus, we propose the following hypothesis:

H9: GDP growth affects bank profitability in the GCC countries.

Inflation

Inflation affects bank profitability through its impact on interest rates and operational costs (Anbar & Alper, 2011; Chowdhury & Rasid, 2017; Jara-Bertin et al., 2014; Masood et al., 2012). If inflation is anticipated, banks can adjust their interest rates more quickly than their costs (e.g., wages and administrative expenses) rise, which leads to higher margins and profitability (Bourke, 1989; Molyneux & Thornton, 1992). If inflation is unanticipated, rising costs may outpace banks' ability to adjust lending rates, thereby reducing earnings (Naceur & Omran, 2011). Barth et al. (2004) find that moderate inflation has a positive impact on profitability, while high inflation erodes gains. Thus, we propose the following hypothesis:

H10: Inflation affects bank profitability in the GCC countries

Rule of Law

The Rule of Law reflects the extent to which legal and regulatory frameworks are transparent, enforceable, and stable. A strong rule of law describes an institutional environment that protects property rights and combats corruption, which reduces information asymmetries. Empirical evidence suggests that better institutional quality improves banking performance by reducing default risks (Barro, 2000; Acemoglu & Johnson, 2005). Thus, we propose the following hypothesis:

H11: Rule of law affects bank profitability in the GCC countries

Major Events (Dummy Variables)

The 2007–08 Global Financial Crisis (GFC)

The Global Financial Crisis (GFC) was triggered by the collapse of the US housing market and the subsequent failure of major financial institutions. It led to a global economic downturn characterised by liquidity shortages, reduced credit availability, and increased financial uncertainty (Dkle & Lee, 2015; Fu et al., 2014). Al-Muharrami & Matthews (2009) and Hasan & Dridi (2011) indicate that the crisis negatively impacted GCC bank profitability due to lower interest income and rising NPLs.Thus, the following hypothesis is tested:

H12: The 2007–08 Global Financial Crisis negatively affected GCC banking profitability.

The 2014–15 Oil Crisis (GOC)

A change in oil prices captures a significant external shock to the GCC's economies. Oil revenues influence GDP growth, government revenues, and spending (Miyajima, 2020). An oversupply of crude oil and weaker global demand triggered the 2014–15 oil price collapse. Declining oil exports led to tighter liquidity conditions, which in turn affected banks' ability to expand credit. Empirical evidence suggests that oil price volatility significantly affects the performance of banks in oil-dependent economies (Bouri et al., 2020). Since GCC banks have a high exposure to government-related deposits and lending, the 2014–15 oil crisis likely constrained profitability. We test the following hypothesis:

H13: The 2014–15 oil crisis had a negative impact on the profitability of GCC banks.

The COVID-19 Lockdown (2020–21)

The COVID-19 pandemic causes widespread economic disruptions due to government-imposed lockdowns and travel restrictions. Studies on the banking sector during COVID-19 (Srairi, 2021) suggest that profitability declined due to higher provisioning costs and economic uncertainty. Thus, the following hypothesis is proposed:

H14: The COVID-19 lockdown hurt the profitability of GCC banks.

Regression Results and Discussion

Table 5.16 reports the models with ROE as the dependent variable; Table 5.17 summarises the results for the ROA models; and Table 5.18 displays the estimations for NIM. Following Rashid & Jabeen (2016), we estimate several specifications for each profitability measure. Each table presents five specifications of Eq. 5.1 for robustness. Model 1 includes bank-specific variables; Model 2 augments Model 1 by adding macroeconomic variables; Model 3 incorporates the institutional variable RULE_OF_LAW into Model 2; Model 4 introduces crisis dummy variables; and Model 5 considers the Islamic dummy variable.

The diagnosis information supports that all estimated models fit the panel data. The Wald test yields a significant statistic indicating that all models fit the panel data. The Hansen overidentification test presents evidence that the underlying overidentifying restrictions are valid. The significance levels of the Hansen test of exogeneity of instruments suggest that the endogeneity problem is mitigated. Finally, the Arellano-Bond test for serial correlation in the first-differenced residuals presents no evidence of model misspecification.

The results in Table 5.16 and Table 5.17 show a positive and significant impact of size, diversification, capitalisation, liquidity, concentration, and economic growth on bank profitability. The results also show that lower credit risk is associated with higher profitability in GCC banking. Other variables, including RULE_OF_LAW, INFLATION, and the ISLAMIC dummy, as well as the dummies for GFC, GOC, and COVID, are not statistically significant.

There are common estimates across the three models, summarised in Table 5.15.

The coefficients on the one-year-lagged dependent variables for ROE, ROA, and NIM are all positive and significant, indicating that profit persistence occurs. Since the coefficients are closer to 0.5, this may suggest that GCC countries have less competitive banking sectors with significant market power (Athanasoglou et al., 2005; Hamid, 2017; Le & Ngo, 2020).

Bank size is significant and positive across all models, suggesting that larger GCC banks benefit from economies of scale. Masood & Ashraf (2012), Growe et al. (2014), Ahamed (2017), Al-Homaidi et al. (2018), and Karadžić & Đalović (2021) report similar findings. This result is supported by the significant and positive coefficient

Table 5.15 Summary of the signs and significance of variables in the profitability models

Variable	*ROE*	*ROA*	*NIM*
Constant	+, sig	+, sig	–, sig
Lag_dependent	+, sig	+, sig	+, sig
Size	+, sig	+, sig	+, insig
Diversification	+, sig	+, sig	–, insig
Capital	Insig	+, sig	+, sig
Liquidity	+, insig	+, sig in 2 models	+, sig in 1 model
Credit risk	–, insig	–, sig	–, sig in 2 models
Cost efficiency	–, +, Insig	Insig	+, insig
Concentration (competition)	+, sig	+, sig	+, 1 sig in 1 model
GDP Growth	+, sig	+, sig in 1 model	–, insig
Inflation	–, insig	–, insig	Mixed, insig
Rule of law	insig	insig	insig
Global Financial Crisis (2009)	insig	insig	insig
Global Oil Crisis (2015)	insig	insig	insig
COVI19 (2020)	insig	insig	insig
ISLAMIC type	insig	insig	insig

on market CONCENTRATION, implying a positive concentration-profitability nexus in GCC banking. Larger banks and greater market concentration allow dominant banks to maintain higher profit margins, consistent with the Structure-Conduct-Performance (SCP) paradigm (Molyneux & Thornton, 1992; Smirlock, 1985).

Capitalisation has a positive and significant impact on ROA and NIM, implying that profitable banks tend to have a high level of capitalisation (Bourke, 1989; Angbazo, 1997; Demirgüç-Kunt & Huizinga, 1999; Drakos, 2003; Maudos & De Guevara, 2004; Saunders & Schumacher, 2000; Hamid, 2017). Higher capital may incentivise banks to undertake riskier but profitable activities, which is inconsistent with the moral hazard hypothesis (Le & Ngo, 2020).

The coefficient on credit risk, captured by the LLP ratio, is negative and significant, indicating that credit risk reduces bank ROE and ROA in the GCC countries. This finding is consistent with Miller and Noulas (1997), Athanasoglou et al. (2008), and Abdulla and Ebrahim (2024). This finding may reflect improved economic conditions and enhanced institutional frameworks for credit in the post-financial crisis

Table 5.16 Estimation results for the ROE models

	Model 1	*Model 2*	*Model 3*	*Model 4*	*Model 5*
CONSTANT	1.2597 (0.001)***	1.7279 (0.000)***	1.77 (0.000)***	1.6325 (0.000)***	1.6052 (0.000)***
LAG_ROE	0.445 (0.002)***	0.293 (0.031)**	0.2899 (0.021)**	0.3339 (0.004)***	0.3433 (0.003)***
SIZE	0.0016 (0.006)***	0.0017 (0.003)***	0.0017 (0.002)***	0.0016 (0.002)***	0.0015 (0.002)***
DIVERSIFICATION	0.041 (0.000)***	0.0351 (0.000)***	0.0295 (0.014)**	0.0261 (0.042)**	0.0272 (0.031)**
CAPITAL	0.0087 (0.901)	–0.0457 (0.628)	–0.0637 (0.587)	–0.0423 (0.581)	–0.0394 (0.608)
LIQUIDITY	0.0003 (0.492)	0.0005 (0.338)	0.0004 (0.471)	0.0006 (0.272)	0.0007 (0.219)
LLP	–0.0007 (0.031)**	–0.0008 (0.015)**	–0.0006 (0.100)*	–0.0006 (0.044)**	–0.0006 (0.049)**
EFFICIENCY	–0.001 (0.375)	–0.0007 (0.495)	–0.0008 (0.461)	0.0003 (0.787)	–0.0002 (0.836)
CONCENTRATION	0.0189 (0.001)***	0.0162 (0.003)***	0.015 (0.019)**	0.0138 (0.008)***	0.0135 (0.011)**
GDPGROWTH		0.0591 (0.006)***	0.0635 (0.005)***	0.0499 (0.042)**	0.0453 (0.074)*
INFLATION		–0.0024 (0.452)	0.0008 (0.772)	–0.001 (0.600)	–0.001 (0.674)
RULE_OF_LAW			–0.0027 (0.402)	–0.0016 (0.610)	0.0011 (0.722)
GFC				–0.0031 (0.187)	–0.0035 (0.135)
GOC				0.0016 (0.295)	0.0017 (0.272)
COVID				–0.0011 (0.619)	–0.0014 (0.708)
DUMMY_ISLAMIC					0.0006 (0.495)
Diagnostics					
No. of obs	674	674	674	674	674
No. of banks	55	55	55	55	55
Arellano-Bond test for AR(1)	–2.62 (0.009)***	–2.66 (0.008)***	–3.19 (0.000)***	–2.65 (0.008)***	–2.66 (0.008)***
Arellano-Bond test for AR(2)	–0.82 (0.414)	–0.05 (0.962)	–0.48 (0.634)	–0.33 (0.743)	–0.35 (0.727)
Hansen test of overid	**20.83** **(0.234)**	**21.95** **(0.523)**	**17.54** **(0.418)**	**17.37** **(0.429)**	**17.17** **(0.443)**
Hansen test of exogeneity	5.43 (0.490)	5.11 (0.529)	4.21 (0.649)	5.14 (0.526)	5.30 (0.506)

Statistical significance: *** for 1%, ** for 5% and * for 10%

Table 5.17 Estimation results for the ROA models

	Model 1	*Model 2*	*Model 3*	*Model 4*	*Model 5*
CONSTANT	0.7258 (0.000)***	0.9235 (0.000)***	0.9156 (0.000)***	0.8908 (0.000)***	0.8968 (0.000)***
LAG_ROA	0.4696 (0.000)***	0.372 (0.000)***	0.3658 (0.000)***	0.3769 (0.000)***	0.375 (0.000)***
SIZE	0.0003 (0.002)***	0.0003 (0.032)**	0.0004 (0.018)**	0.0004 (0.005)***	0.0003 (0.015)**
DIVERSIFICATION	0.0083 (0.000)***	0.0062 (0.015)**	0.0058 (0.017)**	0.0052 (0.061)*	0.005 (0.097)*
CAPITAL	0.0819 (0.001)***	0.0653 (0.044)**	0.0749 (0.008)***	0.0787 (0.001)***	0.0774 (0.003)***
LIQUIDITY	0.0001 (0.330)	0.0002 (0.089)*	0.0001 (0.169)	0.0002 (0.11)	0.0002 (0.077)*
LNP	–0.0002 (0.006)***	–0.0002 (0.001)***	–0.0002 (0.095)	–0.0002 (0.047)**	–0.0002 (0.056)**
EFFICIENCY	–0.0003 (0.275)	–0.0003 (0.200)	0.0002 (0.305)	0.0001 (0.639)	–0.0001 (0.589)
CONCENTRATION	0.0042 (0.001)***	0.0032 (0.189)	0.0038 (0.057)*	0.0034 (0.037)**	0.0033 (0.055)*
GDPGROWTH		0.0155 (0.065)*	–0.0227 (0.474)	0.0108 (0.245)	0.0111 (0.308)
INFLATION		–0.0009 (0.472)	–0.0005 (0.671)	–0.0004 (0.680)	–0.0005 (0.674)
RULE_OF_LAW			–0.0012 (0.353)	–0.0009 (0.452)	–0.001 (0.494)
GFC				–0.0007 (0.198)	–0.0007 (0.168)
GOC				0.0004 (0.230)	0.0004 (0.215)
COVID				–0.0002 (0.694)	–0.0002 (0.708)
DUMMY_ISLAMIC					0.0000 (0.809)
Diagnostics					
No. of obs	674	674	674	674	674
No. of banks	55	55	55	55	55
Arellano–Bond test for AR(1)	–2.87 (0.004)***	–3.09 (0.002)***	–3.19 (0.000)***	–3.10 (0.002)***	–3.10 (0.002)***
Arellano-Bond test for AR(2)	–0.74 (0.461)	–0.53 (0.597)	–0.48 (0.634)	–0.66 (0.512)	–0.66 (0.509)
Hansen test of overid	27.85 (0.221)	24.62 (0.370)	23.85 (0.412)	22.63 (0.482)	22.89 (0.467)
Hansen test of exogeneity	8.68 (0.193)	2.62 (0.855)	2.98 (0.812)	2.30 (0.890)	2.63 (0.854)

Statistical significance: *** for 1%, ** for 5% and * for 10%

Table 5.18 Estimation results for the NIM models

Variable	*Model 1*	*Model 2*	*Model 3*	*Model 4*	*Model 5*
CONSTANT	–0.4592 (0.024)**	–0.5272 (0.000)***	–0.5059 (0.052)***	–0.5036 (0.043)**	–0.5634 (0.043)**
LAG_NIM	0.1958 (0.288)	0.2685 (0.078)*	0.2411 (0.083)*	0.2734 (0.054)**	0.2681 (0.084)*
SIZE	–0.0002 (0.776)	0.0005 (0.472)	0.0002 (0.797)	0.0003 (0.724)	0.0003 (0.694)
DIVERSIFICATION	–0.0136 (0.442)	–0.0195 (0.224)	–0.017 (0.268)	–0.0156 (0.325)	–0.0161 (0.35)
CAPITAL	0.2794 (0.009)***	0.3085 (0.030)**	0.2973 (0.029)**	0.2942 (0.023)**	0.3261 (0.026)**
LIQUIDITY	0.0009 (0.157)	0.001 (0.155)	0.0011 (0.077)*	0.001 (0.132)	0.0011 (0.147)
LNP	–0.0002 (0.599)	–0.0000 (0.931)	–0.0003 (0.505)	–0.0002 (0.047)**	–0.0002 (0.056)*
EFFICIENCY	0.0004 (0.789)	0.0008 (0.552)	0.0008 (0.533)	0.0001 (0.639)	–0.0001 (0.589)
CONCENTRATION	–0.0017 (0.726)	0.0019 (0.79)	–0.0017 (0.825)	–0.0016 (0.839)	0.0033 (0.055)*
GDPGROWTH		–0.0146 (0.668)	–0.0227 (0.474)	0.0003 (0.787)	–0.0156 (0.605)
INFLATION		0.0049 (0.417)	0.0055 (0.306)	0.001 (0.600)	–0.0005 (0.674)
RULE_OF_LAW			0.0056 (0.239)	–0.0009 (0.452)	–0.001 (0.494)
GFC				–0.0031 (0.187)	–0.0007 (0.168)
GOC				0.0018 (0.174)	0.0015 (0.26)
COVID				–0.0001 (0.968)	–0.0002 (0.708)
DUMMY_ISLAMIC					0.0016 (0.343)
Diagnostics					
No. of obs	674	674	674	674	674
No. of banks	55	55	55	55	55
Arellano-Bond test for AR(1)	–1.14 (0.256)	–1.75 (0.080)*	–3.19 (0.000)***	–1.90 (0.057)*	–1.81 (0.070)*
Arellano-Bond test for AR(2)	–0.43 (0.665)	–0.70 (0.483)	–0.48 (0.634)	–0.56 (0.575)	–0.51 (0.609)
Hansen test of overid	29.88 (0.153)	32.86 (0.084)*	31.75 (0.105)	31.88 (0.103)	33.77 (0.069)*
Hansen test of exogeneity	5.16 (0.523)	3.83 (0.700)	5.21 (0.517)	4.20 (0.649)	5.11 (0.529)

Statistical significance: *** for 1%, ** for 5% and * for 10%

period. It may also suggest that GCC managers have become competent at allocating risk and managing uncertainty in their markets.

The overhead ratio has an insignificant effect on bank profitability across all models. This may suggest that GCC banks' operating costs are not high enough to affect their profitability significantly. It may also suggest that GCC banks can control their operating costs and overheads without affecting profitability. The transition from relying on a branch network for business to channels that rely on digital and AI technologies may also help neutralise the adverse effect of costs on profitability.

The coefficients for LIQUIDITY are positive across all specifications but are statistically significant only in the ROA and NIM regressions. This indicates that ROA and NIM increase with liquidity levels. Income diversification has a positive and significant impact on the ROE and ROA estimations. This result is consistent with the findings of DeYoung and Roland (2001), Smith et al. (2003), and Stiroh (2004). Banks that engage in non-interest income activities, driven by the expansion of non-hydrocarbon sectors, tend to perform better.

The dummy variable for Islamic banks is insignificant across all models, suggesting no systematic difference in profitability between Islamic and conventional banks in the GCC. Both banking systems achieve comparable profitability levels due to regulatory harmonisation and market competition.

GDP growth has a positive and significant effect on ROE and ROA, supporting the pro-cyclical nature of bank profitability (Demirgüç-Kunt & Huizinga, 1999; Goddard et al., 2004a; Flamini et al., 2009; Trujillo-Ponce, 2013; Dietrich & Wanzenried, 2014). During periods of economic expansion, banks increase lending, thereby improving their performance. On the other hand, inflation is insignificant in all models, suggesting that monetary policy in the GCC has a neutral effect on bank profitability.

The Rule of Law is insignificant in all models, suggesting that governance in the GCC has no direct impact on bank profitability. This can be attributed to the region's stable and high institutional quality. Ullah et al. (2024) find that the rule of law has adverse, albeit insignificant, effects on financial stability. Ben Naceur and Omran (2011) found that improvements in law and order in the MENA region do not affect bank performance.

The results in Tables 5.16, 5.17 and 5.18 show that all dummy variables controlling for the three significant events of the global financial crisis (DUMMY_Y2009), the oil crisis (DUMMY_Y2015), and the COVID-19 lockdown (DUMMY_Y2020) have insignificant coefficients. This indicates that GCC banks were resilient to significant financial, oil and health shocks. Our results align with those of Erfani and Vasigh (2018), who found that the financial crisis had no significant impact on the profitability of Islamic banks. Bourkhis and Nabi (2013) examine the stability of 34 Islamic banks and 34 commercial banks. The authors found no significant difference in the effect of the recent global financial crisis on the stability of the two types of banks. Similarly, the IMF (2015) reports that the recent 2014–15 oil shock did not significantly affect the profitability of Saudi banks, due to their robust liquidity and capital buffers. Naimy & Kattan (2020) find that the oil price decline in 2014–15 had no significant impact on the profitability indicators of Saudi and Qatari banks. Miyajima (2020) claims that the global oil crisis helped Saudi banks to reduce their holdings of "excess liquidity", enhancing lending growth. In addition, Alhassan et al. (2022) and Alkhazali et al. (2024) find that banks entering the COVID-19 crisis had superior capital and liquidity buffers.

Abdulla and Ebrahim (2024) investigate the effect of COVID-19 on the performance of Islamic and conventional banks in each GCC country separately. The results demonstrate an adverse effect for banks in Saudi Arabia and the UAE, but an insignificant effect for banks in Kuwait and Qatar.

Conclusion

The findings of this study indicate that higher levels of capital, diversification, bank size, market concentration, and economic growth enhance profitability. While credit risk is detrimental, other factors are insignificant. The study suggests that managers and policymakers should focus on enhancing bank-specific factors to improve profitability. For future research, because decisions by their respective sovereigns influence banks, exploring the state ownership-profitability nexus should help prepare the argument for state disengagement from the banking sector.

CHAPTER 6

Impact of ESG on Bank Profitability in GCC Banking

Introduction

In the GCC region, it is highly relevant to examine the relationship between sustainability performance, measured by Environmental, Social, and Governance (ESG) ratings, and the profitability of financial institutions. Over the last decade, several GCC banks have voluntarily or under national government initiatives integrated sustainability principles into their activities. For instance, systemically important banks such as First Gulf Bank, National Bank of Kuwait, Saudi National Bank, and Gulf International Bank have revealed their commitment to increasing their sensitivity to ESG-influenced business models. Nevertheless, while ESG initiatives respond to stakeholder demands, driven by regulators and the green community, it is uncertain whether they serve the interests of bank shareholders. This may imply that adopting ESG creates a conflict between the traditional shareholder-primacy model, which favours value creation for owners, and stakeholder expectations, which regard banks as societal assets serving sustainable goals.

Empirical ESG studies on the stakeholder-shareholder dichotomy yield mixed results. Studies advocating the stakeholder theory argue that ESG engagement has positive effects on bank performance (Scholtens, 2009; Batae, Dragomir, & Feleaga, 2021; Agnese, Cerciello, Oriani, & Teddeo, 2024; Arshed, Bakkar, De Siscto, Iqbal, & Ul-Durar, 2025;

A. Bakhouche, *Banking in the GCC*, Palgrave Macmillan Studies in Banking and Financial Institutions,
https://doi.org/10.1007/978-3-032-21737-0_6

Grau, Castelo-Branco, & Bel-Oms, 2025; Khamisu, Paluri, & Sonwaney, 2024; Liaqat, Floreani, & Naseer, 2026). The effect is channelled through green lending, reputational benefits, social legitimacy, cost efficiencies, lower funding costs, and improved competition. By contrast, supporting Freedom's traditional shareholder doctrine (Friedman, 1970), several studies document negative impact due to implementation costs, information asymmetries and agency conflicts (Yuen et al., 2022; Menicucci & Paolucci, 2023; Wang et al., 2023). Divergent findings reflect variations in methodological approaches, regulatory environments, and institutional maturity. ESG tends to enhance bank performance when supported by strong regulatory frameworks, market incentives, and reputational benefits. However, it may hinder performance in early-stage or compliance-driven settings where costs outweigh potential benefits.

For the GCC countries, empirical evidence is growing but remains limited, constrained by small datasets and, at times, inadequate controls for endogeneity (Al-Jalahma et al., 2020; Michael et al., 2023; Khatatbeh et al., 2025; Srairi, 2025). The disparate progress in ESG policies across the region also contributes to the limited evidence. While the UAE and Saudi Arabia have established regulatory frameworks with mandatory disclosure for most institutions, other GCC states maintain reporting guidelines for systemically important institutions. This study addresses these limitations by analysing 52 GCC banks from 2012 to 2022 using the system GMM. Our findings indicate that, although ESG achievements are not significantly associated with conventional profitability measures (ROA, ROE, NIM), we provide preliminary evidence of the cost implications of ESG and socially responsible governance compliance. We also provide evidence supporting that ESG enhances Islamic banks' profitability, supporting the "*Israf-avoidance*"[1] hypothesis.

The paper proceeds as follows: Sect. "ESG Developments in the GCC" summarises ESG development across GCC countries; Sect. "Theoretical Foundations and ESG Dimensions in the GCC Banking" presents the theoretical framework; Sect. "Literature Review" reviews the relevant literature; Sect. "Methodology" outlines the methodology; Sect. "Empirical Results and Discussion" discusses the empirical results; and Sect. "Conclusion" concludes and offers recommendations.

[1] Iraf is an Arabic for waste.

ESG Developments in the GCC

Saudi Arabia

Saudi Arabia's commitment to sustainable development surfaced in 2016 with the launch of Vision 2030, which promotes economic diversification and decarbonisation (Ali et al., 2025). This policy framework provided the foundation for alignment with international standards in sustainability reporting and practices, climate risk management, and access to sustainable finance for financial and non-financial institutions. Institutions began implementing this framework in 2019, when the Capital Market Authority issued guidelines that organised voluntary sustainability reporting. This was followed by the Saudi Exchange's publication of the ESG Disclosure Guidelines in 2021, which urged listed firms to report on their sustainability practices. In 2025, the Capital Market Authority further published guidelines requiring issuers to subject their green, social, and sustainability-linked instruments to a globally aligned external review. In parallel, the Saudi Central Bank and the Public Investment Fund (PIF) issued further guidelines under the broader Saudi Green Initiative (SGI) to strengthen commitment to environmental goals. Both rely on mobilising private capital, sustainable investments, and international green finance standards to align the Saudi financial sector with climate targets, including 50% renewable energy by 2030 and net-zero by 2060 (Islam & Ali, 2024). The Saudi Central Bank (SAMA) *Sustainable Finance Framework (2021)* focuses on fostering a green economy through two pillars: (i) embedding sustainability into financial decision-making and risk management and (ii) developing a robust market for sustainable financial products. The Public Investment Fund (PIF) *Green Financing Framework (2024)* provides guidelines for the issuance of green bonds and loans, with a focus on channelling funds towards climate-friendly projects, including clean transportation, renewable energy, and sustainable resource management.

These institutional efforts encouraged several banks to integrate ESG principles into their structures, lending policies, and sustainability reporting. For instance, the Saudi National Bank, Saudi Awwal Bank, Al Rajhi Bank, and Riyadh Bank have expanded renewable energy financing through capital mobilisation and the issuance of sustainability-linked sukuk and have expanded female participation in their labour forces.

Despite this progress, ESG adoption remains partially compliance-driven, with long-term financial effects yet to fully emerge.[2]

UAE

The UAE's efforts to build a diversified, environmentally friendly economy capable of achieving social development and quality-of-life goals are enshrined in several national policy frameworks, including the UAE Green Agenda 2030,[3] the National Climate Change Plan (2017–50),[4] and the Net Zero 2050 Strategy.[5] Consequently, the UAE has emerged as the region's largest issuer of green and sustainability-linked bonds, along with Saudi Arabia, with about USD 10 billion in 2025.[6] The UAE accounts for approximately one-third of MENA's green finance issuance, with diverse organisations across the energy, real estate, and financial sectors. In the financial and non-financial sectors, sustainability efforts focus on promoting institutional incentives to adopt ESG principles and on aligning financial and market regulatory frameworks with international recommendations on ESG taxonomies and reporting standards, moving from optional to compulsory adoption. In 2023, the Central Bank of the UAE (CBUAE) issued Guidelines on Sustainable Finance, which explicitly outline its ESG expectations for the banking sector across areas such as sustainability-linked financial instruments, corporate governance, climate risk management, stress testing, and ESG disclosure. The CBUAE aims to mobilise USD 272 billion in sustainable finance by 2030.[7]

Banks have actively aligned with these institutional efforts to integrate sustainability values as a value-creating asset rather than merely a compliance-driven activity. First Abu Dhabi Bank, Emirates NBD, Dubai Islamic Bank, and Mashreq have established sustainability committees and

[2] https://esgmena.com/saudi-arabia-puts-esg-at-the-heart-of-its-economic-agenda/.

[3] https://u.ae/en/about-the-uae/strategies-initiatives-and-awards/strategies-plans-and-visions/environment-and-energy/the-uaes-green-agenda-2030.

[4] https://u.ae/en/about-the-uae/strategies-initiatives-and-awards/strategies-plans-and-visions/environment-and-energy/national-climate-change-plan-of-the-uae.

[5] https://u.ae/en/about-the-uae/strategies-initiatives-and-awards/strategies-plans-and-visions/environment-and-energy/the-uae-net-zero-2050-strategy.

[6] https://www.arabianbusiness.com/gcc/saudi-arabia/saudi-arabia-uae-leads-9-47bn-mena-sustainable-bond-market-in-h1-2025.

[7] https://www.centralbank.ae/en/our-operations/sustainable-finance/.

integrated ESG risk assessments into credit underwriting. While conventional banks have issued green bonds and promoted retail sustainable deposits, Islamic banks have emphasised the sustainability of their Islamic finance and sukuk.[8]

Qatar

Under Qatar National Vision 2030,[9] launched in 2008, Qatar set a long-term goal to mobilise its hydrocarbon-generated financial resources for ESG-based economic diversification, social development, and environmental preservation. The financial sector's contribution to the gradual achievement of ESG goals is institutionally supervised by the Qatar Central Bank (QNB), the Qatar Financial Centre Regulatory Authority (QFCRA), and the country's financial regulator. In 2022, Qatar Financial Centre (QFC)[10] developed a Sustainable Sukuk and Bonds Framework that integrates local ESG disclosure requirements and green finance features with ICMA's globally accepted standards[11] to ensure that sovereign and corporate debt instruments meet their green objectives. In 2025, the QNB issued the Sustainable Finance Strategy (2025)[12] to outline regulatory expectations for banks regarding climate-related risk management, governance, and disclosure. In parallel, the QFCRA introduced the General Rules (Corporate Sustainability Reporting) and the Minor and Technical Amendments Rules 2025 to align with international corporate sustainability reporting standards.[13] Effective from 2026, the Rules require large financial institutions to treat sustainability reporting with the same degree of rigour and governance as traditional financial reporting under the International Sustainability Standards Board

[8] https://www.khaleejtimes.com/uae/cop28-in-uae-how-banks-are-spearheading-sustainability-drive-with-51-billion-in-green-financing.

[9] https://www.gco.gov.qa/en/state-of-qatar/qatar-national-vision-2030/our-story/.

[10] https://www.qfc.qa/-/media/project/qfc/qfcwebsite/documentfiles/publications/research-insights-2022/qfc-sustainable-sukuk-and-bonds-frame-work.pdf.

[11] International Capital Markets Association (ICMA) adopted Green Bond Principles (GBP), Social Bond Principles (SBP), and Sustainable Bond Guidelines (SBG).

[12] https://www.qcb.gov.qa/Documents/Sustainable%20Lending%20-%20English.pdf.

[13] https://www.qfcra.com/news/notification-qfc-regulatory-authority-issues-the-gene-corporate-sustainability-reporting-and-minor-and-technical-amendments-rules-2025/.

(ISSB) IFRS S1 and S2.[14] This regulatory ecosystem, which requires ESG reporting by large banks and allows voluntary reporting by others, has shaped financial institutions' involvement in ESG initiatives through green finance, digital transformation, social responsibility programmes, and alignment with Qatar National Vision 2030. For instance, the Commercial Bank of Qatar (CBQ) issued a $260 million green bond in 2024 for projects in sustainable water management, green buildings, and clean transportation (The Asian Banker, 2024). Qatar National Bank (QNB) supervised the issuance of Qatar's first sovereign green bond, worth USD 2.5 billion, and introduced green residential mortgages (ESG New Survey, 2025). In 2022, Dukhan Bank launched a Shariah-compliant green and sustainable real estate finance programme (The Peninsula, 2022). Additionally, a few banks reported positive results in decarbonisation, financial inclusion, customer satisfaction, and governance. Qatar National Bank,[15] Qatar Islamic Bank,[16] Doha Bank,[17] and Commercial Bank of Qatar[18] have established ESG governance structures, implemented board-level sustainability oversight, and made ESG-related disclosures. Nevertheless, Qatar's ESG transition is shaped by mandatory ESG integration across large institutions, leading to uneven, size-constrained implementation (The Oath, 2025).

Kuwait

The ESG goals of Kuwait are linked to economic diversification, social development, and the expansion of renewable energy, as outlined in the economic vision, New Kuwait 2035, issued in 2017.[19] This development

[14] IFRS S1 (General Requirements for Disclosure of Sustainability-related Financial Information) focuses on general requirements for disclosing material sustainability-related risks and opportunities. IFRS S2 (Climate-related Disclosures) focuses specifically on climate-related risks and opportunities.

[15] https://www.qnb.com/sites/qnb/qnbqatar/page/en/engovernanceandmanagement.html.

[16] https://www.qib.com.qa/wp-content/uploads/2025/07/QIB_SR-2024_Web.pdf.

[17] https://ae.dohabank.com/wp-content/uploads/sites/12/Doha-Bank-Annual-Report-2024-En-V2.pdf.

[18] https://www.cbq.qa/-/media/project/cbq/cbqwebsite/documents/sustainability-reports/cbq-sustainability-report-2024.pdf.

[19] https://www.mofa.gov.kw/en/pages/kuwait-vision-2035.

plan relies on the Central Bank of Kuwait (CBKQ) and the Capital Market Authority (CMA or Boursa Kuwait) to facilitate the integration of ESG goals into the financial sector's institutional ecosystem. Boursa Kuwait issues an ESG Reporting Guide to support transparent, regular ESG reporting by listed firms, as expected by various stakeholders, including investors, customers, suppliers, and regulators.[20] Larger listed firms have been required to transition from optional to mandatory ESG reporting and adopt international standards, such as the Global Reporting Initiative (GRI) or the Integrated Reporting (IR) framework.

The ESG efforts of the banking sector consist of aligning with global sustainability standards and Kuwait's national development goals, integrating ESG into corporate governance, developing sustainable financial products, reducing operational environmental footprints, and promoting social initiatives. Regarding governance, many banks have established dedicated sustainability and climate change committees and subcommittees, with exposure to Board-level oversight, to execute their ESG strategies. This is accompanied by the integration of ESG KPIs into management responsibilities and credit assessment processes for corporate clients, and by alignment with global reporting guidelines, such as the Task Force on Climate-related Financial Disclosures (TCFD) (Hijazeen, 2023). In addition, banks are increasingly offering eco-friendly loans for electric vehicles and housing. Islamic banks, such as Kuwait Finance House (KFH), have developed Sharia-compliant ESG financial products that leverage the alignment between Sharia principles and sustainability goals.[21] In addition, many banks, such as NBK, are increasingly engaged in decarbonisation through recycling, digitalisation, and renewable energy, including solar. The National Bank of Kuwait (NBK) has committed to expanding its sustainable assets from $3.65 billion in 2023 to USD 10 billion by 2030.[22]

Regarding the Social pillar of ESG, women-supportive policies, financial inclusion initiatives, and community engagement are increasingly prevalent in the banking sector. For example, women constitute 35% of the banking sector's workforce and hold approximately 26% of senior

[20] https://www.boursakuwait.com.kw/en/resources/e-publications/esg-reporting-guide.

[21] https://www.kfh.com/en/home/Personal/news/2025/KFH-Highlights-Islamic-Finance-as-a-Catalyst-for-Sustainable-Development-.html.

[22] https://www.nbk.com/sustainability/overview/esg-at-nbk.html.

management roles.[23] NBK, run the "*Diraya*" or "*Let's Be Aware*" campaign to promote financial literacy across society.[24] Kuwait International Bank (KIB) has introduced initiatives, including the *KIB Mubader Centre* and targeted financing, to support domestic entrepreneurship and SMEs.[25] Banks expanded their community engagement to invest in community and charitable programmes. Examples include KIB's "*Iftar Saem*"[26] meal distribution during the holy month of Ramadan and NBK's extensive partnerships with the *LOYAC Foundation* to empower youth.[27]

However, the focus on larger banking institutions has led to uneven, scale-driven adoption of ESG reporting across the broader banking sector (Alremaidhi, 2023).

Bahrain

Bahrain's sustainable efforts are promoted in its Bahrain Economic Vision 2030,[28] launched in 2008, which emphasises justice, competition, institutional governance, private-sector-led growth, human capital development, and environmental protection. The Vision guides Bahrain's transition towards a greener economy through three goals: a 30% reduction in emissions by 2035, a net-zero target for the hydrocarbons sector by 2050, and net-zero emissions by 2060. Achieving these targets would require allocating financial resources to acquire ESG-sensitive technologies, particularly for water desalination, and to develop projects to increase the share of clean, sustainable energy in its power mix. This would require the Central Bank of Bahrain (CBB) and the Bahrain Bourse (BB) to prepare a globally aligned domestic ESG ecosystem for the corporate and

23 https://e.gov.kw/sites/kgoenglish/Pages/ApplicationPages/NewsDetail.aspx?nid=6097695.

24 https://www.nbk.com/kuwait/news-and-insights/media-relations/news.html?news=nbk-supports--let-S-be-aware--campaign-in-raising-awareness-about-the-risks-of-dealing-in-virtual-assets.

25 https://www.kib.com.kw/en/home/Personal/Bank/other-services/KIB-Mubader.html.

26 https://www.kib.com.kw/en/home/Personal/news/news-330.html.

27 https://nbk.com/kuwait/news-and-insights/media-relations/news.html?news=nbk-sponsors-loyac-S--kilma--program-to-empower-youth-through-debate-and-critical-thinking.

28 https://www.mofne.gov.bh/en/project-initiatives/bahrain-economic-vision-2030/.

financial sectors. In 2021, the CBB introduced *ESG Reporting Guidelines*,[29] a regulatory framework that establishes ESG reporting requirements for financial institutions. This was followed by the issuance of the *Bahrain Bourse ESG Reporting Guide*,[30] which recommends optional ESG reporting aligned with global frameworks such as GRI, SASB, and TCFD.[31]

Several banks, including NBB, SICO Bank, Bank ABC, Ahli United Bank, and Bahrain Islamic Bank, are involved in financing renewable energy and social development initiatives, as well as in sustainability and climate-risk reporting. For instance, NBB has a dedicated committee to supervise its ESG initiatives,[32] including reducing its carbon footprint and energy consumption using renewable energy. The Bank supports social infrastructure by funding education projects, social housing initiatives, and youth-empowering sponsorships. Bank ABC adopted ESG principles in its green sukuk and financing of renewable energy projects. It also trains its employees to deepen their understanding of clients' ESG risks,[33] which are considered in the credit approval process. SICO Bank aims to achieve gender balance in its workforce, with the proportion of women employed projected to reach approximately 44% in 2024.[34] Islamic banks have also been focused on developing Sharia-compliant, sustainable instruments to expand the issuance of green and social Sukuk.[35] However, ESG reporting quality and integration across the Bahraini

[29] https://www.cbb.gov.bh/wp-content/uploads/2023/08/ESG-Reporting-Guidelines-Document.pdf.

[30] https://bahrainbourse.com/resources/files/Sustainability/ESG_11%20June%202020.pdf.

[31] The GRI is a globally accepted principles-based approach that encourages engagement with a broader range of stakeholders, including employees, customers, regulators, and the public. SASB helps identify the financial consequences of sustainability-related risks by encouraging the integration of ESG into investment strategies and asset classes. TCFD is a framework for reporting climate-related financial risks. These efforts have advanced the ESG agenda among domestic banks.

[32] https://nbbonline.com/news/14877/.

[33] https://www.bank-abc.com/en/AboutABC/Sustainability/Documents/BH2412025%20Bank%20ABC%20Sustainable%20Finance%20Framework-Final_Digital.pdf.

[34] https://www.sicobank.com/en/our-people.

[35] https://oxfordbusinessgroup.com/reports/kuwait/2024-report/islamic-banks-are-witnessing-the-benefits-of-the-ongoing-regional-and-global-expansion-in-green-financing-overview/

banking sector appear uneven. While leading institutions have increased their ESG engagement, smaller banks have made limited progress (Manju et al., 2024).

Oman

In 2021, Oman launched its economic plan, Vision 2040,[36] which focuses on diversifying the economy by expanding sustainable infrastructure and renewable energy projects. The Vision assigned multiple institutions to support the broader ESG commitment across the real and financial sectors. For instance, the Capital Market Authority (CMA), through the Muscat Stock Exchange (MSX), requires all listed firms to submit a separate sustainability report, in line with the GRI Universal Standards.[37] In 2024, the Central Bank of Oman (CBO) introduced the *Sustainable Finance Framework*[38] and the *Sustainable and Green Financial Practices framework.*[39] Both regulations support banks in integrating ESG risks into credit processes and in promoting sustainable finance instruments to fund ESG-friendly projects, such as green, social, sustainability, and blue loans, bonds, and sukuk, as well as Waqf sukuk. As a result, banks are embedding climate-related risk assessments and conducting stress tests for climate exposure. Larger banks have responded to this policy and regulatory pressures through several initiatives. For instance, Oman's largest bank, Bank Muscat, has established a Sustainability Committee,[40] reported reductions in its own emissions and electricity consumption,[41]

[36] https://www.oman2040.om/?lang=en.

[37] https://www.threepillarsgroup.com/single-blog/the-practical-guide-the-muscat-stock-exchange-msx-sustainability-reporting-requirements.

[38] https://www.mof.gov.om/UploadsAll/ProjectsSectionsTabs/17243240940731704881175957Sustainable%20Finance%20Frameworkcompressed.pdf.

[39] https://cbo.gov.om/sites/assets/Documents/Global/Circulars/2024/2024-10-13%20BM%201208-%20%20Promoting%20Sustainable%20and%20Green%20Finanical%20Practices%20%20-%20Annex%20(Searchable).pdf.

[40] https://www.bankmuscat.com/en/about/SiteAssets/BM_Sustainability_Report_2024_EN.pdf.

[41] https://www.bankmuscat.com/en/about/SiteAssets/SustainabilityReport_2022_Eng.pdf.

and initiated financial literacy programmes and support for SMEs.[42] It is also involved in financing renewable energy and water conservation projects.[43] Sohar International has secured long-term financing for climate-focused projects.[44]

ESG integration across the GCC banking sector has expanded significantly over the past decade. National development visions, alignment with international regulatory frameworks, and growing investor demand for sustainable finance support it. All countries have issued ESG frameworks in line with international standards. However, progress towards a full ESG integration can be categorised into three patterns. First, the UAE and Saudi Arabia made significant progress in institutionalising ESG commitment. Both shifted from optional to mandatory integration, expanding the markets for ESG-compliant financial instruments. Second, Qatar and Bahrain have introduced ESG guidance, but implementation remains optional and confined to leading institutions. Third, Kuwait and Oman have introduced their own regulatory ESG frameworks but remain primarily driven by sovereign national initiatives. Overall, the experience with ESG activities in the GCC banking system indicates that ESG exposure is highly concentrated among large domestic banks with greater international exposure. This may suggest that smaller institutions face constraints related to costs, data availability, and technical expertise (Table 6.1).

Theoretical Foundations and ESG Dimensions in the GCC Banking

According to the Refinitiv methodology that underpins the empirical measures in this study, ESG achievement scores rely on approximately 186 indicators to assess the extent to which banks perform in environmental responsibility (E), social conduct (S), and governance quality (G). The following sections propose hypotheses linking each dimension to bank profitability.

[42] https://www.bankmuscat.com/en/about/csr/Documents/Sustainability_Report__2020_En.pdf.

[43] https://www.zawya.com/en/business/bank-muscat-launches-omans-first-green-finance-scheme-cjfeeoif.

[44] https://ewsdata.rightsindevelopment.org/projects/47713-sohar-international-financing/.

Table 6.1 ESG regulatory and institutional frameworks, and ESG achievements in the GCC banking sector

Country	*National sustainability vision*	*Central bank ESG policies*	*Market-level ESG guidance*	*Environmental achievements (Examples)*	*Social achievements (Examples)*	*Governance Achievements (Examples)*	*Sustainable Finance Instruments*	*Stage of ESG Integration*
UAE	Green Agenda 2030; Net Zero 2050	CBUAE *Guidelines on Sustainable Finance* (2023)	ADGM *Sustainability Disclosure Rules* (2023); DFM ESG Reporting Guide (2020)	FAB issued USD 1.5bn green bonds and financed UAE clean energy projects; ADCB implemented energy-efficient branch operations	Dubai Islamic Bank (DIB) expanded financial inclusion via low-income household financing; Mashreq implemented workforce diversity programmes	Emirates NBD enhanced board oversight and ESG risk-management disclosures, aligning with the GRI and SASB frameworks	Green bonds; sustainability-linked bonds; transition finance	Most advanced; partially mandatory
Saudi Arabia	Vision 2030; Net Zero 2060	SAMA Sustainable Finance Framework (2021)	Tadawul ESG Disclosure Guidelines (2021); CMA TCFD/SASB-aligned guidance	SNB financed large-scale renewable projects; Al Rajhi Bank implemented solar installations and green building upgrades	Saudi Awwal Bank (SAB) invested in financial literacy and SME inclusion programmes	Riyad Bank issued verified sustainability reports and strengthened governance practices under CMA	Green sukuk; sustainability-linked sukuk; green bonds	Advanced, rapidly expanding, compliance-driven

Country	*National sustainability vision*	*Central bank ESG policies*	*Market-level ESG guidance*	*Environmental achievements (Examples)*	*Social achievements (Examples)*	*Governance Achievements (Examples)*	*Sustainable Finance Instruments*	*Stage of ESG Integration*
Qatar	Qatar National Vision 2030	QCB Sustainable & Green Finance Strategy (2022)	QFC ESG Reporting Framework (2021)	QNB invested in solar PV financing and sustainable infrastructure; Masraf Al Rayan reduced operational emissions	QIB community programmes, SME social financing, QNB workforce well-being initiatives	QNB produced TCFD-aligned disclosures; Doha Bank advanced risk governance reforms	Green bonds; sustainability-linked loans	Moderately advanced; concentrated in top-tier banks
Kuwait	New Kuwait Vision 2035	CBK voluntary ESG disclosure guidance	Boursa Kuwait ESG Guide (2021)	Kuwait Finance House (KFH) developed Shariah-based green-financing products; NBK provided renewable energy project loans	NBK launched financial education initiatives and women's empowerment programmes	KFH strengthened Shariah governance and GRI-linked reporting	Limited green sukuk; sustainability reporting	Developing; institution-led

(continued)

Table 6.1 (continued)

Country	*National sustainability vision*	*Central bank ESG policies*	*Market-level ESG guidance*	*Environmental achievements (Examples)*	*Social achievements (Examples)*	*Governance Achievements (Examples)*	*Sustainable Finance Instruments*	*Stage of ESG Integration*
Bahrain	Economic Vision 2030	CBB ESG Reporting Guidelines (2021)	Bahrain Bourse ESG Guidance (2020)	Bank ABC financed renewable energy and carbon-saving projects; Bahrain Islamic Bank introduced green operations	Ahli United Bank supported community health and inclusion projects	Bank ABC published comprehensive ESG governance disclosures	Green sukuk; social financing	Moderate; voluntary ESG adoption
Oman	Oman Vision 2040	CBO Sustainable Finance Framework (2023)	FSA (formerly CMA) sustainability guidance	Bank Muscat issued green loans for residential solar; Oman Arab Bank invested in water conservation projects	Bank Muscat SME support programmes; community development funds	Oman Arab Bank enhanced governance via ESG risk integration and transparent reporting	Green loans; early sustainability-linked products	Early-stage; capacity-building

Environmental Performance (E) and Bank Profitability

The environmental dimension includes measures to reduce the ecological footprint, mitigate climate-related risks, and support decarbonised economic activities. It considers the degree of resource efficiency, lending policies towards environmentally intensive sectors, and the provision of green financial instruments. In the literature, Albertini (2013) and Gangi et al. (2019) find a positive relationship between environmental performance and financial performance. Huang (2019) indicates that environmental factors have a more pronounced effect on financial performance than social or governance factors.

Two theoretical frameworks may support the positive impact of environmental policies on bank performance. First, the Resource-Based View (RBV) holds that environmental resources, including energy-efficient processes, climate-risk mitigation systems, and green-financing expertise, constitute assets that enhance a bank's financial performance and competitive advantage (Cao, Zhu, & Yu, 2024; dos Reis Cardillo & Cruz Basso, 2025). Second, Stakeholder theory suggests that the size of environmental assets signals a commitment to other stakeholders' interests, thereby improving profitability by strengthening stakeholder confidence, market share, and reputation. By contrast, Agency Theory (Jensen & Meckling, 1976) and Shareholder wealth (Friedman, 1970) predict that overinvestment in environmental initiatives may negatively affect profitability and efficiency. This occurs because managers may pursue non-financial objectives at the expense of the shareholders (Friedman, 1970).

In the GCC, the decarbonisation plans contained in national development strategies, such as the UAE Net Zero 2050 and Saudi Vision 2030, provide banks with regulatory and reputational incentives to enhance cost-saving environmental performance. These may support a positive link between environmental achievement and bank performance. Hence, the first hypothesis is as follows:

H1: Environmental performance positively influences the financial performance of GCC banks.

Social Performance (S) and Bank Profitability

The social dimension focuses on banks' contributions to the nation's social development, including ethical lending, financial education, customer protection, and workforce diversity. Several studies have identified a positive link between social engagement and bank performance, driven by strong stakeholder orientation (Wu & Shen, 2013; Belasri et al., 2020), supporting the stakeholder theory (Freeman, 1984). Social investments generate intangible assets—such as reputation, trust, and loyalty—that strengthen legitimacy and alignment with societal goals (Campbell, 2007; Cheung et al., 2020). However, the impact of the social factor on bank performance is not always positive. Menicucci and Paolucci (2023) suggest that managers who focus on serving other stakeholders' interests would lead to increased bank cost inefficiencies and information asymmetries. This is consistent with the predictions of Shareholder and Agency Theories that corporate social policies may reflect managerial preferences rather than value creation for shareholders.

In the GCC, banks' focus on social investment appears to be driven by family- and state-linked expectations, religious compliance, and financial inclusion activities (Khémiri et al., 2024). These conditions may affect the relevance of social commitments to bank performance. Therefore, the second hypothesis is formulated:

> H2: Social performance positively affects the financial performance of GCC banks.

Governance Quality (G) and Bank Profitability

The governance practices encompass board composition, oversight effectiveness, risk governance, ethics, and transparency. Under agency theory, sound governance should improve profitability by enhancing internal monitoring and reducing moral hazard through aligning managerial incentives with shareholder interests (Macey & Hara, 2003). Several studies show that board independence (Rashid, 2018), gender diversity (Giráldez-Puig & Samaniego-Medina, 2025; Sahu et al., 2025), audit quality (Nguyen & & Nguyen, 2024; Gyimah & Owusu-Afriyie, 2025), and non-executive oversight (Harkin et al., 2020) improve firm performance. In the GCC, the governance regimes are characterised by concentrated ownership, state influence, and cross-board memberships

(Faqera et al., 2025). Accordingly, we may argue that governance is expected to strengthen bank performance. The following hypothesis is tested:

H3: Governance quality is positively associated with bank financial performance in the GCC.

ESG Combined and Financial Profitability

The ESG Combined measure aggregates the impact of the three individual dimensions: Environmental, Social, and Governance. Theoretically, higher-quality sustainability practices should enhance bank profitability by reducing risk (Cantero-Saiz et al., 2024), lowering the cost of capital (Raza et al., 2024), generating reputational gains (Singh & Misra, 2021), and improving market power and operational efficiency (Torre-Olmo et al., 2021). Theoretically, the Resource-Based View (RBV) suggests that ESG commitments generate intangible assets, while Stakeholder and Legitimacy theories emphasise compliance with institutional and stakeholder influences. The Agency and Shareholder perspectives contend that ESG engagement creates moral hazard, diverting managers from serving owners' interests. The Cost–Benefit Theory argues that ESG investments involve upfront costs that can reduce short-term profitability and hurt owners. The literature provides mixed empirical evidence. While Buallay (2019) documents a positive ESG-performance relation in Europe, Buallay (2020) finds a neutral or negative effect globally.

In the GCC banking system, ESG practices remain in the early stages of adoption and investment, thereby limiting their positive impact on bank performance. However, the literature suggests that ESG policies have a positive impact on bank profitability. Therefore, we test the following hypothesis:

H4: ESG combined performance is positively associated with the financial performance of GCC banks.

Interaction Between ESG and Islamic Banking

Given the substantial alignment between Shariah principles and the objectives underlying ESG, Islamic banks may employ sustainability practices as an extension of their ethical mandates, emphasising responsible conduct, risk-sharing, and resource preservation (Khamisu et al., 2025). From a resource-based perspective, Islamic banks employ their Shariah governance systems, ethical screening mechanisms, and reputational capital to lower the marginal cost of adopting ESG practices (Milena & Stefan, 2025), and create economies of scope between sustainability activities and religious mandates (Shalhoob, 2025). In this context, ESG engagement may improve cost efficiency and enhance stakeholder trust, thereby increasing financial performance (PwC, 2022). Based on the principles of Maqasid al-Sharia (Salin & Ali, 2025), we propose the **Israf-Avoidance Hypothesis**, which posits that ESG initiatives aligned with the prohibition of waste (*israf*) and the requirement of honest conduct can operate as strategic assets for Islamic banks.

Conversely, an alternative view emphasises the possibility of a deterioration in cost efficiency arising from ESG adoption (Alghafes et al., 2024). Islamic banks already operate within extensive compliance structures, and the introduction of ESG frameworks may impose additional documentation requirements, reporting burdens, and layered governance mechanisms to ensure consistency between ESG practices and Shariah principles (Milena & Stefan, 2025). This **Islamic Compliance-Cost Hypothesis** suggests that the need to harmonise ESG processes with religious governance may generate incremental expenses that offset, or even outweigh, financial gains (Pujiastuti et al., 2024). Taken together, these competing channels suggest that ESG may exert differential effects across conventional and Islamic banks. Reflecting the empirical evidence that Islamic banks respond uniquely to ESG engagement, the following hypothesis is proposed:

> H5: The interaction between ESG performance and Islamic bank status positively influences bank financial performance.

Interaction Between Bank Size and ESG Performance

Bank size may be a significant moderating factor in the ESG-performance relationship (Njuguna et al., 2025). Smaller banks may lack sufficient resources and organisational infrastructure to profit from ESG activities. By contrast, larger banks exhibit higher economies of scale, greater access to capital, broader stakeholder visibility, and high-quality risk management and governance systems (Bolibok, 2024). These advantages may enable them to improve profitability by reducing reputational risks and absorbing ESG-related costs. The resource-based view predicts that size advantages make it easier for larger banks to access the resources needed to promote ESG engagement. Stakeholder and legitimacy theories argue that larger institutions use ESG incentives to enhance their reputational capital with different internal and external stakeholders (Itan et al., 2025). Consistent with global evidence (Yuen et al., 2022; Pham & Nguyen, 2025), ESG engagement may be more profitable for larger banks than smaller banks. The following hypothesis is formulated:

> H6: Bank size positively moderates the relationship between ESG performance and financial performance.

Literature Review

The empirical literature on the relationship between ESG engagement and bank performance can be divided into two principal strands. The first reports a positive association between ESG strategies and financial outcomes. A landmark meta-analysis by Friede et al. (2015), synthesising evidence from approximately 2,000 empirical studies, concludes that ESG achievements are most often positively or neutrally related to financial performance. Several banking-specific studies corroborate this view. Brogi and Lagasio (2019) document that environmental factors positively influence the ROA of US banks. Similarly, Shakil et al. (2019) find a favourable association between ESG and financial performance using a sample of 93 banks from emerging markets. El Khoury et al. (2021) report that ESG scores positively affect ROE and ROA for 46 listed international banks. Torre-Olmo et al. (2021) show that banks adopting the United Nations Principles for Responsible Banking achieve higher profitability, while Gurol and Lagasio (2022) find that governance-related features—such as board size, gender diversity, and board independence—are positively associated with bank profitability.

The second strand reveals insignificant or negative impacts of ESG on bank performance. Yuen et al. (2022), drawing on data from 487 banks in 51 countries, report that stronger social and governance engagement tends to reduce profitability, interpreting ESG investments as compliance costs rather than as value-creating activities. Di Tommaso and Thornton (2020) show that ESG efforts in large European banks depress both market and book value, owing to their cost-intensive nature, supporting the overinvestment view of ESG. Menicucci and Paolucci (2023) similarly document a negative relationship between ESG performance and performance among Italian banks. Agnese et al. (2024) find that European banks with high exposure to ESG controversies paradoxically exhibit stronger profitability ratios, while Bătae et al. (2021) report that improvements in governance, environmental costs, and product responsibility adversely affect financial performance. Harkin et al. (2020) find no significant effect of governance on ROA for US banks. Recent studies extend this insight. Lamanda and Tamásné (2024) show that banks in the Visegrad region tend to embrace sustainability for financial motives, yet ESG disclosure lacks demonstrable links to performance. Humaidan and Naser (2025) find that ESG hurts NIM in British banks, with environmental scores reducing both ROE and NIM. Using data from 384 banks across 62 countries, Pyka et al. (2025) demonstrate that the implementation costs of ESG activities reduce ROA and ROE, primarily through the social and governance channels. Yuen et al. (2022), in a GMM framework, further uncover a U-shaped ESG-profitability relationship, suggesting that while ESG may initially reduce profitability, long-term gains may emerge once a threshold of sustainability investment is reached.

Several studies examine the mechanisms through which ESG affects bank performance. Cantero-Saiz (2025) argues that ESG generates value through improved reputation, investor confidence, and customer loyalty. Wen et al. (2025) highlight ESG's ability to influence bank risk-taking through reputational channels and information asymmetry, though higher implementation costs may offset these benefits. Evidence also supports a positive relationship between ESG and risk. Cantero-Saiz et al. (2024) find that ESG strategies reduce non-performing loans among 96 major banks. Di Tommaso and Thornton (2020) similarly show that ESG scores are associated with lower risk-taking. Chiaramonte et al. (2022) find that stronger ESG engagement improves bank stability, especially during financial crises. Several studies emphasise efficiency channels. Azmi et al. (2021) show that ESG improves profitability by reducing cost inefficiencies across emerging markets. Agnese et al. (2023) report that ESG reduces banks' cost of capital and supports long-term profitability. Liang et al. (2024) and Algeri et al. (2025) find that ESG promotes long-run efficiency, despite higher upfront expenses. Nguyen et al. (2025) identify governance as a key driver of efficiency in Vietnamese banks, while social initiatives are beneficial only when supported by diversified income structures.

The moderating role of country, firm, and market characteristics has also been explored. Cantero-Saiz et al. (2025) show that national sustainability achievements shape the ESG-profitability relationship across 159 banks in 42 economies. In developing countries, the relationship shifts from negative to insignificant, and ultimately to positive, as national sustainability improves. Other moderators include liquidity (Ahmad et al., 2025), which appears to have no meaningful moderating effect, and size, which Shakil et al. (2024) find to influence the link between ESG pillars and stock returns across MENA banks. Alqudah et al. (2025) document that ESG and FinTech integration can jointly depress short-term financial performance.

Research focusing on the GCC and Islamic banking sectors remains limited but is expanding. Drawing on data from 48 GCC banks, Sraiti (2025) finds that ESG commitments reduce profitability, but the negative impact weakens for Islamic banks, partly due to the mediating role of FinTech adoption. Sendi et al. (2024) show that environmental practices matter for conventional banks, whereas the social pillar is more relevant to the stability of Islamic banks. Alam et al. (2022) report that environmental scores enhance cost efficiency for Islamic banks. Alghafes et al. (2024) find that ESG scores of 29 GCC Islamic banks do not significantly affect overall financial performance, although social and governance factors correlate with profitability. Nizam et al. (2019) find no significant differences in the relationship between ESG and performance between Islamic and conventional banks. Michael et al. (2023) show that ESG scores are negatively associated with ROA among GCC banks due to high implementation costs. Smaoui et al. (2025) find that ESG improves performance in both Islamic and conventional banks in dual-banking systems, with governance being more significant for Islamic banks. Yudaruddin et al. (2025) show that ESG risks have a more adverse effect on Islamic banks than on conventional ones in Indonesia.

The mixed empirical evidence suggests that the financial effects of ESG engagement depend on bank characteristics, institutional conditions, and the maturity of sustainability frameworks. Positive ESG–profitability findings tend to occur where disclosure regimes, market incentives, and stakeholder demand are well developed; null or negative results are more common where ESG adoption is compliance-driven and cost-intensive. Against this backdrop, the present study tests four core hypotheses: H1–H3 posit that the environmental, social and governance pillars (respectively) are positively associated with bank performance only when institutional and operational conditions enable profit-making; H4 posits that the composite ESG score is positively associated with performance once ESG investments cross a materiality threshold.

Additionally, building on the literature that emphasises heterogeneity by bank type, the study proposes the *israf-avoidance hypothesis*. This indicates that Islamic banks are more likely than conventional banks to translate ESG engagement into profits, owing to embedded ethical mandates and dual monitoring structures (H5). Finally, based on studies that identify size as a moderator of ESG effects, the analysis tests whether bank size moderates the ESG-profitability nexus in the GCC banking (H6). Owing to greater resources and diversification, larger banks are expected to absorb initial ESG costs more effectively and realise efficiency and reputational gains. In contrast, smaller banks may face diminishing returns from extensive ESG commitments. These hypotheses, therefore, synthesise prior empirical findings and theoretical perspectives (RBV, stakeholder, and agency frameworks) and set the stage for testing heterogeneous ESG effects across pillars, bank types, and scales in the GCC context.

Methodology

Sample and Data

The sample comprises all banks in the GCC region for which at least three consecutive years of financial and ESG data are available in Refinitiv Eikon (Thomson Reuters). Institutions with missing financial data are excluded to avoid bias from incomplete records. The final dataset comprises 52 banks—17 Islamic and 35 conventional—operating across the six GCC countries during 2012–2022. Including both banking types enables the analysis to capture heterogeneous ESG-performance mechanisms in dual-banking environments, a key structural feature of the GCC financial system.

Baseline Regression Model

The empirical specification examining the relationship between ESG performance and bank profitability is grounded in the dealership model of Ho and Saunders (1981) and follows previous banking studies summarised in Table 6.2. The baseline model is expressed as:

$$\begin{aligned} PROFITABILITY_{i,t} = \beta_0 + \beta_1 PROFITABILITY_{i,t-1} \\ + \beta_2 ESG_{i,t} + \beta_3 SIZE_{i,t} + \beta_4 CAPITAL_{i,t} \\ + \beta_5 LIQUIDITY_{i,t} + \beta_6 CREDIT_{i,t} \\ + \beta_7 GROWTH_{i,t} + \beta_8 ISLAMIC_{i,t} \\ + \beta_9 COVID_{i,t} + \mu_i + \lambda_t + \varepsilon_{i,t} \end{aligned} \quad (6.1)$$

In Eq. (6.1), we distinguish between three sets of variables.

First, PROFITABILITY is proxied by ROA, ROE, and NIM, for bank i in year t. ROE captures shareholder returns, ROA reflects operational efficiency relative to asset size, and NIM measures intermediation margins and pricing power. Using multiple profitability indicators strengthens robustness (Buallay, 2019; Batae et al., 2021; Menicucci & Paolucci, 2023). To address profit persistence and potential endogeneity, profitability is lagged by one period.

Second, ESG refers to the combined and pillar-level (environmental, social, governance) scores published by Refinitiv, based on roughly 186 indicators across ten thematic categories. The scores assess a bank's exposure to environmental, social, and governance risks and its effectiveness in managing them relative to peers. Letter-grade ratings are converted to a numerical scale from 1 (D–) to 11 (A). Higher ESG scores may enhance reputation, reduce financing costs, and improve profitability, although ESG investments can also generate additional costs that dampen returns (Ullman, 1985).

Third, SIZE is measured by total assets. Larger banks may benefit from economies of scale (Smirlock, 1985), although size can also reduce profitability due to higher monitoring and bureaucratic costs (Pasiouras & Kosmidou, 2007). CAPITAL is the equity-to-assets ratio, LIQUIDITY is liquid assets relative to total assets, and CREDIT risk is proxied by loan loss provisions to total loans. GROWTH captures each country's annual real GDP growth. COVID is a dummy equal to 1 in 2020 and 2021, capturing pandemic-related disruptions.

Table 6.2 Summary of recent empirical studies on ESG and bank performance

Author(s)	*Country, data, and period*	*Methodology*	*Dependent variable*	*Key control variables*	*Main findings*
Nizam et al. (2019)	713 banks from 75 countries over the period 2013–2015	Panel regression	ROA, ROE	Ownership, capital	No difference between Islamic and conventional banks
Brogi and Lagasio (2019)	36 listed European banks, 2011–2016	Panel regression	ROA, ROE, Tobin's Q	Size, leverage, liquidity	ESG disclosure improves performance, with the most potent effect on ROA
Di Tommaso and Thornton (2020)	19 European banks (2007–2018)	Fixed effects	Tobin's Q, market value	Size, leverage	ESG reduces market and book value due to the cost burden
Di Franco et al. (2020)	Global listed banks	Panel regression	Profitability	Risk, size	Underinvestment in ESG harms profitability by increasing reputational risk
Azmi et al. (2021)	251 banks, 44 emerging markets (2011–2017)	System GMM, 2SLS	ROA, ROE, NIM, TQ	Size, CAR, NPLs, GDP	ESG improves profitability and efficiency, but diminishing returns set in beyond a threshold
Chiaramonte et al. (2022)	84 European banks (2005–2017)	IV-2SLS	Distance to Default	Risk, liquidity, regulation	ESG reduces fragility; the social pillar is the most influential

Author(s)	*Country, data, and period*	*Methodology*	*Dependent variable*	*Key control variables*	*Main findings*
Alam et al. (2022)	98 Islamic & conventional banks incl. GCC (2010–2019)	SFA, GMM	Efficiency	Size, macro	The environmental pillar improves Islamic bank efficiency
Yuen et al. (2022)	487 banks, 51 countries (2006–2021)	System GMM	ROA, ROE, TQ	Bank structure, macro	Social and governance scores reduce profitability; U-shaped ESG-profitability link
Agnese et al. (2023)	63 European banks, 2006–2021	Panel regression	ROA, cost of capital	Size, leverage, GDP	ESG lowers the cost of capital and enhances profitability
Menicucci and Paolucci (2023)	105 Italian banks (2016–2020)	FE/RE	ROA, ROE, TQ	Size, deposits, capital	ESG negatively affects performance; systems remain immature
Michael et al. (2023)	29 GCC banks (2010–2022)	OLS, FE/RE	ROA	Size, LLPs, GDP	ESG is negatively associated with ROA due to high implementation costs
Alghafes et al. 2024	GCC Islamic banks	Panel regression	ROE, ROA, TQ	Bank-specific	ESG insignificant overall; social positive; governance improves ROE; environmental increases TQ
Gutiérrez-Ponce and Wibowo (2024)	19 banks from Southeast Asia for 2010–20	Panel regression methods: OLS, FE, GLS	ROE, ROA, TQ	Size, debt to equity ratio	ESG has a significant adverse effect on all profitability indicators
Liang et al. (2024)	55 European banks (2010–2020)	SFA + regression	Cost efficiency	Size, risk	ESG enhances cost efficiency
Sendi et al. (2024)	Islamic vs conventional GCC banks	GMM	Z-score	Size, CAR	The social pillar stabilises Islamic banks; the environmental pillar stabilises conventional

(continued)

Table 6.2 (continued)

Author(s)	*Country, data, and period*	*Methodology*	*Dependent variable*	*Key control variables*	*Main findings*
Cantero-Saiz et al. (2025)	159 banks (42 countries)	GMM	ROAA, ROAE	Sustainability index, size, capital, risk, macro	ESG harms profitability in low-sustainability economies; the effect reverses in high-sustainability settings
Humaidan and Naser (2025)	12 UK banks, 2015–2022	GLS	ROA, ROE, NIM	Bank-specific	ESG and the environmental pillar reduce NIM; the environmental pillar reduces ROE
Smaoui et al. (2025)	67 banks in 13 dual-banking systems (2009–2019)	GMM	ROA, ROE, NIM	CAR, size, macro	ESG improves performance; governance is most relevant for Islamic banks
Srairi (2025)	48 GCC commercial banks (2013–2022)	GMM, mediation analysis	ROA, ROE	Size, liquidity, capital, macro	ESG negatively affects performance; FinTech strengthens the ESG-profitability channel, particularly for Islamic banks
Yudaruddin et al. (2025)	148 Indonesian banks (2003–2022)	Panel regression	ROA, ROE, NIM	Size, CAR, liquidity	ESG risk reduces profitability, with more substantial adverse effects for Islamic banks

The terms μ_i and λ_t denote bank-specific and time-specific fixed effects, respectively, and $\varepsilon_{i,t}$ is the idiosyncratic error.

Interaction-Effect Models

ESG × ISLAMIC Banks Interaction Model

To examine whether ESG affects Islamic and conventional banks differently (Uracil, 2019; Smaoui et al., 2025), the following model is estimated:

$$\begin{aligned} PROFITABILITY_{i,t} = {} & \beta_0 + \beta_1 PROFITABILITY_{i,t-1} \\ & + \beta_2 ESG_{i,t} + \beta_3 SIZE_{i,t} + \beta_{28}(ESG_{i,t} x ISLAMIC_{i,t}) \\ & + \beta_4 CAPITAL_{i,t} + \beta_5 LIQUIDITY_{i,t} + \beta_6 CREDIT_{i,t} \\ & + \beta_7 GROWTH_{i,t} + \beta_8 ISLAMIC_{i,t} \\ & + \beta_9 COVID_{i,t} + \mu_i + \lambda_t + \varepsilon_{i,t} \end{aligned} \tag{6.2}$$

In Eq. 6.2, β_2 captures the ESG effect for conventional banks, β_{28} captures the differential ESG effect for Islamic banks, and $(\beta_2 + \beta_{28})$ gives the total effect for Islamic institutions. In line with Hypothesis 5, and consistent with stakeholder, legitimacy, and Sharia-compliance perspectives, the model evaluates whether Islamic banks derive distinct performance benefits from ESG commitments.

ESG × SIZE Interaction Model

To test whether bank size moderates the ESG-profitability relationship, the following specification is estimated:

$$\begin{aligned} PROFITABILITY_{i,t} = {} & \beta_0 + \beta_1 PROFITABILITY_{i,t-1} \\ & + \beta_2 ESG_{i,t} + \beta_3 SIZE_{i,t} + \beta_{23}(ESG_{i,t} x SIZE_{i,t}) \\ & + \beta_4 CAPITAL_{i,t} + \beta_5 LIQUIDITY_{i,t} \\ & + \beta_6 CREDIT_{i,t} + \beta_7 GROWTH_{i,t} \\ & + \beta_8 ISLAMIC_{i,t} + \beta_9 COVID_{i,t} + \mu_i + \lambda_t + \varepsilon_{i,t} \end{aligned} \tag{6.3}$$

Equation 6.3 evaluates whether larger banks benefit more from ESG implementation or whether diseconomies and overinvestment costs outweigh the benefits. The coefficient on the interaction term,6_{23}, measures the moderating effect. If B6_{23} > 0, then larger banks derive greater benefits from ESG, consistent with RBV and stakeholder theory.

Larger banks may exhibit economies of scale in ESG implementation, reputational visibility, regulatory pressure, and resource availability. However, if $\beta_{23} < 0$, larger banks experience diseconomies or overinvestment costs, consistent with agency theory.

Equations 6.1, 6.2, and 6.3 are estimated using the two-step System GMM estimator. This approach accommodates unobserved heterogeneity, profit persistence, dynamic endogeneity, autocorrelation, and simultaneity. Lagged levels and differences of the endogenous regressors serve as instruments, while time and country dummies are treated as exogenous.

Table 6.3 summarises the definition and measurement of the dependent and independent variables. It also explains the expected relationship with the dependent variable.

Empirical Results and Discussion

Descriptive Statistics

Table 6.4 presents descriptive statistics for 279 bank-year observations from 54 GCC banks for 2012–22. ESG performance is moderate, with a mean ESG Combined score of 5.13, corresponding to a mid-range "C" rating under the Refinitiv scale. Governance emerges as the strongest pillar (mean 7.36, "B–"), whereas the Environmental dimension is comparatively weak (mean 3.22, "D+"). Profitability indicators suggest a generally healthy banking system, with a mean ROE of 12.4% and a mean ROA of 1.5%. Banks also exhibit relatively strong capitalisation, liquidity, and credit-risk positions.

The distributional moments indicate considerable heterogeneity across institutions. ROE displays strong negative skewness (–1.52) and excess kurtosis (7.81), indicating that while most banks report positive earnings, some report negative earnings. Total assets are markedly right-skewed (2.02), reflecting the dominance of several large banks within the GCC market structure. Credit-risk provisions are similarly skewed (2.27) with elevated kurtosis (7.28), indicating that loan-quality deterioration is concentrated among a limited subset of banks. Retained earnings also exhibit negative skewness (–1.12), consistent with the presence of banks that accumulate persistent earnings deficits.

Table 6.3 Variable definitions and measurement

Variable	*Definition*	*Measurement/ Formula*	*Rationale/Expected effect*
ROE	Return on Equity	Net income/ Shareholders' equity	Captures profitability to owners; sensitive to leverage and capital structure
ROA	Return on Assets	Net income/Total assets	Measures operating profitability and asset-use efficiency. Often used in banking studies owing to its stability
NIM	Net Interest Margin	Net interest income/Total assets	Reflects intermediation efficiency and pricing power
ESG Combined	Overall ESG performance	Refinitiv ESG Combined score (186 indicators across 10 categories)	Captures aggregate sustainability commitment; widely used in ESG-performance literature
Environmental (E)	Environmental practices	Refinitiv environmental pillar score (resource use, emissions, innovation)	Reflects environmental stewardship; expected to affect risk, cost efficiency, and long-term returns
Social (S)	Workforce, human rights, community impact	Refinitiv social pillar score	Influences labour productivity, reputational capital, and community engagement
Governance (G)	Board quality and organisational governance	Refinitiv governance pillar score	Strong governance is associated with lower risk-taking and improved performance
SIZE	Bank size	Total assets	Larger banks have economies of scale, visibility, and greater capacity for ESG investment
CAPITAL	Capital risk	Equity/Total assets	Well-capitalised banks exhibit lower risk and more stable profitability
LIQUIDITY	Liquidity risk	Liquid assets/ Total assets	Reflects bank risk appetite and liquidity management
LLPs	Credit risk	Loan loss provisions/Total assets	Captures asset quality; higher LLP indicates higher credit risk

(continued)

Table 6.3 (continued)

Variable	*Definition*	*Measurement/ Formula*	*Rationale/Expected effect*
GROWTH	Macroeconomic conditions	Annual real GDP growth rate	Stronger growth environments generally improve bank performance
RE	Retained earnings ratio	Total retained earnings to total profit	A measure of organic growth
ISLAMIC	Islamic banking	1 = Islamic bank; 0 = Conventional bank	Allows testing for differential ESG effects in dual-banking systems
COVID	Time-specific shocks	1 = Year 2020, 0 = otherwise	Controls for the COVID-19 effects

Table 6.4 Descriptive statistics for the full sample

	Mean	*Std Dev*	*Min*	*Max*	*Skewness*	*Kurtosis*
No. of banks: 54, No. of obs: 281						
Profitability						
ROE	0.124	0.056	−0.464	0.292	−1.52	7.81
ROA	0.015	0.007	−0.029	0.040	−0.83	4.02
NIM	0.024	0.005	0.011	0.043	0.45	0.84
ESG variables						
ESG Combined	5.13	2.21	1.00	11.00	0.42	−0.51
Environmental	3.22	2.41	1.00	10.00	0.87	0.17
Social	4.41	2.43	1.00	11.00	0.54	−0.33
Governance	7.36	2.47	1.00	12.00	−0.14	−0.67
Control variables						
Total Assets (bn)	57.23	64.89	2.70	300.16	2.02	4.31
Capital Ratio	0.126	0.025	0.034	0.210	0.58	0.26
Liquidity	0.089	0.050	0.005	0.278	1.23	1.52
PPLs	0.009	0.010	−0.009	0.059	2.27	7.28
RE Ratio	0.056	0.027	−0.203	0.212	−1.12	6.83
GDP Growth	0.013	0.037	−0.093	0.084	−0.77	0.45

Table 6.5 presents the means and standard deviations for Islamic and conventional banks (Panel 1) and for size-based groups (Panel 2). Islamic banks score higher on governance (7.74 vs 7.22), consistent with Sharia-based oversight and decision-making structures. Conversely, conventional

banks outperform in the Environmental and Social dimensions, yielding a marginally higher ESG Combined score (5.20 vs 4.93). Profitability levels between the two groups are broadly similar.

In Panel 2, ESG performance increases substantially with bank size. Large banks report the highest ESG Combined scores (5.45), with stronger performance across all ESG pillars, particularly environmental indicators. Profitability also rises with size: large banks exhibit higher ROE (0.135) and ROA (0.016), lower LLPs, and higher retained earnings. These patterns are consistent with economies of scale and scope in the GCC banking sector.

Correlation

Table 6.6 presents the correlation matrix. ROE and ROA are almost perfectly correlated ($r = 0.964$, $p < 0.01$), indicating that both capture similar dimensions of bank profitability. NIM shows a positive correlation with ROA ($r = 0.503$, $p < 0.01$), underscoring the importance of intermediary activities in shaping performance. Credit-risk provisions exhibit strong negative correlations with ROA and ROE (both –0.75, $p < 0.01$), confirming that deteriorating asset quality has a detrimental impact on profitability.

The ESG Combined score is highly correlated with its underlying pillars (environmental: 0.759; social: 0.888; governance: 0.746; all $p < 0.01$), indicating that the composite measure captures broad variation across sustainability dimensions. However, ESG measures show no significant correlation with profitability indicators. This may suggest that ESG engagement has not yet yielded measurable profitability effects in GCC banks, consistent with the emerging neutrality hypothesis in early- to mid-stage ESG environments.

Bank size is positively correlated with ROA (0.374, $p < 0.05$) and all ESG pillars, suggesting that larger institutions exhibit both stronger financial performance and greater capacity to invest in ESG activities. The Islamic-bank dummy correlates positively with NIM (0.311, $p < 0.05$) and negatively with capitalisation and ESG scores, particularly the social pillar, indicating that Islamic banks may still be converging towards international ESG disclosure standards.

Table 6.5 Mean and standard deviation (between brackets) of the dependent and independent variables for bank type and size groups

	Panel 1: Bank type		*Panel 2: Size*		
Variable	*Islamic*	*Conventional*	*Small*	*Medium*	*Large*
Profitability					
ROE	0.124 (0.054)	0.124 (0.057)	0.104 (0.052)	0.123 (0.056)	0.135 (0.055)
ROA	0.014 (0.007)	0.015 (0.007)	0.012 (0.006)	0.015 (0.007)	0.016 (0.007)
NIM	0.025 (0.005)	0.024 (0.005)	0.023 (0.004)	0.024 (0.005)	0.024 (0.005)
ESG Scores					
ESG Combined	4.93 (2.16)	5.20 (2.23)	4.86 (2.16)	4.89 (2.15)	5.45 (2.24)
Environmental	2.76 (2.22)	3.37 (2.45)	2.96 (2.24)	2.91 (2.24)	3.56 (2.56)
Social	4.07 (2.38)	4.52 (2.44)	4.11 (2.31)	4.14 (2.34)	4.75 (2.50)
Governance	7.74 (2.44)	7.22 (2.47)	7.20 (2.51)	7.16 (2.48)	7.59 (2.43)
Control variables					
Total Assets (bn)	51.23 (59.12)	59.35 (66.79)	12.35 (8.91)	31.57 (18.45)	112.46 (82.12)
Capital Ratio	0.130 (0.027)	0.125 (0.024)	0.132 (0.026)	0.128 (0.025)	0.121 (0.024)
Liquidity	0.077 (0.042)	0.093 (0.052)	0.088 (0.050)	0.087 (0.049)	0.091 (0.051)
PPLs	0.008 (0.009)	0.009 (0.010)	0.011 (0.011)	0.009 (0.010)	0.008 (0.009)
Retained Earnings (RE) ratio	0.050 (0.027)	0.058 (0.027)	0.052 (0.027)	0.055 (0.026)	0.059 (0.027)
GDP Growth	0.019 (0.034)	0.019 (0.034)	0.018 (0.033)	0.019 (0.033)	0.020 (0.035)

Table 6.6 Correlation matrix

	ROE	*ROA*	*NIM*	*ESG Combined*	*Environment*	*Social*	*Governance*	*SIZE (Total Assets)*	*Capital*	*Liquidity*	*PPLs*	*RE ratio*	*GDP growth*
ROA	0.964 (0.000)***	1.000											
NIM	0.420 (0.004)***	0.503 (0.000)***	1.000										
ESG Combined	0.022 (0.888)	0.015 (0.925)	−0.179 (0.239)	1.000									
Environmental	0.146 (0.339)	0.103 (0.502)	−0.044 (0.772)	0.759 (0.000)***	1.000								
Social	0.021 (0.890)	0.025 (0.871)	−0.114 (0.455)	0.888 (0.000)***	0.711 (0.000)***	1.000							
Governance	−0.064 (0.676)	−0.066 (0.665)	−0.259 (0.086)*	0.746 (0.000)***	0.337 (0.023)**	0.420 (0.004)***	1.000						
SIZE (Total Assets)	0.416 (0.004)***	0.374 (0.011)**	−0.018 (0.904)	0.390 (0.008)***	0.490 (0.001)***	0.404 (0.006)***	0.152 (0.319)	1.000					
Capital	−0.020 (0.897)	0.189 (0.213)	0.285 (0.058)*	0.010 (0.949)	−0.043 (0.778)	0.005 (0.973)	0.044 (0.776)	−0.107 (0.486)	1.000				
Liquidity	−0.124 (0.417)	−0.084 (0.584)	−0.220 (0.146)	0.202 (0.183)	0.039 (0.801)	0.229 (0.130)	0.221 (0.145)	0.227 (0.134)	0.004 (0.977)	1.000			
PPLs	−0.754 (0.000)***	−0.757 (0.000)***	−0.150 (0.324)	−0.115 (0.450)	−0.195 (0.199)	−0.046 (0.766)	−0.120 (0.432)	−0.240 (0.112)	−0.074 (0.631)	0.168 (0.271)	1.000		
RE ratio	0.346 (0.020)**	0.361 (0.015)**	0.121 (0.429)	0.168 (0.269)	0.209 (0.168)	0.194 (0.201)	0.090 (0.556)	0.332 (0.026)**	0.257 (0.089)*	−0.147 (0.336)	−0.156 (0.307)	1.000	

(continued)

Table 6.6 (continued)

	ROE	*ROA*	*NIM*	*ESG Combined*	*Environment*	*Social*	*Governance*	*SIZE (Total Assets)*	*Capital*	*Liquidity*	*PPLs*	*RE ratio*	*GDP growth*
GDP growth	0.291 (0.053)*	0.335 (0.025)**	0.308 (0.039)**	−0.069 (0.652)	−0.005 (0.976)	−0.163 (0.285)	0.050 (0.744)	0.098 (0.522)	0.231 (0.126)	−0.133 (0.382)	−0.280 (0.063)*	0.270 (0.073)*	1.000
Islamic	0.157 (0.304)	0.142 (0.353)	0.311 (0.038)**	−0.226 (0.135)	−0.212 (0.163)	−0.229 (0.130)	−0.166 (0.275)	−0.050 (0.743)	−0.320 (0.032)**	−0.074 (0.630)	−0.015 (0.921)	−0.195 (0.199)	−0.119 (0.438)

Statistical significance: *** for 1%, ** for 5% and * for 10%

GDP growth correlates positively with profitability (ROA: 0.335; NIM: 0.308; both $p < 0.05$) and negatively with LLPs (–0.280, $p < 0.10$). It suggests that favourable macroeconomic conditions support bank earnings and reduce credit-risk pressures.

Finally, the correlation matrix indicates no multicollinearity concerns. Correlations among independent variables are below the conventional 0.80 threshold. The strong correlation among ESG pillars reinforces the decision not to include all three simultaneously within a single regression model.

Regression Results

Baseline Effects of ESG on Bank Profitability

Table 6.7 shows the results of the baseline models from Model 1 to Model 12 with different specifications of the ESG variables (Combined, Environmental, Social, and Governance) and profitability indicators (ROE, ROA, and NIM).

The baseline models 1, 5 and 9 report an insignificant but negative relationship between the Combined ESG score and the three profitability measures. Similarly, in Models 2, 6, and 10, which capture the Environmental-profitability nexus, Environmental performance has a slight negative but insignificant effect on ROE, ROA, and NIM. This may suggest that environmental reporting, carbon disclosures, and green operations upgrades incur immediate costs without producing short-term financial benefits. The Social pillar in Models 3, 7, and 11, which captures the Social-profitability relationship, also shows insignificant influence on profitability. This may imply that workforce initiatives, community spending, and customer protection mechanisms are not sufficiently integrated to support banks' profitability.

These findings suggest that ESG adoption in the GCC banking sector has not yet matured into a profit-generating asset, supporting the ESG-profitability neutrality hypothesis and aligning with legitimacy theory (Ching & Gerab, 2017). The results are consistent with the compliance-cost argument rather than the strategically embedded (Gutiérrez-Ponce & Wibowo, 2024). This contrasts with the stakeholder theory, which argues that ESG should enhance productivity, customer loyalty, and risk management.

However, Models 4 and 8 show that Governance is negatively significantly associated with ROE (-0.0027, $p = 0.041$) and ROA (-0.0006,

Table 6.7 Regressions of the impact of ESG on profitability (ROE, ROA, NIM) in GCC banking

Profitability variables	*ROE*				*ROA*				*NIM*			
Variable	*Model 1: ESG combined*	*Model 2: Environmental*	*Model 3: Social*	*Model 4: Governance*	*Model 5: ESG combined*	*Model 6: Environmental*	*Model 7: Social*	*Model 8: Governance*	*Model 9: ESG combined*	*Model 10: Environmental*	*Model 11: Social*	*Model 12: Governance*
CONSTANT	0.7589 (0.042) **	1.2429 (0.056) *	0.5661 (0.221)	0.4639 (0.190)	0.6811 (0.001)***	0.8311 (0.001) ***	0.6188 (0.017) **	0.6011 (0.001) ***	−1.0134 (0.009) ***	−0.9174 (0.036) **	−1.0675 (0.010) **	−1.0326 (0.029) **
Lag_ PROFITABILITY	0.3633 (0.032) **	0.3580 (0.021) **	0.4363 (0.008) ***	0.4109 (0.010) **	0.3667 (0.009) ***	0.3278 (0.008) ***	0.3888 (0.016) **	0.3690 (0.004) ***	0.5745 (0.009) ***	0.6383 (0.001) ***	0.5864 (0.016) **	0.6255 (0.008) ***
ESG term	−0.0015 (0.307)	−0.0014 (0.110)	−0.0003 (0.744)	−0.0027 (0.041) **	−0.0003 (0.484)	−0.0003 (0.178)	−0.0000 (0.985)	−0.0006 (0.087) *	0.0010 (0.540)	−0.0004 (0.389)	0.0014 (0.250)	−0.0008 (0.705)
SIZE	0.0008 (0.078) *	0.0014 (0.024) **	0.0006 (0.274)	0.0009 (0.018) **	0.0001 (0.221)	0.0003 (0.049) **	0.0001 (0.416)	0.0002 (0.063) *	−0.0004 (0.336)	−0.0002 (0.559)	−0.0006 (0.144)	−0.0002 (0.489)
CAPITAL	−0.3577 (0.000) ***	−0.2992 (0.004) ***	−0.2754 (0.003) ***	−0.2275 (0.015) **	0.0188 (0.289)	0.0377 (0.107)	0.0380 (0.122)	0.0445 (0.075) *	0.1858 (0.086) *	0.1889 (0.056) *	0.1861 (0.091) *	0.1940 (0.136)
LIQUIDITY	0.0014 (0.010) ***	0.0011 (0.010) ***	0.0010 (0.033) **	0.0014 (0.011) **	0.0003 (0.011) **	0.0003 (0.006) ***	0.0003 (0.042) **	0.0004 (0.005) ***	0.0004 (0.515)	0.0004 (0.261)	0.0002 (0.651)	0.0005 (0.419)
LLPs	−0.0008 (0.092) *	−0.0011 (0.030) **	−0.0008 (0.083) *	−0.0008 (0.049) **	−0.0002 (0.061) *	−0.0003 (0.024) **	−0.0002 (0.071) *	−0.0002 (0.020) **	0.0001 (0.562)	0.0001 (0.602)	0.0000 (0.857)	0.0001 (0.549)
GROWTH	0.0206 (0.007) ***	0.0354 (0.008) ***	0.0263 (0.001) ***	0.0216 (0.012) **	0.0058 (0.000) ***	0.0081 (0.007) ***	0.0072 (0.002) ***	0.0054 (0.004) ***	0.0110 (0.250)	0.0119 (0.137)	0.0129 (0.213)	0.0079 (0.341)

Profitability variables	*ROE*				*ROA*				*NIM*			
Variable	*Model 1: ESG combined*	*Model 2: Environmental*	*Model 3: Social*	*Model 4: Governance*	*Model 5: ESG combined*	*Model 6: Environmental*	*Model 7: Social*	*Model 8: Governance*	*Model 9: ESG combined*	*Model 10: Environmental*	*Model 11: Social*	*Model 12: Governance*
RE	0.5857 (0.006) ***	0.3429 (0.187)	0.5284 (0.013) **	0.5587 (0.007) ***	0.1414 (0.002) ***	0.0911 (0.127)	0.1364 (0.018) **	0.1527 (0.001) ***	0.2821 (0.035) **	0.2388 (0.142)	0.3040 (0.062) *	0.2830 (0.053) *
ISLAMIC	0.0023 (0.011) **	0.0016 (0.083) *	0.0023 (0.014) **	0.0021 (0.010) ***	0.0006 (0.001) ***	0.0005 (0.028) **	0.0006 (0.005) ***	0.0006 (0.000) ***	0.0020 (0.033) **	0.0016 (0.047) **	0.0022 (0.042) **	0.0017 (0.074) *
COVID	−0.0019 (0.035) **	−0.0013 (0.232)	−0.0018 (0.038) **	−0.0023 (0.012) **	−0.0005 (0.014) **	−0.0004 (0.139)	−0.0004 (0.082) *	−0.0005 (0.014) **	0.0002 (0.826)	0.0001 (0.875)	0.0003 (0.734)	−0.0002 (0.753)
Diagnostics												
No. of obs	215	215	215	215	215	215	215	215	215	215	215	215
No. of banks	44	44	44	44	44	44	44	44	44	44	44	44
No. of instruments	16	16	16	16	16	16	16	16	16	16	16	16
Arellano–Bond AR(1)	−2.00 (0.045)**	−2.36 (0.018)**	−2.15 (0.031)**	−2.31 (0.021)**	z = −1.90 (0.058) *	−2.00 (0.045) **	−1.92 (0.055) *	−2.04 (0.041) **	−1.67 (0.094) *	−1.67 (0.095) *	−1.69 (0.091) *	−1.62 (0.105)
Arellano-Bond AR(2)	−0.19 (0.851)	0.10 (0.917)	0.15 (0.885)	0.06 (0.950)	−0.08 (0.933)	−0.01 (0.993)	0.05 (0.960)	−0.09 (0.925)	−0.35 (0.730)	−0.08 (0.940)	−0.34 (0.734)	−0.16 (0.873)

(continued)

Table 6.7 (continued)

Profitability variables	*ROE*				*ROA*				*NIM*			
Variable	*Model 1: ESG combined*	*Model 2: Environmental*	*Model 3: Social*	*Model 4: Governance*	*Model 5: ESG combined*	*Model 6: Environmental*	*Model 7: Social*	*Model 8: Governance*	*Model 9: ESG combined*	*Model 10: Environmental*	*Model 11: Social*	*Model 12: Governance*
Sargan test	5.14	3.20	4.65	4.27	2.78	4.26	9.65	3.68	2.31	2.09	3.37	0.33
	(0.399)	(0.669)	(0.460)	(0.511)	(0.733)	(0.513)	(0.086)	(0.596)	(0.804)	(0.836)	(0.644)	(0.997)
Hanen test	2.38	1.72	0.38	0.10	2.40	1.12	1.08	0.10	0.72	1.38	1.07	0.03
	(0.304)	(0.423)	(0.827)	(0.951)	(0.302)	(0.572)	(0.581)	(0.951)	(0.697)	(0.501)	(0.585)	(0.986)

Notes ***, **, and * denote significance at the 1%, 5%, and 10% levels, respectively; *p*-values are reported in parentheses; All models include year and bank fixed effects, and robust standard errors are used

$p = 0.087$). This suggests that enhanced board oversight, audit structures, and regulatory compliance increase monitoring costs, thereby reducing short-term profitability, consistent with agency theory and the shareholder-expense perspective. The findings also reflect that the GCC banks have invested in governance reforms to align with international standards.

Generally, the control variables exhibit expected signs. Lagged profitability is significant, confirming profit persistence consistent due to market concentration. Size positively affects ROA and ROE, supporting the economies-of-scale argument. Capitalisation is negatively associated with ROE, reflecting the lower risk–return profile of well-capitalised institutions. Loan loss provisions (LLPs) reduce profitability, indicating the importance of credit-quality management. Retained earnings consistently strengthen profitability, supporting internal capital accumulation. GDP growth significantly improves ROE and ROA, confirming the pro-cyclical nature of GCC banking.

ESG-Islamic Interaction Models

Table 6.8 presents the results of the *ESG* × *ISLAMIC* interaction models. Models 13–16 estimate effects on ROE, Models 17–20 on ROA, and Models 21–24 on NIM. Across the Combined ESG, Social pillar, and NIM specifications, the coefficients for ESG, the Islamic-bank dummy, and their interaction are uniformly insignificant. These findings reinforce the neutrality of overall ESG engagement and social initiatives, indicating that Islamic and conventional banks behave similarly when adopting broad ESG practices.

By contrast, the Environmental and Governance models yield more differentiated patterns. In the Environmental specifications (Models 13 and 17), the Environmental pillar shows a negative, significant main effect, suggesting that environmental upgrades impose short-term costs on conventional banks. However, the *ESG* × *ISLAMIC* interaction term is positive and significant for both ROE and ROA. This indicates that Islamic banks convert environmental initiatives into financial gains more effectively than their conventional counterparts. Such an advantage aligns with resource-based and stakeholder perspectives, as environmental stewardship and the avoidance of israf (wastefulness) are embedded in Islamic ethical norms, thereby enabling cost efficiency, reputational benefits, and enhanced trust.

Table 6.8 Results of regressions of the impact of the ESG-ISLAMIC interaction on profitability (ROE, ROA, NIM) in the GCC banking systems

Profitability variables	*ROE*				*ROA*				*NIM*			
Variable	*Model 12: ESG × Islamic*	*Model 13: Environmental × Islamic*	*Model 14: Social × Islamic*	*Model 15: Governance × Islamic*	*Model 16: ESG × Islamic*	*Model 17: Environmental × Islamic*	*Model 18: Social × Islamic*	*Model 19: Governance × Islamic*	*Model 20: ESG × Islamic*	*Model 21: Environmental × Islamic*	*Model 22: Social × Islamic*	*Model 23: Governance × Islamic*
CONSTANT	0.6936 (0.053) *	1.4693 (0.028) **	0.5326 (0.362)	0.3086 (0.408)	0.6600 (0.001) ***	0.9162 (0.000) ***	0.6248 (0.053) *	0.5578 (0.001) ***	−0.9351 (0.023) **	−0.9488 (0.044) **	−1.0884 (0.027) **	−1.2216 (0.046) **
Lag_ PROFITABILITY	0.3567 (0.033) **	0.3922 (0.008) ***	0.4635 (0.006) ***	0.3922 (0.012) **	0.3716 (0.007) ***	0.3293 (0.009) ***	0.3814 (0.070) *	0.3610 (0.003) ***	0.5849 (0.008) ***	0.6287 (0.001) ***	0.5261 (0.027) **	0.5971 (0.009) ***
ESG/Pillar term	−0.0023 (0.253)	−0.0026 (0.029) **	0.0000 (0.994)	−0.0036 (0.040) **	−0.0005 (0.456)	−0.0006 (0.065) *	0.0001 (0.898)	−0.0009 (0.097) *	0.0016 (0.432)	−0.0002 (0.724)	0.0027 (0.294)	−0.0016 (0.552)
Interaction term: Islamic x ESG/Pillar	0.0023 (0.261)	0.0023 (0.038) **	0.0001 (0.972)	0.0035 (0.044) **	0.0005 (0.320)	0.0005 (0.066) *	−0.0001 (0.918)	0.0009 (0.077) *	−0.0016 (0.398)	−0.0003 (0.651)	−0.0029 (0.236)	0.0023 (0.371)
SIZE	0.0008 (0.077) *	0.0017 (0.007) ***	0.0005 (0.564)	0.0008 (0.022) **	0.0001 (0.258)	0.0004 (0.018) **	0.0001 (0.709)	0.0002 (0.073) *	−0.0004 (0.290)	−0.0003 (0.560)	−0.0008 (0.184)	−0.0003 (0.350)
CAPITAL	−0.3675 (0.000) ***	−0.3167 (0.006) ***	−0.2532 (0.024) **	−0.2484 (0.011) **	0.0168 (0.380)	0.0274 (0.345)	0.0411 (0.217)	0.0439 (0.110)	0.1835 (0.083) *	0.1924 (0.053) *	0.2093 (0.036) **	0.2045 (0.108)
LIQUIDITY	0.0014 (0.010) ***	0.0011 (0.010) ***	0.0009 (0.064) *	0.0013 (0.018) **	0.0003 (0.013) **	0.0003 (0.011) **	0.0003 (0.107)	0.0004 (0.006) ***	0.0003 (0.511)	0.0004 (0.250)	0.0003 (0.607)	0.0005 (0.393)
LLPs	−0.0008 (0.075) *	−0.0010 (0.017) **	−0.0008 (0.092) *	−0.0008 (0.045) **	−0.0002 (0.047) **	−0.0002 (0.012) **	−0.0002 (0.081) *	−0.0002 (0.015) **	0.0001 (0.506)	0.0001 (0.590)	0.0001 (0.487)	0.0001 (0.552)

Profitability variables	*ROE*				*ROA*				*NIM*			
Variable	*Model 12: ESG × Islamic*	*Model 13: Environmental × Islamic*	*Model 14: Social × Islamic*	*Model 15: Governance × Islamic*	*Model 16: ESG × Islamic*	*Model 17: Environmental × Islamic*	*Model 18: Social × Islamic*	*Model 19: Governance × Islamic*	*Model 20: ESG × Islamic*	*Model 21: Environmental × Islamic*	*Model 22: Social × Islamic*	*Model 23: Governance × Islamic*
GROWTH	0.0195 (0.013) **	0.0323 (0.001) ***	0.0289 (0.002) ***	0.0193 (0.041) **	0.0055 (0.001) ***	0.0077 (0.006) ***	0.0081 (0.009) ***	0.0047 (0.036) **	0.0120 (0.220)	0.0123 (0.132)	0.0133 (0.219)	0.0072 (0.399)
RE	0.6268 (0.002) ***	0.2303 (0.388)	0.4982 (0.041) **	0.6578 (0.003) ***	0.1483 (0.001) ***	0.0632 (0.339)	0.1366 (0.071) *	0.1766 (0.000) ***	0.2513 (0.076) *	0.2493 (0.170)	0.2965 (0.120)	0.3537 (0.081) *
ISLAMIC	−0.0012 (0.740)	−0.0005 (0.713)	0.0021 (0.065) *	−0.0042 (0.219)	−0.0002 (0.801)	−0.0000 (0.963)	0.0007 (0.558)	−0.0010 (0.282)	0.0044 (0.138)	0.0019 (0.107)	0.0065 (0.076) *	−0.0023 (0.578)
COVID	−0.0018 (0.041) **	−0.0016 (0.090) *	−0.0017 (0.041) **	−0.0024 (0.012) **	−0.0005 (0.015) **	−0.0004 (0.100) *	−0.0003 (0.140)	−0.0006 (0.021) **	0.0002 (0.779)	0.0002 (0.808)	0.0002 (0.826)	−0.0002 (0.754)
Panel/instrument info												
No. of obs	215	215	215	215	215	215	215	215	215	215	215	215
No. of banks in the regression	44	44	44	44	44	44	44	44	44	44	44	44
No. of instruments	17	17	17	17	17	17	17	17	17	17	17	17
Arellano-Bond AR(1)	−2.02 (0.044) **	−2.54 (0.011) **	−1.94 (0.052) *	−2.30 (0.022) **	−1.92 (0.054) *	−2.09 (0.037) **	−1.80 (0.072) *	−2.04 (0.041) **	−1.67 (0.095) *	−1.67 (0.095) *	−1.63 (0.104)	−1.64 (0.100)
Arellano-Bond AR(2)	−0.21 (0.831)	0.28 (0.778)	0.19 (0.851)	0.04 (0.967)	−0.09 (0.929)	−0.01 (0.991)	0.01 (0.990)	−0.12 (0.904)	−0.30 (0.767)	−0.11 (0.916)	−0.64 (0.524)	−0.26 (0.792)
Sargan test	5.22 (0.390)	2.20 (0.821)	5.28 (0.382)	4.44 (0.488)	2.87 (0.720)	3.02 (0.696)	9.96 (0.076)	3.80 (0.578)	2.27 (0.811)	2.15 (0.828)	4.45 (0.486)	0.44 (0.994)
Hansen test	2.37 (0.306)	0.83 (0.662)	0.07 (0.965)	0.22 (0.895)	2.26 (0.324)	0.30 (0.861)	0.54 (0.764)	0.18 (0.916)	0.57 (0.753)	1.29 (0.524)	1.70 (0.428)	2.54 (0.637)

Notes ***, **, and * denote significance at the 1%, 5%, and 10% levels, respectively; *p*-values are reported in parentheses; All models include year and bank fixed effects, and robust standard errors are used

A similar asymmetry emerges in the Governance interaction estimates in Models 15–19. Governance scores have significant adverse effects, indicating that stronger oversight and compliance increase monitoring costs and reduce short-run profitability. Nevertheless, the *GOVERNANCE* × *ISLAMIC* interaction is positive and significant, suggesting that stronger ESG governance raises the profitability of Islamic. This may be because Islamic banks find it easier to integrate ESG frameworks, as they are highly compatible with Islamic principles and objectives.

Overall, the interaction models reveal a clear difference between bank types. Conventional banks experience neutral or cost-absorbing effects from ESG engagement, whereas Islamic banks convert environmental and governance commitments into financial gains. This underscores the strategic role of Sharia-aligned governance and resource stewardship in shaping the ESG-profitability nexus within dual-banking systems.

ESG-Size Interaction Model

Table 6.9 reports the results from Models 24–35, which examine whether bank size moderates the ESG-profitability relationship, i.e., *ESG* × *SIZE*. Across the ROE, ROA, and NIM specifications, the direct effect of ESG is statistically insignificant, indicating that ESG engagement does not systematically enhance bank profitability regardless of bank scale. This reinforces the neutrality observed in the baseline models and is consistent with the argument that ESG practices in the GCC remain evolving and not yet sufficiently integrated to generate immediate financial gains. The exception is Model 28, in which the coefficients on SG-Combined and Size are positive and significant for ROA. This suggests that larger banks may exploit resource complementarities, operational efficiencies, and reputational advantages for marginal improvements in asset-based profitability.

However, the interaction term in Model 28 is negative and significant, implying that although larger banks benefit from ESG adoption, the incremental profit effect weakens as scale increases. This pattern suggests diminishing marginal returns to ESG at larger sizes. Larger institutions may face greater organisational complexity, more extensive reporting requirements, and possible inertia in adapting ESG processes, all of which can dilute the financial impact of sustainability initiatives. The absence of significant interaction effects in ROE and NIM specifications indicates that size-related heterogeneity is specific to combined ESG engagement and cost-related activities embedded in ROA. Overall,

Table 6.9 Results of regressions of the impact of the ESG-SIZE interaction on profitability (ROE, ROA, NIM)

Profitability variables	*ROE*			
Variable	*Model 24: ESG × Size*	*Model 25: Environmental × Size*	*Model 26: Social × Size*	*Model 27: Governance × Size*
CONSTANT	2.1535 (0.092)*	–0.2570 (0.662)	1.0622 (0.140)	1.8381 (0.504)
Lag_PROFITABILITY	0.2737 (0.248)	0.5200 (0.005)***	0.4590 (0.006)***	0.2109 (0.624)
ESG/Pillar term	0.0460 (0.175)	–0.0231 (0.137)	0.0150 (0.331)	0.0667 (0.662)
Interaction term: Size x ESG/Pillar	–0.0046 (0.174)	0.0022 (0.143)	–0.0015 (0.329)	–0.0066 (0.660)
SIZE	0.0088 (0.155)	–0.0018 (0.272)	0.0029 (0.254)	0.0135 (0.640)
CAPITAL	–0.5403 (0.006)***	–0.1676 (0.163)	–0.3380 (0.003)***	–0.5061 (0.263)
LIQUIDITY	0.0010 (0.102)	0.0011 (0.002)***	0.0010 (0.037)**	0.0004 (0.841)
LLPs	–0.0013 (0.038)**	–0.0005 (0.253)	–0.0008 (0.060)*	–0.0016 (0.427)
GROWTH	0.0215 (0.001)***	0.0254 (0.005)***	0.0270 (0.000)***	0.0208 (0.193)
RE	0.2112 (0.515)	0.7097 (0.002)***	0.3432 (0.164)	0.3535 (0.575)
ISLAMIC	0.0006 (0.661)	0.0032 (0.001)***	0.0013 (0.304)	0.0022 (0.302)
COVID	–0.0013 (0.161)	–0.0020 (0.041)**	–0.0017 (0.060)*	–0.0011 (0.332)
No. of obs	215	215	215	215
No. of banks	44	44	44	44
No. of instruments	17	17	17	17
Arellano-Bond AR(1)	–1.47 (0.142)	–2.44 (0.015)**	–2.26 (0.024)**	–0.86 (0.391)
Arellano-Bond AR(2)	–0.07 (0.943)	0.55 (0.582)	0.34 (0.733)	–0.26 (0.795)
Sargan test	5.19 (0.393)	3.16 (0.675)	5.42 (0.367)	4.66 (0.459)
Hansen test	0.57 (0.753)	1.07 (0.586)	0.04 (0.980)	0.90 (0.638)

(continued)

Table 6.9 (continued)

Profitability variables	*ROA*			
Variable	*Model 28: ESG × Size*	*Model 29: Environmental × Size*	*Model 30: Social × Size*	*Model 31: Governance × Size*
CONSTANT	1.1153 (0.013)**	0.4617 (0.047)**	0.7166 (0.005)**	1.2054 (0.267)
Lag_PROFITABILITY	0.2739 (0.159)	0.4226 (0.002)***	0.4350 (0.003)***	0.1542 (0.698)
ESG/Pillar term	0.0115 (0.099)*	−0.0046 (0.214)	0.0042 (0.254)	0.0201 (0.603)
Interaction term: Size x ESG/Pillar	−0.0012 (0.098)*	0.0004 (0.222)	−0.0004 (0.252)	−0.0020 (0.601)
SIZE	0.0022 (0.088)*	−0.0003 (0.400)	0.0008 (0.192)	0.0039 (0.585)
CAPITAL	−0.0136 (0.615)	0.0502 (0.047)**	0.0132 (0.535)	−0.0005 (0.994)
LIQUIDITY	0.0003 (0.088)*	0.0004 (0.000)***	0.0003 (0.028)**	0.0001 (0.789)
LLPs	−0.0003 (0.020)**	−0.0002 (0.130)	−0.0002 (0.023)**	−0.0005 (0.339)
GROWTH	0.0054 (0.000)***	0.0061 (0.001)***	0.0068 (0.000)***	0.0044 (0.278)
RE	0.0445 (0.542)	0.1700 (0.003)**	0.0816 (0.158)	0.0719 (0.697)
ISLAMIC	0.0002 (0.654)	0.0008 (0.000)***	0.0003 (0.333)	0.0005 (0.378)
COVID	−0.0004 (0.077)*	−0.0005 (0.036)**	−0.0004 (0.046)**	−0.0003 (0.291)
No. of obs	215	215	215	215
No. of banks	44	44	44	44
No. of instruments	17	17	17	17
Arellano-Bond AR(1)	−1.64 (0.100)	−2.07 (0.038)**	−2.05 (0.040)**	−0.92 (0.357)
Arellano-Bond AR(2)	−0.06 (0.952)	0.40 (0.689)	0.24 (0.812)	−0.32 (0.746)
Sargan test	2.71 (0.745)	4.58 (0.470)	10.92 (0.053)	3.54 (0.618)
Hansen test	0.16 (0.923)	0.97 (0.617)	0.12 (0.941)	0.53 (0.768)

Profitability variables	*NIM*			
Variable	*Model 31: ESG × Size*	*Model 33: Environmental × Size*	*Model 34: Social × Size*	*Model 35: Governance × Size*
CONSTANT	−0.7782 (0.399)	−1.6110 (0.026)**	−0.7580 (0.572)	−0.8642 (0.448)
Lag_PROFITABILITY	0.5046 (0.032)**	0.8026 (0.000)***	0.4715 (0.021)**	0.6461 (0.226)
ESG/Pillar term	0.0131 (0.732)	−0.0195 (0.191)	0.0147 (0.726)	0.0035 (0.969)
Interaction term: Size x ESG/Pillar	−0.0013 (0.731)	0.0019 (0.196)	−0.0015 (0.723)	−0.0004 (0.969)
SIZE	0.0020 (0.750)	−0.0022 (0.169)	0.0020 (0.754)	0.0005 (0.979)
CAPITAL	0.1704 (0.207)	0.2498 (0.047)**	0.1357 (0.552)	0.1632 (0.079)*
LIQUIDITY	0.0005 (0.403)	0.0003 (0.439)	0.0004 (0.438)	0.0003 (0.801)
LLPs	0.0000 (0.996)	0.0002 (0.350)	0.0000 (0.972)	0.0001 (0.929)
GROWTH	0.0071 (0.378)	0.0143 (0.078)*	0.0073 (0.430)	0.0099 (0.140)
RE	0.1911 (0.562)	0.4779 (0.046)**	0.2112 (0.618)	0.2340 (0.650)
ISLAMIC	0.0017 (0.187)	0.0019 (0.075)*	0.0015 (0.500)	0.0015 (0.101)
COVID	0.0000 (0.997)	0.0001 (0.911)	0.0002 (0.864)	−0.0000 (0.995)
No. of obs	215	215	215	215
No. of banks	44	44	44	44
No. of instruments	17	17	17	17
Arellano-Bond AR(1)	−1.63 (0.103)	−1.71 (0.087)	−1.54 (0.124)	−0.92 (0.358)
Arellano-Bond AR(2)	−0.14 (0.889)	−0.11 (0.909)	−0.48 (0.632)	−0.07 (0.946)
Sargan test	2.12 (0.832)	1.10 (0.954)	5.41 (0.368)	0.65 (0.985)
Hansen test	1.48 (0.477)	0.29 (0.863)	2.90 (0.234)	0.08 (0.960)

Notes ***, **, and * denote significance at the 1%, 5%, and 10% levels, respectively; *p*-values are reported in parentheses; All models include year and bank fixed effects, and robust standard errors are use the ESG–Size results indicate two main findings: (i) Size and ESG have an individual positive impact on profitability, and (ii) size has a negative moderating impact on the ESG-profitability relationship through the economies-of-scale channel.

Conclusion

This study employed a dynamic GMM framework to investigate how ESG ratings influence the profitability of banks in the GCC using 458 bank-year observations from 2012 to 2022. The evidence shows that overall ESG performance, as well as its environmental, social, and governance pillars, has an adverse, statistically significant effect on ROE and ROA. These findings suggest that ESG implementation in the GCC banking sector incurs short-term financial burdens, primarily driven by technological upgrades, environmental initiatives, and strengthened governance systems required for compliance and reporting. In this respect, sustainability practices appear to be at a stage where they primarily serve regulatory compliance rather than as profit-enhancing assets. Despite ambitious national sustainability agendas—such as Saudi Vision 2030, the UAE Net Zero Strategy 2050, and Qatar National Vision 2030—the financial gains from ESG investments have yet to materialise.

The analysis also reveals that ESG effects vary by bank type and size. First, Islamic banks benefit from positive environmental and governance interaction effects, consistent with the israf-avoidance hypothesis, which emphasises cost-saving ethical conduct. Their dual monitoring structures, combining conventional oversight with Shariah supervision, appear to facilitate more effective transformation of ESG initiatives into financial gains. Second, Size effects are similarly important. The interaction results indicate that smaller banks obtain greater marginal improvements in ROA from ESG adoption than their larger rivals. This may reflect the relatively low ESG investment burden on smaller institutions, particularly during a period when ESG disclosure remained largely optional. Overall, the results underscore that ESG transmission into bank performance in the GCC is shaped by institutional characteristics rather than being uniform across the sector.

This study has several policy implications. First, aligning domestic ESG disclosure frameworks with international standards would weaken reporting asymmetries and increase investor confidence. Second, policymakers could promote the expansion of green finance through targeted incentives, thereby aligning sustainability efforts with profitability goals. Third, larger and conventional banks may need to focus on ESG practices that generate financial gains. Investments in energy-efficient infrastructure, digital transformation, and ESG-driven credit assessment could help reduce the cost burden associated with ESG integration. Although it can harm smaller banks, the transition from voluntary to mandatory ESG implementation across all financial institutions may also support more consistent adoption across the banking sector. From another perspective, integrating ESG responsibilities into a KPI system would enable banks not only to monitor ESG performance more systematically but also to align their ESG objectives with their KPIs.

Future research should extend these findings in two ways. First, the significant ESG–Size interaction for ROA suggests that cost efficiency may serve as an operational channel through which ESG affects performance. This calls for an investigation into the links between ESG and cost efficiency. Second, examining how ESG interacts with broader factors—such as competition, regulatory intensity, and macroeconomic conditions—would deepen understanding of the mechanisms underpinning ESG-profitability dynamics. Finally, accounting for potential nonlinearities may reveal whether ESG generates threshold effects, diminishing returns, or scale-dependent impacts in banking performance.

CHAPTER 7

Globalisation, Institutional Quality, and Bank Stability in the GCC

Introduction

Over the past two decades, GCC banks have undergone significant transformations, shaped by several factors, including increased globalisation, institutional reforms triggered by external shocks, and a focus on economic diversification. These transformations might have had repercussions for the stability of banks in a region where banks contribute to economic growth and development. As GCC countries continue to embrace globalisation, understanding how it interacts with institutional quality to shape banking stability is important.

The GCC region is highly integrated into the global economy, with foreign trade-to-GDP exceeding 100%, owing to its strategic location, extensive hydrocarbon exports, significant sovereign wealth funds, a large expatriate population, and strong trade ties with key international markets. While the GCC countries are trading partners of many countries, they have signed numerous free trade agreements (FTAs) with individual countries, such as China, the US, the UK, and the EU, as well as with trading blocs such as the European Free Trade Association (EFTA). They are also key members of multilateral organisations such as the World Trade Organisation (WTO) and the Organisation of Islamic

A. Bakhouche, *Banking in the GCC*, Palgrave Macmillan Studies in Banking and Financial Institutions,
https://doi.org/10.1007/978-3-032-21737-0_7

Cooperation (OIC). These factors may enhance bank stability by facilitating cross-border financial flows, foreign bank participation, and the transfer of human and technological capital.

However, globalisation also carries risks. Greater integration into international financial markets exposes GCC banks to external shocks, volatile capital flows, and increased competition from foreign financial institutions. The 2008 GFC revealed the vulnerabilities of banks overexposed to international credit markets, while the COVID-19 crisis highlighted the risks of reliance on external funding and on global financial conditions. At the same time, the rise of financial technology (fintech) and digital banking has disrupted traditional banking models, forcing banks to adapt to heightened competition and an evolving regulatory landscape.

Institutional quality plays a decisive role in determining how GCC banks respond to these challenges. This study focuses on three key institutional factors—control of corruption, regulatory quality, and rule of law—which influence banking stability by shaping regulatory enforcement, governance effectiveness, and investor confidence. Stronger institutions, as seen in the UAE and Qatar, have allowed these nations to adopt international best practices, implement adequate financial supervision, and enhance banking stability. Conversely, weaker institutions in Bahrain and Oman have led to regulatory gaps, governance inefficiencies, and heightened financial risks, contributing to greater instability in their banking systems.

The interaction between institutional quality and globalisation remains underexplored in the GCC context. While some studies suggest that foreign bank entry and financial integration enhance stability by improving risk diversification and efficiency, others warn that financial openness may increase systemic vulnerabilities, particularly in economies with weaker regulatory frameworks. The question remains: Does strong institutional quality help GCC banks harness the benefits of globalisation while mitigating its risks?

To address this gap, this chapter examines the relationship among institutional quality, globalisation, and bank stability in the GCC from 2002 to 2022. It assesses the impact of institutional quality (control of corruption, regulatory quality, and rule of law) on banking stability in the GCC. It examines the effects of globalisation (economic, social, and political dimensions) on banking stability. It analyses how the interaction between institutional quality and globalisation influences stability, identifying whether strong governance enhances the benefits of globalisation or mitigates its risks.

This study makes several key contributions. First, it provides an in-depth empirical analysis of how institutional quality and globalisation affect banking stability in the GCC, using a comprehensive panel dataset spanning two decades. Second, it introduces a novel perspective by examining the interaction between governance and globalisation, offering insights into whether strong institutions amplify the stabilising effects of financial integration or shield banks from external risks. Third, it presents policy recommendations for strengthening banking resilience in an era of increasing global financial integration, with a focus on regulatory enhancements, risk management, and financial-sector development.

The findings of this study have significant policy implications. Given that the GCC is actively pursuing economic diversification under initiatives such as Saudi Vision 2030, the UAE's Centennial 2071, and Qatar National Vision 2030, a stable and competitive banking sector is essential to financing these long-term development goals. Policymakers must ensure that regulatory reforms keep pace with financial globalisation to prevent instability while leveraging the benefits of integration to enhance the banking sector's performance.

The remainder of this chapter is structured as follows. The next section reviews the theoretical and empirical literature on institutional quality, globalisation, and banking stability. The subsequent section describes the data sources, variable selection, and methodology used in the empirical analysis. The findings are then presented and discussed, with a focus on institutional quality and globalisation—both individually and interactively. The last section concludes.

Theoretical Foundations

The relationship between institutional quality, globalisation, and banking stability is rooted in multiple strands of economic and financial literature. Strong institutional and regulatory frameworks are fundamental to financial stability as they reduce information asymmetries, mitigate excessive risk-taking, and enhance contract enforcement (North, 1990). The economic and financial liberalisation hypothesis (McKinnon, 1973; Shaw, 1973) posits that global integration fosters competition, strengthens financial intermediation, and improves banking efficiency through open markets, free capital movement, and the adoption of advanced regulatory standards. However, Stiglitz (2000) warns that in the absence of strong institutional quality, globalisation can lead to financial instability, capital outflows, and economic vulnerability.

Institutional Quality and Bank Stability

Institutions play a critical role in financial stability by enforcing prudential regulations, ensuring transparency, and mitigating moral hazard. Law and finance theory (La Porta et al., 1998) posits that legal frameworks shape financial market outcomes, particularly in emerging economies where institutional weaknesses persist. In the GCC region, variations in institutional quality have influenced banking stability: the UAE and Saudi Arabia exhibit stronger financial resilience due to robust regulatory frameworks, whereas weaker institutional oversight in other countries has heightened financial vulnerabilities.

The institutional complementarity theory (Hall & Soskice, 2001) suggests that financial institutions are more effective when aligned with broader governance structures. In the GCC, state-led economic models, oil dependence, and hybrid governance systems—combining conventional, Islamic, and state-controlled financial institutions—affect banking stability. Central banks regulate financial activities, while government-backed entities influence credit allocation. As such, institutional quality plays a crucial role in shaping financial-sector resilience, particularly in response to economic shocks and globalisation.

Regulatory arbitrage theory (Houston et al., 2012) further highlights how banks operating in weak institutional environments exploit regulatory loopholes to engage in riskier activities that undermine financial stability. Conversely, strong institutions enforce regulations and sound risk-management practices (Alqahtani & Mayes, 2022), thereby reducing financial instability risks. In the GCC, disparities in regulatory strength have created challenges, as financial institutions often shift activities to less-regulated jurisdictions to maximise profitability (Barth et al., 2006).

Globalisation and Banking Stability

The impact of globalisation on banking stability is multifaceted, yielding both stabilising and destabilising effects depending on the institutional and regulatory environment. The financial openness hypothesis

(McKinnon, 1973; Shaw, 1973) argues that integration into global financial markets enhances stability by diversifying risks, attracting foreign investment, and improving capital allocation. Increased financial openness in the GCC has facilitated economic growth, expanded financial markets, and enhanced liquidity. However, it has also heightened exposure to external shocks, such as capital flight, financial crises, and economic downturns.

Financial globalisation has intensified competition in the banking sector, fostering efficiency and innovation. However, it has also pressured profit margins, encouraging riskier lending strategies. Regulatory challenges—including the heavy reliance of GCC economies on oil revenues—exacerbate concerns about banking stability. Exchange rate policies add further complexity, as most GCC countries peg their currencies to the US dollar, thereby limiting their ability to pursue independent monetary policy. This exposes banks to global financial shocks, particularly fluctuations in interest rates and oil prices.

The global financial cycle hypothesis (Rey, 2015) suggests that integration into global financial markets increases vulnerability to external shocks, regardless of domestic policies. Between 2002 and 2022, GCC banks experienced liquidity surpluses during global periods of low interest rates, followed by funding pressures as financial conditions tightened, including during the 2008 financial crisis and the post-2015 US Federal Reserve rate hikes. Similarly, oil price fluctuations have significantly influenced banking stability. During high-revenue periods (2002–2008, 2010–2014), strong bank lending prevailed, whereas oil price crashes (2008–2009, 2014–2016, 2020) reduced government deposits, constrained liquidity, and increased non-performing loans.

The varieties of capitalism theory (Hall & Soskice, 2001) provide further insights into how institutional differences affect financial stability. It distinguishes between liberal market economies, which rely on competitive market coordination, and coordinated market economies, where state intervention plays a significant role. The GCC represents a hybrid model in which state-driven financial systems coexist with market-oriented reforms. This unique institutional structure shapes how global financialisation affects banking stability, as state-led policies and regulatory quality determine the resilience of financial institutions.

Interplay Between Institutional Quality, Globalisation, and Banking Stability

While many studies examine the independent effects of institutional quality and globalisation on banking stability, fewer explore their interaction, particularly in the GCC. The substitution hypothesis (Acemoglu et al., 2005) suggests that international political integration can compensate for weak domestic governance, but with a marginal effect in countries with already strong regulatory institutions. In the GCC, economic openness is high—trade-to-GDP ratios exceed 90%—but institutional strength varies. Countries such as the UAE and Saudi Arabia have leveraged robust governance frameworks to manage financial liberalisation effectively. In contrast, Bahrain and Oman have experienced greater instability due to weaker regulatory controls.

Empirical studies highlight the significance of integrated approaches. Chinn and Ito (2008) find that financial openness enhances banking performance only when supported by strong institutional frameworks. Similarly, Beck et al. (2013) note that social globalisation fosters financial inclusion, but its effectiveness depends on regulatory quality. This underscores the need for balanced policy strategies that leverage the benefits of global integration while mitigating associated risks.

The 2008 financial crisis and the COVID-19 pandemic demonstrated that strong institutional frameworks help mitigate external shocks, whereas weak regulatory environments increase exposure to financial instability (Beck et al., 2010). Countries with effective macroprudential policies, such as the UAE and Saudi Arabia, have reduced systemic risks through capital adequacy requirements and enhanced risk management. In contrast, countries with weaker institutions have experienced greater financial imbalances and risk accumulation. The 2014–16 oil price crash further highlighted these vulnerabilities, as declining government revenues led to liquidity constraints and rising non-performing loans (IMF, 2016).

Literature Review

The relationship between institutional quality, globalisation, and banking stability has been widely studied, yet research on this nexus within the GCC remains relatively underexplored. Existing empirical evidence presents mixed findings: some studies highlight the stabilising effects of strong institutions and financial integration, whereas others caution against the risks posed by globalisation, particularly in weak-governance environments. This section reviews key empirical studies, categorising findings as positive, negative, or neutral, and considers the interplay between institutional quality and globalisation in shaping banking stability.

Positive Effects of Institutional Quality and Globalisation on Banking Stability

Globalisation has significantly influenced the banking sector by fostering financial integration, advancing communication technologies, and enhancing capital mobility. The internationalisation of banking has allowed financial institutions to capitalise on economies of scale and mitigate risks associated with domestic market volatility (Claessens & van Horen, 2014). Focarelli and Pozzolo (2005) argue that bank internationalisation is primarily driven by profit opportunities and institution-specific characteristics, with large banks being more likely to expand internationally due to their diversified customer base and enhanced risk-sharing capabilities (Berger et al., 1995).

Empirical studies indicate that foreign bank entry enhances banking system stability by improving risk diversification and operational efficiency (Claessens & van Horen, 2014). In emerging markets, Jemric and Vujcic (2002) and Havrylchyk (2006) find that foreign-owned banks tend to operate more efficiently than domestic banks, owing to superior risk-management practices and access to international capital markets. Similarly, Al-Qudah and Jaradat (2013) report that increased financial openness in Qatar and the UAE contributed to greater banking stability by attracting foreign investment and encouraging the adoption of international best practices.

Institutional quality plays a pivotal role in enhancing banking stability by reducing corruption, strengthening legal enforcement, and improving regulatory oversight. Beck et al. (2006) demonstrated that countries with strong governance structures experience fewer banking crises, as effective regulation limits excessive risk-taking. In the GCC, Alqahtani et al. (2020) find that improvements in regulatory quality and transparency in Saudi Arabia contributed to greater banking stability, particularly following the 2008 global financial crisis. Similarly, Al-Khouri and Arouri

(2019) show that robust institutional frameworks in the UAE helped mitigate financial risks, enhancing the resilience of the banking sector.

Moreover, financial globalisation has facilitated greater access to capital, reducing liquidity constraints for banks in the GCC. Kabir et al. (2021) find that deeper integration with global financial markets strengthened financial resilience by providing alternative funding sources and improving credit availability. This aligns with Chinn and Ito's (2008) findings that financial openness enhances banking performance when supported by strong institutional frameworks.

Negative Effects of institutional quality and Globalisation on Banking Stability

Despite its benefits, globalisation also introduces systemic risks, particularly in the absence of strong regulatory oversight. Bhatti et al. (2021) argue that financial liberalisation without adequate institutional safeguards can lead to excessive risk-taking and financial volatility. This concern is particularly relevant in GCC countries with weaker regulatory enforcement, such as Bahrain and Oman, where banks faced greater instability during the 2008 crisis due to weaker capital buffers and reliance on foreign funding (Bitar et al., 2022).

Allen et al. (2017) noted that excessive dependence on global financial flows increases banks' exposure to external shocks, as seen during the COVID-19 pandemic, when sudden capital withdrawals disrupted financial markets. In the GCC, Safiullah and Shamsuddin (2021) find that financial globalisation increased systemic risks, particularly for banks with high foreign liabilities, leading to credit market volatility. Similarly, the rise of fintech and digital banking, driven by globalisation, has intensified competition and, at times, undermined the stability of traditional banking (Cornelli et al., 2020).

Yin (2019) examined foreign bank penetration across 129 countries between 1995 and 2013 and found that greater foreign bank presence was associated with higher banking risk, as reflected in lower Z-scores. This suggests that while financial openness enhances competition, it may also heighten financial fragility if not accompanied by effective prudential regulation. Additionally, Sufian and Kamarudin (2016) found that economic globalisation positively influences banking performance, but social and political globalisation can negatively affect bank profitability, particularly in countries with underdeveloped financial systems.

The relationship between institutional quality and banking stability is also complex. While stricter rule of law generally improves financial stability in developing economies, its effects in developed markets appear ambiguous. Some studies suggest that at higher levels, stringent regulations may increase insolvency risk by limiting banks' flexibility in responding to financial shocks (Rodrik, 1999).

No Significant Relationship Between Institutional Quality, Globalisation, and Banking Stability

Several studies suggest that the relationship between institutional quality, globalisation, and banking stability is not straightforward and may depend on broader macroeconomic conditions. Demirgüç-Kunt and Detragiache (2002) find that financial openness alone does not determine banking stability unless accompanied by sound macroeconomic policies and strong financial supervision. Similarly, Almarzoqi et al. (2020) report that, although globalisation and digital transformation influenced competition in the GCC banking sector, their direct impact on stability was statistically insignificant after controlling for factors such as capital adequacy and asset quality.

In a study of GCC banks, Alshubiri et al. (2023) find that while foreign bank entry increased competition, it did not necessarily improve financial stability, as domestic banks' risk-management strategies played a more critical role. This supports the notion that financial stability depends on both external and internal institutional factors, rather than on globalisation alone.

The Interplay Between Institutional Quality, Globalisation, and Banking Stability

While the individual effects of institutional quality and globalisation on banking stability are well documented, their interaction remains under-explored, particularly in the GCC. Some studies suggest that strong institutions can amplify the positive effects of globalisation while mitigating its risks. Alqahtani and Mayes (2022) argue that well-regulated banking environments reduce information asymmetries and enhance financial transparency, thereby ensuring that the benefits of globalisation outweigh its risks. Conversely, in weak institutional environments, financial integration may lead to greater financial fragility, as evidenced in

Bahrain and Oman during periods of economic turbulence (Bhatti et al., 2021).

Regulatory arbitrage theory (Houston et al., 2012) suggests that banks operating in weak institutional environments may exploit regulatory loopholes, increasing systemic risks. This is particularly relevant in the GCC, where economic openness is high but institutional strength varies. Alshubiri et al. (2023) propose that banks will benefit from harmonising regulatory frameworks across GCC countries by reducing market fragmentation. This aligns with the GCC Common Market initiative, which seeks to integrate financial markets and enhance cross-border banking stability. However, regulatory divergence among member states continues to pose challenges in supervision and enforcement.

Methodology

Data, Sample, and Variables

To examine the relationship among institutional quality, globalisation, and banking stability, we construct a panel dataset covering 60 banks in the GCC from 2002 to 2022, yielding 1,107 bank-year observations. The dataset integrates bank-level financial indicators, macroeconomic variables, institutional quality measures, and external shocks to ensure a comprehensive empirical framework.

Bank-specific financial data are obtained from Thomson Reuters (Orbis Bank Focus). The sample is refined by retaining only commercial banks, bank holding companies, and Islamic banks while excluding investment banks and other financial institutions. To ensure consistency, I keep only consolidated financial statements and include banks with at least four consecutive years of data. Observations with missing key variables or obvious errors (e.g., negative total assets) are excluded.

Country-level variables are sourced from multiple databases. The KOF Globalisation Index from ETH Zurich captures economic, social, and political globalisation. Institutional quality is proxied by Regulatory Quality and Rule of Law, as measured by the Worldwide Governance Indicators (WGI). Macroeconomic controls, such as GDP per capita growth and inflation rate, are extracted from the World Bank's World Development Indicators (WDI).

The study also considers dummy variables for the 2008–2009global financial crisis and the 2020–2021 COVID-19 lockdown period, to capture the impact of financial distress and economic disruptions on banking stability. The final dataset provides a framework for assessing the interplay among globalisation, institutional quality, and bank performance in the GCC (Table 7.1).

Empirical Model

The empirical model examines the effects of institutional quality and globalisation, and their interaction, on bank stability using GCC banking data from 2002 to 2022. The regression model is specified as follows:

$$\begin{aligned} STABILITY_{i,t} = {} & \alpha + \beta 1INSTITUTION_{it} + \beta 2GLOBALISATION_t \\ & + \beta 3(INSTITUTION \times GLOBALISATION)_t \\ & + \beta 3X_{i,t} + Z + \varepsilon i \end{aligned} \tag{7.1}$$

Where $\text{STABILITY}_{\text{i,t}}$ denotes banking stability of a bank *i* in a country in year t, INSTITUTION denotes institutional quality measures, GLOBALISATION captures globalisation indicators, and $\text{X}_{\text{i,t}}$ denotes a set of control variables. We consider three bank-specific variables to proxy for different dimensions of banks: SIZE, proxied by total assets to examine potential scale effects; credit risk captured by the ratio of loan loss provisions to total loans (LLPs); and cost INEFFICIENCY, measured by the ratio of total costs to total income. ISLAMIC banks are controlled for using a dummy variable. We also include the HHI of assets to control for market structure. The impact of economic and adverse shocks on bank stability is captured by annual GROWTH in real GDP per capita, INFLATION, two dummy variables capturing the global financial crisis (GFC) and the COVID lockdown.

The GMM estimator is employed to address dynamic panel bias and ensure robustness. This approach improves the reliability of estimates by reducing the effect of unobserved heterogeneity, autocorrelation, and reverse causality.

Main Variables

Examining the relationship among institutional quality, globalisation, and bank characteristics in the GCC requires focusing on variables that capture the unique dynamics of the region's banking sector. The GCC countries have highly open economies, significant state involvement in

Table 7.1 Summary of variables and data sources

Variable		*Definition*	*Source*
STABILITY	Bank Stability	The Z-score is calculated as (return on assets + equity asset ratio) / standard deviation of return on assets. It measures a bank's risk of insolvency	Thomson Reuters
SIZE	Size	Total assets	Thomson Reuters
LLPs	Loan Loss Provisions**ratio**	The ratio of Loan loss provisions to total loans. It measures credit risk	Thomson Reuters
ISLAMIC	Islamic banks Dummy	1 for Islamic banks, 0 for conventional banks	Bank websites
INEFFICIENCY	Cost Inefficiency	Cost-to-assets ratio	Thomson Reuters
KOFGI	KOF Overall Globalisation Index	KOF Index	KOF Index[1]
KOFECGI	Economic Globalisation Index	Trade and capital flow openness	
KOFSOGI	Social Globalisation Index	Cross-border cultural and information exchange	
KOFPOGI	Political Globalisation Index	Diplomatic ties and policy integration	
REG_QUL	Regulatory Quality	Perception of regulatory effectiveness	World Bank Worldwide Governance Indicators (WGI)
ROL	Rule of Law	Strength of the legal framework	World Bank Worldwide Governance Indicators (WGI)
HHI	Herfindahl–Hirschman Index Assets	A measure of the country-level level of competition in the banking sector	Calculated from a previous chapter
GROWTH	GDP per capita growth	A country's GDP per capita in thousands of 2015 constant USD	World Bank World Development Indicators (WDI)
INFLATION	Inflation Rate	Annual percentage change in national CPI	WDI
GFC	Global Financial Crisis**, Dummy**	1 for 2008–2009, 0 otherwise	Based on the literature
COVID	COVID-19 Lockdown, dummy	1 for 2020–2021, 0 otherwise	Based on the literature

[1] kof.ethz.ch/en/forecasts-and-indicators/indicators/kof-globalisation-index.html.

banking, and financial markets deeply influenced by globalisation and institutional frameworks. Given this context, the variables selected must be directly relevant to explaining how institutional and global forces shape competition among banks.

Bank Stability of GCC Banks: Z-score

The Z-score is a widely used indicator of bank stability. It measures the distance from insolvency by combining profitability, capitalisation, and earnings volatility. Higher Z-scores indicate greater stability and a lower probability of bank failure (Bakhouche, 2024; Boyd & Runkle, 1993; Laeven & Valencia, 2018). Table 7.2 shows the evolution of Z-scores across GCC countries between 2002 and 2022. It reveals substantial heterogeneity in both levels and volatility of banking system stability.

At the GCC level, stability improved from the early 2000s until the mid-2010s, but it declined sharply during the COVID-19 period and recovered thereafter. The GCC average rises from about 54 in 2002 to over 260 in 2013, driven by favourable conditions, including high oil prices, strong fiscal buffers, and regulatory post-crisis strengthening. However, the upward trend was interrupted during global and regional shocks, notably the Global Financial Crisis (2008–09), the oil price collapse (2014–16), and the COVID-19 pandemic (2020). Each of these events is associated with a decline in bank stability.

The decline in the average GCC Z-score to about 41 in 2020 may reflect the region's exposure to Cobid-10 lockdown, which affected both real activity and fiscal revenues. However, the recovery in 2021–22 may have been driven by policy support measures and the rebound in oil prices (IMF, 2022). Overall, the Z-score evidence indicates that GCC banking systems are stable but are exposed to cyclical risks. Therefore, in the GCC region, bank stability may appear closely linked to oil prices, fiscal factors, and regulatory frameworks.

Bahrain exhibits the lowest average Z-score among GCC countries over the sample period, with high volatility. Although stability improved and peaked in 2013, these gains were not sustained through subsequent shocks. This can be due to its smaller banking system, limited fiscal buffers, and greater exposure to regional financial stress (IMF, 2021).

Kuwait has one of the highest average Z-scores, but with higher volatility and extreme outliers, such as in 2017. This may reflect a banking system characterised by very high capital and liquidity ratios, driven by strong sovereign wealth fund backing. In addition, Kuwait's long-term

Table 7.2 Stability of GCC banks between 2002 and 2022, measured by the Z-score

Year	*Bahrain*	*Kuwait*	*Oman*	*Qatar*	*Saudi Arabia*	*UAE*	*Average GCC*
2002	23.46	42.78	49.10	33.28	56.18	83.80	54.02
2003	25.23	44.21	54.20	35.62	55.16	93.19	60.74
2004	43.61	51.08	58.33	41.49	46.35	90.31	63.19
2005	41.24	36.42	67.25	41.53	22.73	45.84	42.39
2006	51.95	109.22	41.25	32.16	23.54	34.94	49.69
2007	47.39	55.93	93.64	33.89	24.20	29.45	42.84
2008	21.00	22.82	51.18	52.86	18.80	35.01	31.76
2009	23.38	47.43	33.99	83.65	31.52	52.58	45.49
2010	28.27	62.19	56.15	115.57	121.41	68.98	76.24
2011	186.32	67.18	49.96	229.75	98.04	89.53	114.88
2012	192.58	69.81	159.36	118.00	82.83	151.00	126.89
2013	588.68	203.68	122.54	85.40	104.59	380.89	264.51
2014	301.29	104.63	152.86	178.81	122.64	170.61	167.84
2015	198.87	171.40	81.66	291.72	160.50	71.42	149.42
2016	400.70	223.00	105.47	54.28	174.60	82.79	165.94
2017	300.42	1,548.71	106.22	74.14	166.90	91.33	384.20
2018	191.00	146.66	199.77	118.22	109.85	88.71	133.42
2019	295.56	128.09	189.33	135.91	78.59	94.34	141.68
2020	27.47	29.33	76.94	58.52	38.99	31.53	40.84
2021	33.44	34.49	107.03	58.03	50.00	46.15	52.15
2022	44.18	64.13	95.64	204.96	90.89	85.01	93.71
Average	160.26	163.58	97.87	105.51	85.30	92.16	115.00

Z-score is calculated as the sum of the capital ratio and ROA divided by the standard deviation of ROA. ROA is calculated as after-tax profit divided by total assets

stability may be supported by a limited exposure to speculative real estate lending (Čihák & Hesse, 2010).

Regarding Oman, Z-scores are moderate and relatively stable compared to those of other GCC countries. While Omani banks maintained adequate levels of capitalisation, they are highly exposed to environmental factors, including oil price fluctuations and adverse shocks.

In Qatar, bank stability has improved in the aftermath of the Global Financial Crisis (2008–09), supported by substantial state support, rapid balance-sheet expansion, and non-financial firm profitability (IMF, 2020). The use of substantial gas revenues to finance fiscal expansion and infrastructure investment helped Z-score remain at higher levels.

Regarding Saudi banks, their average Z-score is consistently high, with fewer extreme fluctuations than in Kuwait or Bahrain, possibly due to Saudi Arabia's larger and more diversified economy. Stability improved after 2010 but declined during oil price downturns and the pandemic, underscoring the close link between bank stability and fiscal-oil cycles.

Banks in the UAE exhibit high average Z-scores with two major trends. Between 2011 and 2014, bank stability rose due to post-crisis recapitalisation and regulatory tightening (Al-Hassan et al., 2014). However, the subsequent declines may reflect real estate market adjustments and external shocks.

Differences in bank stability across GCC countries can be attributed to several interconnected factors. First, fiscal capacity and sovereign backing play a central role. The presence of significant sovereign wealth funds and stronger fiscal positions contributes to the stability of the banking systems, especially during downturns. Second, the structure and concentration of the banking system matter. Systems in the UAE with greater exposure to specific sectors, such as real estate, exhibit relatively greater volatility. Third, government ownership and improvements in regulatory quality influence levels of stability. Countries with more conservative lending practices and stronger prudential oversight tend to exhibit higher and more stable Z-scores (Beck et al., 2006). Finally, dependence on hydrocarbon revenues amplifies cyclical effects, as oil price shocks transmit rapidly to bank profitability and capital through fiscal channels.

Globalisation Variable: The KOF Globalisation Index and Its Dimensions in the GCC

Globalisation shapes competition in banking through financial integration, trade openness, and the diffusion of technology and business practices. The GCC is one of the most open economic regions globally, with extensive trade and investment linkages. To assess the extent of globalisation in the region, I employ the KOF Globalisation Index, a widely used measure developed by the Swiss Economic Institute (KOF). The index captures the economic, social, and political dimensions of globalisation, offering a comprehensive view of a country's integration into global systems. It enables the analysis of how different aspects of globalisation influence financial stability and interact with institutional quality.

The KOF Globalisation Index is structured around three key dimensions: Economic Globalisation, Social Globalisation, and Political Globalisation. These dimensions help identify the specific drivers shaping financial and economic outcomes. Table 7.3 presents the KOG globalisation data for GCC countries in 2023.

Economic globalisation measures a country's integration into global markets through trade, investment, and financial flows. It consists of two sub-components: Actual flows and Restrictions. The Actual Flows capture fundamental economic interactions, including trade in goods and services (as a percentage of GDP), foreign direct investment (FDI) inflows and outflows, portfolio investments, and income payments to foreign nationals. The Restrictions reflect barriers to global economic integration, including tariffs, non-tariff barriers, capital controls, and trade taxes.

Within economic globalisation, two key pillars stand out. First, financial globalisation, which reflects cross-border financial flows, foreign investment in financial services, and the extent of integration into global financial markets. The presence of foreign banks in the GCC enhances competition, exposing local banks to international best practices. Second, trade globalisation, which captures the reliance on trade and its influence on banking competition. Open trade policies in the GCC facilitate cross-border financial services and attract foreign banks, intensifying competition and driving efficiency.

Economic globalisation plays an important role in the GCC, as the region's economies are heavily dependent on trade and foreign investment. The UAE and Qatar lead in this dimension, with high trade-to-GDP ratios and significant FDI inflows. Saudi Arabia and Oman, while still integrated into global trade, rely more on oil exports, limiting their economic diversification.

Social globalisation measures the diffusion of ideas, information, and human interactions across borders. It consists of three sub-components: i) personal contacts, which reflect direct cross-border interactions, including international tourism, remittances, and communication flows; ii) information flows, capturing the exchange of knowledge through internet usage, media access, and trade in cultural goods; and iii) cultural proximity, measuring cultural integration through indicators such as the number of global retail chains (e.g., McDonald's, IKEA), trade in cultural products, and the presence of international NGOs. In the GCC, Table 7.3 shows that the UAE and Qatar rank highest in social globalisation, driven by large expatriate populations, strong tourism sectors, and a globally connected media landscape. Bahrain and Kuwait exhibit moderate levels, while Saudi Arabia and Oman remain more conservative in cultural exchange and media openness.

Table 7.3 GCC Countries' performance in the KOF globalisation index and its pillars in 2023

Country	*KOF Index*	*Economic globalisation*	*Social globalisation*	*Political globalisation*	*Key Features*
Bahrain	75.2	78.5	72.8	74.1	–Economic: Financial hub, open trade policies, high FDI inflows
		–Trade: 80% of GDP	–Personal Contacts: High expatriate population, tourism	–Embassies: Hosts foreign embassies	–Social: Moderate cultural exchange, limited media openness
		–FDI: Strong inflows	–Information Flows: high internet usage	–Treaties: Active in regional agreements	–Political: Active in GCC and international diplomacy
Kuwait	68.9	70.3	67.5	69.0	–Economic: Oil exports dominate trade, moderate FDI
		–Trade: 70% of GDP	–Personal Contacts: Moderate tourism, expatriates	–Embassies: Strong diplomatic presence	–Social: Limited cultural exchange, conservative media policies
		–FDI: Moderate inflows	–Information Flows: high internet penetration	–Treaties: Active in OPEC and GCC	–Political: Strong regional influence, moderate global engagement
Oman	66.7	69.8	64.2	65.5	–Economic: Economic diversification efforts, moderate trade
		–Trade: 65% of GDP	–Personal Contacts: Moderate tourism, expatriates	–Embassies: Hosts foreign embassies	–Social: Limited cultural exchange, conservative social policies
		–FDI: Moderate inflows	–Information Flows: Low media openness	–Treaties: Neutral diplomacy, fewer treaties	–Political: Neutral stance, limited global engagement

(continued)

Table 7.3 (continued)

Country	*KOF Index*	*Economic globalisation*	*Social globalisation*	*Political globalisation*	*Key Features*
Qatar	80.1	82.4	78.6	79.3	–Economic: Strong trade, high FDI, global events (FIFA World Cup 2022)
		–Trade: 85% of GDP	–Personal Contacts: High tourism, expatriates	–Embassies: Strong global diplomatic presence	–Social: High cultural exchange, global media presence
		–FDI: Very high inflows	–Information Flows: High internet and media usage	–Treaties: Active in global treaties and organisations	–Political: Global mediation, strong international influence
Saudi Arabia	65.4	68.2	63.0	64.5	–Economic: Oil exports dominate, Vision 2030 reforms
		–Trade: 60% of GDP	–Personal Contacts: Moderate tourism, expatriates	–Embassies: Strong regional diplomatic presence	–Social: Conservative social policies, limited cultural exchange
		–FDI: Moderate inflows	–Information Flows: Moderate internet usage	–Treaties: Active in OPEC and GCC	–Political: Strong regional influence, limited global engagement
UAE	85.6	88.0	84.2	84.5	–Economic: Global trade hub, high FDI, diversified economy
		–Trade: 90% of GDP	–Personal Contacts: High tourism, expatriates	–Embassies: Strong global diplomatic presence	–Social: High cultural exchange, global media presence
		–FDI: Very high inflows	–Information Flows: High internet and media usage	–Treaties: Active in global treaties and organisations	–Political: Global influence, active in international diplomacy

Political globalisation assesses a country's involvement in international political structures and agreements. It includes: i) embassies and international organisations, measuring membership in entities such as the United Nations (UN), World Trade Organisation (WTO), and regional blocs like the GCC; ii) participation in UN peacekeeping missions, reflecting contributions to global peace initiatives; and iii) international treaties and agreements, indicating engagement in diplomatic and economic treaties.

Table 7.3 shows that the UAE and Qatar demonstrate intense political globalisation, actively participating in global governance and international organisations. Bahrain and Kuwait place greater emphasis on regional engagement, whereas Saudi Arabia and Oman maintain a more limited international diplomatic presence.

A comparison of GCC countries in the 2023 KOF Globalisation Index, which is available in Table 7.3, highlights notable differences in their global integration. The UAE emerges as the most globalised GCC country, with the highest overall score of 85.6, driven by its status as a global trade and financial hub. Qatar follows with 80.1, benefiting from strong economic integration and international engagement. Bahrain (75.2) and Kuwait (68.9) exhibit moderate levels of globalisation, with Bahrain's financial openness and Kuwait's trade-focused economy driving their rankings. Oman (66.7) and Saudi Arabia (65.4) remain the least globalised, with their scores constrained by conservative social policies and lower levels of political engagement.

The varying degrees of globalisation among the GCC countries reflect differences in economic diversification strategies, social openness, and political participation. While the UAE and Qatar have embraced global integration across all three dimensions, Saudi Arabia and Oman are gradually increasing their global presence through economic reforms and international partnerships. These distinctions highlight the diverse pathways through which globalisation shapes economic and financial stability in the region.

Institutional Quality (World Bank Governance Indicators) for GCC Countries

In the GCC, where state intervention in financial markets is significant, institutional quality, as captured by regulatory frameworks and the rule of law, may influence the performance of the banking sector. In this study, we retain two proxies of institutional quality: regulatory quality and rule of law. First, *regulatory quality* measures the ability of governments to formulate and implement policies that support private-sector development. In the banking sector, well-designed regulations promote fair competition, profitability, and solvency by preventing monopolistic practices, ensuring equal access to financial markets, and enforcing capital adequacy requirements. In the GCC, where government policies significantly shape banking outcomes, regulatory quality may be a key determinant of stability. Second, the rule of law encompasses contract enforcement and the protection of property rights. A strong legal environment reduces uncertainty, lowers operational risks, and ensures that financial institutions operate under fair and predictable conditions. In the GCC, where legal traditions differ from Western markets, the rule of law can influence how banks operate, particularly in enforcing lending contracts and resolving disputes.

These two institutional quality indicators provide a comprehensive view of how governance affects banking stability. Strong institutions promote stable market conditions, whereas weaker institutions may lead to inefficiencies, regulatory capture, and market distortions, thereby increasing risk exposure. Table 7.4 present the performance of each GCC country in the two key institutional indicators—Regulatory Quality and Rule of Law—as obtained from the World Bank's Worldwide Governance Indicators (WGI). Higher values indicate better performance.

The GCC countries exhibit varying performance across governance indicators, particularly in Regulatory Quality and Rule of Law, reflecting

Table 7.4 GCC Countries' performance in governance indicators (WGI) in 2023–24

Country	*Regulatory quality*	*Rule of Law*
Bahrain	68.7 (Strong regulatory frameworks, especially in finance)	65.4 (Moderate legal system, with some rigidity)
Kuwait	60.2 (Moderate, with room for improvement in business regulations)	58.9 (Moderate, with some inefficiencies in the legal system)
Oman	62.5 (Moderate, with efforts to improve business regulations)	61.0 (Moderate, with a focus on legal reforms)
Qatar	75.3 (Strong, with efficient business regulations)	72.8 (Strong, with a well-functioning legal system)
Saudi Arabia	64.8 (Moderate, with reforms under Vision 2030)	63.2 (Moderate, with ongoing legal reforms)
UAE	78.9 (Strong, with efficient and business-friendly regulations)	76.5 (Strong, with a well-functioning legal system)

differences in institutional frameworks and legal systems. The United Arab Emirates (UAE) leads the region, with outstanding scores in Regulatory Quality (78.9) and Rule of Law (76.5). Its business-friendly regulatory environment and efficient legal system have established the UAE as a global hub for trade, finance, and investment. Similarly, Qatar ranks second, with strong scores in Regulatory Quality (75.3) and Rule of Law (72.8). Qatar's practical regulatory framework and well-functioning legal system have supported its economic diversification and global influence, particularly in energy, finance, and tourism.

Bahrain, Saudi Arabia, and Oman demonstrate moderate performance in these governance indicators. Bahrain scores well in Regulatory Quality (68.7) and performs moderately in Rule of Law (65.4), with a strong regulatory framework, particularly in the financial sector, though its legal system shows some rigidity. Saudi Arabia, with Regulatory Quality (64.8) and Rule of Law (63.2), has made significant progress under its Vision 2030 reforms, improving its regulatory environment and legal system, though further enhancements are needed. Oman, with Regulatory Quality (62.5) and Rule of Law (61.0), has focused on legal and regulatory reforms to support economic diversification but lags behind the UAE and Qatar in governance performance.

Kuwait has the lowest governance scores in the GCC, with Regulatory Quality (60.2) and Rule of Law (58.9) ranking lowest. While Kuwait has made efforts to improve its regulatory environment, its legal system remains inefficient, and further reforms are needed to enhance governance. Overall, the UAE and Qatar lead in regulatory quality and the rule of law, whereas Bahrain, Saudi Arabia, and Oman exhibit moderate performance. Kuwait trails behind, highlighting the need for continued reforms to strengthen its governance framework.

The GCC countries exhibit significant differences in governance performance, with the UAE and Qatar leading in regulatory quality, rule of law, and control of corruption. Bahrain, Saudi Arabia, and Oman show moderate performance, while Kuwait lags. These differences highlight the need for targeted reforms to strengthen governance frameworks, particularly in Kuwait and Oman. Improving governance indicators will be critical for enhancing economic diversification, attracting investment, and ensuring sustainable development across the GCC.

Interaction Between Globalisation and Institutional Quality
Based on the statistics provided for the KOF Globalisation Index (economic, social, and political globalisation) and the World Bank's Worldwide Governance Indicators (WGI) (regulatory quality and rule of law), we can identify three combinations of globalisation pillars and governance dimensions that are likely to affect bank stability in the GCC region.

Economic globalisation and regulatory quality
Economic globalisation measures a country's integration into the global economy through trade, investment, and financial flows. Regulatory quality reflects the government's ability to formulate and implement sound policies and regulations that enable and promote private-sector development. Therefore, countries with high economic globalisation (e.g., the UAE and Qatar) and strong regulatory quality (e.g., the UAE and Qatar) are better equipped to manage risks associated with cross-border financial flows, such as capital flight and foreign exchange volatility. Strong regulatory frameworks ensure that banks adhere to international standards, reducing the likelihood of financial crises. For example, in the UAE, the robust regulatory environment has helped its banking sector remain stable despite global economic shocks. On the other hand, poorer regulatory quality in countries could exacerbate risks from economic globalisation, such as exposure to volatile international markets or inadequate oversight of foreign investments.

Political globalisation and the rule of law

enlargethispage-24ptPolitical globalisation reflects a country's participation in international political institutions and agreements, whereas the rule of law measures the extent to which laws are applied and enforced fairly. Countries with high political globalisation (e.g., the UAE and Qatar) and strict rule of law (e.g., the UAE and Qatar) are more likely to attract foreign investment and maintain stable banking systems. For instance, Qatar's active role in international diplomacy and its strong legal system have bolstered investor confidence in its banking sector. A weak rule of law can undermine the benefits of political globalisation by creating legal uncertainties and reducing investor confidence. This can increase risks for banks, including non-performing loans and reduced foreign capital inflows. However, a strict rule of law ensures that contracts are enforced, property rights are protected, and disputes are resolved fairly, all of which are critical for bank stability.

Political globalisation and regulatory quality

Political globalisation reflects a country's engagement in international diplomacy and institutions, while regulatory quality measures the effectiveness of government policies and regulations. Against this backdrop, countries with high political globalisation (e.g., the UAE and Qatar) and strong regulatory quality (e.g., the UAE and Qatar) are better able to implement international best practices in banking regulation. For example, the UAE's active participation in global financial institutions has helped it adopt robust regulatory standards. Poor regulatory quality can limit the benefits of political globalisation by creating regulatory gaps that increase risks for banks. However, strong regulatory quality helps ensure that banks comply with international standards, thereby reducing the likelihood of financial instability.

Results and Discussion

To examine the influence of globalisation on the stability of the GCC banking sector, we consider the overall globalisation index (KOFGI in Table 7.5) along with its three dimensions: economic (KOFECGI in Table 7.6), social (KOFSOGI in Table 7.7) and political (KOFPOGI in Table 7.8). Economic globalisation captures long-distance flows of goods, capital, and services, as well as the exchange of information and perceptions that accompany market transactions. Social globalisation reflects the spread of ideas, information, images, and people across borders, while political globalisation characterises the diffusion of government policies (Gygli et al., 2019).

We further disentangle economic (trade: KOFTRGI in Table 7.9; financial: KOFFIGI in Table 7.10), social (Interpersonal: KOFIPGI in Table 7.11) and Cultural (KOFCUGI in Table 7.12) globalisation indices. Given the high correlation among these sub-indices and to mitigate severe multicollinearity issues, we analyse the three dimensions of globalisation separately in our regression models (Dreher, 2006). For each index, we estimate four models, varying by the institutional quality proxy and the inclusion of interaction terms. Model 1 assesses the direct effects of globalisation and regulatory quality, whereas Model 2 extends this by

Table 7.5 Regression results of KOF Overall Globalisation Index (KOFGI)

Variable	*Model 1 (Regulatory Quality)*	*Model 2 (Regulatory Quality + Interaction)*	*Model 3 (Rule of Law)*	*Model 4 (Rule of Law + Interaction)*
CONSTANT	−3.3709 (1.9046)	26.5930*** (7.4453)	−2.8270 (1.8732)	23.4531** (9.2792)
Lag.STABILITY	0.7527*** (0.0519)	0.7501*** (0.0510)	0.7620*** (0.0534)	0.7629*** (0.0517)
KOFGI	0.9731** (0.3882)	3.5206*** (0.6375)	0.7690** (0.3635)	2.8988*** (0.7891)
ROL	–	–	−0.4309*** (0.1501)	6.0752** (2.2389)
REG_QUA	−0.4781*** (0.1262)	7.9893*** (1.9824)	–	–
KOFGI x ROL	–	–	–	−8.0131*** (2.7135)
ROFGI x REG_QUA	–	−9.2676*** (2.1311)	–	–
SIZE	0.0143 (0.0187)	0.0255 (0.0194)	0.0277* (0.0165)	0.0417** (0.0175)
LLPs	−0.5004*** (0.0202)	−0.4995*** (0.0198)	−0.5049*** (0.0210)	−0.4887*** (0.0209)
INEFFICIENCY	−0.2285*** (0.0712)	−0.2451*** (0.0697)	−0.2280*** (0.0697)	−0.2475*** (0.0687)
ISLAMIC	−0.1156** (0.0569)	−0.1155** (0.0579)	−0.0857* (0.0487)	−0.0862 (0.0555)
HHI	0.1380** (0.0543)	0.0847 (0.0589)	0.1515** (0.0589)	0.1619** (0.0713)
GROWTH	1.3948** (0.6669)	1.5159** (0.6739)	1.2112* (0.6683)	1.3086* (0.6699)
INFLATION	0.4050 (0.2359)	0.3308 (0.2377)	0.4457* (0.2445)	0.4043 (0.2434)
GFC	−0.3236 (0.1979)	−0.3648* (0.1952)	−0.3385* (0.1943)	−0.3403* (0.2003)
COVID	−0.6773*** (0.1407)	−0.6752*** (0.1427)	−0.7049*** (0.1410)	−0.6961*** (0.1420)
Diagnostics				
Arellano–Bond AR(1)	−6.50*** (0.000)	−6.49*** (0.000)	−6.52*** (0.000)	−6.56*** (0.000)
Arellano-Bond AR(2)	−2.26** (0.024)	−2.26** (0.024)	−2.23** (0.026)	−2.26** (0.024)
Sargan Test (*p*-value)	0.829	0.816	0.771	0.809
Hansen Test (*p*-value)	0.709	0.695	0.556	0.590

Notes ***, **, and * denote significance at the 1%, 5%, and 10% levels, respectively. Standard errors are reported in parentheses. The dependent variable is STABILITY. All models include year and bank fixed effects, and robust standard errors are used. Instruments for the GMM estimation are consistent across models, with lagged dependent variables and exogenous variables used as instruments

Table 7.6 Regression results of KOF Economic Globalisation Index (KOFECGI)

Variable	*Model 1 (Regulatory quality)*	*Model 2 (Regulatory quality + Interaction)*	*Model 3 (Rule of Law)*	*Model 4 (Rule of Law + Interaction)*
CONSTANT	–3.2185** (1.5784)	17.8692** (7.8881)	11.4860 (26.8061)	32.5270 (28.3096)
Lag.STABILITY	0.7434*** (0.0498)	0.7350*** (0.0481)	0.8525*** (0.1720)	0.8046*** (0.1551)
KOFECGI	0.9024*** (0.3005)	2.2122*** (0.5344)	0.7115* (0.4216)	2.0117** (0.8154)
REG_QUA	–0.6289*** (0.1550)	3.5559** (1.5257)	–	–
KOFECGI_REG_QUA	–	–5.5724*** (1.9835)	–	–
ROL	–	–	–0.6147* (0.3349)	4.0690** (1.8940)
KOFECGI_ROL	–	–	–	–6.8265** (2.8619)
SIZE	0.0299* (0.0160)	0.0433*** (0.0156)	0.0352** (0.0174)	0.0548*** (0.0161)
INEFFICIENCY	–0.2618*** (0.0727)	–0.2976*** (0.0743)	–0.2059** (0.1033)	–0.2676*** (0.0984)
LLPs	–0.4978*** (0.0196)	–0.4959*** (0.0190)	–4.7277 (8.3473)	–2.8445 (7.2146)
ISLAMIC	–0.1027* (0.0534)	–0.0924* (0.0552)	–0.0598 (0.0396)	–0.0499 (0.0434)
HHI	0.1219** (0.0502)	0.0320 (0.0696)	0.1517** (0.0654)	0.0972 (0.0647)
GROWTH	1.5498** (0.6688)	1.6712** (0.6716)	1.4129** (0.7043)	1.4584** (0.6901)
INFLATION	0.3945* (0.2314)	0.2871 (0.2376)	0.6167 (0.3711)	0.4561 (0.3428)
GFC	–0.3470* (0.1940)	–0.4100** (0.1993)	–0.2655 (0.2343)	–0.3432 (0.2207)
COVID	–0.6514*** (0.1387)	–0.6559*** (0.1413)	–0.6312*** (0.1849)	–0.6398*** (0.1792)
Diagnostics				
Arellano-Bond AR(1)	–6.46*** (0.000)	–6.40*** (0.000)	–1.05 (0.295)	–1.17 (0.243)
Arellano-Bond AR(2)	–2.28** (0.023)	–2.22** (0.026)	0.21 (0.833)	–0.03 (0.980)
Sargan Test (p-value)	0.899	0.789	0.907	0.843
Hansen Test (p-value)	0.902	0.769	0.882	0.832

Notes ***, **, and * denote significance at the 1%, 5%, and 10% levels, respectively. Standard errors are reported in parentheses. The dependent variable is STABILITY. All models include year and bank fixed effects, and robust standard errors are used. Instruments for the GMM estimation are consistent across models, with lagged dependent variables and exogenous variables used as instruments

Table 7.7 Regression results of KOF Social Globalisation Index (KOFSOGI)

Variable	*Model 1 (Regulatory quality)*	*Model 2 (Regulatory quality + Interaction)*	*Model 3 (Rule of Law)*	*Model 4 –(Rule of Law + Interaction)*
Constant	–17.6496** (7.1107)	-9.7856 (8.9576)	–11.1549* (6.0969)	-2.9172 (7.7209)
Lag.STABILITY	0.7622*** (0.0516)	0.7598*** (0.0508)	0.7706*** (0.0520)	0.7690*** (0.0514)
KOFSOGI	3.4307*** (1.2878)	6.5984*** (1.6638)	2.1647** (1.0905)	4.5648*** (1.5505)
REG_QUA	–0.5353*** (0.1356)	3.3174* (1.8909)	–	–
KOFSOGI x REG_QUA	–	–5.2308** (2.4974)	–	–
ROL	–	–	–0.4292*** (0.1425)	2.4498 (1.5808)
KOFSOGI x ROL	–	–	–	-10.409
SIZE	0.0185 (0.0161)	0.0248 (0.0164)	0.0329** (0.0146)	0.0410*** (0.0145)
INEFFICIENCY	–0.2362*** (0.0717)	–0.2520*** (0.0709)	–0.2336*** (0.0700)	–0.2480*** (0.0716)
LLPs	–0.5034*** (0.0198)	–0.5032*** (0.0194)	–0.5075*** (0.0201)	–0.5078*** (0.0199)
ISLAMIC	–0.005	–0.0852 (0.0533)	–0.0655 (0.0487)	–0.0606 (0.0474)
HHI	0.1244** (0.0519)	0.0915 (0.0588)	0.1317** (0.0538)	0.1373** (0.0542)
GROWTH	1.3367** (0.6776)	1.4191** (0.6777)	1.1651* (0.6690)	1.2122* (0.6709)
INFLATION	0.3786 (0.2382)	0.3110 (0.2360)	0.4423* (0.2455)	0.4104* (0.2426)
GFC	–0.2671 (0.2028)	–0.2809 (0.2025)	–0.2921 (0.1965)	–0.2995 (0.1945)
COVID	–0.6807*** (0.1452)	–0.6832*** (0.1462)	–0.7005*** (0.1463)	–0.6907*** (0.1466)
Diagnostics				
Arellano-Bond AR(1)	–6.48*** (0.000)	–6.48*** (0.000)	–6.52*** (0.000)	–6.52*** (0.000)
Arellano-Bond AR(2)	–2.26** (0.024)	–2.25** (0.024)	–2.23** (0.026)	–2.21** (0.027)
Sargan Test (*p*-value)	0.653	0.659	0.682	0.726
Hansen Test (*p*-value)	0.434	0.472	0.432	0.497

Notes ***, **, and * denote significance at the 1%, 5%, and 10% levels, respectively. Standard errors are reported in parentheses. The dependent variable is STABILITY. All models include year and bank fixed effects, and robust standard errors are used. Instruments for the GMM estimation are consistent across models, with lagged dependent variables and exogenous variables used as instruments

Table 7.8 Regression results of KOF Political Globalisation Index (KOFPOGI)

Variables	Model 1 (Regulatory Quality)	Model 2 (Regulatory Quality + Interaction)	Model 3 (Rule of Law)	Model 4 (Rule of Law + Interaction)
CONSTANT	0.228 (3.870)	1.260 (3.738)	–2.283 (4.140)	–1.300 (4.968)
Lag.STABILITY	0.743*** (0.050)	0.743*** (0.050)	0.754*** (0.051)	0.753*** (0.051)
KOFPOGI	0.120 (0.690)	4.179** (1.882)	0.533 (0.732)	1.689 (2.243)
REG_QUA	–0.319*** (0.102)	3.151** (1.495)	–	–
KOFPOGI × REG_QUA	–	–4.948** (2.084)	–	–
ROL	–	–	–0.293** (0.139)	0.662 (1.949)
KOFPOGI × ROL	–	–	–	–1.531 (3.058)
SIZE	0.032** (0.016)	0.033* (0.017)	0.033** (0.016)	0.033** (0.016)
LLPs	–0.495*** (0.020)	–0.492*** (0.020)	–0.500*** (0.020)	–0.499*** (0.021)
INEFFICIENCY	–0.232*** (0.071)	–0.227*** (0.069)	–0.229*** (0.070)	–0.226*** (0.069)
ISLAMIC	–0.088 (0.056)	–0.101* (0.058)	–0.076 (0.052)	–0.079 (0.052)
HHI	0.087* (0.050)	0.091* (0.051)	0.118** (0.058)	0.126** (0.058)
GROWTH	1.405** (0.652)	1.414** (0.655)	1.284** (0.657)	1.290** (0.658)
INFLATION	0.432* (0.237)	0.411* (0.237)	0.461* (0.241)	0.454* (0.238)
GFC	–0.316 (0.197)	–0.350 (0.192)	–0.327 (0.195)	–0.334 (0.195)
COVID	–0.656*** (0.138)	–0.656*** (0.140)	–0.693*** (0.135)	–0.692*** (0.135)
Diagnostics				
Arellano-Bond AR(1)	–6.54 (0.000)	–6.54 (0.000)	–6.53 (0.000)	–6.53 (0.000)
Arellano-Bond AR(2)	–2.28 (0.022)	–2.29 (0.022)	–2.25 (0.024)	–2.25 (0.024)
Sargan Test (p-value)	0.949	0.975	0.963	0.964
Hansen Test (p-value)	0.944	0.971	0.926	0.930

Notes ***, **, and * denote significance at the 1%, 5%, and 10% levels, respectively. Standard errors are reported in parentheses. The dependent variable is STABILITY. All models include year and bank fixed effects, and robust standard errors are used. Instruments for the GMM estimation are consistent across models, with lagged dependent variables and exogenous variables used as instruments

including an interaction term between the globalisation proxy and regulatory quality. Model 3 examines the impact of globalisation and the rule of law, and Model 4 adds an interaction term between a globalisation proxy and the rule of law.

Results of the Impact of Globalisation on Bank Stability

The results in Table 7.5 show that overall globalisation (KOFGI) has a positive, statistically significant effect across all models, suggesting that greater integration into global spheres enhances banking stability. This aligns with the literature, which suggests that global openness encourages regulatory improvements, enhances risk diversification, and attracts capital inflows, thereby strengthening banking resilience (Baltagi et al., 2009). To identify the specific sources of this positive effect, we further examine the three dimensions of globalisation: economic, social, and political.

Economic Globalisation and Bank Stability

Regression results in Tables (7.6, 7.9, and 7.10) confirm that economic globalisation—encompassing trade flows, foreign direct investment (FDI), portfolio investment, and capital restrictions—positively and significantly influences banking stability. This finding supports the economic integration hypothesis, which posits that economic globalisation enhances stability by facilitating access to international capital markets, improving risk diversification, and increasing banking efficiency (Kose et al., 2009).

However, the disaggregated results for trade and financial globalisation in Tables 7.9 and 7.10 reveal nuanced effects. Trade globalisation, measured by exports and imports of goods and services as a share of GDP, has an insignificant coefficient across all models (Table 7.9). Similarly, financial globalisation, defined by capital flows and stocks of foreign assets and liabilities, also exhibits an insignificant coefficient (Table 7.10). These results suggest that the influence of economic globalisation on banking systems in the GCC is primarily channelled through financial openness, which supports banking-sector stability by deepening financial integration and promoting efficient capital allocation. Bekaert et al. (2011) similarly demonstrate that financial globalisation reduces capital costs and strengthens risk-sharing mechanisms.

Table 7.9 Regression results of KOF Trade Globalisation Index (KOFTRGI)

Variable	*Model 1 (Regulatory quality)*	*Model 2 (Regulatory quality + Interaction)*	*Model 3 (Rule of Law)*	*Model 4 (Rule of Law + Interaction)*
CONSTANT	−6.0437 (5.3520)	−0.8349 (7.4646)	−1.9049 (3.8209)	3.8851 (7.1892)
Lag.STABILITY	0.7333*** (0.0482)	0.7310*** (0.0490)	0.7512*** (0.0504)	0.7489*** (0.0498)
KOFTRGI	1.2115 (0.9116)	3.0672* (1.7046)	0.4303 (0.6268)	2.0912 (2.0408)
REG_QUA	−0.4832** (0.1826)	1.8322 (1.9534)	–	–
KOFTRGI x REG_QUA	–	−3.1230 (2.5324)	–	–
ROL	–	–	−0.3393** (0.1645)	1.6645 (2.3186)
KOFTRGI x ROL	–	–	–	−2.9978 (3.3696)
SIZE	0.0352** (0.0145)	0.0385*** (0.0147)	0.0412*** (0.0139)	0.0472*** (0.0139)
LLPs	−0.4933*** (0.0192)	−0.4931*** (0.0192)	−0.4997*** (0.0201)	−0.4988*** (0.0199)
INEFFICIENCY	−0.2424*** (0.0729)	−0.2822*** (0.0763)	−0.2418*** (0.0707)	−0.2587*** (0.0767)
ISLAMIC	−0.0911* (0.0534)	−0.1102** (0.0555)	−0.0642 (0.0481)	−0.0593 (0.0482)
HHI	0.1515** (0.0720)	0.0978 (0.1030)	0.1270* (0.0662)	0.1034 (0.0754)
GROWTH	1.5011** (0.6787)	1.4871** (0.6970)	1.3346** (0.6630)	1.3604** (0.6719)
INFLATION	0.3737 (0.2298)	0.2953 (0.2459)	0.4521* (0.2358)	0.4010 (0.2509)
GFC	−0.3562* (0.1956)	−0.3043 (0.1899)	−0.3303* (0.1932)	−0.3613* (0.1969)
COVID	−0.6202*** (0.1396)	−0.5921*** (0.1429)	−0.6788*** (0.1332)	−0.6662*** (0.1361)
Diagnostics				
Arellano-Bond AR(1)	−6.44*** (0.000)	−6.32*** (0.000)	−6.49*** (0.000)	−6.48*** (0.000)
Arellano-Bond AR(2)	−2.27** (0.023)	−2.26** (0.024)	−2.24** (0.025)	−2.20** (0.028)
Sargan Test (*p*-value)	0.849	0.713	0.974	0.960
Hansen Test (*p*-value)	0.777	0.440	0.969	0.962

Notes ***, **, and * denote significance at the 1%, 5%, and 10% levels, respectively. Standard errors are reported in parentheses. The dependent variable is STABILITY. All models include year and bank fixed effects, and robust standard errors are used. Instruments for the GMM estimation are consistent across models, with lagged dependent variables and exogenous variables used as instruments

Table 7.10 Regression results of KOF Financial Globalisation Index (KOFFIGI)

Variable	*Model 1 (Regulatory quality)*	*Model 2 (Regulatory quality + Interaction)*	*Model 3 (Rule of Law)*	*Model 4 (Rule of Law + Interaction)*
CONSTANT	–11.7236*** (3.4713)	–3.1415 (4.0657)	–7.9450*** (2.8998)	6.7774 (4.3366)
Lag.STABILITY	0.7567*** (0.0527)	0.7555*** (0.0506)	0.7650*** (0.0540)	0.7644*** (0.0523)
KOFFIGI	2.4419*** (0.6379)	6.3799*** (1.2664)	1.6404*** (0.5205)	5.3279*** (1.2042)
REG_QUA	–0.5806*** (0.1270)	3.4080*** (1.1139)	–	–
KOFFIGI x REG_QUA	–	–6.0507*** (1.6798)	–	–
ROL	–	–	–0.4437*** (0.1355)	3.7295*** (1.1458)
KOFFIGI x ROL	–	–	–	–7.0202*** (1.9048)
SIZE	0.0267 (0.0173)	0.0414** (0.0161)	0.0398** (0.0156)	0.0590*** (0.0156)
LLPs	–0.5014*** (0.0207)	–0.5035*** (0.0199)	–0.5054*** (0.0214)	–0.5095*** (0.0207)
INEFFICIENCY	–0.2545*** (0.0721)	–0.2876*** (0.0719)	–0.2449*** (0.0711)	–0.2809*** (0.0735)
ISLAMIC	–0.1078** (0.0547)	–0.0887 (0.0551)	–0.0723 (0.0502)	–0.0564 (0.0506)
HHI	0.0288 (0.0474)	–0.0555 (0.0565)	0.0679 (0.0501)	0.0501 (0.0521)
GROWTH	1.4353** (0.6661)	1.6683** (0.6628)	1.2505* (0.6743)	1.3804** (0.6815)

Variable	*Model 1 (Regulatory quality)*	*Model 2 (Regulatory quality +* ***Interaction)***	*Model 3 (Rule of Law)*	*Model 4 (Rule of Law + Interaction)*
INFLATION	0.4349* (0.2387)	0.3481 (0.2402)	0.4821* (0.2473)	0.4259* (0.2472)
GFC	–0.3236* (0.1955)	–0.3420* (0.1941)	–0.3328* (0.1936)	–0.3342* (0.1917)
COVID	–0.6988*** (0.1425)	–0.7160*** (0.1447)	–0.7267*** (0.1425)	–0.7145*** (0.1428)
Diagnostics				
Arellano-Bond AR(1)	–6.44*** (0.000)	–6.41*** (0.000)	–6.47*** (0.000)	–6.49*** (0.000)
Arellano-Bond AR(2)	–2.31** (0.021)	–2.29** (0.022)	–2.26** (0.024)	–2.17** (0.030)
Sargan Test (p-value)	0.798	0.834	0.755	0.813
Hansen Test (p-value)	0.558	0.656	0.452	0.513

Notes ***, **, and * denote significance at the 1%, 5%, and 10% levels, respectively. Standard errors are reported in parentheses. The dependent variable is STABILITY. All models include year and bank fixed effects, and robust standard errors are used. Instruments for the GMM estimation are consistent across models, with lagged dependent variables and exogenous variables used as instruments

Table 7.11 Regression results of KOF Interpersonal Globalisation Index (KOFIPGI)

Variable	*Model 1 (Regulatory quality)*	*Model 2 (Regulatory quality + Interaction)*	*Model 3 (Rule of Law)*	*Model 4 (Rule of Law + Interaction)*
CONSTANT	−31.5670*** (5.8031)	−26.8949*** (8.7094)	−17.1889*** (4.0886)	−13.6242** (5.1844)
Lag.STABILITY	0.7371*** (0.0495)	0.7352*** (0.0493)	0.7562*** (0.0517)	0.7496*** (0.0500)
KOFIPGI	6.1117*** (1.0770)	7.2788*** (1.4785)	3.3222*** (0.7384)	3.8213*** (0.8728)
REG_QUA	−0.7986*** (0.1477)	0.8125 (1.8045)	–	–
KOFIPGI x REG_QUA	–	−2.2655 (2.4851)	–	–
ROL	–	–	−0.5051*** (0.1370)	0.3355 (0.7802)
KOFIPGI x ROL	–	–	–	−1.2542 (1.1588)
SIZE	0.0437** (0.0164)	0.0456*** (0.0158)	0.0507*** (0.0155)	0.0580*** (0.0164)
LLPs	−0.4978*** (0.0194)	−0.4975*** (0.0192)	−0.5041*** (0.0205)	−0.5028*** (0.0198)
INEFFICIENCY	−0.2062*** (0.0669)	−0.2095*** (0.0665)	−0.2191*** (0.0672)	−0.2237*** (0.0668)
ISLAMIC	−0.0893* (0.0536)	−0.0847 (0.0532)	−0.0514 (0.0536)	−0.0540 (0.0527)
HHI	0.1141** (0.0496)	0.0974* (0.0578)	0.1236** (0.0526)	0.1063* (0.0568)
GROWTH	1.5497** (0.6490)	1.5658** (0.6426)	1.3204** (0.6648)	1.2677* (0.6518)
INFLATION	0.4757** (0.2302)	0.4487* (0.2305)	0.5228** (0.2407)	0.5128** (0.2375)
GFC	−0.2365 (0.1909)	−0.2476 (0.1926)	−0.2777 (0.1894)	−0.3044 (0.1914)
COVID	−0.5594*** (0.1334)	−0.5683*** (0.1326)	−0.6545*** (0.1333)	−0.6088*** (0.1423)
Diagnostics				
Arellano-Bond AR(1)	−6.45*** (0.000)	−6.46*** (0.000)	−6.47*** (0.000)	−6.59*** (0.000)
Arellano-Bond AR(2)	−2.32** (0.020)	−2.31** (0.021)	−2.25** (0.024)	−2.25** (0.024)
Sargan Test (p-value)	0.969	0.974	0.877	0.954
Hansen Test (p-value)	0.911	0.929	0.685	0.923

Notes ***, **, and * denote significance at the 1%, 5%, and 10% levels, respectively. Standard errors are reported in parentheses. The dependent variable is STABILITY. All models include year and bank fixed effects, and robust standard errors are used. Instruments for the GMM estimation are consistent across models, with lagged dependent variables and exogenous variables used as instruments

Table 7.12 Regression results of KOF Cultural Globalisation Index (KOFFIGI)

Variables	*Model 1 (Regulatory quality)*	*Model 2 (Regulatory quality + Interaction)*	*Model 3 (Rule of Law)*	*Model 4 (Rule of Law + Interaction)*
CONSTANT	–2.425 (3.817)	17.021** (8.609)	–1.870 (4.143)	3.717 (6.635)
Lag.STABILITY	0.745*** (0.050)	0.716*** (0.048)	0.754*** (0.051)	0.756*** (0.051)
KOFCUGI	0.611 (0.678)	2.694*** (0.840)	0.455 (0.726)	1.708 (1.240)
REG_QUA	–0.357*** (0.107)	4.099** (1.623)	–	–
KOFCUGI × REG_QUA	–	–6.617*** (2.342)	–	–
ROL	–	–	–0.320** (0.151)	1.001 (1.193)
KOFCUGI × ROL	–	–	–	–2.505 (2.192)
SIZE	0.029* (0.015)	0.088*** (0.026)	0.037** (0.014)	0.044*** (0.014)
LLPs	–0.496*** (0.020)	–0.482*** (0.019)	–0.500*** (0.020)	–0.501*** (0.020)
INEFFICIENCY	–0.238*** (0.071)	–0.325*** (0.082)	–0.239*** (0.070)	–0.249*** (0.073)
ISLAMIC	–0.092* (0.052)	–0.034 (0.063)	–0.070 (0.046)	–0.063 (0.045)
HHI	0.090* (0.046)	–0.036 (0.090)	0.107** (0.052)	0.121** (0.054)
GROWTH	1.429** (0.667)	1.624** (0.685)	1.307** (0.666)	1.335** (0.673)
INFLATION	0.417* (0.234)	0.278 (0.237)	0.455* (0.238)	0.430* (0.239)
GFC	–0.308 (0.200)	–0.337 (0.203)	–0.314 (0.195)	–0.313 (0.195)
COVID	–0.660*** (0.139)	–0.622*** (0.147)	–0.689*** (0.137)	–0.687*** (0.137)
Diagnostics				
Arellano-Bond AR(1)	–6.51*** (0.000)	–6.54*** (0.000)	–6.51*** (0.000)	–6.52*** (0.000)
Arellano-Bond AR(2)	–2.26** (0.024)	–2.27** (0.023)	–2.24** (0.025)	–2.23** (0.026)
Sargan Test (*p*-value)	0.943	0.592	0.961	0.964
Hansen Test (*p*-value)	0.946	0.333	0.925	0.919

Notes ***, **, and * denote significance at the 1%, 5%, and 10% levels, respectively. Standard errors are reported in parentheses. The dependent variable is STABILITY. All models include year and bank fixed effects, and robust standard errors are used. Instruments for the GMM estimation are consistent across models, with lagged dependent variables and exogenous variables used as instruments

Social Globalisation and Bank Stability

Regression results in Tables 7.7, 7.11, and 7.12 confirm that social globalisation, with its two interpersonal and cultural components, has a positive impact on bank stability. The results indicate that social globalisation, as measured by personal contacts, information flows, and cultural proximity, significantly enhances stability across most models. This aligns with globalisation theory, which posits that increased cross-border interactions facilitate knowledge transfer, innovation, and risk diversification, thereby strengthening financial resilience (Dreher, 2006). Beck et al. (2007) argue that social networks and cross-border relationships contribute to financial stability by enhancing information flow, reducing transaction costs, and improving access to external financial resources.

The differentiated impact of the sub-components of social globalisation—interpersonal globalisation and cultural globalisation—on bank stability suggests that not all aspects of social globalisation contribute equally to financial-sector outcomes in the GCC. The consistently positive and significant coefficient on interpersonal globalisation implies that increased cross-border social interactions, including migration, communication networks, and personal connections, play a stabilising role in the banking sector. This is likely due to the enhanced exchange of financial knowledge, remittances, and international business linkages that accompany greater interpersonal connectivity. Migrant workers and expatriates, who constitute a substantial share of the GCC population, contribute to financial-sector resilience through steady remittance inflows, increased demand for financial services, and broader financial inclusion. Empirical studies, such as those by Aggarwal et al. (2011), show that remittances help stabilise banking systems by providing banks with a steady source of deposits and reducing reliance on volatile external funding.

By contrast, cultural globalisation exhibits an insignificant impact on bank stability, except in Model 2, where it becomes significant when interacted with regulatory quality. This suggests that mere exposure to global cultural influences does not affect financial stability unless accompanied by strong regulatory frameworks. This finding aligns with institutional theories, which posit that cultural integration may enhance bank stability when coupled with effective governance structures that facilitate the adoption of global financial norms (Acemoglu & Robinson, 2012).

Political Globalisation and Bank Stability

The results in Table 7.8 indicate that political globalisation (KOFPOGI) has a positive but statistically insignificant effect in Models 1, 3, and 4. This suggests that, in isolation, factors associated with political globalisation—such as diplomatic ties and international treaties—do not significantly influence banking stability. However, in Model 2, where political globalisation interacts with regulatory quality, the coefficient becomes positive and significant. This indicates that political globalisation enhances bank stability when accompanied by strong regulatory institutions, aligning with theories suggesting that global political integration can improve financial stability when regulatory mechanisms are robust.

Results of the Impact of Regulatory Quality and Rule of Law on Bank Stability

Across the GMM regression tables, the findings reveal a complex relationship between institutional quality—measured by regulatory quality and the rule of law—and bank stability in the GCC. In non-interaction models, regulatory quality and the rule of law exhibit negative, significant coefficients. This suggests that, in isolation, stronger institutions may be associated with less banking-sector stability. This result may reflect the unique economic structures of GCC economies, in which stringent regulations and heavy government intervention may constrain banking operations, potentially weakening the conditions of profit-making.

However, in the interaction models, globalisation proxies, regulatory quality, and the rule of law are positively and significantly associated with bank stability. This indicates that institutional quality enhances bank stability in a highly globalised context, possibly due to *spillover effects*. This means that while strong institutions may introduce constraints in a closed economy, they become instrumental in promoting financial stability when integrated into global financial networks. These findings align with the institutional complementarity framework (Rajan & Zingales, 2003), which supports the view that globalisation incentivises regulatory improvements that bolster financial stability.

Results of the Impact of the Interaction Between Measures of Globalisation and Institutional Quality on Bank Stability

In regression tables, the significant negative coefficient on the interaction term between measures of globalisation and institutional quality suggests that, although globalisation and strong institutions promote bank stability individually, their combined effect is complex. One explanation is that globalisation, when coupled with stringent institutional frameworks, may create rigidities that limit banks' adaptability to global financial dynamics, leading to inefficiencies or credit constraints. This finding is consistent with Stiglitz (2000) and Rajan and Zingales (2003), who argue that financial liberalisation without adaptive regulatory reforms can generate instability.

Results for the Control Variables

The regression results across specifications show that bank-specific characteristics significantly influence banking stability.

The strong significance of the lagged dependent variable across all models indicates that stability is highly persistent over time (Arellano & Bond, 1991). The resource-based view supports this result, as banks with a history of stability likely possess superior risk-management capabilities, established customer relationships, and institutional expertise.

Bank SIZE, measured by total assets, is positively associated with stability in most models, supporting the *too-big-to-fail* hypothesis. Larger banks benefit from economies of scale, greater diversification, and enhanced access to capital markets (Boyd & Runkle, 1993). Market concentration, measured by the Herfindahl–Hirschman Index (HHI), is positively associated with stability. This supports the *franchise value hypothesis*, which argues that reduced competition discourages excessive risk-taking (Keeley, 1990).

Cost inefficiency, measured by total costs per asset, negatively affects stability, suggesting that efficient banks are more resilient. Credit risk, as proxied by LLPs, is consistently negative and significant, suggesting that high credit risk is associated with deterioration in bank stability (Bushman & Williams, 2012). Islamic banks exhibit a weakly significant negative relationship with stability (Beck et al., 2013; Bakhouche et al., 2022).

Economic GROWTH positively impacts stability (Levine, 2005), while INFLATION has an insignificant effect (Boyd et al., 2001). The 2008–09 global financial crisis (GFC) had significant negative effects (Laeven & Valencia, 2013), but COVID exerted a larger destabilising impact. This underscores GCC banks' exposure to external shocks, particularly those linked to oil markets and global trade.

These findings underscore the importance of regulatory flexibility in ensuring that the benefits of globalisation are fully realised in the GCC banking sector. While globalisation supports stability by fostering competition and diversification, rigid regulatory frameworks may hinder banks' ability to capitalise on these benefits. Policymakers should consider adaptive regulatory strategies that balance oversight with market responsiveness, ensuring that global integration enhances rather than undermines financial stability. The findings indicate that while globalisation can enhance stability, its benefits are contingent on strong regulatory frameworks. This underscores the need to strengthen institutional governance and regulatory oversight to leverage the advantages of globalisation fully. The findings align with the substitution hypothesis, which suggests that globalisation can compensate for weak institutions but has a diminished impact in countries with strong governance. Additionally, the complementarity hypothesis is supported by evidence that globalisation and institutional quality interact to shape financial stability.

Conclusion

The findings of this study highlight the significant role that globalisation plays in influencing the stability of the GCC banking sector. Globalisation has a strong positive effect on bank stability, supporting the view that deeper integration into global markets enhances resilience. However, when examined in greater detail, it becomes clear that economic, social, and political globalisation affect banking stability through distinct mechanisms. Economic globalisation promotes stability by providing access to international capital markets and encouraging financial integration, while social globalisation—primarily through personal connections—enhances resilience via remittances and financial inclusion. In contrast, political globalisation contributes to stability only when it is supported by robust regulatory frameworks, indicating that the quality of institutions plays a vital mediating role.

The results also highlight the importance of institutional quality for bank resilience. While regulatory quality and rule of law alone appear to introduce constraints in the GCC context, their interaction with globalisation is positive and significant. This suggests that globalisation can catalyse institutional improvements, reinforcing the stability of the banking sector when regulatory frameworks are effectively aligned with global financial standards. The persistence of bank stability over time, alongside the role of bank-specific factors such as size, cost efficiency, and risk management, further reinforces the notion that both external integration and internal structural characteristics are critical determinants of financial resilience.

enlargethispage-24ptFrom a policy perspective, these findings offer several important recommendations. First, policymakers should focus on strengthening the regulatory environment to ensure that global financialisaton translates into stability. Strengthening risk-based supervision, improving transparency, and aligning banking regulations with international standards, such as Basel III, will help mitigate vulnerabilities associated with increased financial integration. Second, fostering greater financial inclusion through policies that support remittances and migrant banking services can harness the stabilising effects of interpersonal globalisation. Initiatives that facilitate digital banking, cross-border payment systems, and financial literacy among expatriate populations could further enhance resilience.

Additionally, given the significant role of institutional quality, policymakers should prioritise governance reforms that enhance the effectiveness of regulatory institutions. Strengthening the independence and capacity of financial regulatory bodies, enhancing legal frameworks for contract enforcement, and improving judicial efficiency will create a more robust financial environment that can better absorb external shocks. The findings also suggest that while larger banks tend to be more stable, regulators must remain vigilant against excessive risk-taking, particularly amid global financial market fluctuations.

Future research should examine the long-term effects of globalisation on banking stability, particularly in light of emerging financial technologies and evolving geopolitical risks. Investigating the role of fintech, digital currencies, and cross-border financial innovations could provide further insights into how technological globalisation influences financial resilience. Additionally, examining the heterogeneous effects of globalisation across different banking models, including Islamic and conventional banks, would offer a more nuanced understanding of stability dynamics within the GCC. Further research could also examine how environmental, social, and governance (ESG) factors interact with globalisation to shape the stability of the banking sector in the region.

This study highlights the complex interplay between globalisation, institutional quality, and banking stability in the GCC. While global integration offers opportunities to enhance resilience, the effectiveness of regulatory and institutional frameworks remains a key determinant of stability. Policymakers must therefore adopt a proactive approach that balances financial openness with robust governance to ensure a stable and resilient banking sector.

CHAPTER 8

Cost Efficiency and Returns to Scale in GCC Banking

Introduction

From the early 2000s to the post-pandemic era, the global focus has shifted towards the GCC economies due to their geopolitical significance and rapid economic and social transformations. The region has evolved from a hydrocarbon-dependent economy into an increasingly diversified investment destination, shaped by tourism, infrastructure development, financial market expansion, and digitalisation (Ben Hassen, 2025). In GCC finance, financial intermediaries remain the primary channel for financing production and consumption, making banking performance essential to financial and economic stability. Several factors, including deregulation, institutional strengthening, global financial shocks, oil price volatility, and accelerated technological change, have influenced the performance of GCC financial intermediation (IMF, 2025; Khandelal et al., 2016). During the 2007–09 global financial crisis, policymakers reaffirmed the relevance of the Schumpeterian view that financial institutions contribute effectively to growth only when they operate under conditions of competition and efficient resource allocation (Claessens et al., 2010; Martyniszyn, 2025). As a result, the stability of banking systems depends not only on capital adequacy but also on institutions' ability to operate at higher levels of efficiency. Reform measures in the post-GFC phase reflected this reaffirmation, which provides a

A. Bakhouche, *Banking in the GCC*, Palgrave Macmillan Studies in Banking and Financial Institutions,
https://doi.org/10.1007/978-3-032-21737-0_8

basis for enhancing the conditions under which banks conduct their intermediation function at minimum cost (Nasim et al., 2025).

In GCC countries, banking-sector reforms have been undertaken not only to enhance efficiency and stability but also to strengthen integration, advance convergence, and prepare the foundations for a prospective monetary union (Laabas & Limam, 2002; Sturm & Siegfried, 2005; Takagi, 2012). In the absence of such convergence, structural asymmetries may undermine collective stability and prevent deeper integration (De Grauwe, 2018). The empirical literature on bank performance highlights the importance of efficiency for profitability, resilience, and survival (Bayeh et al., 2021; Chaffai & Coccorese, 2019; González et al., 2019). In non-crisis times, banks employ cost efficiency to reduce the risk of failure and enhance profitability during subsequent financial crises (Assaf et al., 2019).

Efficiency measures managerial and organisational quality by capturing a bank's ability to minimise costs relative to a best-practice frontier (Shamshur & Weill, 2019). In this context, efficient banks can allocate capital more productively, absorb shocks, and support sustainable growth (Berger & Humphrey, 1997). Over time, more efficient banks are likely to expand, and less efficient institutions lose market share, reshaping the financial landscape.

This study addresses the following question: *How efficient are GCC banks, and what factors have shaped their performance over the period 2002–2022?* Using two-stage analysis, the study applies Data Envelopment Analysis (DEA) to estimate and examine cost efficiency for a panel of 71 GCC banks from 2002 to 2022 (Charnes et al., 1978; Coelli et al., 1998). The DEA decomposes overall cost efficiency (CE) into allocative (AE), pure technical (TE), and scale (SE) efficiencies, allowing separation of managerial performance from structural constraints related to size and input prices (Farrell, 1957; Kumbhakar & Lovell, 2000). In the second-stage analysis, the study assesses the impact of size, diversification, ownership, inflation, the rule of law, and three global crisis events during 2002–22 on cost efficiency.

In addition, during the period under study, the GCC banking systems experienced size-related events, including significant asset growth, mergers and acquisitions (M&As), and the emergence of large national institutions alongside small and medium-sized ones, which might have impacted whether banks are operating at an appropriate size. Accordingly, the analysis further aims to identify the type of return to scale—constant (CRS), increasing (IRS), or decreasing (DRS)—for individual GCC banks. Under CRS, banks operate at their most productive scale, implying that proportional increases in inputs generate proportional increases in outputs. The IRS indicates that banks are too small relative to their operations and could reduce average costs through expansion. By contrast, DRS reflects diseconomies of scale, in which further growth leads to rising unit costs due to managerial complexity, coordination failures, and regulatory burdens. RTS can be used to design sound merger and competition policies and set regulatory thresholds. If CRS is less widespread, expansion may proceed under the assumption of inherent scale economies, leading to inefficiency and systemic fragility rather than enhancing competitiveness and resilience.

Three stylised facts emerge from this study on GCC banking. First, GCC banks exhibit lower but uneven cost efficiency, with cross-country heterogeneity. Second, scale inefficiency is recurrent, and larger banks do not systematically outperform smaller peers, suggesting the presence of diseconomies of scale. Third, efficiency is shaped not only by bank-specific characteristics but also by economic and institutional factors. The findings from this study offer policymakers a framework to strengthen the resilience, competitiveness, and convergence of financial systems.

The remainder of the paper is organised as follows. Section 8.2 reviews the literature on bank efficiency. Section 8.3 outlines the methodological framework. Section 8.4 presents the efficiency estimates, scale properties, and regression analysis. Section 8.5 concludes and recommends.

Literature Review

Globalisation, consolidation, the adoption of international regulatory standards, and the integration of ICT and AI have shaped global banking over the past few decades. These factors are expected to have a profound effect on the cost efficiency of banking institutions. The literature has paid attention to such issue with a strong focus on banks in developed countries such as the US, the UK, and Europe (Berger et al., 1993; Kaparakis et al., 1994; Mester, 1996; Mitchell & Onvural, 1996; Shamshur & Weill, 2019), the more recent studies analyse bank efficiency in emerging and developing countries in Asia, MENA, Latin America, and EEC. Generally, studies on bank efficiency can be categorised into two main groups: SFA and DEA. This study focuses on DEA studies on GCC banking.

Several empirical studies examine cost efficiency in GCC banking markets and compare their levels across bank types and countries (Alexakis et al., 2019; Kamarudin et al., 2014; Maghyereh & Awartani, 2014; Mostafa, 2007; Rosman et al., 2014; Tai, 2014; Srairi, 2010; Zeitun, 2012; Zeitun et al., 2013). An earlier DEA study by Limam (2002) reported technical efficiency ranging from 82 to 94% in 1999, with significant sensitivity to capital and size. Mostafa (2007) applies DEA to 50 GCC banks in 2005 and reports an average technical efficiency of 73%. Turk-Ariss et al. (2007) find that the mean cost efficiency for GCC banks is 77.59%, driven by both allocative (86.12%) and technical (88.13%) efficiencies. Maghyereh and Awartani (2014) find that, between 2000 and 2009, the average technical efficiency for GCC banks was 86%, with a drop in 2007–08. Aghimien et al. (2016) investigate the DEA-based efficiency of 43 GCC banks over 2007–2011. The findings suggest that GCC banks have exhibited a mean technical inefficiency of 17.4%. This level was attributed to pure technical inefficiency (12.3%) and scale inefficiency (5.1%). Gattoufi et al. (2009) examine the cost efficiency of 10 banks involved in mergers and acquisitions (M&A) during 2003–2007. The results show that their technical efficiency improved from 82.37% in 2003 to 85.86% in 2007.

Mohanty et al. (2016) show that cost efficiency varies widely across the GCC countries between 1999 and 2020. Grigorian and Manole (2005) find that banks in Bahrain are, on average, the most technically efficient in the GCC. However, Ariss et al. (2007) show that Omani banks were the most efficient from 1999 to 2004, followed by those in Bahrain and Kuwait.

The literature also compares cost efficiency between Islamic and conventional banks. Covering the period 2001–06, Sufian and Noor (2009) find that technical inefficiency was widespread in Islamic banks and is primarily attributable to pure technical inefficiency rather than scale inefficiency. This finding was consistent with findings reported by Srairi and Kouki (2012) and Aghmien et al. (2016) on their samples. Hamdani et al. (2014) compare the DEA-based cost efficiency of Islamic and conventional banks in GCC countries. The findings indicate that conventional banks outperform Islamic banks, with an average technical efficiency score of 81% versus 95.57%. Mohanty et al. (2016) find that while conventional and Islamic banks exhibit similar average cost efficiency, Islamic banks' efficiency is more volatile than that of conventional banks. Miah and Uddin (2017) show that conventional banks are more efficient than Islamic banks from 2005 to 2014.

Alrafadi et al. (2014) observed that efficiency deteriorated following the 2008–09 turbulence, primarily due to allocative and scale inefficiencies. Hamdani et al. (2014) show that the efficiency of conventional banks has declined since 2008, whereas Islamic banks' efficiency has increased since 2009. Alqahtani et al. (2017) observe that during the 2007–09 GFC, Islamic banks were more efficient than conventional banks due to constraints on trading in non-Sharia-compliant assets (Table 8.1).

Methodology

Sample

The data were extracted from the nonconsolidated balance sheets and income statements for 2002–2022, reported in USD. The branches of foreign banks and non-commercial financial institutions were excluded. The sample comprises an unbalanced panel of 71 banks with a total of 1,145 years of observation over the period 2002–22. While Oman experienced an increase in the number of banks over this period, the UAE saw a decrease in the number of banks post-2016 due to Mergers and Acquisitions.

This study examines cost efficiency performance and scale dynamics in GCC banking systems over the period 2002–2022. Table 8.2 shows that the total number of banks in our sample is 71. Some of these banks were involved in mergers and acquisitions. The UAE is the most represented in our sample, with 21 banks, followed by Saudi Arabia with 13. There are 47 conventional banks in our sample, of which 30 banks are government-owned. Islamic banks are predominantly owned by domestic capital. There are no *small* foreign banks in the sample, nor are there any foreign or small banks operating in Qatar.

Definition of Costs, Outputs, and Inputs

This study employs the intermediation approach, developed by Sealey and Lindley (1977), to define input and output variables (Berger & Humphrey, 1997). The approach views a bank as a financial intermediary producing two outputs: total loans (Y1) and other earning assets

Table 8.1 Selected DEA studies on GCC bank efficiency: 2009–2023

Author	*Country/data*	*Period*	*Output*	*Input/Input prices*	*Method*	*Results (sample)*
Sufian and Noor (2009)	16 Islamic banks from the MENA region	2001–2006	Financing, investments, income	Deposits, assets	DEA	-Mean technical efficiency of 66.7%, with scale technical efficiency outweighing pure technical efficiency -Tobit: A Positive relationship was found between bank efficiency and loan intensity, size, capitalisation, and profitability
Olson and Zoubi (2011)	80 banks in GCC, Egypt, Jordan, Lebanon and Morocco	2000–2008	Net loans Securities and other earning assets	Price of deposit: interest expense/deposits Price of labour: personnel expenditures/total assets Depreciation and other non-labour operating expenses/fixed assets	SFA	Mean cost efficiency of 0.703 with model A without country dummies, and 0.735 (Model B) with country dummies

Author	*Country/data*	*Period*	*Output*	*Input/Input prices*	*Method*	*Results (sample)*
Kamarudin et al. (2014)	74 GCC banks (47 conventional and 27 Islamic banks)	2007 - 2011	Loans (total of short-term and long-term loans); Income (gross interest and dividends)	Deposits (deposits and short-term funding); Labour (personnel expenses) Price of deposits (total interest expenses/ deposits) Price of labour (personnel expenses/ total assets)	DEA	Conventional banks (mean CE: 71.9%) are more cost-efficient than Islamic banks (Mean CE 38.4%
Alqahtan et al. (2017)	80 banks in 6 GCC countries	1999–2012	Loans Other earning assets	Deposits Labour	DEA	Average cost efficiency 0.71, with conventional (0.7175) and Islamic (0.6877)
Ghosh (2018)	96 banks, of which 26 are Islamic, in 12 MENA countries	2001–2012	Total customer loans Other earning assets (investment securities, Interbank funds and other investments)	Price of capital: operating cost net of personnel expense/total fixed asset Price of funds: total interest expense/ total deposits Price of labour: personnel expense /total asset	SFA	Mean efficiency of 0.632

(continued)

Table 8.1 (continued)

Author	*Country/data*	*Period*	*Output*	*Input/Input prices*	*Method*	*Results (sample)*
González et al. (2019)	201 banks in 19 MENA countries	2005–2012	Loans Other off-balance-sheet activities (OBS)	Deposits, Labour, and Physical Capital Price of deposits: interest expenses over total customer deposits Price of labour: total salaries and staff expenses over total assets Price of capital: other operating expenses over total assets	SFA	Mean cost efficiency of 0.77
Mansour and El Moussawi (2020)	199 banks in 12 Arab countries	2000–2014	Total earning assets, total customer deposits, and impaired loans	Physical capital (Fixed assets), financial capital (total interest expenses), and labour (personnel expenses)	DEA	Technical, allocative of and cost efficiencies 87%, 79% and 70% respectively

Table 8.2 Number of banks used in the sample between 2002 and 2022

	Bahrain	*Kuwait*	*Oman*	*Qatar*	*Saudi Arabia*	*UAE*	*Number of banks*
I- Conventional	**5**	**6**	**7**	**5**	**9**	**15**	**47**
a. Foreign	**1**	**1**	**1**	–	**3**	–	**6**
Large	1	–	–	–	3	–	4
Medium	–	1	1	–	–	–	2
b. Government	**4**	**2**	**3**	**3**	**6**	**12**	**30**
Large	3	1		1	5	7	17
Medium		1	3	2	1	1	8
Small	1	–	–	–	–	4	5
c. Private	–	**3**	**3**	**2**	–	**3**	**11**
Large	–	1	1	1	–	1	4
Medium	–	2	2	1	–	1	6
Small	–	–	–	–	–	1	1
II- Islamic	**4**	**4**	**2**	**4**	**4**	**6**	**24**
a. Foreign	**1**	–	–	–	–	–	**1**
Medium	1	–	–	–	–	–	1
b. Government	–	**3**	**1**	**3**	**1**	**6**	**14**
Large	–	1	–	1	–	2	4
Medium	–	1	–	2	1	3	7
Small	–	1	1		–	1	3
c. Private	**3**	**1**	**1**	**1**	**3**	–	**9**
Large	–	–	–	–	1	–	1
Medium	–	–	–	1	2	–	3
Small	3	1	1	–	–	–	5
III- Number of banks	**9**	**10**	**9**	**9**	**13**	**21**	**71**

(Y2), using three inputs: purchased funds (X1), labour, proxied by total employee expenses (X2), and physical capital, proxied by total fixed assets (X3). The intermediation approach may be superior for evaluating entire financial institutions because it includes interest expenses, which typically account for more than half of total costs (Berger & Humphrey, 1997). The price of purchased funds is calculated as the ratio of total interest expenses to total deposits; the price of labour is proxied by the ratio of total employees' expenses to total assets; and the price of physical capital is measured as the ratio of total depreciation and other operating expenses to total fixed assets. The sum of interest expenses, labour expenses, depreciation, and other operating expenses represents the bank's total cost.

Table 8.3 provides descriptive statistics for the outputs, inputs, and input prices used to estimate efficiency measures. They indicate differences in the scale, cost structure, and production technology of GCC banks over the period 2002–22. On average, banks operating in Saudi Arabia, Qatar, and the UAE exhibit larger assets, loans, and purchased funds than those in Bahrain and Oman. This may reflect differences in economic size and financial depth. Conventional banks are larger than Islamic banks, and government-owned banks are substantially bigger than banks with other types of ownership.

For input prices, banks in Bahrain paid the highest interest (2.5%), followed by Kuwait (2.08%) and Qatar (2.06%). Saudi banks faced the lowest cost of purchased funds (approximately 1%). Larger GCC banks face a lower cost of funds than smaller banks. Government banks also incurred lower interest costs than private and foreign banks. No substantial differences in costs of funds between conventional and Islamic banks.

As for labour, it is cheaper in Qatar, Kuwait, and Saudi Arabia, and more expensive in Oman, the UAE, and Bahrain. Other results suggest that Islamic banks, smaller banks, private and government banks pay higher labour rates than their respective counterparts.

Regarding physical capital, it is more expensive in Oman and Bahrain and cheaper in Kuwait and Saudi Arabia. Islamic, smaller, and private banks incur higher expenses on their fixed assets than their counterparts.

DEA Approach to Measurement of Cost Efficiency

Cost efficiency measures the difference between a bank's actual cost and its optimal cost for producing the same bundle of outputs. This difference provides insight into inefficiencies in the production process and the optimality of the chosen input mix. The two most widely used methods for estimating bank efficiency are parametric stochastic frontier analysis (SFA) and non-parametric data envelopment analysis (DEA) (Iosifidi et al., 2021).

DEA is a non-parametric frontier-based mathematical programming method used to estimate cost efficiency (CE) values for decision-making units such as banks (Charnes et al., 1978; Farrell, 1957; Sherman & Gold,

Table 8.3 Average values of output, input, and input prices used to estimate efficiency measures in the GCC banking systems between 2002 and 2022. All values are in millions of USD. Standard deviation values are between brackets

	No. of obs	*Total assets*	*Interest expense*	*Depreciation, depletion & amortisation*	*Loans*	*Investments*	*Purchased funds*	*Labour expenses*	*Physical capital*	*Price of purchased funds (P1)*	*Price of labour (P2)*	*Price of physical capital (P3)*
Panel 1: Country												
Bahrain	157	11,873.09 (11,306.12)	274.21 (323.41)	16.36 (22.67)	6,769.85 (6,974)	2,717.62 (2866.9)	10,025.76 (9,614.3)	105.05 (104.01)	119.49 (133.05)	0.0247 (0.0126)	0.0093 (0.0025)	0.2365 (0.367)
Kuwait	179	22,027.79 (23,473.07)	350.07 (344.48)	34.51 (55.73)	13,359.51 (13,170)	3,887.71 (6010.94)	18,555.01 (19,605.08)	156.41 (171.26)	336.56 (560.25)	0.0208 (0.0131)	0.0073 (0.0029)	0.1175 (0.0668)
Oman	128	7,357.66 (7,580.63)	116.64 (115.72)	9.68 (10.39)	5,474.95 (5,525.54)	800.88 (930.81)	6,058.27 (6,152.85)	69.45 (61.81)	60.74 (54.83)	0.0191 (0.0093)	0.0112 (0.0052)	0.2164 (0.191)
Qatar	125	36,123.22 (60,549.6)	684.33 (1652.06)	28.44 (44.28)	25,171.89 (42,571.98)	5,688.12 (7,593.75)	29,784.23 (52,999.82)	151.24 (216.95)	221.62 (349.18)	0.0206 (0.0121)	0.0052 (0.0021)	0.15 (0.0932)
Saudi Arabia	227	46,936.3 (38,698.97)	320.89 (301.01)	65.52 (73.89)	29,033.25 (23,280.03)	11,842.76 (11,307.99)	38,605.38 (31,751.05)	341.61 (239.07)	523.06 (580.11)	0.01 (0.0078)	0.0084 (0.0032)	0.1402 (0.051)
UAE	329	27,377.27 (44,194.62)	347.06 (546.02)	27.97 (44.84)	16,404.8 (22,988.07)	4,842.62 (9,708.47)	22,428.05 (36,264.57)	195.65 (238.56)	204.17 (263.3)	0.0188 (0.0099)	0.0098 (0.0047)	0.1568 (0.1097)
Panel 2: Bank type												
Conventional	771	31,029.17 (44,102.36)	407.78 (790.01)	33.31 (52.92)	19,139.48 (26,404.63)	6,132.02 (9,733.78)	25,733.46 (36,863.33)	202.37 (232.31)	254.75 (361.59)	0.0188 (0.0112)	0.0080 (0.0031)	0.1471 (0.1175)
Islamic	374	18,723.01 (23,932.12)	210.72 (271.48)	31.91 (51.53)	12,119.48 (15,597.26)	3,983.52 (6,224.5)	15,228.95 (19,939.27)	155.54 (174.11)	278.01 (513.25)	0.0178 (0.0123)	0.0101 (0.0053)	0.1996 (0.2454)
Panel 3: Size												
Large	511	48,540.38 (50,031.93)	589 (937.02)	57.53 (68.91)	29,707.61 (30,217.95)	10,239.87 (11,310.59)	40,208.21 (41,901.71)	324.85 (255.06)	458.9 (550.72)	0.0163 (0.0104)	0.0079 (0.003)	0.1397 (0.0569)
Medium	436	12,254.31 (88,15.18)	182.27 (164.96)	16.61 (18.07)	8,262.8 (6,149.43)	1,966.49 (1,962.15)	9,992.68 (7,351.58)	95.15 (69.95)	133.73 (128.4)	0.0202 (0.0128)	0.0087 (0.0037)	0.1607 (0.1572)
Small	198	3,933.74 (2,988.74)	64.45 (58)	4.93 (4.2)	2,555.87 (1,980.1)	644.75 (570.38)	3,196.57 (2,586.63)	33.93 (20.24)	38.29 (40.8)	0.0201 (0.0108)	0.0108 (0.0061)	0.2353 (0.3192)
Panel 4: Ownership												
Government	681	31,536.08 (46,049.28)	412.74 (838.37)	36.47 (59.46)	19,403.43 (27,462.56)	6,648.71 (10,456.58)	26,062.13 (3,8591.37)	210.01 (244.32)	275.23 (424.85)	0.0179 (0.0105)	0.0087 (0.0043)	0.1549 (0.1131)

(continued)

Table 8.3 (continued)

	No. of obs	*Total assets*	*Interest expense*	*Depreciation, depletion & amortisation*	*Loans*	*Investments*	*Purchased funds*	*Labour expenses*	*Physical capital*	*Price of purchased funds (P1)*	*Price of labour (P2)*	*Price of physical capital (P3)*
Private	336	18,037.5	215.7	26.09	11,551.31	29,77.73	14,853.66	140.82	236.83	0.0199	0.0091	0.1877
		(25,574.81)	(264)	(42.14)	(16,785.16)	(4,955.77)	(21,315.62)	(171.4)	(432.83)	(0.0128)	(0.0039)	(0.2537)
Foreign	128	26,478.31	309.85	31.34	17,142.6	5,385.46	21,851.45	186.47	260.8	0.0175	0.0080	0.1524
		(19,303.23)	(245.21)	(31.22)	(12,192.93)	(4,825.94)	(15,167.69)	(122.5)	(322.85)	(0.0131)	(0.0029)	(0.1604)
Average	1,145	27,009.51	343.41	32.85	16,846.49	5,430.24	22,302.29	187.07	262.35	0.0184	0.0087	0.1642
		(39,105.35)	(672.79)	(52.45)	(23,652.49)	(8,798.88)	(32,688.95)	(216.08)	(417.15)	(0.0116)	(0.0041)	(0.1719)

1985). It computes relative efficiency as the ratio of the weighted sum of outputs to the sum of the weighted inputs. It does not require specifying a regression model, nor does it make prior assumptions regarding functional forms or distributional assumptions that require residuals (Casu & Molyneux, 2003). DEA-based cost efficiency (CE) measures the proportional reduction in costs that would be achieved if the bank were both technically and allocatively efficient. In this context, cost efficiency (CE) can be decomposed into overall technical (OTE) and allocative (AE). While OTE measures the proportional reduction in input usage, AE measures the proportional reduction in costs that banks achieve by selecting the optimal input mix. OTE can also be decomposed into pure technical efficiency (TE) and scale efficiency (SE) (Isik & Hassan, 2002). Thus, CE can be represented by:

$$CE = AE\ X\ TE\ X\ SE \tag{8.1}$$

DEA efficiency scores are bounded between zero and one, with a value of one indicating that a bank lies on the efficient frontier. Scores below unity indicate relative inefficiency relative to the best-performing banks in the sample. All efficiency measures are computed annually to capture temporal variation and to account for changes in market, regulatory, and economic conditions. DEA enables the decomposition of sources of inefficiency and the examination of scale effects across countries, bank types, size classes, and ownership categories. We construct sub-samples for these dimensions to allow comparison.

Following the intermediation approach to banking, banks are modelled as financial intermediaries that use labour, physical capital, and funds to produce loans and other earning assets. The DEA cost efficiency model is estimated under both variable returns to scale (VRS) and constant returns to scale (CRS) assumptions. The VRS specification accounts for differences in scale across banks and yields measures of technical efficiency (TE) under VRS. In contrast, the CRS specification assumes that inputs and outputs are proportional and yields technical efficiency under CRS.

Formally, for each bank i,the cost-minimisation DEA problem is solved by minimising total cost subject to producing at least the observed level of outputs, given input prices and the technology defined by the sample. Scale efficiency (SE) is then computed as the ratio of TE_CRS to TE, capturing the extent to which inefficiency is attributable to operating at a non-optimal scale.

Returns to Scale (RTS) Analysis

The RTS properties for each bank are derived by comparing its technical efficiency scores under constant (TE_CRS) and variable (TE_VRS) returns-to-scale assumptions. Based on this comparison, banks are classified as operating under increasing returns to scale (IRS), constant returns to scale (CRS), or decreasing returns to scale (DRS). This classification helps identify whether a bank is operating below, at, or above its optimal scale and assesses the role of size in shaping efficiency levels. For managers and regulators, the IRS suggests that a bank could lower its average costs by expanding, supporting arguments for consolidation or organic growth. By contrast, widespread DRS may indicate inefficiencies arising from exceeding an optimal size, possibly signalling a need for restructuring.

Second Stage Analysis: Regression

Following Casu and Molyneux (2003), we employ a two-step approach to investigate the determinants of GCC bank efficiency further. The efficiency measures derived from the DEA are retained as the dependent variable, and we then estimate the following Tobit regression model:

$$\begin{aligned} EFFICIENCY = {} & \beta_0 + \beta_1\, LAG\_EFFICIENCY + \beta_2\, SIZE \\ & + \beta_3\, DIVERSIFICATION + \beta_4 GOVERNMENT \\ & + \beta_5\, INFLATION + \beta_6\, RULE\ OF\ LAW \\ & + \beta_7\, GFC + \beta_8\, GOC + \beta_9\, COVID + \varepsilon \end{aligned} \tag{8.2}$$

where: SIZE is total assets in logarithmic terms, DIVERSIFICATION is total non-interest income to total income to measure the level of specialisation in intermediary; Government is a dummy variable capturing government-owned banks, INFLATION measures economic conditions; Rule of Law proxies country-level institutional policies; GFC, GOC, and COVID are dummy variables that measure the impact of the Global Financial Crisis 2007–09, the Global Oil Crisis 2014–15, and COVID-19, respectively, on bank efficiency. Inflation rates and Rule of Law data are obtained from the World Bank.

To estimate Eq. 8.2, *we use the GMM estimator because bank variables are endogenously determined by* unobserved heterogeneity across banks

Table 8.4 Average values of cost efficiency types in the GCC banking systems between 2002 and 2022, using the DEA approach

	CE	*AE*	*TE*	*SE*		*CE*	*AE*	*TE*	*SE*
Annual trend					**Country**				
2002	0.306	0.338	0.762	0.738	Bahrain	0.378	0.441	0.790	0.786
2003	0.441	0.507	0.822	0.739	Kuwait	0.250	0.345	0.744	0.787
2004	0.311	0.342	0.792	0.727	Oman	0.367	0.396	0.855	0.795
2005	0.373	0.500	0.692	0.713	Qatar	0.314	0.405	0.758	0.824
2006	0.348	0.441	0.700	0.731	Saudi Arabia	0.249	0.447	0.567	0.779
2007	0.289	0.354	0.725	0.748	UAE	0.244	0.322	0.722	0.764
2008	0.310	0.367	0.767	0.843	**Bank type**				
2009	0.412	0.616	0.683	0.694	Conventional	0.268	0.381	0.702	0.776
2010	0.303	0.514	0.634	0.689	Islamic	0.323	0.391	0.765	0.800
2011	0.286	0.336	0.812	0.832	**Ownership**				
2012	0.335	0.353	0.870	0.921	Foreign	0.308	0.454	0.670	0.801
2013	0.301	0.414	0.661	0.684	Government	0.258	0.365	0.691	0.778
2014	0.237	0.282	0.781	0.842	Private	0.333	0.396	0.806	0.789
2015	0.302	0.464	0.619	0.651	**Size**				
2016	0.290	0.317	0.842	0.881	Small	0.365	0.375	0.912	0.810
2017	0.177	0.330	0.583	0.770	Medium	0.287	0.348	0.776	0.780
2018	0.186	0.365	0.612	0.755	Large	0.254	0.419	0.604	0.777
2019	0.196	0.364	0.583	0.697	**Regime of scale**				
2020	0.335	0.413	0.768	0.865	CRS	0.564	0.571	0.972	1.000
2021	0.228	0.254	0.829	0.907	DRS	0.290	0.385	0.732	0.849
2022	0.230	0.312	0.744	0.934	IRS	0.159	0.300	0.607	0.660
Average	**0.286**	**0.384**	**0.723**	**0.784**	**Average**	**0.286**	**0.384**	**0.723**	**0.784**

(omitted variables), reverse causality, endogeneity bias, and highly persistent efficiency effects. Hansen's (1982) test of overidentifying restrictions is used to assess the reliability of the GMM procedure and the validity of the instruments. The Arellano-Bond (AR) test is used to ensure the absence of second-order autocorrelation.

Results and Discussion

DEA-Based Efficiency Estimates

Tables 8.4 and 8.5 present the results of the DEA-based efficiency estimates for GCC banks for the period 2002–22. Table 8.4 presents annual GCC-level averages of cost efficiency (CE), allocative efficiency (AE),

Table 8.5 Average values of DEA-based bank cost efficiency types (CE, AE, TE, SE) of the individual GCC countries between 2002 and 2022

	Bahrain				*Kuwait*				*Oman*			
Efficiency type	*CE*	*AE*	*TE*	*SE*	*CE*	*AE*	*TE*	*SE*	*CE*	*AE*	*TE*	*SE*
Panel 1: Year												
2002	0.439	0.446	0.797	0.762	0.320	0.383	0.725	0.718	0.368	0.381	0.829	0.476
2003	0.496	0.573	0.816	0.804	0.353	0.489	0.682	0.749	0.548	0.586	0.878	0.691
2004	0.247	0.256	0.819	0.576	0.471	0.476	0.925	0.901	0.438	0.443	0.858	0.640
2005	0.259	0.324	0.743	0.634	0.179	0.422	0.510	0.782	0.420	0.420	1.000	0.881
2006	0.482	0.541	0.795	0.769	0.216	0.377	0.609	0.588	0.481	0.481	1.000	0.923
2007	0.313	0.364	0.805	0.747	0.285	0.378	0.644	0.698	0.538	0.550	0.870	0.973
2008	0.464	0.500	0.748	0.954	0.281	0.336	0.791	0.827	0.640	0.640	1.000	0.987
2009	0.473	0.576	0.801	0.637	0.215	0.436	0.665	0.633	0.564	0.691	0.779	0.639
2010	0.391	0.527	0.852	0.768	0.335	0.457	0.708	0.700	0.619	0.748	0.795	0.874
2011	0.517	0.523	0.973	0.826	0.273	0.348	0.718	0.793	0.333	0.361	0.870	0.606
2012	0.605	0.620	0.956	0.986	0.373	0.392	0.857	0.884	0.257	0.260	0.968	0.895
2013	0.426	0.461	0.843	0.736	0.311	0.405	0.753	0.706	0.548	0.579	0.838	0.780
2014	0.154	0.183	0.806	0.794	0.131	0.166	0.785	0.892	0.287	0.299	0.879	0.687
2015	0.565	0.636	0.798	0.751	0.191	0.369	0.629	0.767	0.416	0.462	0.725	0.715
2016	0.288	0.323	0.842	0.799	0.179	0.210	0.782	0.857	0.457	0.459	0.881	0.788
2017	0.181	0.254	0.700	0.809	0.130	0.298	0.610	0.794	0.203	0.208	0.857	0.846
2018	0.485	0.573	0.805	0.961	0.181	0.293	0.725	0.606	0.179	0.199	0.874	0.769
2019	0.199	0.308	0.618	0.620	0.334	0.442	0.817	0.655	0.204	0.245	0.762	0.908
2020	0.348	0.473	0.693	0.786	0.362	0.424	0.873	0.951	0.292	0.375	0.756	0.855
2021	0.334	0.370	0.701	0.887	0.159	0.179	0.868	0.964	0.163	0.167	0.905	0.773
2022	0.279	0.389	0.655	0.909	0.172	0.220	0.847	0.967	0.402	0.418	0.922	0.904
Panel 2: Bank type												
Conventional	0.322	0.409	0.719	0.763	0.246	0.359	0.736	0.771	0.317	0.349	0.833	0.775
Islamic	0.454	0.484	0.886	0.817	0.258	0.322	0.756	0.813	0.676	0.686	0.989	0.921
Panel 3: Size												
Small	0.540	0.542	0.973	0.870	0.311	0.318	0.951	0.810	0.676	0.686	0.989	0.921
Medium	0.322	0.415	0.695	0.749	0.246	0.320	0.751	0.774	0.333	0.362	0.855	0.786
Large	0.280	0.377	0.687	0.737	0.227	0.395	0.630	0.794	0.234	0.285	0.720	0.719

	Bahrain				*Kuwait*				*Oman*			
Efficiency type	***CE***	***AE***	***TE***	***SE***	***CE***	***AE***	***TE***	***SE***	***CE***	***AE***	***TE***	***SE***
Panel 4: Ownership												
Government	0.342	0.403	0.750	0.773	0.205	0.288	0.707	0.776	0.310	0.351	0.829	0.739
Private	0.511	0.513	0.968	0.846	0.288	0.389	0.783	0.779	0.386	0.414	0.825	0.847
Foreign	0.283	0.423	0.646	0.736	0.299	0.429	0.732	0.884	0.467	0.467	1.000	0.805
Panel 5: Areas of scale												
DRS	0.353	0.433	0.756	0.823	0.244	0.375	0.697	0.812	0.250	0.275	0.887	0.886
CRS	0.688	0.690	0.980	1.000	0.432	0.435	0.977	1.000	0.648	0.654	0.993	1.000
IRS	0.191	0.287	0.681	0.640	0.182	0.302	0.665	0.697	0.169	0.217	0.741	0.618
Average	**0.378**	**0.441**	**0.790**	**0.786**	**0.250**	**0.345**	**0.744**	**0.787**	**0.367**	**0.396**	**0.855**	**0.795**

	Qatar				*Saudi Arabia*				*UAE*			
Efficiency type	***CE***	***AE***	***TE***	***SE***	***CE***	***AE***	***TE***	***SE***	***CE***	***AE***	***TE***	***SE***
Panel 1: Year												
2002	1.000	1.000	1.000	1.000	0.292	0.356	0.676	0.721	0.107	0.120	0.767	0.827
2003	0.510	0.510	1.000	0.974	0.476	0.539	0.842	0.752	0.373	0.428	0.809	0.645
2004	1.000	1.000	1.000	1.000	0.143	0.235	0.598	0.646	0.249	0.272	0.809	0.787
2005	1.000	1.000	1.000	1.000	0.401	0.644	0.560	0.704	0.406	0.505	0.691	0.640
2006	0.433	0.445	0.915	0.630	0.322	0.524	0.526	0.844	0.328	0.366	0.709	0.699
2007	0.050	0.071	0.763	0.957	0.235	0.337	0.617	0.586	0.273	0.324	0.769	0.800
2008	0.123	0.165	0.800	0.817	0.262	0.374	0.673	0.863	0.211	0.253	0.760	0.720
2009	0.600	0.806	0.705	0.862	0.364	0.746	0.528	0.743	0.428	0.558	0.718	0.701
2010	0.147	0.173	0.772	0.525	0.261	0.722	0.400	0.764	0.234	0.400	0.602	0.586
2011	0.359	0.393	0.876	0.971	0.126	0.190	0.717	0.907	0.258	0.317	0.812	0.781
2012	0.206	0.224	0.881	0.935	0.478	0.502	0.907	0.922	0.169	0.189	0.773	0.909
2013	0.221	0.354	0.643	0.786	0.232	0.470	0.428	0.553	0.216	0.318	0.622	0.650
2014	0.248	0.274	0.837	0.907	0.292	0.417	0.604	0.902	0.260	0.290	0.813	0.839
2015	0.337	0.506	0.599	0.574	0.205	0.559	0.387	0.559	0.248	0.364	0.656	0.619
2016	0.402	0.427	0.918	0.960	0.236	0.273	0.804	0.958	0.256	0.285	0.845	0.883
2017	0.171	0.373	0.469	0.825	0.204	0.533	0.311	0.618	0.172	0.279	0.628	0.781

(continued)

Table 8.5 (continued)

	Qatar				*Saudi Arabia*				*UAE*			
Efficiency type	*CE*	*AE*	*TE*	*SE*	*CE*	*AE*	*TE*	*SE*	*CE*	*AE*	*TE*	*SE*
2018	0.107	0.327	0.532	0.608	0.128	0.533	0.247	0.692	0.143	0.296	0.636	0.854
2019	0.266	0.501	0.536	0.552	0.130	0.491	0.253	0.745	0.126	0.244	0.608	0.687
2020	0.475	0.508	0.905	0.918	0.210	0.307	0.688	0.911	0.342	0.418	0.730	0.803
2021	0.262	0.280	0.908	0.925	0.262	0.314	0.779	0.970	0.219	0.240	0.823	0.891
2022	0.311	0.378	0.779	0.931	0.167	0.291	0.635	0.953	0.167	0.269	0.687	0.927
Panel 2: Bank type												
Conventional	0.306	0.432	0.699	0.814	0.231	0.468	0.509	0.794	0.249	0.321	0.750	0.760
Islamic	0.323	0.373	0.826	0.836	0.292	0.398	0.704	0.745	0.231	0.325	0.654	0.772
Panel 3: Size												
Small	–	–	–	–	–	–	–	–	0.218	0.234	0.849	0.752
Medium	0.307	0.359	0.820	0.816	0.275	0.362	0.700	0.764	0.261	0.320	0.749	0.763
Large	0.329	0.509	0.617	0.842	0.238	0.485	0.507	0.786	0.251	0.376	0.631	0.771
Panel 4: Ownership												
Government	0.297	0.401	0.706	0.833	0.209	0.442	0.516	0.771	0.253	0.338	0.716	0.775
Private	0.342	0.411	0.844	0.810	0.319	0.428	0.699	0.755	0.194	0.234	0.753	0.706
Foreign	–	–	–	–	0.265	0.477	0.542	0.823	–	–	–	–
Panel 5: Areas of scale												
DRS	0.321	0.357	0.861	0.844	0.291	0.413	0.683	0.858	0.282	0.368	0.728	0.856
CRS	0.575	0.579	0.977	1.000	0.607	0.634	0.901	1.000	0.483	0.491	0.966	1.000
IRS	0.175	0.330	0.609	0.725	0.160	0.439	0.431	0.688	0.121	0.227	0.610	0.619
Average	**0.314**	**0.405**	**0.758**	**0.824**	**0.249**	**0.447**	**0.567**	**0.779**	**0.244**	**0.322**	**0.722**	**0.764**

technical efficiency under variable returns to scale (TE), and scale efficiency (SE). Table 8.5 presents the estimates for each country. Both tables present efficiency measures disaggregated by bank type, size, ownership, and RTS classification. Table 8.6 summarises the distribution of RTS regimes across key sub-periods. All DEA efficiency results are relative to the GCC common frontier.

Table 8.6 Areas of scale of GCC banks between 2002 and 2022, using the DEA approach

Panel / Dimension	*2002–2007 (Pre-Crisis)*	*2008–2010 (Global Crisis)*	*2011–2014 (Recovery)*	*2015–2019 (Stagnation)*	*2020–2022(Pandemic)*	*2002–2022 (Overall Dominant Scale)*
PANEL 1: Country						
UAE	IRS	DRS	IRS	DRS	DRS	IRS
Saudi Arabia	IRS	DRS	IRS	DRS	DRS	IRS
Kuwait	IRS	MIX (IRS/DRS)	IRS	MIX (IRS/ CRS)	MIX (IRS/CRS)	IRS
Qatar	MIX (IRS/CRS)	MIX (IRS/CRS)	IRS	MIX (CRS/ DRS)	MIX (CRS/DRS)	IRS
Oman	MIX (IRS/CRS)	MIX (CRS/ DRS)	MIX (IRS/CRS)	MIX (IRS/ CRS/DRS)	MIX (IRS/CRS/ DRS)	MIX (IRS/CRS)
Bahrain	MIX (CRS/ DRS)	MIX (CRS/IRS)	CRS	MIX (IRS/ CRS)	MIX (IRS/CRS)	CRS
PANEL 2: Bank type						
Conventional	IRS	MIX (IRS/DRS)	IRS	MIX (IRS/ DRS)	MIX (IRS/DRS)	IRS
Islamic	MIX (IRS/CRS)	MIX (IRS/CRS)	IRS	MIX (IRS/ DRS)	MIX (IRS/DRS)	IRS
PANEL 3: Bank size						
Large	IRS	DRS	IRS	DRS	DRS	IRS
Medium	MIX (IRS/CRS)	MIX (IRS/CRS)	IRS	MIX (IRS/ CRS/DRS)	MIX (IRS/CRS/ DRS)	IRS
Small	MIX (CRS/ DRS)	MIX (CRS/IRS)	MIX (IRS/CRS)	MIX (IRS/ CRS)	MIX (IRS/CRS)	MIX (IRS/CRS)
PANEL 4: Ownership						
Government	IRS	DRS	IRS	DRS	DRS	IRS
Private	MIX (IRS/CRS)	MIX (IRS/CRS)	IRS	MIX (IRS/ CRS)	MIX (IRS/CRS)	IRS
Foreign	IRS	DRS	IRS	DRS	DRS	IRS
MOST dominant per sub-period	**IRS**	**DRS**	**IRS**	**MIX (IRS/ CRS/DRS, but IRS slightly more frequent)**	**DRS**	**IRS**

Table 8.4 shows that the mean CE for GCC banking systems ranges from 0.25 to 0.37, suggesting that GCC banks could reduce costs by approximately 63–75% while maintaining the same output levels. Mean annual CE exceeded 0.40 only in 2003 and 2008, whereas it was below 0.20 during 2017–19. CE experienced its most significant declines during the sub-periods 2003–07, 2009–11, 2015–17, and 2019–20, all of which were periods of global and regional turbulence. This may point to a pro-cyclical feature of banking efficiency, consistent with the literature on bank performance. In addition, CE ranged from approximately 0.25 in the UAE, Saudi Arabia, and Kuwait to approximately 0.37 in Bahrain and Oman, and 0.31 in Qatar. On average, Islamic banks (0.323), private banks (0.333), and small banks (0.365) are more cost-efficient than their counterparts. In addition, banks operating under CRS (0.564) are more cost-efficient than those operating under DRS (0.29) and IRS (0.159).

Tables 8.4 and 8.5 indicate that the modest levels of CE are attributable to AE more than TE. The mean AE (0.384) indicates that suboptimal input mix choices are an important source of inefficiency in GCC banking. In contrast, the higher mean TE (0.723) indicates that banks are relatively better at converting inputs into outputs. The mean SE of 0.784 indicates that GCC banks operate relatively close to their optimal scale. These results suggest that inefficiency in GCC banking systems is driven primarily by allocative distortions rather than by managerial inefficiencies or inappropriate scale. These results align with prior studies on banking efficiency in GCC economies, which show that institutional and market constraints often prevent the adoption of continuous cost-reducing behaviour. It is consistent with the X-inefficiency hypothesis, which predicts that limited competition in bank-dominated and state-influenced financial systems reduces incentives to minimise costs. The evidence strongly supports the hypothesis that *GCC banks are primarily constrained by allocative inefficiencies rather than managerial and scale inefficiencies.*

The decomposition of CE into TE and AE helps identify the underlying sources of inefficiency in GCC banking. Panel 2 shows that TE is consistently high across countries and years, ranging from 0.855 in Oman to 0.567 in Saudi Arabia. TEs of other countries ranged from 0.722 to 0.79. Islamic banks (0.765), private banks (0.806), small banks (0.912), and banks operating under CRS (0.972) have higher TE than their counterparts. The results may indicate that GCC banks employ better managerial practices and production technologies in transforming inputs into outputs. However, the low AE estimates (mean of 0.384) indicate that cost inefficiency in GCC banking is driven predominantly by suboptimal input allocation decisions rather than by pure technical waste. Tables 8.4 and 8.5 show that the largest falls in AE were observed during 2005–07, 2009–11, 2013–14, 2015–19, and 2020–21. AE is highest in Saudi Arabia (0.447) and Bahrain (0.441), whereas it is lower in the UAE (0.322) and Kuwait (0.345). Foreign banks (0.454) exhibit higher AE levels than private (0.396) and government (0.365) banks. Larger banks (0,419) than small (0.375) and medium-sized (0.348) banks.

Tables 8.4 and 8.5 also show that the average SE in GCC banking is approximately 0.784, suggesting that the average bank can operate with 20% lower costs by adjusting its size. SE ranges from 0.824 in Qatar to 0.764 in the UAE. While there are no substantial differences in SE across bank types, bank size, and ownership, the results suggest that banks operating under IRS (0.66) are less scale-efficient than banks operating under IRS (0.849). The results suggest that the IRS is the dominant regime throughout the sample period, supporting the view that expansion in GCC banking may generate economies-of-scale benefits.

Cyclical Effects

The annual trends in Tables 8.3, 8.4 and 8.5 support the hypothesis that the types of returns to scale (DRS, CRS and IRS) *and efficiency levels in GCC banks are time-varying and sensitive to systemic shocks*. First, during the pre-crisis period (2002–07), TE and SE improved with IRS dominating across countries and bank types. This reflects credit growth, financial deepening, and favourable macroeconomic conditions. Second, the global financial crisis (2008–10) was accompanied by a decline in CE to approximately 0.30, with DRS emerging as the dominant scale regime in most sub-samples. This IRS-to-DRS shift suggests that "bigger is better"-based recourse allocation is unproductive due to overcapacity and managerial complexity. Third, in the post-GFC phase (2011–14), TE and SE improved, and SE exceeded 0.90. IRS prevailed, signalling that PFC restructuring measures stimulated exploitation of scale economies. Fourth, the period of oil price decline (2015–2019) and the pandemic period (2020–2022) are characterised by prevailing DRS, particularly among large banks, reflecting excess capacity under adverse conditions.

The analysis suggests that GCC banks make efficiency gains during stable periods, but these gains are often eroded during adverse economic conditions.

Cross-Country Differences in Banking Efficiency

The efficiency results in Tables 8.3, 8.4 and 8.5 indicate variations in efficiency types across GCC countries. Oman has the highest TE with a mean of 0.855, reflecting sound operational management. Bahrain has a higher CE of 0.378, attributable to its mature financial sector and more competition. In contrast, despite their large banking sectors, Saudi Arabia and the UAE have the lowest efficiency values. Saudi Arabia is associated with low SE levels, possibly due to market fragmentation or regulatory constraints. The UAE's mean CE of 0.244 may reflect high operating costs associated with serving as a regional financial centre. These cross-country disparities may reflect differences in country-level factors, including regulatory and governance environments, market concentration, and economic diversification strategies.

Islamic Versus Conventional Banks

The results show that Islamic banks outperform conventional banks across all efficiency types. In Tables 8.3 and 8.4, Islamic banks have higher mean CE scores (0.323 vs. 0.268), driven by TE (0.765 vs. 0.702) and SE (0.800 vs. 0.776). Table 8.5 shows that Islamic banks are more associated with CRS or IRS regimes. This evidence aligns with studies on Islamic banking, which document the relative resilience and efficiency of Islamic banks during periods of financial stress. Islamic banks exhibit more stable funding, lower leverage, and sharia-compliant governance structures (Boulanouar et al., 2026). These results weaken the hypothesis that Islamic banks are less efficient than conventional banks *due to* operational and compliance constraints. Therefore, a Sharia-based business model may mitigate inefficiencies rather than exacerbate them.

Bank Size

The empirical results in Tables 8.3 and 8.4 show that bank size is inversely related to TE but positively associated with AE. For instance, small banks have the highest TE (0.912) and SE (0.810), suggesting better managerial effectiveness, and operation closer to the optimal scale. In contrast, large banks are associated with higher AE (0.419) but with lower SE (0.78). This implies that large banks can benefit from economies of scope and better input pricing, but they may be overextended or operationally constrained. These results enhance the finding that large banks are more likely to experience DRS.

Bank Ownership

Tables 8.3 and 8.4 yield different efficiency results across ownership types. First, private banks have the highest mean of TE (0.806), likely due to stronger profit incentives. Second, foreign banks exhibit the highest mean AE (0.454), possibly reflecting advanced managerial practices in pricing and global benchmarking. Third, government-owned banks, which are larger in asset size, have lower levels of TE and AE, possibly due to government intervention and directed lending, or less competitive pressure. The persistence of DRS among these banks suggests that size expansion in the GCC has exceeded their optimal scale. These results are consistent with agency theory, which holds that organisational complexity, weaker monitoring, and implicit state guarantees can erode efficiency gains in large and government-owned institutions.

Scale Analysis

Tables 8.3, 8.4 and 8.5 have evidence on the distribution and dominance of regimes of returns to scale (DRS, CRS and IRS). First, banks operating under CRS (*CRS banks*) achieve higher CE, TE, and AE, reflecting optimal scale and technology. Second, banks operating under IRS (*IRS banks*) display lower TE and AE, indicating substantial unrealised scale economies. Banks experiencing IRS should either improve their scale efficiency through internal expansion or mergers and acquisitions (Aghimien et al., 2016). Third, banks operating under DRS (*DRS banks*) exhibit higher SE and TE than IRS banks, suggesting overcapacity and greater reliance on technology. Generally, CRS banks operate in Bahrain, whereas mixed regimes are common among small- and medium-sized banks. This is consistent with Aghimien et al. (2016), who indicate that large GCC banks tend to operate at CRS or DRS, whereas small banks tend to operate at CRS or IRS.

Matrix 8.1 Pairs for M&A based on empirical results

Target bank profile	*Preferred acquirer*	*Expected outcome*
Small, IRS, low AE	Medium CRS, private/Islamic	CRS convergence
Conventional IRS	Islamic CRS/IRS	AE + governance gains
Government IRS	Private CRS	Cost discipline
Large DRS	None (restructuring preferred)	Avoid merger

Matrix 8.2 Pairs candidates for cross-border M&A based on empirical results

Acquirer country	*Target country*	*Primary efficiency rationale*
Qatar	Oman	Acquisition of high-TE banks to enhance operational efficiency
UAE	Saudi Arabia	Transfer of cost management and digital expertise to a large but inefficient bank
Bahrain	Kuwait	Transfer of cost efficiency and managerial discipline
Saudi Arabia	Bahrain	Access to advanced regulatory frameworks and managerial practices

Table 8.6 reveals that in the long run (2002–22), IRS dominates across most GCC banking systems, suggesting that banks could benefit from consolidation or organic growth (Aghimien et al., 2016). However, it appears that dominant scale regimes vary over time: IRS predominates during expansionary phases, whereas DRS becomes prevalent during the global financial crisis (2008–10) and the pandemic era (2020–22).

The Case for Consolidation as a Response to Low Efficiency

The uneven distribution of efficiency among GCC banks suggests that inefficiency is linked to specific institutional, structural, and cyclical factors. GCC banks are affected mainly by allocative and, to a lesser extent, scale inefficiencies, particularly among small, conventional, and government-owned banks in Saudi Arabia and the UAE. From a production-theory perspective, IRS and DRS banks are sub-optimally sized and therefore benefit from restructuring. In this context, mergers and acquisitions (M&As) may emerge as a mechanism to improve efficiency in GCC banking. However, caution is warranted against indiscriminate consolidation, as efficiency-enhancing M&A requires complementarity rather than similarity. Matrix 8.1 and Matrix 8.2 provide some guidance. First, Matrix 8.1 proposes mergers between pairs with different RTS regimes, or between allocatively inefficient institutions and technically efficient counterparts. Matrix 8.1 cautions against consolidating solely by country, size, ownership, or RTS. For this case, a merger among small and medium-sized conventional IRS banks, characterised by lower CE and SE, can help them transition to CRS.

Matrix 8.2 proposes four cross-border M&As pairings based on efficiency differences and scale complementarities reported in Tables 8.3, 8.4 and 8.5. Bahrain and Oman are opportunity-driven environments in which high TE can be leveraged both domestically and for export. Saudi Arabia and the UAE host necessity-driven environments in which consolidation is necessary to address fragmentation and high operating costs. Kuwait and Qatar exhibit a case characterised by limited urgency for efficiency-driven consolidation.

Regression Results and Discussion

The empirical results of the factors that influence efficiency in GCC banking systems from the GMM models are presented in Table 8.7. The GMM models (CE, AE, TE, and SE) are generally well identified, as diagnostics indicate endogeneity bias is addressed. The Hansen test statistics (ranging from 5.11 to 10.63, $p > 0.10$) confirm instrument validity, and the absence of second-order serial correlation (AR(2) test p-values all > 0.05) satisfies a critical assumption for consistency.

The GMM results in Table 8.7 show statistically insignificant lagged dependent variable coefficients across all specifications, suggesting less persistence in cost efficiency. This implies that cost efficiency in GCC banking systems exhibits less inertia and is more immediately influenced by current managerial, institutional, and environmental factors.

Regarding size and diversification, the GMM regressions show that both are negatively associated with CE, AE, and TE, but positively associated with SE. This result shows that scale expansion and income diversification in GCC banking have not translated into cost advantages and may instead generate managerial and organisational inefficiencies. However, the efficiency-size and efficiency-diversification relationships are

Table 8.7 GMM model for the determinants of cost efficiency measures in GCC banking between 2002 and 2022

	Cost Efficiency (CE)	*Allocative Efficiency (AE)*	*Technical Efficiency (TE)*	*Scale Efficiency (SE)*
CONSTANT	0.8188 (0.193)	1.3911 (0.074)*	1.0313 (0.001)***	–0.7542 (0.122)
LAG. DEPENDENT	0.4844 (0.218)	0.0838 (0.845)	0.1043 (0.648)	0.0606 (0.921)
LOG. ASSETS	–0.0632 (0.25)	–0.0947 (0.132)	–0.0398 (0.062)*	0.1386 (0.122)
DIVERSIFICATION	–0.1006 (0.411)	–0.093 (0.541)	–0.1373 (0.098)*	0.1929 (0.274)
GOVERNMENT	–0.0235 (0.472)	–0.0113 (0.743)	–0.0711 (0.041)**	–0.0455 (0.229)
INFLATION	–0.0032 (0.039)**	–0.0049 (0.000)***	0.0025 (0.003)***	0.0054 (0.001)***
RULE OF LAW	–0.0733 (0.383)	–0.2678 (0.067)*	0.1797 (0.009)***	0.2223 (0.098)*
GFC	0.0364 (0.525)	–0.0136 (0.835)	0.0629 (0.050)**	0.1088 (0.075)*
GOC	0.0015 (0.975)	–0.1034 (0.035)**	0.1595 (0.000)***	0.1449 (0.26)
COVID	0.0137 (0.742)	–0.0481 (0.297)	0.1427 (0.000)***	0.0958 (0.026)**
Diagnostics				
No. of obs:	1,047	1,047	1,047	1,047
No. of banks	71	71	71	71
No. of instruments	16	16	16	16
Arellano-Bond test for AR(1)	–2.18 (0.030)**	–1.31 (0.191)	–2.12 (0.034)**	–1.01 (0.315)
Arellano-Bond test for AR(2)	1.48 (0.14)	0.34 (0.734)	0.30 (0.761)	0.20 (0.843)
Hansen test of overid	9.93 (0.127)	5.11 (0.529)	8.71 (0.191)	10.63 (0.101)
Hansen test for exogeneity	6.15 (0.015)	1.72 (0.633)	3.42 (0.331)	9.08 (0.028)**

Statistical significance: *** for 1%, ** for 5% and * for 10%

significant only in the TE specification. These findings suggest that larger banks and greater involvement in non-interest income activities increase operational complexity and overhead costs, reducing cost efficiency rather than enhancing it. This may be supported by the Agency theory, which holds that increases in size and non-core activities increase agency costs and dilute monitoring (Jensen & Meckling, 1976). Consequently, traditional deposit and loan activities are associated with higher cost efficiency in GCC banking.

For ownership, the Government dummy shows a negative relationship with all efficiency measures and is statistically significant only in the TE regression (-0.0711, p = 0.041). This suggests that government-owned banks incur higher operational costs than private and foreign banks. This negative effect may often be linked to factors such as non-economic goals overriding profit maximisation, inefficient resource allocation, or bureaucratic hurdles.

Inflation, as a proxy for macroeconomic stability, is a significant factor for all measures of cost efficiency, consistent with the theory of inflation's non-neutrality (Converse & Jain, 2024).. However, it hurts AE but has a positive effect on TE and SE. The results show that higher inflation is significantly detrimental to AE due to higher operating costs from uncertainty in inflationary environments. Bergant et al. (2025) argue that the impact of inflation on bank performance on cost efficiency varies significantly across countries due to differences in contracting conventions, regulatory frameworks, business models, and competitive pressures. Inflation influences the operating environment for banks by affecting operating expenses and interest rates. In the GCC, policy rates and price stability are anchored to the USD under pegged exchange rate regimes. Wexler (2021) argues that inflation may push up banks' wages and total non-interest expenses more rapidly than bank revenues in other periods.

The variable proxying the quality of institutions, the Rule of Law, has a negative and significant impact on AE, but a positive and significant effect on TE and SE. This result suggests that the current institutional environment influences banks' cost structures and operational efficiency. This aligns with institutional theory (North, 1990), which posits that a strong institutional environment reduces uncertainty and enhances resource allocation. Maghyereh and Awartani (2014) suggest links between efficiency gains and enhanced institutional conditions.

Crisis dummy variables (GFC, GOC, and COVID) exhibit asymmetric effects. The GFC and COVID shocks have positive and significant effects on SE and TE, while the GOC has a significant negative effect on AE and a positive and significant effect on TE. Khediri et al. (2015) also noted that oil shocks forced GCC banks to enhance resilience and cost management. These results indicate that banks may employ a crisis as an opportunity to restructure operations, reduce costs, and adjust portfolios. The significance of the global oil crisis on AE underscores the importance of oil revenues for the operating environment of GCC banking.

Conclusion

This study shows that GCC banks exhibit higher levels of cost inefficiency, primarily driven by allocative rather than technical or scale factors. Country-level analysis indicates relatively limited divergence, although Oman and Kuwait exhibit higher levels of technical and allocative efficiencies. While conventional banks marginally outperform Islamic banks in technical efficiencies, Islamic banks demonstrate comparable allocative efficiency and stronger scale performance.

These findings have important implications. First, due to technical and scale inefficiencies, reforms should focus on technological upgrading, improved managerial practices, and restructuring to exploit economies of scale. The widespread allocative inefficiencies indicate that banks should consider more effective management of input combinations under prevailing market conditions. Second, the sensitivity of efficiency to sudden external shocks underscores the need to strengthen resilience in normal times to safeguard performance during periods of turbulence. Regulatory frameworks should enhance proactive risk management, capital buffers, and liquidity requirements. Policymakers should develop frameworks that treat crises as potential catalysts for operational improvement. Third, persistent scale inefficiency across indicates that market fragmentation is one important feature of GCC banking. The coexistence of large state-owned institutions and smaller banks may not enable economies of scale, thereby justifying consolidation. However, consolidation should be accompanied by safeguards to promote competition and prevent excessive concentration and the abuse of market power. In parallel, bank managers should address the diseconomies of scale that prevail in GCC banking. This may be achieved by shifting focus from asset growth to operational efficiency, restructuring to mitigate bureaucratic inefficiencies, and considering divestitures of non-core units. Authorities should develop merger and acquisition guidelines that promote operations at constant returns to scale, introduce tax incentives for banks operating at optimal scale, and incorporate regular scale-efficiency audits into the supervisory review process.

In addition, policymakers should focus on improving institutional quality. measures can include promoting transparency in different institutions to reduce contractual enforcement costs; enhancing governance codes; and ensuring that regulatory bodies operate with clear, independent enforcement powers. They should also implement management incentive structures linked to efficiency gains in government-owned banks and consider the complete privatisation of these banks.

Additionally, given inflation's pervasive impact—eroding allocative efficiency while improving technical and scale efficiency—banks need to focus on hedging against it. The adoption of inflation-adjusted pricing models and the investment in technological infrastructure can harness operational benefits during inflationary periods.

References

Abbas, Z., Afshan, G., & Mustifa, G. (2022). The effect of financial development on economic growth and income distribution: An empirical evidence from lower-middle and upper-middle-income countries. *Development Studies Research, 9*(1), 117–128. https://doi.org/10.1080/21665095.2022.2065325

Abdelkawy, N. A. (2024). Diversification and the resource curse: An econometric analysis of GCC Countries. *Economies, 12*(287). https://doi.org/10.3390/economies12110287

Aghimien, P. A., Kamarudin, F., Hamid, M., & Noordin, B. (2016). Efficiency of Gulf Cooperation Council Banks. *Review of International Business and Strategy, 25*(1), 118–126. https://doi.org/10.1108/RIBS-11-2013-0111

Agnese, P., Cerciello, M., Oriani, R., & Teddeo, S. (2024). ESG controversies and profitability in the European banking sector. *Finance Research Letters, 61*, Article 105042. https://doi.org/10.1016/j.frl.2024.105042

Agosin, M. R., Alvarez, R., & Bravo-Ortega, C. (2011). Determinants of export diversification around the world: 1962–2000. *35*(3), 295–315. https://doi.org/10.1111/j.1467-9701.2011.01395.x

Alfaihani, S., Badunenko, O., & Jaffry, S. (2024). Market power, optimal scale and competition promotion in banking: Analysis in the GCC region. *International Journal of Finance & Economics*. https://doi.org/10.1002/ijfe.2990

Alghafes, R., Karim, S., Aliani, K., Qureishi, N., & Alkayed, L. (2024). Influence of key ESG factors on Islamic banks' financial performance: Evidence from

A. Bakhouche, *Banking in the GCC*, Palgrave Macmillan Studies in Banking and Financial Institutions,
https://doi.org/10.1007/978-3-032-21737-0

GCC countries. *International Review of Economics & Finance, 96*, Article 103629. https://doi.org/10.1016/j.iref.2024.103629

Ali, M. N., Mohammed, H. M., Mohammed, K. A., Almutiri, A. A., & Ali, M. A. (2025). The Effect of Environmental, Social, and Governance (ESG) Disclosure on the profitability of Saudi-Listed firms: Insights from Saudi Vision 2030. *Sustainability,* (17), 2977. https://doi.org/10.3390/su17072977

Al-Jalahma, A., Al-Fadhel, H., Al-Muhanadi, M., & Al-Zaimoor, N. (2020). Environmental, Social, and Governance (ESG) disclosure and firm performance: Evidence from GCC Banking sector. *2020 International Conference on Decision Aid Sciences and Application (DASA)*, (pp. 54–58). Sakheer, Bahrain. https://doi.org/10.1109/DASA51403.2020.9317210

Alremaidhi, y. (2023). ESG disclosures and Kuwait Banking industry performance. *Diversified Science Research, 2*(1), 169–180. https://journalrrsite.com/index.php/Myjrr/article/view/47

Alsayegh, O. (2023). *How Economic and political factors drive the oil strategy of Gulf Arab States.* Center for Energy Studies, Edward P. Djerejian Center for the Middle East . https://www.bakerinstitute.org/research/how-economic-and-political-factors-drive-oil-strategy-gulf-arab-states

Alssadek, M., & Benhin, J. (2021). Oil boom, exchange rate and sectoral output: An empirical analysis of Dutch disease in oil-rich countries. *Resources Policy, 74*, Article 102362. https://doi.org/10.1016/j.resourpol.2021.102362

Amar, J., Lecourt, C., & Carpantier, J.-F. (2022). GCC Sovereign Wealth Funds: Why do they take control? *Journal of International Financial Markets, Institutions and Money, 77*, 101494. https://doi.org/10.1016/j.intfin.2021.101494

Amjed, S., & Shah, I. A. (2021). Does financial system development, capital formation and economic growth induces trade diversification? *Journal of Economics and Development, 23*(3), 222–237.

Antwi-Boateng, O., & Al jaberi, N. H. (2022). The post-oil strategy of the UAE: An examination of diversification strategies and challenges. *Politics & Policy, 50*(2), 380–407. https://doi.org/10.1111/polp.12457

Arestis, P., & Demetriades, P. (1997). Financial development and economic growth: Assessing the evidence. *The Economic Journal, 107*(442), 783–799. https://doi.org/10.1111/j.1468-0297.1997.tb00043.x

Ari, I., Akkas, E., Asutay, M., & Koç, M. (2019). Public and private investment in the hydrocarbon-based rentier economies: A case study for the GCC countries. *Resources Policy, 62*, 165–175. https://doi.org/10.1016/j.resourpol.2019.03.016

Arshed, N., Bakkar, Y., De Siscto, M., Iqbal, M., & Ul-Durar, S. (2025). *The role of ESG in shaping the impact of financial development on Banks' Performance. 70037*. https://doi.org/10.1111/eufm.70037

Asteriou, D., Pilbeam, k., & Tomuleasa, I. (2021). The impact of corruption, economic freedom, regulation and transparency on bank profitability and bank stability: Evidence from the Eurozone area. *Journal of Economic Behavior & Organization, 184*, 150–177. https://doi.org/10.1016/j.jebo.2020.08.023

Athanasoglou, P. P., Brissimis, S. N., & Delis, M. D. (2008). Bank-specific, industry-specific and macroeconomic determinants of bank profitability. *Journal of International Financial Markets, Institutions and Money, 18*(2), 121–136. https://doi.org/10.1016/j.intfin.2006.07.001

Atil, A., Nawaz, K., Lahiani, A., & Roubaud, D. (2020). Are natural resources a blessing or a curse for financial development in Pakistan? The importance of oil prices, economic growth and economic globalization. *Resources Policy, 67*, 101683. https://doi.org/10.1016/j.resourpol.2020.101683

Auty, R. M. (1993). *Sustaining development in mineral economies: The resource curse thesis*. Routledge.

Auty, R. M. (2001). Resource abundance and economic development. *Oxford University Press*. https://doi.org/10.1093/0199275785.001.0001

Auty, R., & Warhurst, A. (1993). Sustainable development in mineral exporting economies. *Resources Policy, 19*(1), 4–29. https://doi.org/10.1016/0301-4207(93)90049-S

Badeeb, R. A., Lean, H. H., & Clark, J. (2017). The evolution of the natural resource curse thesis: A critical literature survey. *Resources Policy, 51*, 23–124. https://doi.org/10.1016/j.resourpol.2016.10.015

Bain, J. S. (1951). Relation of profit-rate to industry concentration: American manufacturing, 1936–1940. *Quarterly Journal of Economics, 65*(3), 293–324. https://doi.org/10.2307/1882217

Bakhouche, A. (2024). Competition, stability and the efficiency channel in the Tunisian banking system. *International Journal of Accounting, Auditing and Performance Evaluation, 20*(1/2), 121–154. https://doi.org/10.1504/IJAAPE.2024.10061069

Bakhouche, A., El Ghak, T., & Alshiab, M. (2022). Does Islamicity matter for the stability of Islamic banks in dual banking systems? *Heliyon, 8*(4), Article e09245. https://doi.org/10.1016/j.heliyon.2022.e09245

Banwo, O., Harrald, P., & Medda, F. (2019). Understanding the consequences of diversification on financial stability. *Journal of Economic Interaction and Coordination, 14*, 273–292. https://doi.org/10.1007/s11403-018-0216-9

Barry, F. (2014). Diversifying external linkages: The exercise of Irish economic sovereignty in long-term perspective. *Oxford Review of Economic Policy, 30*(2), 208–222. https://doi.org/10.1093/oxrep/gru011

Basile, R., Giallonardo, L., Girardi, A., & Mantegazzi, D. (2024). Access to credit and economic complexity: Evidence from Italian provinces. *Journal of Regional Science, 64*(4), 1183–1204. https://doi.org/10.1111/jors.12698

Batae, O. M., Dragomir, V. D., & Feleaga, L. (2021). The relationship between environmental, social, and financial performance in the banking sector: A European study. *Journal of Cleaner Production, 290*, Article 125791. https://doi.org/10.1016/j.jclepro.2021.125791

Bayeh, A., Bitar, M., Burlacu, R., & Walker, T. (2021). Competition, securitization, and efficiency in US banks. *The Quarterly Review of Economics and Finance, 80*, 553–576. https://doi.org/10.1016/j.qref.2021.04.004

Beck, R., & Fidoa, M. (2008). The impact of sovereign wealth funds on global financial markets. *Intereconomics: Review of European Economic Policy, 43*, 349–358. https://doi.org/10.1007/s10272-008-0268-5

Beck, T. (2011). *Finance and Oil: Is There a resource curse in financial development?* European Banking Center Discussion Paper No. 2011–004. https://doi.org/10.2139/ssrn.1769803

Beck, T., & Demirguc-Kunt, A. (2006). Small and medium-size enterprises: Access to finance as a growth constraint. *Journal of Banking & Finance, 30*(11), 2931–2943. https://doi.org/10.1016/j.jbankfin.2006.05.009

Beck, T., & Levine, R. (2002). Industry growth and capital allocation: Does having a market- or bank-based system matter? *Journal of Financial Economics, 64*(2), 147–180. https://doi.org/10.1016/S0304-405X(02)00074-0

Beck, T., & Levine, R. (2004). Stock markets, banks, and growth: Panel evidence. *Journal of Banking & Finance, 28*(3), 423–442. https://doi.org/10.1016/S0378-4266(02)00408-9

Beidas-Strom, S., Rasmussen, T., Robinson, D. O., Charap, J., Cherif, A., Khamis, M., … Sidahmed, R. (2011). *Gulf Cooperation Council Countries (GCC): Enhancing Economic Outcomes in an Uncertain Global Economy.* IMF. Retrieved 8 22, 2024, from www.imf.org/external/pubs/ft/dp/2011/1101mcd.pdf

Belasri, S., Gomes, M., & Pijourlet, G. (2020). Corporate social responsibility and bank efficiency. *Journal of Multinational Financial Management, 54*, Article 100612. https://doi.org/10.1016/j.mulfin.2020.100612

Ben Hassen, T. (2025). The GCC economies in the wake of COVID-19: Toward post-oil sustainable knowledge-based economies? *Sustainability, 14*(18), 11251. https://doi.org/10.3390/su141811251

Ben Saad, M., Brahim, M., Shaffar, A., Guesmi, K., & Ben Saad, R. (2023). Economic complexity, diversification and economic development: The strategic factors. *Research in International Business and Finance, 101840*,. https://doi.org/10.1016/j.ribaf.2022.101840

Berger, A. N. (1995). The profit-structure relationship in banking–Tests of market-power and efficient-structure hypotheses. *Journal of Money, Credit and Banking, 27*(2), 404–431. https://doi.org/10.2307/2077876

Bhattacharyya, S., & Hodler, R. (2014). Do natural resource revenues hinder financial development? The role of political institutions. *World Development, 57*(C), 101–113. https://doi.org/10.1016/j.worlddev.2013.12.003

Bikker, J. A., & Haaf, K. (2002). Competition, concentration and their relationship: An empirical analysis of the banking industry. *Journal of Banking & Finance, 26*(11), 2191–2214. https://doi.org/10.1016/S0378-4266(02)00205-4

Bolibok, P. M. (2024). Does firm size matter for ESG risk? Cross-sectional evidence from the banking industry. *Sustainability, 16*(2), 1–26.

Bolt, W., & Humphrey, D. (2015). Assessing bank competition for consumer loans. *Journal of Banking & Finance, 61*, 127–141. https://doi.org/10.1016/j.jbankfin.2015.09.004

Boone, J. (2008). A new way to measure competition. *The Economic Journal, 118*(531), 1245–1261. https://doi.org/10.1111/j.1468-0297.2008.02168.x

Boschini, A. D., Pettersson, J., & Roine, J. (2007). Resource curse or not: A question of appropriability. *The Scandinavian Journal of Economics, 109*(3), 593–617. https://doi.org/10.1111/j.1467-9442.2007.00509.x

Boulanouar, Z., Grassa, R., Nouar, A., & El Ammari, A. (2026). Does Sharia governance deter bank risk-taking? Evidence from profit-sharing accounts and board financial expertise. *Journal of Financial Reporting and Accounting*. https://doi.org/10.1108/JFRA-05-2025-0419

Bouri, E., Hammoud, R., & Abou Kassm, C. (2023). The effect of oil implied volatility and geopolitical risk on GCC stock sectors under various market conditions. *Energy Economics, 120*, Article 106617. https://doi.org/10.1016/j.eneco.2023.106617

BP. (2023). *Statistical review of world energy 2023*. www.bp.com

Brixiová, Z., Kangoye, T., & Yogo, T. U. (2020). Access to finance among small and medium-sized enterprises and job creation in Africa. *Structural Change and Economic Dynamics, 55*, 177–189. https://doi.org/10.1016/j.strueco.2020.08.008

Campbell, J. L. (2007). Why would corporations behave in socially responsible ways? An institutional theory of corporate social responsibility. *Academy of Management Review, 32*(3), 946–967. https://doi.org/10.5465/amr.2007.25275684

Cantero-Saiz, M., Polizzi, S., & Scannella, E. (2024). ESG and asset quality in the banking industry: The moderating role of financial performance. *Research in International Business and Finance, 69*, Article 102221. https://doi.org/10.1016/j.ribaf.2024.102221

Cao, Q., Zhu, T., & Yu, W. (2024). ESG investment and bank efficiency: Evidence from China. *Energy Economics, 133*, Article 107516. https://doi.org/10.1016/j.eneco.2024.107516

Caporale, G. M., Lodh, S., & Nandy, M. (2017). The performance of banks in the MENA region during the global financial crisis. *Research in International Business and Finance, 42*, 583–590. https://doi.org/10.1016/j.ribaf.2017.07.003

Casu, B., & Girardone, C. (2006). Bank competition, concentration and efficiency in the single European market. *The Manchester School, 74*(4), 441–468.

Casu, B., & Molyneux, P. (2003). A comparative study of efficiency in European banking. *Applied Economics, 35*(17), 1865–1876. https://doi.org/10.1080/0003684032000158109

Chaffai, M., & Coccorese, P. (2019). How far away is the MENA banking system? Efficiency comparisons with international banks. *The North American Journal of Economics and Finance, 49*, 378–395. https://doi.org/10.1016/j.najef.2019.04.013

Charfeddine, L., & Barkat, K. (2020). Short- and long-run asymmetric effect of oil prices and oil and gas revenues on the real GDP and economic diversification in oil-dependent economy. *Energy Economics, 86*, Article 104680. https://doi.org/10.1016/j.eneco.2020.104680

Charnes, A., Cooper, W. W., & Rhodes, E. (1978). Measuring the efficiency of decision making units. *European Journal of Operational Research, 2*(6), 429–444. https://doi.org/10.1016/0377-2217(78)90138-8

Chen, Y., Khurshid, A., Raud, A., Yang, H., & Calin, A. C. (2023). Natural resource endowment and human development: Contemporary role of governance. *Resources Policy, 81*, Article 103334. https://doi.org/10.1016/j.resourpol.2023.103334

Cherif, R., Hasanov, F., & Zhu, M. (2016). Breaking the oil spell: The Gulf Falcon's path to diversification. *IMF*. https://doi.org/10.5089/9781513537863.071

Cheung, Y.-L., Tan, W., & Wang, W. (2020). Where do banks value corporate social responsibility more? Evidence on the role of national culture. *Journal of Banking & Finance, 118*, Article 105810. https://doi.org/10.1016/j.jbankfin.2020.105810

Ching, H. Y., & Gerab, F. (2017). Sustainability reports in Brazil through the lens of signaling, legitimacy and stakeholder theories. *Social Responsability Journal, 13*(1), 95–110. https://doi.org/10.1108/SRJ-10-2015-0147

Chronopoulos, D. K., Liu, F. H., McMillan, F. J., & Wilson, J. O. (2015). The dynamics of US bank profitability. *European Journal of Finance, 21*(5), 426–443. https://doi.org/10.1080/1351847X.2013.838184

Claessens, S., & Laeven, L. (2004). What drives bank competition? Some international evidence. *Journal of Money, Credit and Banking, 36*(3), 563–583. https://doi.org/10.1353/mcb.2004.0044

Cocks, L., & Francken, N. (2016). Natural resources: A curse on education spending? *Energy Policy, 92*, 394–408. https://doi.org/10.1016/j.enpol.2016.02.027

Collier, P., & Goderis, B. (2012). Commodity prices and growth: An empirical investigation☆. *European Economic Review, 56*(6), 1241–1460. https://doi.org/10.1016/j.euroecorev.2012.04.002

Converse, N., & Jain, A. K. (2024). *Do banks gain from inflation? Evidence from inflation surprises*. American Economic Association.

Corden, W. M., & Neary, J. P. (1982). Booming sector and de-industrialisation in a small open economy. *The Economic Journal, 92*(368), 825–848. https://doi.org/10.2307/2232670

Delechat, C. C., Melina, G., Newiak, M., Papageorgiou, C., & Spatafora, N. (2024). *Economic diversification in developing countries: lessons from country experiences with broad-based and industrial policies*. IMF. www.imf.org/en/Publications/Departmental-Papers-Policy-Papers/Issues/2024/07/20/Economic-Diversification-in-Developing-Countries-Lessons-from-Country-Experiences-with-532135

Dell'Anno, R., & Maddah, M. (2022). Natural resources, rent seeking and economic development. An analysis of the resource curse hypothesis for Iran. *Macroeconomics and Finance in Emerging Market Economies, 15*(1), 47–65. https://doi.org/10.1080/17520843.2020.1806093

Demirguc-Kunt, A., & Huizinga, H. (1999). Determinants of commercial bank interest margins and profitability: Some international evidence. *The World Bank Economic Review, 13*, 379–408. https://doi.org/10.1093/wber/13.2.379

Demsetz, H. (1973). Industry structure, market rivalry, and public policy. *Journal of Law and Economics, 16*(1), 1–9.

Destek, M. A., Hossain, M. R., Aydin, S., Shakib, M., & Destek, G. (2023). Investigating the role of economic complexity in evading the resource curse. *Resources Policy, 86*(B), 104131. https://doi.org/10.1016/j.resourpol.2023.104131

Diallo, B., & Al-Titi, O. (2017). Local growth and access to credit: Theory and evidence. *Journal of Macroeconomics, 54*(B), 410–423. https://doi.org/10.1016/j.jmacro.2017.07.005

Dietrich, A., & Wanzenried, G. (2011). Determinants of bank profitability before and during the crisis: Evidence from Switzerland. *Journal of International Financial Markets, Institutions & Money, 21*, 307–327. https://doi.org/10.1016/j.intfin.2010.11.002

Dogan, E., Altinoz, B., & Tzeremes, P. (2020). The analysis of 'Financial Resource Curse' hypothesis for developed countries: Evidence from asymmetric effects with quantile regression. *Resources Policy, 68*, Article 101773. https://doi.org/10.1016/j.resourpol.2020

dos Reis Cardillo, M. A., & Cruz Basso, L. F. (2025). Revisiting knowledge on ESG/CSR and financial performance: A bibliometric and systematic review of moderating variables. *Journal of Innovation & Knowledge, 10*(1), Article 100648. https://doi.org/10.1016/j.jik.2024.100648

Douglas, S., & Walker, A. (2017). Coal mining and the resource curse in the eastern United States. *Journal of Regional Science, 57*(4), 568–590. https://doi.org/10.1111/jors.12310

Dreher, A. (2006). Does globalization affect growth? Evidence from a new index of globalization. *Applied Economics, 38*(10), 1091–1110. https://doi.org/10.1080/00036840500392078

Dwumfour, R. A., & Ntow-Gyamfi, M. (2018). Natural resources, financial development and institutional quality in Africa: Is there a resource curse? *Resources Policy, 59*, 411–426. https://doi.org/10.1016/j.resourpol.2018.08.012

EIA. (2014). *World oil reserves overview*. U.S. Energy Information Administration. www.eia.gov

EIA. (2023). *Strait of Hormuz as a strategic chokepoint*. U.S. Energy Information Administration. www.eia.gov

El Anshasy, A. A., & Bradley, M. D. (2012). Oil prices and the fiscal policy response in oil-exporting countries. *Journal of Policy Modeling, 34*(5), 605–620. https://doi.org/10.1016/j.jpolmod.2011.08.021

Elbadawi, I. A., & Soto, R. (2012). *Resource rents, political institutions and economic growth*. Economic Research Forum (ERF) Working Paper No. 678. https://erf.org.eg/app/uploads/2014/08/678.pdf

Erdoğan, S., Yıldırım, D. Ç., & Gedikli, A. (2020). Natural resource abundance, financial development and economic growth: An investigation on Next-11 countries. *Resources Policy, 65*, Article 101559. https://doi.org/10.1016/j.resourpol.2019.101559

ESG New Survey. (2025, August 14). *Qatar expands green finance strategy with first sovereign green bonds*. https://esgnews.com/qatar-expands-green-finance-strategy-with-first-sovereign-green-bonds/

Faqera, A. F., Waemustafa, W., Jadi, D. M., Al-Matari, E. M., & Bin-Nashwan, S. A. (2025). The interplay of financial risk and governance mechanisms in shaping banks' performance: Evidence from major banks in the UAE. *Corporate Governance*. https://doi.org/10.1108/CG-10-2024-0515

Farrell, M. J. (1957). The measurement of productive efficiency. *Journal of the Royal Statistical Society: Series A (General), 120*(3), 253–281. https://doi.org/10.2307/2343100

Fasanya, I. O., Oyewole, O. J., Adekoya, O. B., & Badaru, F. O. (2021). Oil price and stock market behaviour in GCC countries: Do asymmetries and structural breaks matter? *Energy Strategy Reviews, 36*, Article 100682. https://doi.org/10.1016/j.esr.2021.100682

Frankel, J. A. (2012). *The natural resource curse: A survey of diagnoses and some prescriptions*. HKS Faculty Research Working Paper Series, *RWP12-014*.

Freeman, R. E. (1984). Strategic management: A stakeholder approach. *Cambridge University Press*. https://doi.org/10.1017/CBO9781139192675

Friedman, M. (1970, September 13). A Friedman Doctrine—The social responsibility of business is to increase its profits. New York Times Magazine. Retrieved 2025, from www.nytimes.com/1970/09/13/archives/a-friedman-doctrine-the-social-responsibility-of-business-is-to.html

Fuinhas, J. A., Marques, A. C., & Couto, A. P. (2015). Oil rents and economic growth in oil-producing countries: Evidence from a macro panel. *Economic Change and Restructuring, 48*, 257–279. https://doi.org/10.1007/s10644-015-9170-x

Gately, D. (1987). Lessons from the 1986 Oil price collapse. *Brooking Papers on economic activity, 2*, 237–284. www.brookings.edu/wp-content/uploads/1986/06/1986b_bpea_gately_adelman_griffin.pdf

Gelman, M., Goldstein, I., & MacKinlay, A. (2023). *Bank diversification and lending resiliency*. https://doi.org/10.2139/ssrn.4147790

Gilberthorpe, E., & Papyrakis, E. (2015). The extractive industries and development: The resource curse at the micro, meso and macro levels. *The Extractive Industries and Society, 2*(2), 381–390. https://doi.org/10.1016/j.exis.2015.02.008

Giráldez-Puig, P., & Samaniego-Medina, R. (2025). Unveiling the impact of board gender diversity on credit rating. *Management Research Review, 89–111*,. https://doi.org/10.1108/MRR-08-2024-0652

González, L. O., Razia, A., Búa, V. M., & Sestayo, R. L. (2019). Market structure, performance, and efficiency: Evidence from the MENA banking sector. *International Review of Economics & Finance, 64*(C), 84–101.

Grau, A., Castelo-Branco, M., & Bel-Oms, I. (2025). The impacts of ESG reporting, stakeholder engagement and board gender diversity on firm performance: Exploring the moderating role of board independence. *Business Strategy & Development, 8*(3), Article e70159. https://doi.org/10.1002/bsd2.70159

Greenwood, J., & Jovanovic, B. (1990). Financial development, growth, and the distribution of income. *Journal of Political Economy, 98*(5), 1076–1107. https://doi.org/10.1086/261720

Guan, J., Kirikkaleli, D., Bibi, A., & Zhang, W. (2020). Natural resources rents nexus with financial development in the presence of globalization: Is the "resource curse" exist or myth? *Resources Policy, 66*, Article 101641. https://doi.org/10.1016/j.resourpol.2020.101641

Guillén, J., Rengifo, E. W., & Ozsoz, E. (2014). Relative power and efficiency as a main determinant of banks' profitability in Latin America. *Borsa Istanbul Review, 14*(2), 119–125. https://doi.org/10.1016/j.bir.2014.02.003

Guru, B. K., & Yadav, I. S. (2019). Financial development and economic growth: Panel evidence from BRICS. *Journal of Economics, Finance and Administrative Science, 24*(47), 113–126. https://doi.org/10.1108/JEFAS-12-2017-0125

Gutiérrez-Ponce, H., & Wibowo, S. A. (2024). Do sustainability practices contribute to the financial performance of banks? An analysis of banks in Southeast Asia. *Corporate Social Responsibility and Environmental Management, 31*(2), 418–1432. https://doi.org/10.1002/csr.2641

Gyamfi, B. A., Onifade, S. T., haouas, I. H., & Adedoyin, F. F. (2023). The impacts of resource abundance and export diversity on financial development in the South Asian economic bloc. *Heliyon, 9*(4), 15105. https://doi.org/10.1016/j.heliyon.2023.e15105

Gygli, S., Haelg, F., Potrafke, N., & Sturm, J.-E. (2019). The Review of International Organizations. *The Review of International Organizations, 14*, 543–574. https://doi.org/10.1007/s11558-019-09344-2

Gyimah, P., & Owusu-Afriyie, R. (2025). Bank sustainability: Do corporate governance and internal audit quality matter? *World Development Sustainability, 6*, Article 100222. https://doi.org/10.1016/j.wds.2025.100222

Gylfason, T. (2001). Natural resources, education, and economic development. *European Economic Review, 45*(4–6), 847–859. https://doi.org/10.1016/S0014-2921(01)00127-1

Hamdi, H., & Sbia, R. (2013). Dynamic relationships between oil revenues, government spending and economic growth in an oil-dependent economy. *Economic Modelling, 35*(C), 118–125. https://doi.org/10.1016/j.econmod.2013.06.043

Han, J., Raghutla, C. R., Chittedi, K. R., Tan, Z., & Koodhar, M. A. (2022). How natural resources affect financial development? Fresh evidence from top-10 natural resource abundant countries. *Rsources Policy, 76*, Article 102647. https://doi.org/10.1016/j.resourpol.2022.102647

Hao, L., Ahmad, S., Chang, H.-L., & Umar, M. (2021). Knowledge spill-over and institutional quality role in controlling Dutch disease: A case of BRICS countries. *Resources Policy, 72*, Article 102114. https://doi.org/10.1016/j.resourpol.2021.102114

Haque, M. I., Faruk, B. U., & Tausif, M. R. (2022). Growth-finance nexus in oil abundant GCC countries of MENA region. *Cogent Economics & Finance, 10*(1). https://doi.org/10.1080/23322039.2022.2087646

Harkin, S. M., Mare, D. S., & Crook, J. N. (2020). Independence in bank governance structure: Empirical evidence of effects on bank risk and performance. *Research in International Business and Finance, 52*, Article 101177. https://doi.org/10.1016/j.ribaf.2019.101177

Hasanov, F. J., Aliyev, R., Taskin, D., & Suleymanov, E. (2023). Oil rents and non-oil economic growth in CIS oil exporters. The role of financial development. *Resources Policy, 82*, 103523. https://doi.org/10.1016/j.resourpol.2023.103523

Hattendorff, C. (2014). *Natural resources, export concentration and financial development*. Freie Universität Berlin, Fachbereich Wirtschaftswissenschaft. www.econstor.eu/bitstream/10419/104548/1/806879858.pdf

Hendrix, C. S. (2019). Kicking a crude habit: Diversifying away from oil and gas in the twenty-first century. *International Review of Applied Economics, 33*(2), 188–208. https://doi.org/10.1080/02692171.2017.1389862

Herfindahl, O. C. (1950). *Concentration in the U.S. steel industry.* Columbia University.

Hesse, H. (2008). Export diversification and economic growth. *World Bank Publications*. https://econpapers.repec.org/scripts/redir.pf?u=https%3A%2F%2Fopenknowledge.worldbank.org%2Fbitstream%2Fhandle%2F10986%2F28040%2F577210NWP0Box353766B01PUBLIC10gcwp021web.pdf

Hijazeen, I. (2023). *ESG risks and The Kuwaiti financial sector*. Institute of Banking Studies. https://kibs.edu.kw/wp-content/uploads/2023/12/ESG-.pdf

Hirschman, A. O. (1964). The paternity of an index. *The American Economic Review, 54*(5), 761–762. www.jstor.org/stable/1818582

Hunjra, A. I., Azam, M., Bruna, M. G., & Taskin, D. (2022). Role of financial development for sustainable economic development in low middle income countries. *Finance Research Letters, 47*(B). https://doi.org/10.1016/j.frl.2022.102793

Ibrahim, M. H. (2019). Oil and macro-financial linkages: Evidence from the GCC countries. *The Quarterly Review of Economics and Finance, 72*, 1–13. https://doi.org/10.1016/j.qref.2019.01.014

IEA. (2022). *Gas Market Report 2022.* International Energy Agency. www.iea.org

ILO. (2021). *Labour market trends in the GCC.* International Labour Organization. www.ilo.org

IMF. (1996). *Policy Challenges in the Gulf Cooperation Council Countries.* https://www.imf.org/external/pubs/ft/policy/contents.htm

IMF. (2022). *Economic diversification in the GCC.* www.imf.org

IMF. (2023). Gulf Cooperation Council: Economic prospects and policy challenges for the GCC countries. *IMF Staff Country Reports*. https://doi.org/10.5089/9798400263279.002.A001

IMF. (2024). Strengthening bank credit to the private sector while limiting risks to financial sector stability. In IMF, *Togo: Selected Issues* (Vol. 2024). https://doi.org/10.5089/9798400291227.002

Iosifidi, M., Panopoulou, E., & Tsoumas, C. (2021). Mortgage loan demand and banks' operational efficiency. *Journal of Financial Stability, 53*,. https://doi.org/10.1016/j.jfs.2021.100851

Isik, I., & Hassan, K. (2002). Technical, scale and allocative efficiencies of Turkish banking industry. *Journal of Banking & Finance, 26*(4), 719–766.

Islam, M. T., & Ali, A. (2024). Sustainable green energy transition in Saudi Arabia: Characterizing policy framework, interrelations and future research directions. *Next Energy, 5*, Article 100161. https://doi.org/10.1016/j.nxener.2024.100161

Itan, I., Sylvia, S., Septiany, S., & Chen, R. (2025). The influence of environmental, social, and governance disclosure on market reaction: Evidence from emerging markets. *Discover Sustainability, 6*(347). https://doi.org/10.1007/s43621-025-01085-0

Jensen, M. C., & Meckling, W. H. (1976). Theory of the firm: Managerial behavior, agency costs and ownership structure. *Journal of Financial Economics, 3*(4), 305–360. https://doi.org/10.1016/0304-405X(76)90026-X

Jolo, A., Ari, i., & Koç, M. (2022). Driving Factors of Economic diversification in resource-rich countries via panel data evidence. *Sustainability, 14*(5). https://doi.org/10.3390/su14052797

Kainat, R., Hafiz, M. A., Marc, A., & Sumaira, S. (2024). Impact of financial development on export performance: Evidence from South Asia. *MPRA Paper 122474*. https://mpra.ub.uni-muenchen.de/122474/1/MPRA_paper_122474.pdf

Karkowska, R., Korzeb, Z., & Niedziółka, P. (2025). Inflation's dual impact on European banks' profitability. *Journal of Policy Modeling*. https://doi.org/10.1016/j.jpolmod.2024.11.004

Kaufmann, D., Aart, K., & Massimo, M. M. (2010). *The worldwide governance indicators: methodology and analytical issues*. The World Bank. http://papers.ssrn.com/sol3/papers.cfm?abstract_id=1682130

Khamisu, M. S., Paluri, R. A., & Sonwaney, V. (2024). Stakeholders' perspectives on critical success factors for environmental social and governance (ESG) implementation. *Journal of Environmental Management, 365*, Article 121583. https://doi.org/10.1016/j.jenvman.2024.121583

Khamisu, M. S., Yero, J. I., & Paluri, R. A. (2025). Modeling environmental, social, and governance (ESG) adoption enablers: The case of Islamic financial institutions. *Journal of Financial Reporting and Accounting*. https://doi.org/10.1108/JFRA-07-2024-0499

Khan, H. H., Ahmad, R. B., & Gee, C. S. (2016). Bank competition and monetary policy transmission through the bank lending channel: Evidence from ASEAN. *International Review of Economics & Finance, 44*, 19–39. https://doi.org/10.1016/j.iref.2016.03.003

Khatatbeh, I. N., Tayeh, M., Freihat, A. F., & Aldeki, R. G. (2025). ESG and bank stability in Gulf Cooperation Council countries: Empirical evidence from listed commercial banks. *South African Journal of Economic and Management Sciences, 28*(1). https://doi.org/10.4102/sajems.v28i1.6287

Khémiri, W., Chafai, A. A., Tobar, R., & Farid Fouad, H. (2024). Trade-off between financial inclusion and Islamic bank stability in five GCC countries: The moderating effect of CSR. *Cogent Business & Management, 11*(1), 2300524. https://doi.org/10.1080/23311975.2023.2300524

King, R. G., & Levine, R. (1993). Finance and growth: Schumpeter might be right. *The Quarterly Journal of Economics, 108*(3), 717–737. https://doi.org/10.2307/2118406

Klein, P.-O., & Weill, L. (2022). Bank profitability and economic growth. *The Quarterly Review of Economics and Finance, 84*, 183–199. https://doi.org/10.1016/j.qref.2022.01.009

Krugman, P., & Obstfeld, M. (2015). *International economics: Theory and policy*. Pearson.

Kurronen, S. (2015). Financial sector in resource-dependent economies. *Emerging Markets Review, 23*, 208–229. https://doi.org/10.1016/j.ememar.2015.04.010

Le, T. D., & Ngo, T. (2020). The determinants of bank profitability: A cross-country analysis. *Central Bank Review, 20*(2), 65–73. https://doi.org/10.1016/j.cbrev.2020.04.001

Leite, C. A., & Weidmann, J. (1999). Does mother nature corrupt? Natural resources, corruption, and economic growth. *IMF Working Papers 1999/085*. https://www.imf.org/en/Publications/WP/Issues/2016/12/30/Does-Mother-Nature-Corrupt-Natural-Resources-Corruption-and-Economic-Growth-3126

Lerner, A. P. (1934). The concept of monopoly and the measurement of monopoly power. *The Review of Economic Studies, 3*(1), 157–175.

Levine, R. (1997). Financial development and economic growth: Views and agenda. *Journal of Economic Literature, 35*(2), 688. www.jstor.org/stable/2729790

Levine, R. (2002). Bank-based or market-based financial systems: Which is better? *Journal of Financial Intermediation, 11*(4), 398–428. https://doi.org/10.1006/jfin.2002.0341

Li, L., Gao, W., & Gu, W. (2023). Fintech, bank concentration and commercial bank profitability: Evidence from Chinese urban commercial banks. *Finance Research Letters, 57*, Article 104234. https://doi.org/10.1016/j.frl.2023.104234

Liaqat, I., Floreani, J., & Naseer, M. M. (2026). ESG performance and Bank stability: The role of national culture and formal institutions. *Research in*

International Business and Finance, 81, Article 103214. https://doi.org/10.1016/j.ribaf.2025.103214
Lisbinski, F. C., & Burnquis, H. L. (2024). Fernanda Cigainski Lisbinski, Heloisa Lee Burnquis. *Institutions and Financial Development: Comparative Analysis of Developed and Developing Economies, 25*(2), 347–376. https://doi.org/10.1108/ECON-11-2023-0201
Macey, J. R., & Hara, M. (2003). The Corporate Governance of Banks. *FRBNY Economic Policy Review, 9*(1), 91–107. www.newyorkfed.org/medialibrary/media/research/epr/03v09n1/0304mace.pdf
Manju, R. B., Ratnakaram, S. P., & Manikeswari, D. (2024). ESG Integration in Islamic Banking sector in the Kingdom of Bahrain: Paving the path to sustainable finance. In *Business development via AI and digitalization* (pp. 215–229). Springer Nature. https://doi.org/10.1007/978-3-031-62106-2_18
Markowitz, H. (1952). Portfolio selection. *The Journal of Finance, 7*(1), 77–91. https://doi.org/10.2307/2975974
Martínek, S. A. (2021). The impact of Sovereign Wealth Funds on their investees: Methodology limitations. *Research in Globalization, 3*, Article 100072. https://doi.org/10.1016/j.resglo.2021.100072
Mason, E. S. (1939). Price and production policies of large-scale enterprise. *The American Economic Review, 29*(1), 61–74. www.jstor.org/stable/1806955
Matallah, S. (2022). Economic diversification and governance challenges in MENA oil exporters: A comparative analysis. *The Journal of Economic Asymmetries, 26*, Article e00255. https://doi.org/10.1016/j.jeca.2022.e00255
Mateev, M., & Bachvarov, P. (2021). Regulation, ownership and bank performance in the MENA region: Evidence for Islamic and conventional banks. *Emerging Markets Review, 47*, Article 100789. https://doi.org/10.1016/j.ememar.2020.100789
Maudos, J., & De Guevara, J. F. (2007). The cost of market power in banking: Social welfare loss vs. cost inefficiency. *Journal of Banking & Finance, 31*(7), 2103–2125. https://doi.org/10.1016/j.jbankfin.2006.10.028
Mazengia, T., Bezabih, M., & Chekol, F. (2023). Financial development and export diversification in Ethiopia: ARDL approach. *Cogent Economics & Finance, 11*(1), 2163079. https://doi.org/10.1080/23322039.2022.2163079
Mehlum, H., Moene, K., & Torvik, R. (2006). Institutions and the resource curse. *The Economic Journal, 116*(508), 1–20.
Menicucci, E., & Paolucci, G. (2023). ESG dimensions and bank performance: An empirical investigation in Italy. *Corporate Governance, 23*(3), 565–586. https://doi.org/10.1108/CG-03-2022-0094
Metu, A. G., Madichie, C. V., Anyanwu, U. N., Kalu, C. U., & Ihugba, O. A. (2021). Economic diversification and inclusive growth in Nigeria: Does institutional quality matter? In E. S. Osabuohien, E. A. Oduntan, O. Gershon,

O. Onanuga, & O. Ola-David, *Handbook of Research on Institution development for sustainable and inclusive economic growth in Afric* (pp. 90–108). IGI Global. https://doi.org/10.4018/978-1-7998-4817-2.ch006

Michael, J., Awad, A. B., & Abu Khalaf, B. (2023). Exploring Environmental, social, and governance and bank performance in the Gulf Cooperation Council region. *Corporate Law & Governance Review, 5*(2), 192–200. https://doi.org/10.22495/clgrv5i2sip6

Mien, E., & Goujon, M. (2022). 40 Years of Dutch disease literature: Lessons for developing countries. *Comparative Economic Studies* , 351–383.

Milena, W., & Stefan, A. (2025). Enhancing ESG Performance in Islamic Banks: The Impact of Shari'ah governance quality across countries. *Journal International Economic Sharia, 1*(13), 158–174. https://doi.org/10.69725/jies.v1i3.143

Mirzoev, T., Zhu, L., & Yang, Y. (2020). *The future of oil and fiscal sustainability in the GCC region.* IMF. https://www.imf.org/-/media/Files/Publications/DP/2020/English/FOFSGCCEA.ashx

Miyajima, K. (2020). What influences bank lending in Saudi Arabia? *Islamic Economic Studies, 27*(2), 125–155. https://doi.org/10.1108/IES-07-2019-0018

Mlachila, M., & Ouedraogo, R. (2020). Financial resource curse in resource-rich countries. *The Quarterly Review of Economics and Finance, 76*, 84–96. https://doi.org/10.1016/j.qref.2019.04.011

Mohammed, J. I., Karimu, A., Fiador, V. O., & Abor, J. Y. (2020). Oil revenues and economic growth in oil-producing countries: The role of domestic financial markets. *Resources Policy, 69*, Article 101832. https://doi.org/10.1016/j.resourpol.2020.101832

Molyneux, P., & Thornton, J. (1992). Determinants of European bank profitability: A note. *Journal of Banking & Finance, 16*(6), 1173–1178. https://doi.org/10.1016/0378-4266(92)90065-8

Molyneux, P., Lloyd-Williams, M. D., & Thornton, J. (1994). Competitive conditions in European banking. *Journal of Banking & Finance, 18*(3), 445–459. https://doi.org/10.1016/0378-4266(94)90003-5

Molyneux, P., Thornton, J., & Lloyd-Williams, M. D. (1996). Competition and market contestability in Japanese commercial banking. *Journal of Economics and Business, 48*(1), 33–45. https://doi.org/10.1016/0148-6195(95)00047-X

Morakabati, Y., Beavis, J., & Fletcher, J. (2014). Planning for a Qatar without oil: Tourism and economic diversification, a battle of perceptions. *Tourism Planning & Development, 11*(4). https://doi.org/10.1080/21568316.2014.884978

Nganga, M. L. (2021). Effects of the quality of institutions on the economic diversification of the states of the economic and monetary community of Central Africa (CEMAC). *Theoretical Economics Letters, 11*(1), 84–99. https://doi.org/10.4236/tel.2021.111007

Nguyen, C. P., Schinckus, C., & Su, T. D. (2020). The drivers of economic complexity: International evidence from financial development and patents. *International Economics, 164*, 140–150. https://doi.org/10.1016/j.inteco.2020.09.004

Nguyen, Q. M., & & Nguyen, C. V. (2024). Corporate governance, audit quality and firm performance—An empirical evidence. *Cogent Economics & Finance, 12*(1). https://doi.org/10.1080/23322039.2024.2334128

Nieminen, M. (2020). Multidimensional financial development, exporter behavior and export diversification. *Economic Modelling, 93*, 1–12. https://doi.org/10.1016/j.econmod.2020.07.021

Nili, M., & Rastad, M. (2007). Addressing the growth failure of the oil economies: the role of f inancial development. *The Quarterly Review of Economics and Finance, 46*(5), 726–740. https://doi.org/10.1016/j.qref.2006.08.007

Nili, M., & Rastad, M. (2007b). Addressing the growth failure of the oil economies: The role of financial development. *The Quarterly Review of Economics and Finance, 46*(5), 726–740. https://doi.org/10.1016/j.qref.2006.08.007

Njuguna, I. M., Mwangi, L. W., & Waweru, F. W. (2025). The Moderating effect of size of the bank on the relationship between Environmental, Social, and Governance (ESG) Practices and the financial performance of listed Commercial Banks in Africa. *Journal of Finance and Accounting, 5*(11), 36–53. https://doi.org/10.70619/vol5iss11pp36-53-706

North, D. C. (1990). *Institutions, institutional change and economic performance*. Cambridge University Press. https://doi.org/10.1017/CBO9780511808678

Nusair, S. A. (2016). The effects of oil price shocks on the economies of the Gulf Co-operation Council countries: Nonlinear analysis. *Energey Policy, 91*, 256–267. https://doi.org/10.1016/j.enpol.2016.01.013

Nwani, C., Okezie, B. N., Nwali, A. C., Nwokeiwu, J., Duruzor, G. I., & Eze, O. N. (2023). Natural resources, financial development and structural transformation in Sub-Saharan Africa. *Heliyon, 9*(9), Article e19522. https://doi.org/10.1016/j.heliyon.2023.e19522

O'Connell, M. (2023). Bank-specific, industry-specific and macroeconomic determinants of bank profitability: Evidence from the UK. *Studies in Economics and Finance, 40*(1), 155–174. https://doi.org/10.1108/SEF-10-2021-0413

Ogbonna, O. E., Mobosi, I. A., & Ugwuoke, O. W. (2020). Economic growth in an oil-dominant economy of Nigeria: The role of financial system development. *Cogent Economics & Finance, 8*(1). https://doi.org/10.1080/23322039.2020.1810390

Olander, P. (2019). Economic diversification and institutional quality-issues of concentrated interest. *Studies in Comparative International Development, 54*, 346–364. https://doi.org/10.1007/s12116-019-09287-0

OPEC. (2022). *Annual statistical Bulletin 2022.* www.opec.org

OPEC. (2023). *Annual statistical Bulletin 2023.* www.opec.org/opec_web/static_files_project/media/downloads/publications/ASB_2023.pdf

Patrick, H. T. (1966). Financial development and economic growth in underdeveloped countries. *Economic Development and Cultural Change, 14*(2), 174–189. https://doi.org/10.1086/450153

Pham, N. T., & Nguyen, D. T. (2025). Impacts of ESG practices on the operation performance: An empirical study of Vietnamese. *International Journal of Innovative Research and Scientific Studies, 8*(2), 4424–4434. https://doi.org/10.53894/ijirss.v8i2.6376

Poghosyan, P. (2022). *Financial development and growth in the Caucasus and Central Asia*. IMF.

Prieg, L., & Greenham, T. (2013). *Stakeholder Banks benefits of banking diversity.* New Economics Foundation. https://neweconomics.org/uploads/files/e0b3bd2b9423abfec8_pem6i6six.pdf

Pujiastuti, A., Nurhidayah, S. A., & Sulistiyanto, T. J. (2024). Does sharia compliance enhance ESG performance to better firm performance? *Diponegoro International Journal of Business, 7*(2), 177–190. https://doi.org/10.14710/dijb.7.2.2024.177-190

PwC. (2022). Islamic finance & ESG investing: Ready for convergance? www.pwc.com/m1/en/publications/documents/islamic-finance-and-esg-investing.pdf

Rajan, R., & Zingales, L. (2003). The great reversals: The politics of financial development in the twentieth century. *Journal of Financial Economics, 69*(1), 5–50. https://doi.org/10.1016/S0304-405X(03)00125-9

Rashid, A. (2018). Board independence and firm performance: Evidence from Bangladesh. *Future Business Journal, 4*(1), 34–49. https://doi.org/10.1016/j.fbj.2017.11.003

Raza, A., Alavi, A. B., & Asif, L. (2024). Sustainability and financial performance in the banking industry of the United Arab Emirates. *Discover Sustainability, 5*(223). https://doi.org/10.1007/s43621-024-00414-z

Rezvanian, R., & Mehdian, S. (2024). The impact of the 2008 Global financial crisis on the efficiency and profitability of the U.S. small banks. *Finance Research Letters, 67*, 105879. https://doi.org/10.1016/j.frl.2024.105879

Ricardo, D. (1817). *On the principles of political economy and taxation.*

Rodrik, D., Subramanian, A., & Trebbi, F. (2004). Institutions Rule: The primacy of institutions over Geography and integration in economic development. *Journal of Economic Growth, 9*, 131–165. https://doi.org/10.1023/B:JOEG.0000031425.72248.85

Romer, P. (1994). The origins of endogenous growth. *The Journal of Economic Perspectives, 8*(1), 3–22. https://doi.org/10.1257/jep.8.1.3

Ross, M. L. (2012). *The politics of the resource curse: A review Michael L. Ross.* Oxford University Press. https://escholarship.org/content/qt9cm6h1rk/qt9cm6h1rk.pdf

Saborowski, C. (2011). Can financial development cure the Dutch disease? *International Journal of Finacne & Economics, 16*(3), 218–236. https://doi.org/10.1002/ijfe.419

Sachs, J. D., & Warner, A. (2001). The curse of natural resources. *European Economic Review, 45*, 827–838. https://doi.org/10.1016/S0014-2921(01)00125-8

Sachs, J. D., & Warner, A. M. (1995). *Natural resource abundance and economic growth.* NBER Working Papers 5398,. www.nber.org/system/files/working_papers/w5398/w5398.pdf

Sachs, J. D., & Warner, A. M. (1997). *Natural Resource Abundance and Economic Growth* (Working paper). Center for International Development and Harvard Institute for International Development.

Sahay, R., Čihák, M. N., Barajas, A., Bi, R., Ayala, D., Gao, Y., & Yousefi, S. R. (2015). Rethinking financial deepening: Stability and growth in emerging markets. *Revista De Economía Institucional, 17*(33), 73–107. https://doi.org/10.18601/01245996.v17n33.04

Sahu, M., Alahdal, W. M., Panday, D. K., Baatwah, S. R., & Bajaher, M. S. (2025). Board gender diversity and firm performance: Unveiling the ESG effect, *9*, 100493. https://doi.org/10.1016/j.sftr.2025.100493

Saif-Alyousfi, A. Y., Saha, A., & Md-Rus, R. (2020). The impact of bank competition and concentration on bank risk-taking behavior and stability: Evidence from GCC countries. *The North American Journal of Economics and Finance, 51*,. https://doi.org/10.1016/j.najef.2018.10.015

Sala-i-Martin, X., & Subramanian, A. (2013). Addressing the natural resource curse: An illustration from Nigeria. *Journal of African Economies, 22*(4), 570–615. https://doi.org/10.1093/jae/ejs033

Salin, A. S., & Ali, N. B. (2025). Islamic ESG -A conceptual framework. *Journal of Islamic Social Economics and Development, 10*(75), 767–779. https://doi.org/10.55573/JISED.107564

Samargandi, N., Fidrmuc, J., & Ghosh, S. (2014). Financial development and economic growth in an oil-rich economy: The case of Saudi Arabia. *Economic Modelling, 43*, 267–278. https://doi.org/10.1016/j.econmod.2014.07.042

Saona, P. (2016). Intra- and extra-bank determinants of Latin American Banks' profitability. *International Review of Economics & Finance, 45*, 197–214. https://doi.org/10.1016/j.iref.2016.06.004

Schaeck, K., & Čihák, M. (2014). Competition, efficiency and stability in banking. *Financial Management, 43*(1), 215–241. https://doi.org/10.1111/fima.12010

Scholtens, B. (2009). Corporate social responsibility in the international banking industry. *Journal of Business Ethics, 86*, 159–175. https://doi.org/10.1007/s10551-008-9841-x

Schreiber, B. Z. (2024). The impact of revenue diversification on profitability, capital, and risk in US banks by size. *The North American Journal of Economics and Finance, 69*, Article 102000. https://doi.org/10.1016/j.najef.2023.102000

Schumpeter, J. (1911). *The theory of economic development*. Harvard University Press.

Shadab, S. (2023). The New Arab Gulf: Evaluating the success of economic diversification in the UAE. In M. M. Rahman, & A. Al-Azm, *Social Change in the Gulf Region* (pp. 415–430). Springer. https://doi.org/10.1007/978-981-19-7796-1_25

Shalhoob, H. (2025). ESG disclosure and financial performance: Survey evidence from accounting and Islamic Finance. *Sustainability, 17*(4). https://doi.org/10.3390/su17041582

Shawtari, F. A., Elsalem, B. A., Salem, M. A., & Shah, M. E. (2024). Financial development and economic diversification in Qatar: Does Islamic finance matters. *Journal of Islamic Accounting and Business Research, 15*(6), 959–987. https://doi.org/10.1108/JIABR-01-2022-0021

Sherman, H. D., & Gold, F. (1985). Bank branch operating efficiency: Evaluation with data envelopment analysis. *Journal of Banking & Finance, 9*(2), 297–315. https://doi.org/10.1016/0378-4266(85)90025-1

Shome, R., Elbardan, H., & Yazdifar, H. (2024). Banking research in the GCC region and agenda for future research—A bibliometric examination. *Journal of Applied Accounting Research, 25*(5), 1091–1119. https://doi.org/10.1108/JAAR-03-2023-0070

Singh, K., & Misra, M. (2021). Linking Corporate Social Responsibility (CSR) and Organizational Performance: The moderating effect of corporate reputation. *European Research on Management and Business Economics, 27*(1), Article 100139. https://doi.org/10.1016/j.iedeen.2020.100139

Solow, R. M. (1956). A contribution to the theory of economic growth. *The Quarterly Journal of Economics, 70*(1), 65–94. https://doi.org/10.2307/1884513

Srairi, S. (2025). How does ESG performance affect bank performance? A comparative analysis of conventional and Islamic banks in GCC countries.

International Journal of Disclosure and Governance . https://doi.org/10.1057/s41310-025-00319-x

Stiglitz, J., & Weiss, A. (1983). Incentive effects of terminations: Applications to the credit and labor markets. *American Economic Review, 73*(5), 912–927.

Stocker, M., Baffes, J., Some, Y. M., Vorisek, D., & Wheeler, C. M. (2018). The 2014–16 oil price collapse in retrospect: Sources and implications. *The World Bank*. https://doi.org/10.1596/1813-9450-8419

Sun, Z., & Cai, Z. (2020). Does financial development hamper or improve the resource curse? Analysis based on the panel threshold effect model. *Mathematical Problems in Engineering, 1*, 4365205. https://doi.org/10.1155/2020/4365205

Sweidan, O. D., & Elbargathi, K. (2023). Economic diversification in Saudi Arabia: Comparing the impact of oil prices, geopolitical risk, and government expenditures. *International Economics, 175*, 13–24. https://doi.org/10.1016/j.inteco.2023.05.003

SWFI. (2023). *Sovereign wealth fund rankings*. Sovereign Wealth Fund Institute. www.swfinstitute.org

Tan, Y. (2016). The impacts of risk and competition on bank profitability in China. *Journal of International Financial Markets, Institutions and Money, 40*, 85–110. https://doi.org/10.1016/j.intfin.2015.09.003

The Asian Banker. (2024, November 22). *ESG leadership drives Commercial Bank of Qatar's sustainability success*. https://www.theasianbanker.com/updates-and-articles/sustainable-and-green-bank-of-the-year-in-qatar-is-commercial-bank-of-qatar-2024

The Oath. (2025, October). *ESG is moving from voluntary to mandatory*. https://theoath-me.com/esg-is-moving-from-voluntary-to-mandatory/

The Peninsula. (2022, November 14). *Dukhan Bank, GORD introduce Shari'ah compliant Green Finance program*. https://thepeninsulaqatar.com/article/14/11/2022/dukhan-bank-gord-introduce-shariah-compliant-green-finance-program

The US Department of Justice. (2024, Janurary 17). *Herfindahl–Hirschman Index*. https://www.justice.gov/atr/herfindahl-hirschman-index

Torre-Olmo, B., Cantero-Saiz, M., & Azofra, S. S. (2021). Sustainable Banking, market power, and efficiency: Effects on banks' profitability and risk. *Sustainability, 13*(3). https://doi.org/10.3390/su13031298

van der Ploeg, F. (2011). Natural resources: Curse or blessing? *Journal of Economic Literature, 49*(2), 366–420. https://doi.org/10.1257/jel.49.2.366

Vision 2030. (2023). *Saudi Vision 2030 strategic framework*. Government of Saudi Arabia. www.vision2030.gov.sa

Wang, K.-H., Liu, L., Adebayo, T. S., Lobonţ, O.-R., & Claudia, M. N. (2021). Fiscal decentralization, political stability and resources curse hypothesis: A case of fiscal decentralized economies. *Resources Policy, 72*, Article 102071. https://doi.org/10.1016/j.resourpol.2021.102071

Wang, L., Fan, X., & Zhuang, H. (2023). ESG disclosure facilitator: How do the multiple large shareholders affect firms' ESG disclosure? evidence from China. *Frontiers in Environmental Science, 11*, 1063501. https://doi.org/10.3389/fenvs.2023.1063501

Woertz, E. (2018). Bahrain's Economy: Oil prices, economic diversification, Saudi support, and. *Notes Internacionals, 189*, 1–6. https://www.cidob.org/en/publications/bahrains-economy-oil-prices-economic-diversification-saudi-support-and-political: www.cidob.org/sites/default/files/2024-07/NOTES%20189_ECKART%20WOERTZ_CAST.pdf

World Bank. (2022). *Qatar Economic update*. www.worldbank.org

World Bank. (2023). *GCC Economic outlook report 2023*. www.worldbank.org

Wu, M.-W., & Shen, C.-H. (2013). Corporate social responsibility in the banking industry: Motives and financial performance. *Journal of Banking & Finance, 37*(9), 3529–3547. https://doi.org/10.1016/j.jbankfin.2013.04.023

Yıldırım, S., Gedikli, A., & Yıldırım, D. Ç. (2020). Natural resources rents-financial development nexus: Evidence from sixteen developing countries. *Resources Policy, 68*, Article 101705. https://doi.org/10.1016/j.resourpol.2020.101705

Young, B. (2022, July 25). *Why GCC banking systems are resilient to geopolitical stress scenarios*. Retrieved August 09, 2023, from Arabian Business: https://www.arabianbusiness.com/opinion/why-gcc-banking-systems-are-resilient-to-geopolitical-stress-scenario

Yuen, M. K., Ngo, T. L., & Ho, T. H. (2022a). The environment, social and governance (ESG) activities and profitability under COVID-19: Evidence from the global banking sector. *Journal of Economics and Development, 23*(4). https://doi.org/10.1108/JED-08-2022-0136

Yuen, M. K., Ngo, T., Le, T. D., & Ho, T. H. (2022b). The environment, social and governance (ESG) activities and profitability under COVID-19 evidence from the global banking sector. *Journal of Economics and Development, 24*(4), 345–364. https://doi.org/10.1108/JED-08-2022-0136

Yuxiang, K., & Chen, Z. (2011). Resource abundance and financial development: Evidence from China. *Resources Policy, 36*(1), 72–79. https://doi.org/10.1017/S1355770X10000422

Zaidi, S. A., Wei, Z., Gedikli, A., Zafar, M. W., Hou, F., & Iftikhar, Y. (2019). The impact of globalization, natural resources abundance, and human capital on financial development: Evidence from thirty-one OECD countries. *Resources Policy, 64*, Article 101476. https://doi.org/10.1016/j.resourpol.2019.101476

Index

A. Bakhouche, *Banking in the GCC*, Palgrave Macmillan Studies in Banking and Financial Institutions,
https://doi.org/10.1007/978-3-032-21737-0

GPSR Compliance
The European Union's (EU) General Product Safety Regulation (GPSR) is a set of rules that requires consumer products to be safe and our obligations to ensure this.

If you have any concerns about our products, you can contact us on

ProductSafety@springernature.com

In case Publisher is established outside the EU, the EU authorized representative is:

Springer Nature Customer Service Center GmbH
Europaplatz 3
69115 Heidelberg, Germany

www.ingramcontent.com/pod-product-compliance
Ingram Content Group UK Ltd.
Pitfield, Milton Keynes, MK11 3LW, UK
UKHW020115240926
475648UK00011BA/28

* 9 7 8 3 0 3 2 2 1 7 3 6 3 *